CABINETS AND THE BOMB

IN MEMORY OF MARGARET GOWING

AND

FOR LORNA ARNOLD

THEY SHOWED HISTORIANS THE WAY

British Academy Occasional Paper, 11

British Academy Occasional Papers are a series of paperback volumes on topics of current interest.

The British Academy, established by Royal Charter in 1902, is the national academy for the humanities and the social sciences, promoting, sustaining and representing advanced research. As an academy composed of senior scholars throughout the UK, it gives recognition to academic excellence and achievement, and plays a leadership role in representing the humanities and social sciences nationally and internationally. As a learned society, the British Academy seeks to sustain the health and promote the development of the various academic disciplines that make up the humanities and social sciences. And as a grant-giving body, the British Academy facilitates the research of individuals and groups of scholars.

More information can be found at *www.britac.ac.uk*

Cabinets and THE BOMB

PETER HENNESSY

Published for THE BRITISH ACADEMY
by OXFORD UNIVERSITY PRESS

Oxford University Press, Great Clarendon Street, Oxford OX2 6DP

Oxford New York
Auckland Cape Town Dar es Salaam Hong Kong Karachi
Kuala Lumpur Madrid Melbourne Mexico City Nairobi
New Delhi Shanghai Taipei Toronto

With offices in
Argentina Austria Brazil Chile Czech Republic France Greece
Guatemala Hungary Italy Japan Poland Portugal Singapore
South Korea Switzerland Thailand Turkey Ukraine Vietnam

Published in the United States
by Oxford University Press Inc., New York

British Library Cataloguing in Publication Data
Data available

Library of Congress Cataloging in Publication Data
Data available

Typeset by
J&L Composition, Filey, North Yorkshire
Printed in Great Britain
on acid-free paper by
Henry Ling Limited
at the Dorset Press
Dorchester, Dorset

ISBN 978–0–19–726422–5

CONTENTS

Participants at the British Academy, National Archives, Mile End Institute workshop on 'Cabinets and the Bomb', held at the British Academy on 27 March 2007. At the table are: Sir Kevin Tebbit (standing); a serving MOD official; Sir Ronald Mason; Lord Carrington; Sir Michael Quinlan; Professor Peter Hennessy.

PREFACE

The preparation of this study has accumulated a sheaf of debts: to the British Academy for sponsoring it and for hosting the 'Cabinets and the Bomb' workshop on 27 March 2007; to the National Archives for furnishing the documentary raw material; and to the members of the Queen Mary Mile End Group (the seminar wing of the Mile End Institute) for a range of help, encouragement and participation.

Special thanks go to James Rivington and Michael Reade at the British Academy; Natalie Ceeney, David Thomas, Tom Gregan and Tom O'Leary at the National Archives; and to Catherine Haddon of Queen Mary for research assistance, advice and for her wise choice of documents, and to another Mile End grouper, Matt Lyus, for heavy duty word-processing. Chris Walley of *The Times* provided invaluable help with the picture research.

I am grateful, too, to all the participants of the workshop, for providing extra insights and pooling their wisdom after reading the documents reproduced herein. My special thanks go to the pair of retired permanent secretaries who opened and closed it—Sir Michael Quinlan and Sir Kevin Tebbit.

Peter Hennessy
Walthamstow, Mile End, Carlton House Terrace, and Kew
May 2007

Unless you were quite senior in the government, you knew nothing about these things at all. You talk about Parliament being ignorant . . . We were all ignorant about it.

Lord Carrington, speaking at the British Academy, National Archives, Mile End Institute workshop on 'Cabinets and the Bomb', 27 March 2007.

INTRODUCTION

Michael Quinlan

We have in this volume a fascinating set of documents to illustrate the saga of Cabinets and the bomb. For me, the richest jewel is almost at the outset, in the form of Clement Atlee's paper—surely his own work, from the laconic directness of its expression—written for a small number of his colleagues on 28 August 1945. Within weeks of the two bombs on Japan, he has grasped the significance of what has happened with a clarity that some flashier minds still had not equalled decades later: '. . . even the modern conception of war to which in my lifetime we have become accustomed is now completely out of date' and '. . . this invention has made it essential to end wars . . . the whole conception of war [must be] banished from people's minds and from the calculations of government.'

I would like to pick out from this treasure chest eight themes—not in any particular chronological or other order—which readers might like to explore.

The first theme is the *rationale* for Britain's going into the nuclear-weapon business. This has diverse strands discernible. There is prestige, though not in a shallow showy sense: if we have this capability, other countries will continue to take us seriously as we engage in our responsibilities around the globe. There is the seat at the top table, so that we can make ourselves heard in top-level disarmament and arms-control dealings. There is influence with the United States, though interestingly the paths of that are rarely spelled out in any clear analytical way, save perhaps for references to responsibility-sharing in NATO. There is the contribution to Western deterrence capability, and by the 1960s this runs alongside the second-centre-of-decision argument and the concept of independence—though there is some wrestling with what independence needs to mean (it is piquant to compare Harold Wilson in and out of office on this). But, despite the renowned early remark by Ernest Bevin about a Union Jack on the bomb, there is scarcely any trace, at any stage, of what might be called straight Gaullisme—the notion that 'we are a great historic nation that should not put its ultimate trust in anyone else.'

My second theme is that of *challenge* to the policy. This is not confined to periods of Labour government—there are serious doubts about its continuance expressed within the Cabinet in 1962 and 1972, for example, on economic and value-for-money grounds. But of course opposition is most evident under Labour. It is striking to see Wilson in 1974 not only having to explain to Cabinet, almost apologetically, his having authorised a nuclear test but even then having, under pressure, to submit afterwards a paper filling out the explanation.

I find myself wondering just why challenges to nuclear-weapon status were more frequently recurrent, and went deeper, in Britain than in any of the other four Treaty-recognised possessors. I suspect that the answer may lie not in any distinctive positive feature of the British scene, but merely in the absence or relative weakness in Britain of any of the special perceived national imperatives which diversely motivated the other four (the United States, the Soviet Union, France and China).

My third theme is *cost*. This needs little elaboration—it was a continual worry for every Cabinet. Again, though, the comparison with France is notable. While we do not know (or at least I do not) all the detail of France's internal deliberations, it is surely remarkable that France bore with much less agonising—or much less evident agonising—a resource burden almost always several times higher than Britain's. (The opportunity cost of that was seen, of course, in the differences of conventional force contribution to the Atlantic Alliance and in the 1991 Gulf War.)

My fourth theme is *the attitude of the United States*. This varies significantly over time. For a decade from 1946 the McMahon Act holds sway, and there is little or no collaboration, though some discreet dialogue. That changes in 1958 after our weapon tests in the Pacific have demonstrated our technical competence, but reservations persist in some parts of the United States government. The Skybolt episode quite aside, Robert McNamara makes a speech notoriously disobliging to Britain and France at Ann Arbor in 1962, and parts of the State Department, focused on an arms-control agenda, did not like the Polaris deal at Nassau. The papers show Nixon and Kissinger sympathetic to British capability, but uneasy about support in Congress for further aid to it. I myself recall an informal discussion in London in 1979 when Secretary of Defense Harold Brown, asked by Francis Pym what he thought about British continuance in the business, said 'I regard it as modestly advantageous—with the emphasis on the adverb.' But the George W. Bush letter of 7 December 2006 shows no reservations. And it is interesting, throughout the saga, that there never seems to be any trace of a United States' attempt to use their support of our nuclear capability as a lever to secure co-operation in other fields, as over military involvement in the Vietnam War.

My fifth theme concerns *France*. Alongside a gut reluctance to contemplate France as the only West European nuclear power, the idea of Anglo-French co-operation flits in and out of the papers. Harold Macmillan is interested in 1962, and Edward Heath (more markedly) in the early 1970s. But quite aside from French reservations, the close co-operation with the United States, which was always far the greater prize for us, entailed constraints, as the paper of 22 September 1976 brings out—constraints theoretically on both sides of the partnership, though one may legitimately wonder whether the United States observed them as meticulously as we in prudence felt bound to.

My sixth theme is the *ethics* of the whole business. Explicit references to moral concerns are notable mostly for their absence, though there is recorded on 8 July 1954 a significant Cabinet exchange about worries of this kind over the shift to the H-bomb. And there is virtually no discussion about operational aspects (with ethical implications) like targeting; it is apparently taken for granted at least until 1980—when the public document explaining the choice of Trident, not in this volume, contained a low-key but significant choice of words of different import—that the measurement currency of deterrent threat is the destruction of cities.

My seventh theme is *institutional pressure*. There is less of this than critics sometimes supposed. The Royal Air Force was always very keen on the strategic nuclear role, and continued to cherish its remaining capability for over a decade even after the central responsibility had passed to the Royal Navy in 1969. The

Navy itself was occasionally ambivalent—not all sailors found the role itself operationally attractive, and there was recurrent unease about whether the displacement effect of its cost within the defence budget might hurt other things which most of the Navy prized more highly. I myself recall first having been drawn into the 'airborne versus seaborne' debate in 1961, well before Nassau, and the Admiralty's desire to win the debate seemed at that time by no means unqualified. The scientists at Aldermaston and elsewhere were naturally key players as advisers on what was feasible, but contrary to some public suspicion they rarely if ever attempted to drive policy—it is not the case, for example, that they pushed specially for the Chevaline project.

My eighth and final theme is *secrecy*. Though once policy was settled plenty of material was usually—and, once more, contrary to anti-nuclear legend—made available, papers in advance of decision were almost always very closely held, no doubt primarily so as not to give information prematurely to the Soviet Union (the scars of espionage scandals took time to heal). But there can be no doubt that under Labour governments there was an additional strand of motivation in the desire not to expose too much surface to major figures within the Cabinet who were deeply opposed to the whole nuclear business. That was clearly so, for vivid example, during the years when Chevaline was being developed, though there was a further and more externally legitimate reason for that: Chevaline was a technically demanding project that seemed in earlier stages by no means certain to succeed, and it would have been very damaging to the credibility of our deterrent stance to disclose its existence and purpose and then have to admit that we had not managed to make it work. When Francis Pym told Parliament about it in 1980, development had reached a point where we were confident of bringing it to fruition.

A last reflection. It is agreeable, is it not, to read, even under Top Secret classifications, thorough and balanced papers for the Cabinet or its committees, with ensuing discussion coolly and carefully recorded. *Autres temps, autres moeurs*, perhaps.

Sir Michael Quinlan was Permanent Under-Secretary of State at the Ministry of Defence from 1988 to 1992, and Director of the Ditchley Foundation from 1992 to 1999.

THE NUCLEAR CERTIFICATE

Of all the thousands of decisions taken by British Cabinets since 1945, each one carefully recorded and preserved for eventual release at what is now the National Archives, those touching upon the nuclear weapon leave a special trace. Quite apart from the cost, the science and the logistics involved, a bundle of forces come into play in which instinct and emotion jostle with strategy and reality—the whole business overlain by uncertainty about the world, Britain's place in it, and the likelihood of an international clash so serious that actually using the dreadful thing might have to be contemplated. Several sets of ministers of both major parties have been involved in such decision-taking, and in each generation the mixture of motivations and justifications shifts and rearranges itself, though, as in a child's kaleidoscope, many of the particles remain the same. This study is about the *private* impulses and judgements that swirled around the Cabinet Room when big bomb decisions awaited, and the stories ministers told themselves about why this was the moment to get into the nuclear weapons business, or to ensure the country stayed in it decades later unless a disarmament-minded set of successors took their seats around the Cabinet Table in the meantime.

It was a remarkable Frenchman, Raymond Aron, who combined the gifts of a historical sociologist and a journalist with those of a cold-war strategic analyst who, in his post-1945 generation, caught best the specialness of the nuclear factor in high politics and history. In a famous essay on Max Weber, Aron stressed the importance of projecting back into past decisions and decision-makers the same degree of uncertainty *we* feel *today* about the future. 'The effort,' Aron wrote in 1959,

> to avoid the retrospective deterministic illusion regarding events or actions is . . . characteristic of the political historian—the historian who . . . wants to respect the proper dimension of action: namely, uncertainty with regard to the future. . .[1]

Three years earlier, Aron had himself set about untangling the motives behind the British government's determination to upgrade itself from an atomic to a thermonuclear power, with a degree of insight that suggested he had actually seen the Cabinet Secretary's minutes of the discussion which preceded the Churchill administration's decision to commission the building of a UK hydrogen bomb in the spring and summer of 1954 (a decision Whitehall managed to keep secret until the February 1955 Defence White Paper was published[2]).

In his *On War*, Aron depicted the British intention to go thermonuclear as seeking a 'certificate of grandeur', a modern equivalent of the fleets, armies and colonial territories that were required by a nineteenth-century nation wishing to 'enter the exclusive club of the world's masters.'[3] This, as we shall see later, was very much the flavour of the Chiefs of Staff's briefing for the Cabinet and of Churchill's selling of the upgrade from a fission to a fusion weapon in the Cabinet Room.

'Certificates' of several kinds were involved in the six decades of decision-taking encompassed by this book: insurance certificates (lest the United States withdraw its nuclear shield from western Europe); certificates of deterrence (would the Soviet Union risk attacking a stand-alone Britain, even without an American guarantee, if Russia stood to lose tens of its cities in a UK-launched retaliation?); political certificates of various kinds (wouldn't the UK be in a stronger position to restrain the USA in a period of rising international tension if it, too, were a nuclear power? Would the rest of western Europe be happy if, following a unilateral British disarmament, the French were left as the sole continental nuclear-tipped nation?). For the British bomb, ever since the Attlee government decided to go-it-alone and make an atomic weapon without US assistance, has been as much if not more of a political weapon than a military one. And the becoming and remaining a nuclear power is one of the most fascinating running themes of the post-war years. So far, every government has wished to either acquire, retain or renew its nuclear certificate.

Though the bulk of the documents reproduced herein date from 1945, the story does not. By the time Clement Attlee wrote his first memorandum on the bomb in August that year within a few weeks of becoming Prime Minister, another British premier had become the first and the last to authorise the use of an atomic weapon. Yet, till Attlee, no British Cabinet or Cabinet committee had been involved in nuclear decision-taking of any kind. For Winston Churchill, 'Tube Alloys' issues (as the bomb project was codenamed during World War II) were, first and last, a prime ministerial not a Cabinet matter. He declined all suggestions that he should consult even the Service Ministers leading the War Office, the Admiralty and the Air Ministry, let alone a formal group of colleagues, even after the secret Quebec Agreement of 1943. At Quebec, the allies' chief nuclear collaborators, Roosevelt and Churchill (the Canadians were also involved in the Manhattan Project, the cover-name for the bomb's development) agreed that the US President and the UK Prime Minister would need to concur jointly before the weapon, once produced, could be used.

Thanks to Churchill's fading memory a decade later during his twilight premiership, we can piece together the essentials of this example of truly prime ministerial British government. For reasons that are unclear, in January 1953 Churchill asked his scientific adviser, the Paymaster General, Lord Cherwell, to outline for him 'the principal events leading up to the dropping of the atomic bombs at Hiroshima and Nagasaki.'

In his reply, Cherwell began with the constitutional question:

> On March 21, 1944, Sir John Anderson [Churchill's minister for the bomb] suggested that the Tube Alloys programme should be mentioned to the Service Ministers and to the other ministers concerned but you minuted 'I do not agree.' Sir John Anderson was perturbed by your decision and I am fairly certain that in the spring of 1945 he made another attempt to persuade you to bring the matter to Cabinet and that I supported him. No papers bearing on this can however be found. In the event, it seems, the question was never discussed at Cabinet or in the Defence Committee.[4]

Buckingham Palace, however, was informed about work on the bomb though this did not become known until 2005 when the wartime diaries of King George

VI's Private Secretary, Sir Alan ('Tommy') Lascelles, were published. In his entry for 8 February 1945, Lascelles recorded:

> Sir Edward Appleton, FRS, who runs the Government's Scientific Research department came to see me, to advise about 'hush-hush' places which the King wants to visit; a genial little man, who looks like a fox-hunter, and is an ardent Trollopian. I asked him about the progress of harnessing the atom [Lascelles plainly knew about the 'Tube Alloys' project already; but who told him and when and whether Lascelles informed the King we do not know]: apparently you can't do this without about ten acres of laboratories etc., and had the Germans got such a layout, we should certainly know about it. Our own outfit has been transported to the USA, since it was considered too vulnerable for this country during the Blitz [in fact, this decision was taken later]; there, with help readily given by American scientists, there has been rapid development.

Appleton was even more forthcoming about likely future plans to deploy the weapon:

> Appleton did not think that there would be time to use any sort of atom-filled bomb against the Germans, but there might be an opportunity of doing so in Japan. I asked what would be the result. 'Oh,' he answered, 'a couple of them would end the war overnight ~ there is no doubt about that.' I said that it might be a good thing if humanity were given proof of the effects of these fearful engines, as it might convince it that any further indulgence in war would inevitably end in its own annihilation. He said that the deterrent aspect was an important one, and had not been overlooked; but, apart from its military side, the atom had immense commercial possibilities, and was destined to replace the world's already dwindling resources of coal and oil. I wish I understood these things better.[5]

For all the strain on his brain induced by the Appleton briefing, Lascelles knew far more about the bomb in early 1945 than any member of the War Cabinet, Churchill and Anderson apart.

Two months later, as Cherwell's January 1953 minute reminded Churchill, the Manhattan Project was approaching a critical stage:

> In April 1945 Lord Wilson [Whitehall's representative on the Combined Policy Committee which dealt with atomic matters in Washington] telegraphed to Sir John Anderson that the Americans proposed to make a full-scale test in the desert in July and to drop a bomb on the Japanese in August and I told you about this.[6]

At the end of May 1945, after the war in Europe had ended, 'it was agreed that in order to fulfil the Quebec Agreement the concurrence of HMG [His Majesty's Government] should be recorded at a meeting of the Combined Policy Committee.' On 29 June 1945 Anderson reminded Churchill of the agreed procedure. 'In this minute,' Cherwell reminded Churchill, 'he requested authority to instruct our representatives to give the concurrence of HMG in the decision to use the bomb against the Japanese. You initialled the minute on July 1.' On 4 July 1945, Wilson 'formally gave the concurrence' at a meeting of the Combined Policy Committee in Washington.[7]

By the time Churchill took this awesome decision, Britain was over a fortnight into a general election campaign. The country was balloted four days later on 5 July though the result was not announced for another three weeks to give time for the Armed Forces' votes to be gathered and tallied around the world. To his own and his country's surprise Clement Attlee led the Labour Party to victory.[8]

How much did Attlee know about 'Tube Alloys' before becoming Prime Minister? At the time the wartime Coalition Government broke up in June 1945, Attlee, as he recalled in his memoirs, 'did not know then that the atom bomb project was about to come to fruition, for knowledge of it had been kept to a very narrow circle. It looked at that time to be likely that the Japanese would have to be dislodged piecemeal from the wide area which they occupied.'[9] Attlee's official biographer, Kenneth Harris, suggested that is was on 1 August 1945, six days after Attlee had become Prime Minister, that Roosevelt's successor, President Harry Truman, told him in a letter (they were both at the Potsdam Conference in Berlin) that the US Air Force was now ready to drop an atomic bomb on Japan.[10]

Attlee, as he made plain to his former Press Secretary, Francis Williams, 15 year later, had no difficulty with Truman's decision (though how much he knew about the details of the Quebec Agreement or Churchill's decision on 1 July to agree to the bomb's use, remains a matter of conjecture). 'Of course,' he told Williams,

> at the time we knew nothing, I certainly knew absolutely nothing, about the consequences of dropping the bomb except that it was larger than an ordinary bomb and had a much greater explosive force. If were are going back you must look at the situation as it then was. The Japanese were scattered over wide areas and we had no knowledge—I hadn't anyway—that they were likely to collapse. Knowing how they had fought in Burma, the odds were they would fight it out wherever they were with immense loss of life on both sides unless we could get a rescript from the Emperor ordering them to stop. The bomb was a way of getting such a rescript. And in fact we did get it.[11]

Two bombs were dropped on Japan. The first struck Hiroshima on 6 August; the second, Nagasaki on 9 August. As Appleton had predicted, two were enough to end the war in the Far East.

With all the other duties placed upon his shoulders during the first weeks of his premiership, the bomb and those 'consequences' of which he had until so recently known 'absolutely nothing' became a great preoccupation of Attlee's in August 1945. He swiftly commissioned an *ad hoc* ministerial Cabinet Committee on Atomic Energy (GEN 75 in the Cabinet Office's code). And it is with the first paper it took, prepared by Attlee's own hand, that this documentary study begins (apart from a couple of extracts giving the flavour of the Frisch-Peierls memorandum of 1940 and the Maud Report of 1941 which, between them, triggered the British quest for a bomb). For it was in the first weeks of Attlee's Government that the mechanics of Cabinet government became bound into the question of the bomb. The study finishes with the exchange of letters between Prime Minister Tony Blair and President George Bush in December 2006 (and the vote in Parliament in March 2007) which, unless an intervening government on either side of the Atlantic cancels the arrangement, should ensure that the UK will have a nuclear weapon with a 'bloody Union Jack on top of it', to borrow Ernest Bevin's now famous words at a GEN 75 meeting in October 1946,[12] for at least a century from the date of the first atomic test in October 1952.

In between Attlee's August 1945 memorandum and the Blair-Bush correspondence, the documents herein trace the January 1947 decision to make a British atomic bomb; Churchill's amazement at finding, on returning to office in 1951, that Attlee's administration had concealed its £100m budget so successfully from Parliament, through to his own Cabinet's decision to authorise the manufacture of the vastly more powerful hydrogen bomb. The papers illuminate the decision of the Macmillan government in 1960 to purchase the US stand-off Skybolt missile as a way of extending the life of the RAF's 'V' force, and then to secure the submarine-launched Polaris system when the Americans abandoned Skybolt at the end of 1962.

Labour politics became integral to the story once more in the autumn and winter of 1964 when Harold Wilson persuaded his Cabinet, despite the appearance given by a manifesto pledge in the October election that it might be cancelled,[13] to proceed with Polaris. The debate about improving it, through what was to become known as the Chevaline project, designed to penetrate the anti-ballistic missile screen around Moscow, is followed through the Wilson government of 1966–70, and into the Heath administration of 1970–74 and the Labour governments of 1974–79.

A small amount of information is available from the highly secret ministerial group Jim Callaghan convened in 1978 to consider Polaris *replacement*, not merely improvement, once the submarines went out of service in the 1990s—a decision eventually taken by the first Thatcher administration in 1980–81 when it opted for the US Trident missile. Finally the manner in which the Blair government reached its intention of replacing the Trident D5 system, with most likely an updated version of the D5 and a new squadron of Royal Navy submarines to carry them into the 2050s, will be analysed.

Before turning to the documents themselves, a word of caution is needed. Acquiring the declassified papers and minutes of the Cabinets and Cabinet committees involved might, on first acquaintance, give the impression that this, after a suitable lapse of time, is the equivalent of reading the delayed product of a bug or two in the Cabinet Room. Revealing though the Cabinet official record can be, this is not so. For there is a certain austerity about the style of minute-writing practised by the Cabinet Office. For example, nowhere in the GEN 75 record is to be found Bevin's use of the words 'We've got to have the bloody Union Jack on top of it.' For this we needed a BBC *Timewatch* documentary broadcast on 29 September 1982 in which one of the scientific advisers present at the crucial GEN 75 meeting, Sir Michael Perrin, recalled the Foreign Secretary's actual words.[14] Similarly, to appreciate the disarray in Churchill's Cabinet at the first of its H-bomb meetings on 7 July 1954, we had to await the release of Harold Macmillan's diaries to researchers.[15]

That said, there is much to be gleaned from retrospective eavesdropping on this succession of nuclear moments in Downing Street. Each has to be understood in the context of its times and of the personal and political formations of the men and women taking the decision. What it really needs is a substantial study in its own right, a task which I hope a member of the up-and-coming generation of contemporary British historians will undertake. When the young scholar concerned eventually sets to work—hopefully with more evidence to draw on, given that little nuclear-weapons related material is declassified until 30 years have elapsed—this documentary reader will, with luck, provide at the very least some of the fuel that propels his or her project from its launch-pad. In the meantime, it is written as a contribution by the British Academy, the Mile End Institute at Queen Mary, University of London, and the National Archives to the debate stimulated by the decision of the Blair government to replace the current Trident system which is likely to extend over the next few years. The purpose of the study is explanation, *not* advocacy (in any direction) of the wisdom or otherwise of the UK becoming and remaining a certificated nuclear weapons power.

NOTE. The documents have been photographed from copies in the National Archives, and are printed in facsimile to provide a sense of authenticity. In several instances, redundant or tangential pages have been omitted.

CHRONOLOGY

1940

March   Otto Frisch and Rudolf Peierls, a pair of émigré scientists at Birmingham University, complete their memorandum 'On the Construction of a "Super-bomb"; based on a Nuclear Chain Reaction in Uranium', showing that far less uranium than previously thought, if it could be enriched, would be needed to make a bomb of great destructive power producing 'radiations [which] would be fatal to living beings even a long time after the explosion.'

April   The Ministry of Aircraft Production establishes the Maud Committee to examine the feasibility of a uranium bomb on the basis of the Frisch-Peierls Memorandum.

1941

July   The Maud Committee 'considers that the scheme for a uranium bomb is practicable and likely to lead to decisive results in the war. It recommends that this work be continued on the highest priority and on the increasing scale necessary to obtain the weapon in the shortest possible time.'

1942

30 July   Sir John Anderson, minister for 'Tube Alloys' (the weapon's cover name), minutes Churchill advising that the scale and cost of the atomic bomb project requires the UK to 'move our design work and the personnel concerned to the United States. Henceforth, work on the bomb project would be pursued as a combined Anglo-American effort.'

1943

19 August   Churchill and Roosevelt sign the secret Quebec Agreement establishing 'First, that we will never use this agency [the atomic bomb] against each other. Secondly, that we will not use it against third parties without each other's consent. Thirdly, that we will not either of us communicate any information about Tube Alloys to third parties except by mutual consent.' Collaboration between the US and the UK to be overseen by a Combined Policy Committee meeting in Washington.

December   First members of a 19-strong UK team of British scientists arrive at Los Alamos in New Mexico, where the bomb is designed and built in immense secrecy.

1944

19 September   Hyde Park Aide-memoire of conversation between Roosevelt and Churchill at the President's home in upstate New York recording the decision that the 'matter should continue to be regarded as of the utmost secrecy; but when a "bomb" is finally available, it might

perhaps, after mature consideration, be used against the Japanese, who should be warned that this bombardment will be repeated until they surrender' and that '[f]ull collaboration between the United States and the British Government in developing tube alloys for military and commercial purposes should continue after the defeat of Japan unless and until terminated by joint agreement.'

1945

1 July	Churchill gives UK approval for atomic bombs to be dropped on Japan.
16 July	World's first atomic explosion takes place at the Trinity test site in New Mexico.
26 July	Attlee forms a government. Labour majority of 146 in the House of Commons.
6 August	Atomic bomb dropped on Hiroshima.
9 August	Atomic bomb dropped on Nagasaki.
14 August	Japan surrenders.
28 August	Attlee circulates memorandum on 'The Atomic Bomb' to GEN 75, his Cabinet Committee on Atomic Energy. He tells ministers that 'No government has ever been placed in such a position as is ours today. The Governments of the UK and the USA are responsible as never before for the future of the human race' and that 'The answer to an atomic bomb on London is an atomic bomb on another great city.'
18 December	GEN 75 authorises the construction of an atomic pile at Windscale to produce plutonium.

1946

August	US Congress passes the McMahon Act prohibiting the transmission of nuclear information to another country.
25 October	During a GEN 75 meeting, Dalton (Chancellor of the Exchequer) and Cripps (President of the Board of Trade) argue that UK economic recovery could not afford the £30–40 million needed over five years to build a gaseous diffusion plant for the production of Uranium 235. Bevin insists 'We've got to have the bloody Union Jack on top of it' [i.e. the atomic bomb], and prevails.

1947

8 January	GEN 163 meets for the first and only time to authorise 'that research and development work on atomic weapons should be undertaken' in conditions of the utmost secrecy. The decision is taken by Attlee and five ministers. The group does not include Dalton and Cripps.

1948

12 May	Minister of Defence, A. V. Alexander, tells the House of Commons that 'research and developments continue to receive the highest priority in the defence field, and all types of modern weapons, inclu-

ding atomic weapons, are being developed.' He adds that it would not be 'in the public interest' to say more.

1949

29 August	The Soviet Union detonates its first atomic device in Kazakhstan.
23 September	Truman announces the news of the Russian test in Washington.

1950

31 January	Truman makes public his decision taken that day that the US will manufacture 'the so-called hydrogen or superbomb'.
3 February	British nuclear physicist Klaus Fuchs charged with passing nuclear secrets to the Soviet Union.
23 February	General election: Attlee government returned to office with a majority of five.
1 March	Fuchs sentenced to 14 years imprisonment.

1951

25 October	General election: Churchill and the Conservatives returned to power with a majority of 17.
21 November	Churchill briefed on Attlee governments' work on the atomic bomb.
12 December	Churchill briefed on how Attlee governments concealed the cost of the atomic bomb from Parliament.
14 December	Churchill authorises bomb test in Australia.

1952

18 February	Churchill announces that the UK will test an atomic bomb later in the year.
3 October	First British atomic device detonated in the Monte Bello Islands off north-west Australia.
1 November	US tests first hydrogen bomb at Eniwetok in the Pacific. At 10.4 megatons, its power is twice that of all the explosives used in the Second World War.

1953

12 August	Soviet Union tests an H-bomb. (In fact, it was a hybrid device, not a true thermonuclear explosion.)
7 November	First Blue Danube atomic bomb arrives from Aldermaston at RAF Wittering.

1954

1 March	US explodes a 15-megaton H-bomb at Bikini Atoll in the Pacific.
22 March	*Lucky Dragon* returns to Japan from a Pacific fishing voyage with its crew suffering from radiation sickness.

13 April	Churchill tells ministers on the GEN 464 Cabinet Committee he would like the full Cabinet to authorise the manufacture of a British H-bomb.
1 June	Chiefs of Staff brief Churchill and members of his Defence Policy Committee on the danger of the USA starting a 'forestalling' war against the Soviet Union. They also claim that a UK armed with its own H-bomb could 'be on terms with the United States and Russia.'
16 June	Churchill's Defence Policy Committee authorises an H-bomb programme.
7 July	Cabinet breaks up in disarray after discussing proposed talks with the Russians and the making of a British H-bomb. Some ministers complain at lack of consultation.
8 July	Cabinet discusses morality and cost of an H-bomb.
26 July	Cabinet agrees to the manufacture of a British H-bomb.

1955

13 January	Joint Intelligence Committee states that the only warning of an H-bomb attack on the UK will probably be the presence of Russian bombers on RAF and allied radar screens.
17 February	Defence White Paper reveals government's intention to make an H-bomb.
5 April	Churchill resigns. Eden Prime Minister.
26 May	General election: Conservatives increase majority to 59.
22 November	Soviets test a 1.6-megaton hydrogen bomb.

1956

July	First operational Valiant bombers arrive at RAF Wittering.
5 November	Soviet Prime Minister, Bulganin, threatens rockets on Paris and London if Anglo-French invasion of Egypt is not halted.

1957

9 January	Eden resigns.
10 January	Queen appoints Macmillan Prime Minister.
4 April	Sandys Defence White Paper published stressing the primacy of nuclear deterrence and foreshadowing the end of National Service.
15 May	UK tests a thermonuclear device at Christmas Island in the Pacific. It yields 300 kilotons, 30 per cent of the megaton target.
3 October	Bevan heckled at Labour Party Conference for arguing this is not the time for Britain to renounce the H-bomb.
24 October	President Eisenhower agrees to amend the McMahon Act to enable a US-UK exchange of nuclear weapons information during talks in Washington with Macmillan.
8 November	Britain's first megaton H-bomb explodes off Christmas Island yielding 1.8 megatons.

1958

15 January	Meeting at Canon Collins' home near St Paul's Cathedral sees birth of the Campaign for Nuclear Disarmament (CND).
17 February	CND holds its first meeting in Westminster Central Hall.
4 April	4,000 protestors leave Trafalgar Square for the Atomic Weapons Research Establishment at Aldermaston.
7 April	They arrive.
30 June	US Congress repeals those sections of the McMahon Act that prevented nuclear weapons collaboration with the UK.
4 August	US and UK governments conclude the Agreement for Co-operation on the Uses of Atomic Energy for Mutual Defence Purposes.

1959

7 June	Secret meeting at Chequers of military, officials and diplomats chaired by Macmillan rules out unilateral nuclear disarmament and concludes that 'In terms of foreign policy the British contribution to the western deterrent had paid a handsome dividend up to now, but we should have to consider whether it would continue to do so.' Macmillan commissions a *Future Policy Study* to forecast Britain's place in the world by 1970.
8 October	General election: Conservatives increase majority to 100.

1960

13 February	France tests its first atomic bomb in the Algerian Sahara.
24 February	*Future Policy Study* completed. It concludes that: 'Our purpose should be to maintain a strategic nuclear force which is accepted by the Americans, and by the [NATO] Alliance as a whole, as a significant contribution to the western deterrent. . . This would not mean (except in the view of one of those associated with this study [Sir Dermot Boyle, Chief of the Air Staff]) that we were aiming to provide a force capable by itself of deterring Russia.'
13 April	Cabinet told that its Defence Committee, on the advice of the Chiefs of Staff, had decided to abandon the Blue Streak rocket. Cabinet concurs and the decision is announced in the House of Commons the same day.
20 June	Cabinet approves the purchase of the untested US stand-off Skybolt missile which, if it worked, would have a British nuclear warhead and prolong the deterrent capability of the RAF's V-bombers into 'the later 1960s', thereby filling the gap left by the cancellation of Blue Streak.

1962

11 December	Kennedy Administration announces the cancellation of Skybolt.
18 December	Macmillan flies to Nassau to meet President Kennedy in an attempt to persuade his administration to supply submarine-launched Polaris missiles as a replacement for Skybolt.

21 December	Cabinet, chaired by R. A. Butler in Macmillan's absence, considers telegrams from the Prime Minister in Nassau and asking 'for the advice of the Cabinet' on the acceptability of the terms proposed for the purchase of Polaris.
26 December	Macmillan asks Minister of Defence to prepare a paper on UK designed and built alternatives to Polaris if the Nassau agreement collapsed.
31 December	At a meeting of ministers and officials, chaired by Macmillan, Ted Heath says the Skybolt cancellation and the Polaris purchase exposed to the public 'the extent of our dependence on the United States.' If the two governments disagreed strongly on policy, the US might cancel the arrangement. The Minister of Defence, Peter Thorneycroft says the UK would not be able to afford to develop 'a reinsurance system of its own' from scratch.

1963

3 January	Full Cabinet discusses the Nassau deal and authorises the purchase of Polaris, and the arrangement whereby it could be withdrawn from NATO into national service 'if the supreme interests of the country required it'. Macmillan says that, unlike Skybolt, 'Polaris would extend the effectiveness and credibility of the United Kingdom deterrent for an almost indefinite period.'
15 January	Amery, Minister of Aviation, briefs Thorneycroft on the long-term procurement runs and expense needed to develop a UK alternative to Polaris.
28 January	Thorneycroft rules out taking the exercise further.
6 April	Polaris Sales Agreement signed in Washington.

1964

September	Labour's General Election Manifesto says of Polaris: 'It will not be independent and it will not be British and it will not deter. . . We are not prepared any longer to waste the country's resources on endless duplication of strategic nuclear weapons. We shall propose the re-negotiation of the Nassau agreement.'
15 October	General election: Labour wins with a majority of 5. Harold Wilson Prime Minister the following day.
16 October	China explodes an atomic device in Sinkiang Province.
11 November	MISC 16 Cabinet committee on 'Atlantic Nuclear Force' meets (Wilson; Patrick Gordon Walker, Foreign Secretary; Denis Healey, Defence Secretary). Discusses the idea of pooling the UK Polaris submarines with a number of US ones in an Atlantic nuclear force. Decides that 'three submarines would represent the minimum force which would be acceptable to us in the event of the dissolution of the NATO Alliance.' The Conservative Government's proposed five submarines 'would not represent a nuclear force for a world-wide role, but would only meet the requirements of the European theatre.'
21–22 November	Wilson summons a meeting of MISC 17, his Cabinet Committee on Defence Policy, to Chequers to consider the forthcoming defence

review and the future of Polaris. Wilson tells his colleagues that 'of the five submarines which had been planned, two were at an advanced stage of development and short of scrapping it would be impracticable not to complete them.' Debate focuses on desirability of a three or four-boat force.

26 November   Full Cabinet briefed by Wilson on decision to commit 'such Polaris submarines as we might construct' to a proposed Atlantic Nuclear Force... The precise number of these submarines would be for further consideration; but it was relevant to a decision that the construction of some of them was already sufficiently advanced to make it unrealistic to cancel the orders. On the other hand the number to be retained would be smaller than the number which the previous Government had envisaged and would be such as to make it clear that we no longer contemplated the maintenance of an independent nuclear force.' The Cabinet approves the Prime Minister's proposals.

1965

6 January   Healey circulates a paper to the Cabinet's Defence and Oversea Policy Committee arguing that a fleet of four Polaris submarines is preferable to three, and as the fourth boat is already under construction, 'cancellation at this stage would involve the payment of cancellation charges...'

29 January   Cabinet's Defence and Oversea Policy Committee meets (Wilson plus six ministers). Decision taken to build four Polaris submarines partly to ensure that one boat will always be on station when the Royal Navy assumes the main deterrent role in the late 1960s.

1966

March   Labour manifesto says the party 'stands by its pledge to internationalise our strategic nuclear forces' through the proposed Atlantic Nuclear Force (which never materialised).

31 March   General election: Labour returned with a majority of 96.

28 September   First meeting of Wilson's new Cabinet Committee on Nuclear Policy (PN). Discussion on whether UK 'could no longer count on United States co-operation in nuclear defence matters unless we retained a nuclear weapons capability.'

1967

3 August   Healey implements PN committee decision that 'in accordance with the Nassau Agreement our POLARIS missiles will be assigned' to NATO's Supreme Allied Commander Europe, 'as soon as the first submarine becomes operational, i.e., in 1968. Ultimate United Kingdom control of the POLARIS force will not be affected, since control of the firing chain will remain in UK hands; in particular, no submarine commander will be authorised to fire the POLARIS weapons without the Prime Minister's specific authority.'

30 October   *HMS Resolution*, first of the Polaris missile-carrying submarines, is commissioned.

18 November	The pound is devalued by 14 per cent from $2.80 to $2.40 against the US dollar.
1 December	Paper goes to PN on future options for Polaris. Should it be improved to enable the missiles to penetrate the anti-ballistic missile screen the Russians were thought to be planning to protect Moscow? The Ministry of Defence and the Foreign Office say yes. The Treasury and the Department for Economic Affairs urge 'abandonment' of 'the whole of our nuclear capability as quickly as possible. Given our difficult economic situation, the capability is a misuse of the resources it will consume.'
5 December	PN meets. Polaris to continue but 'further studies should be undertaken to clarify the requirements and the costs of alternative programmes for hardening the Polaris warhead and of penetration aids for the Polaris system.' Inquiry to be held 'into the minimum scale of effort' that would be needed at the Atomic Weapons Research Establishment, Aldermaston.

1968

15 February	*HMS Resolution* successfully test fires the first of the Royal Navy's Polaris missiles off Florida.
31 July	Lord Rothschild, in a minority dissenting note to the Kings Norton inquiry into the future of Aldermaston, recommends against improving Polaris as it 'will incur additional open-ended expenditure' as 'No technical considerations have been advanced which lead to the conclusion that hardening or the development of more sophisticated warheads would confer clear-cut and unequivocal advantages on the United Kingdom.'
24 August	France successfully tests an H-bomb at Fangataufa Atoll in the Pacific.
28 September	*HMS Repulse* commissioned.
15 November	*HMS Renown* commissioned.

1969

17 January	Joint Intelligence Committee reports that 'An ABM system is being constructed around Moscow' based on the Galosh missile which 'is expected to provide Moscow with a limited defence against ... Polaris missiles' picked up on radars in the Baltic and the Kola Peninsula.
14 June	Royal Navy Polaris submarines formally take over the primary deterrent role from the RAF V force. *HMS Resolution* had slipped out of Faslane on 30 April.
4 December	*HMS Revenge* commissioned.

1970

| 18 June | General election: Conservatives returned with a majority of 30. Heath becomes Prime Minister the following day and inherits Labour's work on a possible Polaris Improvement Programme codenamed 'Super Antelope'. |

1972

26 May   Signing in Moscow of SALT I treaty limiting the USA and USSR to 200 anti-ballistic missile launchers to protect Washington and Moscow.

1973

12 September   Heath chairs a meeting of three ministers (Douglas-Home, Foreign Secretary; Carrington, Defence Secretary; Barber, Chancellor of the Exchequer) on the future of the deterrent. Funding for 'Super Antelope' research due to run out at the end of the month. Carrington says it's uncertain that the US Congress would approve the sale of Poseidon missiles to the Royal Navy. Heath says 'the maintenance of a credible nuclear deterrent must be regarded as of very great importance in the wider political context.' More money allocated to 'Super Antelope'.

30 October   The same ministerial group approves the development of 'Super Antelope' (later known as 'Chevaline'). Co-operation with France ruled out.

1974

28 February   General election produces a 'hung' result. Labour 301 seats; Conservatives 297; Liberals 14.

4 March   Heath resigns; Wilson appointed Prime Minister in a minority Labour government.

5 April   Wilson, after discussion with Callaghan (Foreign Secretary) and Healey (Chancellor) approves a Chevaline-related test in Nevada planned by the Heath administration.

24 May   UK underground test, codenamed 'Fallon', in Nevada.

13 June   Joint Intelligence Committee reports heavy Soviet R and D and new construction work around Moscow to improve 'the deployed MOSCOW system'.

19 June   Defence Studies Working Party (part of Labour's 1974 defence review) reports that £50m has already been spent on 'Super Antelope' and that the project's cancellation 'would mean that our Polaris missiles could no longer be certain of penetrating Soviet ABM defences throughout the existing life of the submarines; and, although out ability to threaten undefended cities within range would remain, our ultimate determination to go to the limit in confronting the USSR would be in question and the main reason for possessing a strategic deterrent negated.'

15 July   Paper circulated to ministers on the Cabinet's Defence and Oversea Policy Committee arguing that 'peacetime capability' of Polaris needs improving if the UK strategic deterrent is to remain credible. The cost estimated at 'about £170m over the [10-year] LTC [long-term costing] period'.

31 July   Wilson prepares a paper for the Cabinet on a recent British nuclear test in America. 'We knew from technical assessment . . . [of] . . . the nature and rate of Soviet anti-missile defence development that our

missiles would have to be given better penetration capability if we wished to retain a credible deterrent. . . We also specifically agreed that the decision to hold this test was without prejudice to the policy decision of whether to retain our nuclear deterrent which would be taken in the context of the defence review.' (The paper is not shown to the Cabinet until 12 September because of pressure of other business at last pre-recess Cabinet).

18 September	Wilson chairs a meeting of the Defence and Oversea Policy Committee (including Callaghan; Healey; Short, Lord President; Mason, Defence Secretary; Lever, Chancellor of the Duchy). Decides not to lower 'the nuclear threshold'.
10 October	General election; Labour returned with an overall majority of 3. Its manifesto says 'We have renounced any intention of moving towards a new generation of strategic nuclear weapons.'
20 November	Wilson tells the full Cabinet that the DOPC 'had unanimously decided' the UK strategic nuclear deterrent 'should be retained.' Planned improvements 'necessary to ensure the continuing credibility of the present force were relatively cheap; they would not involve either a new generation of missiles or Multiple Independently Targeted Re-entry Vehicles.' Some dissenting views expressed, but Cabinet agrees.

1976

| 4 April | Wilson resigns and Callaghan becomes Prime Minister. |
| December | Substantial defence spending cuts, to meet the terms of an International Monetary Fund loan, fleetingly place 'Chevaline' and the Polaris system in jeopardy. |

1977

Estimates of 'Chevaline' costs rise to £810m (£494m at 1972 prices). Callaghan and a small group of ministers decide to carry on nonetheless.

1978

January	Callaghan sets up Ministerial Nuclear Policy Group (himself; Owen, Foreign Secretary; Healey, Chancellor of the Exchequer; Mulley, Defence Secretary) to consider possible Polaris replacement. Commissions an official Steering Group on Nuclear Matters chaired by the Cabinet Secretary, Hunt.
16 February	The steering group commissions Nuclear Matters Working Party to produce a two-part report: on politico-military requirements for a future UK deterrent led by Sir Antony Duff, a senior diplomat; and on the technical options, led by Professor Sir Ronald Mason, Chief Scientific Adviser to the Ministry of Defence.
13 December	Callaghan's ministerial group meets to consider the Duff-Mason Report which recommends Polaris be replaced by Trident. Owen argues for a cheaper, submarine-launched cruise missile system. Callaghan says: 'To give up our status as a nuclear weapon state would be a momentous step in British history,' but the decision

should go to Cabinet after the general election. Full Cabinet unaware of this discussion.

| 21 December | Ministerial Group meets. |

1979

| 2 January | Ministerial Group meets. |

| 6 January | Callaghan secures agreement from President Carter at a private meeting during the Guadaloupe summit that the US would supply Trident missiles if a UK Cabinet asked for them. |

| April | Labour's manifesto states 'In 1974, we renounced any intention of moving towards the production of a new generation of nuclear weapons or a successor to the Polaris nuclear force; we reiterate our belief that this is the best course for Britain. But many great issues affecting our allies and the world are involved, and a new round of strategic arms limitation negotiations will soon begin. We think it is essential that there must be a full and informed debate about these issues in the country before the necessary decision is taken.' |
| | Conservative manifesto states: 'The SALT [Strategic Arms Limitation Talks] increase the importance of ensuring the continuing effectiveness of Britain's nuclear deterrent.' |

| 3 May | General election: Conservatives win a majority of 43. |

| 4 May | Callaghan leaves instructions in Downing Street that Duff-Mason reports should be made available to Mrs Thatcher who becomes Prime Minister that day. |
| | Mrs Thatcher swiftly convenes her MISC 7 Cabinet committee to examine Polaris replacement. |

| 6 December | MISC 7 decides to opt for the Trident C4 missile. |

1980

| 24 January | Pym (Defence Secretary) reveals 'Chevaline' programme to Parliament and says its costs have risen to £1bn (£530m in 1972 prices). |

| 15 July | Thatcher tells the full Cabinet that MISC 7 has decided to opt for the Trident C4 missile (announcement made in Parliament that afternoon for fear of a leak in the *New York Times*). |
| | Government publishes *The Future United Kingdom Strategic Nuclear Deterrent Force*. Drafted by Michael Quinlan, it stresses the 'second centre of decision-making' argument ('We need to convince Soviet leaders that even if they thought at some critical point as a conflict developed the US would hold back, the British force could still inflict a blow so destructive that the penalty for aggression would have proved too high'). |

1981

| November– January | MISC 7 reopens C4 decision. Decides to opt for the improved D5 missile and a four-boat force. |

1982

January	Full Cabinet briefed on MISC 7 deliberations and concurs.
November	Ministry of Defence announces 'Chevaline' missiles operational at sea.

1993

14 August	*HMS Vanguard*, the first Trident missile carrying submarine, is commissioned.

1994

May	*HMS Vanguard* launches first UK test-firing of a Trident D5 missile off Florida.
December	*HMS Vanguard* sails on first Trident operational patrol.

1995

7 January	*HMS Victorious* commissioned.

1996

13 May	*HMS Repulse* returns to Faslane at the end of the 229th and final Polaris operational patrol.
28 August	Prime Minister John Major visits Faslane for decommissioning ceremony for *HMS Repulse* and the end of Polaris' 27 years of continuous patrols.
10 December	*HMS Vigilant* commissioned.

1999

27 November	*HMS Vengeance* commissioned.

2003

11 December	The Ministry of Defence publishes its White Paper *Delivering Security in a Changing World*, which notes that decisions on replacing Trident 'are not needed in this Parliament but are likely to be required in the next one.'

2004

January	Prime Minister's group on nuclear weapons policy agrees funds to sustain capabilities of the Atomic Weapons Establishment.
21 July	The Defence Secretary, Geoff Hoon, unveils the White Paper *Delivering Security in a Changing World: Future Capabilities*. He tells Parliament that the Government remains committed to keeping open the option to replace Trident until such time as a decision is required, 'probably in the next Parliament' and announces continued funding for Atomic Weapons Establishment, Aldermaston.

2005

13 April	The Labour Manifesto is published, stating 'we are . . . committed to retaining the independent nuclear deterrent. . .'

19 July	The Defence Secretary, John Reid, tells Parliament that an average of an additional £350m per annum will be invested in Aldermaston over three years to maintain its capability.
1 November	John Reid informs the House of Commons Defence Committee that the Government's working assumption is that the UK will keep its nuclear weapons as long as other nuclear states which present a potential threat keep theirs, but that that assumption will be tested before decisions are taken.
16 November	The Official Group on the Future of the Deterrent meets for the first time under the chairmanship of the Cabinet Secretary, Sir Gus O'Donnell.
24 November	The Ministry of Defence submits evidence to the Commons Defence Committee inquiry into the future of the deterrent, on the strategic context.
14 December	The Official Group on the Future of the Deterrent meets for the second time under the chairmanship of Sir Nigel Sheinwald, Foreign Policy Adviser to the Prime Minister.

2006

26 April	The Official Group on the Future of the Deterrent meets for the third time under the chairmanship of O'Donnell.
22 June	The Chancellor of the Exchequer, Gordon Brown, in his Mansion House speech, says the 'strength of national purpose' needed to maintain UK security requires 'retaining our independent nuclear deterrent'.
27 June	The Prime Minister's Group on the Future of the Deterrent meets for the first time.
28 June	The Prime Minister, Tony Blair, tells Parliament that a decision will be taken in 2006.
30 June	The Commons Defence Committee publishes its report *The Future of the UK's Strategic Nuclear Deterrent: the Strategic Context*.
12 July	Tony Blair confirms that Parliament will vote on the future of the deterrent.
26 July	The Government responds to the Commons Defence Committee report on the Strategic Context.
18 September	The Official Group on the Future of the Deterrent meets for the fourth time under the chairmanship of O'Donnell.
17 October	The Official Group on the Future of the Deterrent meets for the fifth time under the chairmanship of Sheinwald.
10 November	The Official Group on the Future of the Deterrent meets for the sixth time under the chairmanship of O'Donnell.
15 November	The Prime Minister's Group on the Future of the Deterrent meets for the second time.

21 November	The Minister for Defence Procurement, Lord Drayson, gives evidence to the Commons Defence Committee inquiry into the Strategic Nuclear Deterrent, on the manufacturing and skills base.
23 November	The Cabinet discusses future threats which might require the retention of nuclear weapons by the UK.
4 December	Full Cabinet decides, without 'any dissenting voices', to authorise construction of a new generation of missile-carrying submarines to sustain UK deterrent over the period 2020–2050. A White Paper, *The Future of the United Kingdom's Nuclear Deterrent* (Cm 6994), is published that afternoon.
6 December	The Commons Defence Committee announces its inquiry into the White Paper.
7 December	President Bush and Tony Blair exchange letters arranging collaboration on Trident's 'life extension programme' under the terms of the 1958 agreement on nuclear co-operation and the 1963 Polaris Sales Agreement, and stating that 'any successor to the D5 system' will be compatible with UK submarine-carried launch systems.
19 December	Tony Blair publishes the UK-US exchange of letters. The Commons Defence Committee publishes its report on the manufacturing and skills base.

2007

| 14 March | House of Commons votes 409–161 to renew the Trident system (88 Labour MPs vote against). |

THE DOCUMENTS

Otto Frisch and Rudolf Peierls: co-authors of the Frisch-Peierls Memorandum, 1940.

FISSION   1940–53

In the spring of 1988, a quiet, softly-spoken scholarly figure in a brown corduroy jacket turned up at the BBC Broadcasting House reception desk a few hundred yards north of Oxford Circus. He was Sir Rudolf Peierls, co-author of the piece of paper with which any account of British government and nuclear weapons must begin. The documentary I was making for BBC Radio 4 with my producer Caroline Anstey, with the title of 'A Bloody Union Jack on Top of It', was to mark the fortieth anniversary of the announcement in the House of Commons that Britain was conducting research into atomic weapons. Sir Rudolf had come to talk about the moment, nearly eight years before the May 1948 parliamentary answer, when he and his fellow refugee scientist at Birmingham University, Otto Frisch, made their crucial theoretical breakthrough on the possibility of atomic fission.

In a basement studio, Sir Rudolf took Caroline and myself through their thought processes during the early months of 1940:

> Nobody had really thought hard about how much separated uranium would be required to make an explosion, what was a critical size, and then one day it occurred to us to ask what would happen if you had a large quantity of separated isotope, and to our surprise if you worked this out on the back of an envelope, the amount came out quite small. Then we asked ourselves, if you could make such an explosion, what would happen? And again, on the back of another envelope, it came out that while you couldn't predict the exact power, the effects would be enormous. We also then pointed out the consequences of this weapon, including the fallout, including the fact that it would probably be very difficult to use it without killing a lot of civilians, and we added for that reason it might never be a suitable weapon for use by this country.[16]

1. The Frisch–Peierls 'Memorandum on the properties of a radioactive "superbomb"' and 'On the construction of a "superbomb", based on a nuclear chain reaction in uranium'.   TNA, PRO, AB 1/210

Memorandum on the properties of a radioactive "super-bomb".

The attached detailed report concerns the possibility of constructing a "super-bomb" which utilizes the energy stored in atomic nuclei as a source of energy. The energy liberated in the explosion of such a super-bomb is about the same as that produced by the explosion of 1000 tons of dynamite. This energy is liberated in a small volume, in which it will, for an instant, produce a temperature comparable to that in the interior of the sun. The blast from such an explosion would destroy life in a wide area. The size of this area is difficult to estimate, but it will probably cover the centre of a big city.

In addition, some part of the energy set free by the bomb goes to produce radioactive substances, and these will emit very powerful and dangerous radiations. The effect of these radiations is greatest immediately after the explosion, but it decays only gradually and even for days after the explosion any person entering the affected area will be killed.

Some of this radioactivity will be carried along with the wind and will spread the contamination; several miles downwind this may kill people.

In order to produce such a bomb it is necessary to treat a few cwt. of uranium by a process which will separate from the uranium its light isotope (U_{235}) of which it contains about 0.7%. Methods for the separation of isotopes have recently been developed. They are slow and they have not until now been applied to uranium, whose chemical properties give rise to technical difficulties. But these difficulties are by no means insuperable. We have not sufficient experience with large-scale chemical plant to give a reliable estimate of the cost, but it is certainly not prohibitive.

It is a property of these super-bombs that there exists a "critical size" of about one pound. A quantity of the separated uranium isotope that exceeds the critical amount is explosive; +++. The bomb would therefore be manufactured in two (or more) parts, each being less than the critical size, and in transport all danger of a premature explosion would be avoided if these parts were kept at a distance of few inches from each other. The bomb would be provided with a mechanism that brings the two parts together when the bomb is intended to go off. Once the parts are joined to form a block which exceeds the critical amount, the effect of the penetrating radiation always present in the atmosphere will initiate the explosion within a second or so.

The mechanism which brings the parts of the bomb together must be arranged to work fairly rapidly because of the possibility of the bomb exploding when the critical conditions have just only been reached. In this case the explosion will be far less powerful. It is never possible to exclude this altogether, but one can easily ensure that only, say, one bomb out of 100 will fail in this way, and since in any case the explosion is strong enough to destroy the bomb itself, this point is not serious.

We do not feel competent to discuss the strategic value of such a bomb, but the following conclusions seem certain:

1. As a weapon, the super-bomb would be practically irresistible. There is no material or structure that could be expected to resist the force of the explosion. If one thinks of using the bomb for breaking through a line of fortifications, it should be kept in mind that the radioactive radiations will prevent anyone from approaching the affected territory for several days; they will equally prevent defenders from reoccupying the affected positions. The advantage would lie with the side which can determine most accurately just when it is safe to re-enter the area; this is likely to be the aggressor, who knows the location of the bomb in advance.

+++ yet a quantity less than the critical amount is absolutely safe.

2.   Owing to the spreading of radioactive substances with
the wind, the bomb could probably not be used without killing
large numbers of civilians, and this may make it unsuitable as a
weapon for use by this country. (Use as a depth charge near a
naval base suggests itself, but even there it is likely that it
would cause great loss of civilian life by flooding and by the
radioactive radiations.)

3.   We have no information that the same idea has also
occurred to other scientists, but since all the theoretical data
bearing on this problem are published, it is quite conceivable that
Germany is, in fact, developing this weapon. Whether this is
the case is difficult to find out, since the plant for the
separation of isotopes need not be of such a size as to attract
attention. Information that could be helpful in this respect would
be data about the exploitation of the uranium mines under German
control (mainly in Czechoslovakia) and about any recent German
purchases of uranium abroad. It is likely that the plant would be
controlled by Dr. K. Clusius (Professor of Physical Chemistry in
Munich University), the inventor of the best method for separating
isotopes, and therefore information as to his whereabouts and
status might also give an important clue.

At the same time it is quite possible that nobody in
Germany has yet realised that the separation of the uranium isotopes
would make the construction of a super-bomb possible. Hence it is
of extreme importance to keep this report secret since any rumour
about the connection between uranium separation and a super-bomb
may set a German scientist thinking along the right lines.

4.   If one works on the assumption that Germany is, or will
be, in the possession of this weapon, it must be realised that
no shelters are available that would be effective and could be used
on a large scale. The most effective reply would be a counter-
threat with a similar bomb. Therefore it seems to us important to
start production as soon and as rapidly as possible, even if it
is not intended to use the bomb as a means of attack. Since the
separation of the necessary amount of uranium is, in the most
favourable circumstances, a matter of several months, it would
obviously be too late to start production when such a bomb is known
to be in the hands of Germany, and the matter seems, therefore,
very urgent.

5.   As a measure of precaution, it is important to have
detection squads available in order to deal with the radioactive
effects of such a bomb. Their task would be to approach the danger
zone zone with measuring instruments, to determine the extent and
probable duration of the danger and to prevent people from entering
the danger zone. This is vital since the radiations kill
instantly only in very strong doses, whereas weaker doses produce
delayed effects, and hence near the edges of the danger zone people
would have no warning until it were too late.

For their own protection, the detection squads would enter
the danger zone in motor-cars or aeroplanes which are armoured
with lead plates, which absorb most of the dangerous radiation. The
cabin would have to be hermetically sealed and oxygen carried in
cylinders because of the danger from contaminated air.

The detection staff would have to know exactly the greatest
dose of radiation to which a human being can be exposed safely for
a short time. This safety limit is not at present known with
sufficient accuracy and further biological research for this
purpose is urgently required.

As regards the reliability of the conclusions outlined
above, it may be said that they are not based on direct experiments,
since nobody has ever yet built a super-bomb, but they are mostly
based on facts which, by recent research in nuclear physics, have
been very safely established. The only uncertainty concerns the

1. (cont.)

critical size for the bomb. We are fairly confident that the critical size is roughly a pound or so, but for this estimate we have to rely on certain theoretical ideas which have not been positively confirmed. If the critical size were appreciably larger than we believe it to be, the technical difficulties in the way of constructing the bomb would be enhanced. The point can be definitely settled as soon as a small amount of uranium has been separated, and we think that in view of the importance of the matter immediate steps should be taken to reach at least this stage; meanwhile it is also possible to carry out certain experiments which, while they cannot settle the question with absolute finality, could, if their result were positive, give strong support to our conclusions.

O. R. Frisch
R. Peierls

The University,
Birmingham.

On the construction of a "super-bomb", based on a nuclear chain reaction in uranium.

5B

The Possible construction of "super-bombs" based on a nuclear chain reaction in uranium has been discussed a great deal and arguments have been brought forward which seemed to exclude this possibility. We wish here to point out and discuss a possibility which seems to have been overlooked in these earlier discussions.

Uranium consists essentially of two isotopes, U_{238} (99.3%) and U_{235} (0.7%). If a uranium nucleus is hit by a neutron, three processes are possible: (1) scattering, whereby the neutron changes direction and, if its energy is above about 0.1 MeV, loses energy; (2) capture, when the neutron is taken up by the nucleus; and (3) fission, i.e. the nucleus breaks up into two nuclei of comparable size, with the liberation of an energy of about 200 MeV.

The possibility of a chain reaction is given by the fact that neutrons are emitted in the fission and that the number of these neutrons per fission is greater than 1. The most probable value for this figure seems to be 2.3, from two independent determinations.

However, it has been shown that even in a large block of ordinary uranium no chain reaction would take place since too many neutrons would be slowed down by inelastic scattering into the energy region where they are strongly absorbed by U_{238}.

Several people have tried to make chain reaction possible by mixing the uranium with water, which reduces the energy of the neutrons still further and thereby increases their efficiency again. It seems fairly certain, however, that even then it is impossible to sustain a chain reaction.

In any case, no arrangement containing hydrogen and based on the action of slow neutrons could act as an effective super-bomb, because the reaction would be too slow. The time required to slow down a neutron is about 10^{-5} sec. and the average time lost before a neutron hits a uranium nucleus is even 10^{-4} sec. In the reaction, the number of neutrons would increase exponentially, like $e^{t/\tau}$ where τ would be at least 10^{-4} sec. When the temperature reaches several thousand degrees the container of the bomb will break and within 10^{-4} sec the uranium would have expanded sufficiently to let the neutrons escape and so to stop the reaction. The energy liberated would, therefore, be only a few times the energy required to break the container, i.e. of the same order of magnitude as with ordinary high explosives.

Bohr has put forward strong arguments for the suggestion that the fission observed with slow neutrons is to be ascribed to the rare isotope U_{235}, and that this isotope has, on the whole, a much greater fission probability than the common isotope U_{238}. Effective methods for the separation of isotopes have been developed recently, of which the method of thermal diffusion is simple enough to permit separation on a fairly large scale.

This permits, in principle, the use of nearly pure U_{235} in such a bomb, a possibility which apparently has not so far been seriously considered. We have discussed this possibility and come to the conclusion that a moderate amount of U_{235} would indeed constitute an extremely efficient explosive.

The behaviour of U_{235} under bombardment with fast neutrons is not known experimentally, but from rather simple theoretical arguments it can be concluded that almost every collision produces fission and that neutrons of any energy are effective. Therefore it is not necessary to add hydrogen, and the reaction, depending on the action of fast neutrons, develops with very great rapidity so that a considerable part of the total energy is liberated before the reactions gets stopped on account of the expansion of the material.

1. (cont.)

The critical radius r_0 – that is, the radius of a sphere in which the surplus of neutrons created by the fission is just equal to the loss of neutrons by escape through the surface – is, for a material with a given composition, in a fixed ratio to the mean free path of the neutrons, and this in turn is inversely proportional to the density. If therefore pays to bring the material into the densest possible form, i.e. the metallic state, probably sintered or hammered. If we assume, for U_{235}, no appreciable scattering, and 2.3 neutrons emitted per fission, then the critical radius is found to be 0.8 times the mean free path. In the metallic state (density 15), and assuming a fission cross-section of $10^{-23} cm^2$, the mean free path would be 2.6 cm. and r_0 would be 2.1 cm, corresponding to a mass of 600 grams. A sphere of metallic U_{235} of a radius greater than r_0 would be explosive, and one might think of about 1 Kg as a suitable size for the bomb.

The speed of the reaction is easy to estimate. The neutrons emitted in the fission have velocities of about 10^9 cm/sec and they have to travel 2.6 cm before hitting a uranium nucleus. For a sphere well above the critical size the loss through neutron escape would be small, so we may assume that each neutron, after a life of 2.6×10^{-9} sec, produces a fission, giving birth to two neutrons. In the expression $e^{t/\tau}$ for the increase of neutron density with time, τ would be about 4×10^{-9} sec, very much shorter than in the case of chain reaction depending on slow neutrons.

If the reaction proceeds until most of the uranium is used up, temperatures of the order of 10^{10} degrees and pressures of about 10^{13} atmospheres are produced. It is difficult to predict accurately the behaviour of matter under these extreme conditions, and the mathematical difficulties of the problem are considerable. By a rough calculation we get the following expression for the energy liberated before the mass expends so much that the reaction is interrupted:

$$E = 0.2 \ M \ (r^2/\tau^2) \ (\sqrt{r/r_0} - 1) \tag{1}$$

(M total mass of uranium, r radius of sphere, r_0 critical radius, τ time required for neutron density to multiply by a factor e). For a sphere of radius 4.2 cm (r_0= 2.1 cm), M = 4700 grams, τ = 4×10^{-9} sec, we find E = 4×10^{20} ergs, which is about one tenth of the total fission energy. For a radius of about 8 cms. (M = 32 Kg) the whole fission energy is liberated, according to formula (1) For small radii the efficiency falls off even faster than indicated by formula (1) because goes up as r approaches r_0. The energy liberated by a 5 Kg bomb would be equivalent to that of several thousand tons of dynamite, while that of a 1 kg bomb, though about 500 times less, would still be formidable.

It is necessary that such a sphere should be made in two (or more) parts which are brought together first when the explosion is wanted. Once assembled, the bomb would explode within a second or less, since one neutron is sufficient to start the reaction and there are several neutrons passing through the bomb in every second, from the cosmic radiation. (Neutrons originating from the action of uranium alpha rays on light-element impurities would be negligible provided the uranium is reasonably pure.) A sphere with a radius less than about 3 cm could be made up in two hemispheres which are pulled together by springs and kept separated by a suitable structure which is removed at the desired moment. A larger sphere would have to be composed of more than two parts, if the parts, taken separately, are to be stable.

It is important that the assembling of the parts should be done as rapidly as possible, in order to minimize the chance of a reaction getting started at a moment when the critical conditions have only just been reached. If this happened, the reaction rate would be much slower and the energy liberation would be considerably reduced; it would, however, always be sufficient to destroy the bomb.

It may be well to emphasize that a sphere only slightly below the critical size is entirely safe and harmless. By experimenting with spheres of gradually increasing size and measuring the number of neutrons emerging from them under a known neutron bombardment, one could accurately determine the critical size, without any danger of a premature explosion.

For the separation of the U_{235}, the method of thermal diffusion, developed by Clusius and others, seems to be the only one which can cope with the large amounts required. A gaseous uranium compound, for example uranium hexafluoride, is placed between two vertical surfaces which are kept at a different temperature. The light isotope tends to get more concentrated near the hot surface, where it is carried upwards by the convection current. Exchange with the current moving downwards along the cold surface produces a fractionating effect, and after some time a state of equilibrium is reached when the gas near the upper end contains markedly more of the light isotype than near the lower end.

For example, a system of two concentric tubes, of 2 mm separation and 3 cm diameter, 150 cm long, would produce a difference of about 40% in the concentration of the rare isotype between its ends, and about 1 gram per day could be drawn from the upper end without unduly upsetting the equilibrium.

In order to produce large amounts of highly concentrated U_{235}, a great number of these separating units will have to be used, being arranged in parallel as well as in series. For a daily production of 100 grams of U_{235} of 90% purity, we estimate that about 100,000 of these tubes would be required. This seems a large number, but it would undoubtedly be possible to design some kind of a system which would have the same effective area in a more compact and less expensive form.

In addition to the destructive effect of the explosion itself, the whole material of the bomb would be transformed into a highly radioactive state. The energy radiated by these active substances will amount to about 20% of the energy liberated in the explosion, and the radiations would be fatal to living beings even long time after the explosion.

The fission of uranium results in the formation of a great number of active bodies with periods between, roughly speaking, a second and a year. The resulting radiation is found to decay in such a way that the intensity is about inversely proportional to the time. Even one day after the explosion the radiation will correspond to a power expenditure of the order ot 1000 KW, or to the radiation of a hundred tons of radium.

Any estimates of the effects of this radiation on human beings must be rather uncertain because it is difficult to tell what will happen to the radioactive material after the explosion. Most of it will probably be blown into the air and carried away by the wind. This cloud of radioactive material will kill everybody within a strip estimated to be several miles long. If it rained the danger would be even worse because active material would be carried down to the ground and stick to it, and persons entering the contaminated area would be subjected to dangerous radiations even after days. If 1% of the active material sticks to the debris in the vicinity of the explosion and if the debris is spread over an area, of, say, a square mile, any person entering this area would be in serious danger, even several days after the explosion.

1. (cont.)

In these estimates, the lethal dose of penetrating radiation was assumed to be 1000 Roentgen; consultation of a medical specialist on X-ray treatment and perhaps further biological research may enable one to fix the danger limit more accurately. The main source of uncertainty is our lack of knowledge as to the behaviour of materials in such a super-explosion, and an expert on high explosives may be able to clarify some of these problems.

Effective protection is hardly possible. Houses would offer protection only at the margins of the danger zone. Deep cellars or tunnels may be comparatiely safe, provided air can be supplied from an uncontaminated area (some of the active substances would be noble gases which are not stopped by ordinary filters).

The irradiation is not felt under hours later when it may be too late. Therefore it would be very important to have an organisation which determines the exact extent of the danger area, by means of ionisation measurements, so that people can be warned from entering it.

O.R.Frisch
R.Peierls

The University,
Birmingham.

Frisch and Peierls, who as recent émigrés from Nazi-occupied Europe, lacked the security clearances to work in Whitehall's secret establishments, showed their memorandum to Professor Mark Oliphant, their Birmingham colleague, who passed it on to Sir Henry Tizard, Chairman of the government's Committee on the Scientific Survey of Air Defence.[17]

Eventually, the Ministry of Aircraft Production established the Maud Committee to evaluate the possibilities outlined by Frisch and Peierls. Its name had nothing to do with its chairman, Professor G. P. Thompson of Imperial College. Its genesis was a bizarre accident. As Margaret Gowing explained in her official history of the project:

> When Denmark was overrun by the Germans Niels Bohr had sent Dr Frisch a telegram, the latter part of which said 'Tell Cockcroft [Professor John Cockcroft of the Cavendish Laboratory, Cambridge] and Maud Ray Kent.' This was believed to be a garbled message about radium . . . and it was only after the war that it was found out that there was in fact a lady called Maud Ray in Kent who had been a governess to the Bohr children and to whom Bohr wanted a message sent. At all events the name Maud was adopted for what was to be a scientific committee of incalculable importance.[18]

The Maud Committee began meeting at the Royal Society in April 1940.[19] Fifteen months later, it reported.

2. 'Report by M.A.U.D. Committee on the use of Uranium for a Bomb'

TNA, PRO, CAB 104/227

27.

S E C R E T

Report by M.A.U.D. Committee
on the use of Uranium for a Bomb

PART I

1. General Statement

      Work to investigate the possibilities of utilising the atomic energy of uranium for military purposes has been in progress since 1939, and a stage has now been reached when it seems desirable to report progress.

      We should like to emphasize at the beginning of this report that we entered the project with more scepticism than belief, though we felt it was a matter which had to be investigated. As we proceeded we became more and more convinced that release of atomic energy on a large scale is possible and that conditions can be chosen which would make it a very powerful weapon of war. We have now reached the conclusion that it will be possible to make an effective uranium bomb which, containing some 25 lbs. of active material would be equivalent as regards destructive effect to 1,800 tons of T.N.T. and would also release large quantities of radioactive substances, which would make places near to where the bomb exploded dangerous to human life for a long period. The bomb would be composed of an active constituent (referred to in what follows as U.235) present to the extent of about 1 part in 140 in ordinary Uranium. Owing to the very small difference in properties (other than explosive) between this substance and the rest of the Uranium, its extraction is a matter of great difficulty and a plant to produce 2¼ lbs (1 kilogram) per day (or 3 bombs per month) is estimated to cost approximately £5,000,000, of which sum a considerable proportion would be spent on engineering requiring labour of the same highly skilled character as is needed for making turbines.

      In spite of this very large expenditure we consider that the destructive effect both material and moral is so great that every effort should be made to produce bombs of this kind. As regards the time required, Imperial Chemical Industries(1) after consultation with Dr. Guy of Metropolitan Vickers, estimate that the material for the first bomb could be ready by the end of 1943. This of course assumes that no major difficulty of an entirely unforeseen character arises. Dr. Ferguson of Woolwich (2) estimates that the time required to work out the method of producing high velocities required for fusing (see para. 3) is 1 – 2 months. As this could be done concurrently with the production of the material no further delay is to be anticipated on this score. Even if the war should end before the bombs are ready the effort would not be wasted except in the unlikely event of complete disarmament since no nation would care to risk being caught without a weapon of such decisive possibilities.

      We know that Germany has taken a great deal of trouble to secure supplies of the substance known as heavy water. In the earlier stages we thought that this substance might be of great importance for our work. It appears in fact that its usefulness in the release of atomic energy is limited to processes which are not likely to be of immediate war value (3), but the Germans may by now have realised this, and it may be mentioned that the lines on which we are now working are such as would be likely to suggest themselves to any capable physicist.

      By far the largest supplies of Uranium are in Canada and the Belgian Congo, and since it has been actively looked for because of the radium, which accompanies it, it is unlikely that any considerable quantities exist which are unknown except possibly in unexplored regions.

(1) Appendix I   (2) Appendix II   (3) Report of M.A.U.D. Committee on use of Uranium as a source of power.

P.8856

2. Principle Involved

This type of bomb is possible because of the enormous store of energy resident in atoms and because of the special properties of the active constituent of uranium. The explosion is very different in its mechanism from the ordinary chemical explosion, for it can occur only if the quantity of U.235 is greater than a certain critical amount. Quantities of the material less than the critical amount are quite stable. Such quantities are therefore perfectly safe, and this is a point which we wish to emphasize. On the other hand, if the amount of material exceeds the critical value it is unstable and a reaction will develop and multiply itself with enormous rapidity, resulting in an explosion of unprecedented violence. Thus all that is necessary to detonate the bomb is to bring together two pieces of the active material each less than the critical size but which when in contact form a mass exceeding it.

3. Method of Fusing

In order to achieve the greatest efficiency in an explosion of this type, it is necessary to bring the 2 halves together at high velocity and it is proposed to do this by firing them together with charges of ordinary explosive in a form of double gun.

The weight of this gun will of course exceed greatly the weight of the bomb itself, but should not be more than 1 ton, and it would certainly be within the carrying capacity of a modern bomber. It is suggested that the bomb (contained in the gun) should be dropped by parachute and that the gun should be fired by means of a percussion device when it hits the ground. The time of drop can be made long enough to allow the aeroplane to escape from the danger zone, and as this is very large, great accuracy of aim is not required.

4. Probable Effect

The best estimate of the kind of damage likely to be produced by the explosion of 1,500 tons of TNT is afforded by the great explosion at Halifax N.S. in 1917. The following account is from the "History of Explosives"[*]. "The ship contained 450,000 lb. of TNT, 122,960 lb. of guncotton, and 4,661,794 lb. of picric acid wet and dry, making a total of 5,234,754 lb. The zone of the explosion extended for about $\frac{3}{4}$ mile in every direction and in this zone the destruction was almost complete. Severe structural damage extended generally for a radius of $1\frac{1}{8}$ to $1\frac{1}{4}$ miles, and in one direction up to $1\frac{3}{4}$ miles from the origin. Missiles were projected to 3 – 4 miles, window glass broken up to 10 miles generally, and in one instance up to 61 miles."

In considering this description it is to be remembered that part of the explosives cargo was situated below water level and part above.

5. Preparation of Material and Cost

We have considered in great detail the possible methods of extracting the U.235 from ordinary Uranium and have made a number of experiments. The scheme which we recommend is described in Part II of this report and in greater detail in Appendix IV. It involves essentially the gaseous diffusion of a compound of Uranium through gauzes of very fine mesh.

In the estimates of size and cost which accompany this report, we have only assumed types of gauze which are at present in existence. It is probable that a comparatively small amount of development would enable gauzes of smaller mesh to be made and this would allow the construction of a somewhat smaller and consequently cheaper separation plant for the same output.

---

[*] Published under the direction of the Institute of Makers of Explosives by the Press of the Charles L. Story Co., Wilmington, Del., U.S.A.

2. (cont.)

Although the cost per lb. of this explosive is so great it compares very favourably (4) with ordinary explosives when reckoned in terms of energy released and damage done. It is, in fact, considerably cheaper, but the points which we regard as of overwhelming importance are the concentrated destruction which it would produce, the large moral effect, and the saving in air effort the use of this substance would allow, as compared with bombing with ordinary explosives.

6. Discussion

One outstanding difficulty of the scheme is that the main principle cannot be tested on a small scale. Even to produce a bomb of the minimum critical size would involve a great expenditure of time and money. We are however convinced that the principle is correct, and whilst there is still some uncertainty as to the critical size it is most unlikely that the best estimate we can make is so far in error as to invalidate the general conclusions. We feel that the present evidence is sufficient to justify the scheme being strongly pressed.

As regards the manufacture of the isotope we have gone nearly as far as we can on a laboratory scale. The principle of the method is certain, and the application does not appear unduly difficult as a piece of chemical engineering. The need to work on a larger scale is now very apparent and we are beginning to have difficulty in finding the necessary scientific personnel. Further, if the weapon is to be available in say two years from now, it is necessary to start plans for the erection of a factory, though no really large expenditure will be needed till the 20 stage model (5) has been tested. It is also important to begin training men who can ultimately act as supervisors of the manufacture. There are a number of auxiliary pieces of apparatus to be developed, such as those for measuring the concentration of the isotope. In addition, work on a fairly large scale is needed to develop the chemical side for the production in bulk of uranium hexafluoride.

It will be seen from the foregoing that a stage in the work has now been reached at which it is important that a decision should be made as to whether the work is to be continued on the increasing scale which would be necessary if we are to hope for it as an effective weapon for this war. Any considerable delay now would retard by an equivalent amount the date by which the weapon could come into effect.

7. Action in U.S.

We are informed that while the Americans are working on the uranium problem the bulk of their effort has been directed to the production of energy as discussed in our report on Uranium as a source of power, rather than to the production of a bomb. We are in fact co-operating with the United States to the extent of exchanging information, and they have undertaken one or two pieces of laboratory work for us. We feel that it is important and desirable that development work should proceed on both sides of the Atlantic irrespective of where it may be finally decided to locate the plant for separating the U.235 and for this purpose it seems desirable that certain members of the committee should visit the United States. We are informed that such a visit would be welcomed by members of the United States committees which are dealing with this matter.

8. Conclusions and Recommendations

(i) The committee considers that the scheme for a Uranium bomb is practicable and likely to lead to decisive results in the war.

(ii) It recommends that this work be continued on the highest priority and on the increasing scale necessary to obtain the weapon in the shortest possible time, and

(iii) That the present collaboration with America should be continued and extended especially in the region of experimental work.

(4) Appendix I.   (5) § 15. Part II

The three way US-UK-Canadian wartime partnership to develop nuclear weapons, the Manhattan Project, was dominated by American money (some $2000 million), technology and manpower. But, as Margaret Gowing noted:

> If it had not been for the brilliant scientific work done in Britain in the early part of the war, by refugee scientists, the Second World War would almost certainly have ended before an atomic bomb was dropped. It had been the cogency and clarity of the British Maud Report in 1941 which had persuaded the Americans of the practical possibility of an atomic bomb and the urgency of making one.[20]

Britain, Professor Gowing concluded, 'had been the midwife' of the atomic bomb.[21]

As official historian of Britain and atomic energy 1939–1952, Margaret Gowing had access to all related papers. She reckoned that '[a]bout seven Ministers in the wartime coalition had been involved in the bomb project in varying degrees and at varying times.' Not all of them were members of the War Cabinet. None of them were Labour.[22]* 'Mr Churchill,' she wrote, 'gave little thought to the post-war implications of the atomic bomb, except in so far as Anglo-American relations were concerned, but even if he had done so it is unlikely that he would have foreseen or imagined the difficulties of a totally unprepared and uninformed Labour Government in office when the first bombs were dropped.'[23]

Labour's 'chief problem was only too clear' in August 1945—'having ended one war with atomic bombs, how was the world to avoid blowing itself to pieces with some more?'[24] By the end of that month, Attlee had turned his mind to exactly that problem at the precise point when the question of the bomb first entered the British Cabinet system in the shape of the Prime Minister's think-piece, prepared as the first paper for his newly created Cabinet Committee on Atomic Energy (GEN 75 in the Cabinet Office's classification).

---

* General de Gaulle, Leader of Fighting France, knew what the British Deputy Prime Minister, Clement Attlee, did not know. At a brief, furtive meeting in Ottawa in July 1944, three French members of the Canadian-based 'Tube Alloys' team 'secretly informed' the General 'of the imminent results' of the Manhattan Project.[25]

3. 'The Atomic Bomb: Memorandum by the Prime Minister', GEN 75/1, 28 August 1945.

TNA, PRO, CAB 130/3

THIS DOCUMENT IS THE PROPERTY OF HIS BRITANNIC MAJESTY'S GOVERNMENT

The circulation of this paper has been strictly limited.

It is issued for the personal use of...

TOP SECRET

Copy No..............

GEN 75/1

28TH AUGUST, 1945

THE ATOMIC BOMB

Memorandum by the Prime Minister

1. A decision on major policy with regard to the atomic bomb is imperative. Until this is taken civil and military departments are unable to plan. It must be recognised that the emergence of this weapon has rendered much of our post-war planning out of date.

2. For instance a redistribution of industry planned on account of the experience of bombing attacks during the war is quite futile in face of the atomic bomb. Nothing can alter the fact that the geographical situation of Britain offers to a Continental Power such targets as London and the other great cities. Dispersal of munition works and airfields cannot alter the facts of geography.

3. Again it would appear that the provision of bomb proof basements in factories and offices and the retention of A.R.P. and Fire Services is just futile waste.

4. All considerations of strategic bases in the Mediterranean or the East Indies are obsolete. The vulnerability of the heart of the Empire is the one fact that matters. Unless its safety can be secured, it is no use bothering about things on the periphery. It is difficult for people to adjust their minds to an entirely new situation. I noticed at Potsdam that people still talked of the line of the Western Neisse although rivers as strategic frontiers have been obsolete since the advent of Air Power. It is infinitely harder for people to realise that even the modern conception of war to which in my lifetime we have become accustomed is now completely out of date.

5. We recognise or some of us did before this war that bombing could only be answered by counter bombing. We were right. Berlin and Magdeburg were the answer to London and Coventry. Both derive from Guernica. The answer to an atomic bomb on London is an atomic bomb on another great city.

6. Duelling with swords and inefficient pistols was bearable. Duelling had to go with the advent of weapons of precision. What is to be done about the atomic bomb? It has been suggested that by a Geneva Convention all nations might agree to abstain from its use. This method is bound to fail as it has failed in the past. Gas was forbidden but used in the first world war. It was not used in World War 2, but the

-1-

belligerents were armed with it. We should have used it, if the Germans had landed on our beaches. It was not used, because military opinion considered it less effective than explosives and incendiaries.

7. Further the banning of the atomic bomb would leave us with the other weapons used in the late war which were quite destructive enough.

8. Scientists agree that we cannot stop the march of discovery. We can assume that any attempt to keep this as a secret in the hands of the U.S.A. and U.K. is useless. Scientists in other countries are certain in time to hit upon the secret.

9. The most we may have is a few years start.

The question is what use are we to make of that few years start.

10. We might presumably on the strength of our knowledge and of the advanced stage reached in technical development in the U.S.A. seek to set up an Anglo-American Hegemony in the world using our power to enforce a world wide rigid inspection of all laboratories and plants.

11. I do not think this is desirable or practicable. We should not be able to penetrate the curtain that conceals the vast area of Russia. To attempt this would be to invite a world war leading to the destruction of civilization in a dozen years or so.

12. The only course which seems to me to be feasible and to offer a reasonable hope of staving off imminent disaster for the world is joint action by the U.S.A., U.K. and Russia based upon stark reality.

13. We should declare that this invention has made it essential to end wars. The new World Order must start now. The work of the San Francisco Conference must be carried much further.

14. While steps must be taken to prevent the development of this weapon in any country, this will be futile unless the whole conception of war is banished from people's minds and from the calculations of governments. This means that every vexed question will have to be settled without the use of force, whether it is Palestine, Venezia Giulia, the Ruhr, India. Every nation must submit to the rule of law. The U.S.S.R. must abandon, if it still holds them, its dreams of revolution by force or intrigue. The U.K. and the U.S.A. must abandon, if they have them, any dreams of overturning Left Governments. All nations must give up their dreams of realising some historic expansion at the expense of their neighbours. They must look to a peaceful future instead of a warlike past.

-2-

3. (cont.)

15. This sort of thing has in the past been considered a Utopian dream. It has become today the essential condition of the survival of civilisation and possibly of life in this planet.

16. No government has ever been placed in such a position as is ours today. The Governments of the U.K. and the U.S.A. are responsible as never before for the future of the human race.

17. I can see no other course than that I should on behalf of the Government put the whole of the case to President Truman and propose that he and I and Stalin should forthwith take counsel together.

The time is short.

We must come to a decision before the meeting of the United Nations Organization.

We cannot plan our future while this major factor is uncertain.

I believe that only a bold course can save civilization.

C.R.A.

———————————————

Cabinet Office, S.W.1.

28TH AUGUST, 1945.

-3-

With characteristic terseness, Attlee outlined the degree to which all politico-military thinking had been rendered 'completely out-of-date' by the new weapon; a new theory of deterrence; the overriding need for international agreement on atomic power; the certainty that other countries, the Soviet Union in particular, would possess the secret within a few years; and the possibility of a civilization-destroying third world war by the mid to late 1950s if international control was not established.

Over the autumn and early winter of 1945, Attlee and his inner group of atomic-primed ministers pursued a twin-track approach. Hopes still existed for an international agreement through the proposed United Nations Atomic Energy Commission. But, at the same time, GEN 75 began the work of creating a UK capacity to make a bomb by authorising funds for the construction of a plutonium pile in Cumberland as a matter of 'the highest urgency and importance'.

To be returned to = Mr M Olley

THIS DOCUMENT IS THE PROPERTY OF HIS BRITANNIC MAJESTY'S GOVERNMENT

The circulation of this paper has been strictly limited.

It is issued for the personal use of............................. *Cl*

TOP SECRET   Copy No. 26

GEN. 75/8th Meeting

CABINET

ATOMIC ENERGY

NOTE of a Meeting of Ministers held at
No. 10 Downing Street, S.W.1,, on
TUESDAY, 18TH DECEMBER, 1945, at 10.45 a.m.

PRESENT:

The Rt. Hon. C.R. Attlee, M.P.,
Prime Minister (In the Chair),

The Rt. Hon. Herbert Morrison,
M.P., Lord President of the
Council.

The Rt. Hon. A. Greenwood, M.P.,
Lord Privy Seal.

The Rt. Hon. Hugh Dalton, M.P.,
Chancellor of the Exchequer.

The Rt. Hon. Sir Stafford Cripps,
K.C., M.P., President of the
Board of Trade,

The Rt. Hon. Viscount Addison,
Secretary of State for
Dominion Affairs,

The Rt. Hon. John Wilmot, M.P.,
Minister of Supply and
Aircraft Production,

ALSO PRESENT:

Sir Edward Bridges,
Secretary of the Cabinet.

Marshal of the Royal Air Force,
Lord Portal of Hungerford,
Chief of the Air Staff.

Mr. Nevile Butler,
Foreign Office.

Mr. D.H.F. Rickett,,......................,,Secretary

1. — LARGE SCALE PRODUCTION

The meeting had before them a Note by the Secretary of the Cabinet (GEN.75/16) circulating a report by the Advisory Committee on Atomic Energy.

THE PRIME MINISTER said that of the four recommendations contained in Section B of the Summary, the most important was the first, namely that either one or two piles should be constructed in this country for the production of plutonium. How many piles should be built depended in part upon the output of bombs which the Government thought necessary. The Committee recommended, however, that if two piles would ultimately be required, they should be built on adjacent sites and their construction should be undertaken simultaneously.

The meeting was informed that the Chiefs of Staff had not yet been able to make a full study of our strategic requirements for bombs and the possibility of making reductions in other forms of armament production. Fuller study might well show, however, that in the light of possible production rates in other countries, the building of a second pile in this country would be justified.

It was pointed out, on the other hand, that the construction of two piles would make heavy demands upon the capacity of the chemical engineering and heavy electrical industries, both of which were of great importance to the revival of our export trade. The programme would also require building labour and machinery, e.g. for heavy excavating, both of which were in very short supply.

As the Advisory Committee had pointed out, if a second pile were to be built, it would be cheaper and more efficient to place it on a site adjacent to the first. It was not essential, however, that a decision to build the second pile should be taken immediately.

The conclusions reached were as follows:—

(1) Approval was given to the building of one pile for the production of plutonium on a suitable site in this country (probably at Drigg in Cumberland). This work should be treated as of the highest urgency and importance.

(2) The work to be undertaken should include the provision of such common services and facilities as would be needed should it be decided later to undertake the building of a second pile. A decision on this point should be postponed until the information referred to in (3) and (4) below was available.

(3) The Chiefs of Staff would submit a report on our requirements for atomic bombs and the possibility of making consequential reductions in other forms of armament production.

—1—

4. (cont.)

    (4)   The Minister of Supply would submit a statement showing as clearly as possible what demands might be made by the construction of one or two piles upon industrial capacity which would otherwise be available for re-construction and the export trade; and what special forms of priority would be needed to secure the completion of the piles within, say, three years.

    (5)   A small number of electro magnetic plant units should be installed in the Research Establishment both for the separation of isotopes and in order to develop the technique of the process.

    (6)   Capacity on a scale sufficient to feed two piles should be provided as soon as possible in this country for:-

        (i)   purification of oxide from uranium concentrates;

        (ii)   production of pure metal from oxide;

        (iii)   production of graphite.

2.   DISCUSSIONS AT MOSCOW

The meeting had before them:-

    (i)   A note by the Secretary of the Cabinet (GEN.75/19) covering a minute from the Foreign Secretary to the Prime Minister dated 12th December 1945; and other papers relating to the discussions at Moscow.

    (ii)   A note prepared in the Foreign Office (GEN.75/17) comparing the American proposals for the terms of reference of the United Nations Commission with those suggested in the Foreign Secretary's minute to the Prime Minister.

In addition, copies of Telegram No.14 WORTHY from the British Delegation at Moscow were handed round at the meeting. It was noted that two further telegrams on this subject **had** been despatched from Moscow but were not yet available.

The Prime Minister said that the first and most important point to be considered was whether the proposed United Nations Commission should report to the Assembly or to the Security Council. The Foreign Secretary, in his minute, preferred the latter alternative. He himself had always been inclined to prefer the former, partly because the deliberations of the Assembly were not subject to the veto, and partly because if the matter were placed in the hands of the Security Council, there was a risk of antagonising the smaller Powers.

Secondly, the proposals put forward by the Americans seemed to treat the matter too much as if it were a simple question of sharing information on the atomic bomb alone with a single Power, namely, Russia. At Washington emphasis had been laid on the need for reciprocity and for building up confidence between all nations by sharing information about all weapons capable of being used for mass destruction. We should also wish to see evidence of a co-operative spirit in the general political field.

-2-

1946 was a year of setbacks. A growing cold war between east and west rendered the chances of an international agreement on atomic matters increasingly unlikely. In the United States in August, Congress, in ignorance of confidential US-UK agreements drawn up in 1943–44 covering the continuation of nuclear collaboration after World War II, passed the McMahon Act prohibiting the sharing of American atomic know-how with *any* other country. The blow was felt particularly hard in Whitehall on the industrial side, requiring the UK to plan and design its own infrastructure for building the weapon and producing its fissile ingredients.

In late October 1946, Attlee's atomic committee had to decide on the construction of a gaseous diffusion plant for the production of enriched uranium. Had the decision been against, Britain's nuclear weapons programme would effectively have been at an end. As during the 18 December 1945 meeting, doubts were raised about the desirability of diverting for bomb purposes scarce technical and industrial resources needed for the UK's post-war economic recovery.

5. Minutes of a meeting of the Cabinet Committee on Atomic Energy, GEN 75, 25 October 1946.
TNA, PRO, CAB 130/2

THIS DOCUMENT IS THE PROPERTY OF HIS BRITANNIC MAJESTY'S GOVERNMENT

The circulation of this paper has been strictly limited.

It is issued for the personal use of........................... *C.L.*

TOP SECRET   Copy No. 26

GEN.75/15th Meeting

CABINET

ATOMIC ENERGY

Note of a Meeting of Ministers held at
No. 10, Downing Street, S.W.1. on
FRIDAY, 25TH OCTOBER, 1946, at 2.15 p.m.

PRESENT:

The Rt. Hon. C.R. Attlee, M.P.,
Prime Minister (In the Chair)

The Rt. Hon. E. Bevin, M.P.,
Secretary of State for
Foreign Affairs

The Rt. Hon. H. Dalton, M.P.,
Chancellor of the Exchequer

The Rt. Hon. Viscount Addison,
Secretary of State for
Dominion Affairs

The Rt. Hon. Sir Stafford Cripps,
K.C., M.P., President of the
Board of Trade

The Rt. Hon. J. Wilmot, M.P.,
Minister of Supply and
Aircraft Production

THE FOLLOWING WERE ALSO PRESENT:

Sir Edward Bridges,
Secretary of the Cabinet

Viscount Portal of Hungerford,
Ministry of Supply

Mr. Neville Butler,
Foreign Office

Mr. W.L. Gorell-Barnes,
Prime Minister's Office

Mr. M.W. Perrin,
Ministry of Supply

SECRETARY:

Mr. D.H.F. Rickett

1. UNITED KINGDOM ATOMIC ENERGY PROGRAMME

Proposal to Build a Gaseous Diffusion Plant

THE MEETING considered a note by the Secretary of the Cabinet (GEN.75/44) covering:-

    (i) A copy of a minute to the Prime Minister from the Minister of Supply dated 28th August, 1946, submitting a Memorandum on the United Kingdom Atomic Energy Programme.

    (ii) A copy of the Report by the Advisory Committee on Atomic Energy commenting on (i) above.

The Memorandum by the Minister of Supply proposed that there should be added to our programme the design and construction of a gaseous diffusion plant for the production of U.235, estimated to cost £30-£40 million spread over a period of 4 to 5 years.

It was explained that there were three main arguments in favour of this proposal:-

    (a) It would enable us to produce from the "pile" the largest possible quantity of fissile material with the limited supplies of uranium which now seemed likely to be available.

    (b) It would provide a stock of material which could be used for fundamental research over a wider field (including the "breeding" of fissile material and the production of industrial power from fast reactors) than would be possible using ~~plutonium~~ alone.

    (c) The "seeding" of the pile with U.235 would provide a measure of insurance that the pile could be made to work at its rated output. Such an insurance was all the more necessary because we had been considerably handicapped by the denial to us of American information.

The Advisory Committee on Atomic Energy supported the proposal on the understanding that the project would be reviewed before any major financial commitment was undertaken for the building of the plant.

In discussion it was urged that we must consider seriously whether we could afford to divert from civilian consumption and the restoration of our balance of payments, the economic resources required for a project on this scale. Unless present trends were reversed we might find ourselves faced with an extremely serious economic and financial situation in two to three years time.

On the other hand it was argued that we could not afford to be left behind in a field which was of such revolutionary importance from an industrial, no less than from a military point of view. Our prestige in the world, as well as our chances of securing American co-operation

-1-

5. (cont.)

would both suffer if we did not exploit to the full a
discovery in which we had played a leading part at the
outset. The development of a new source of industrial
power might strengthen our industrial position very
considerably in the future, particularly at a time when
it was becoming more and more difficult to find labour for
coal-mining.

Other points made in discussion were:-

(a) Would it not be possible to arrange for a
plant of this kind to be constructed in
Canada, where many of the resources necessary,
e.g. abundant water power, were available?

It was explained *or British industrial organisations.* that without extensive help
from American, Canada was unlikely to be
able to carry through an elaborate
engineering project of this kind. Moreover
the plant, which was necessary to the success
of our own programme, would not be under our
control if it were constructed in another
country.

(b) Part of the necessity for the plant arose from
the refusal of the Americans to give us the
"know-how". Should not a decision be
deferred until a further approach had been
made to the President?

THE FOREIGN SECRETARY said that he had discussed
this matter with Mr. Byrnes and would be
willing to take the matter up again as soon
as the elections to Congress were over.
Even with American information, however,
there would still be strong grounds for
proceeding with the construction of the plant.

(c) It would be of assistance in reaching a
decision if a more exact estimate could be
given of the demands which the project
would make for skilled man-power and scarce
materials.

It was pointed out that until a qualified
design staff had been recruited it would be
difficult to add much to the information
given in paragraph 8 of the Minister of
Supply's Memorandum. On a rough estimate
an expenditure of £40 million might be
regarded as equivalent to a labour force
of 25,000 men employed for 4 years.
Rather less than half of these would be
employed on civil engineering work and rather
more than half on electrical and mechanical
engineering. The power consumption required
would be equal to the output of 15% of the
planned increase for one year in installed
capacity for power production.

-2-

(d) Although the immediate outlook for uranium
supplies was disappointing, the long-term
prospects were favourable, since by the
development of new methods, such as "breeding",
we might hope to make a far more efficient use
of the supplies of material available to us,
including thorium.   The present project
would make an important contribution to the
development of such methods, which were likely
to be worked out by other countries also.

(e) It was not proposed that final authority should
now be given for expenditure up to
£30-£40 million.   A preliminary period of
planning and design would first be necessary,
after which there would be an opportunity to
review the matter further.   It was, however,
important that the Minister of Supply should
have authority to place such orders as would
enable him to recruit a fully qualified staff
to work on the project.   Care would be taken,
however, to ensure that the Government was not
finally committed to expenditure exceeding
£500,000, for which the Chancellor was prepared
to give financial sanction at this stage.

(f) It was doubtful whether without the express
approval of Congress the United States
Government would be in a position, since the
passage of the McMahon Act, to supply to us
either information or fissile material.
Much might depend upon the result of the
discussions now proceeding in the United
Nations Atomic Energy Commission.   In the
meantime we were continuing to give them
technical help in various directions, but
we stood to gain by this through the
information which our scientists were
enabled to obtain.

IT WAS AGREED:-

(1) That authority should be given to the Minister
of Supply to proceed with the design and
construction of a gaseous diffusion plant on
the lines proposed in his paper, on the
understanding that the project should be
reviewed again by the Advisory Committee on
Atomic Energy and by Ministers before any
inescapable commitment was undertaken for an
expenditure in excess of £500,000.

(2) That the Prime Minister and the Foreign Secretary
should consider at what point it would be
desirable to take up once more with the
United States Government our claim to full
and effective co-operation in the field of
atomic energy, in accordance with the
undertakings given by the President to the
Prime Minister at Washington in November, 1945.

-3-

The official account gives but a partial flavour of this crucial meeting. When the minutes were copied and taken by Chris Graham and a BBC *Timewatch* team in September 1982 to Sir Michael Perrin, a Ministry of Supply official present at the October 1946 discussion, he filled in the missing detail.[26]

The doubters were the Cabinet's leading economic ministers Hugh Dalton (Chancellor of the Exchequer) and Sir Stafford Cripps (President of the Board of Trade). They appeared to be winning the argument until the Foreign Secretary, Ernest Bevin, waddled in late, having fallen asleep after a heavy lunch. As Perrin recalled for *Timewatch*, Bevin wrenched the discussion right round the other way:

> That won't do at all . . . we've got to have this. . . I don't mind for myself, but I don't want any other Foreign Secretary of this country to be talked to or at by a Secretary of State in the United States as I have just had in my discussions with Mr Byrnes. We've got to have this thing over here whatever it costs. . . We've got to have the bloody Union Jack on top of it.

On the way back to the Ministry of Supply in the Strand from the meeting in No. 10, Lord Portal (Controller of Production of Atomic Energy) turned to Perrin and said: 'You know, if Bevin hadn't come in then, we wouldn't have had that bomb, Michael.'[27]

The minutes, however, capture the arguments which trumped Dalton and Cripps. Atomic energy was of revolutionary industrial as well as military importance. Britain's prestige in the world depended upon its possession of an atomic weapon. American co-operation, severed by the McMahon Act, could not be restored without it. Britain had to 'exploit to the full a discovery in which we had played a leading part at the outset.' The 'elaborate' engineering required to produce the Uranium 235 needed for a bomb had been made more demanding and costly by 'the refusal of the Americans to give us the "know-how".' There was no mention of the Russians.

Bevin had indeed saved the bomb. But, within a few weeks, Portal felt the need to secure specific approval from ministers for the manufacture of a weapon and completed a brief for Attlee and his colleagues on New Year's Eve 1946.

Ernest Bevin and Clement Attlee: placers of a 'bloody Union Jack' on top of the Bomb.

6. 'Note by the Controller of Production of Atomic Energy', Ministry of Supply, 31 December 1946. TNA, PRO, PREM 8/911

Cabinet.

Atomic Energy.

Research on Atomic Weapons.

245

3/1.

January 1947.

MEMORANDUM BY THE MINISTER OF SUPPLY

I forward for the consideration of Ministers a note by the Controller of Production of Atomic Energy.

John Wilmot

Note by the Controller of Production of Atomic Energy

1.   I submit that a decision is required about the development of Atomic weapons in this country.   The Service Departments are beginning to move in the matter and certain sections of the Press are showing interest in it.

2.   My organization is charged solely with the production of "fissile material", i.e. of the "filling" that would go into any bomb that it was decided to develop.   Apart altogether from producing the "filling", the development of the bomb mechanism is a complex problem of nuclear physics and precision engineering on which some years of research and development would be necessary.

3.   I suggest that there are broadly three courses of action to choose from.

    (a) Not to develop the atomic weapon at all.

    (b) To develop the weapon by means of the ordinary agencies in the Ministry of Supply and the Service Departments.

    (c) To develop the weapon under special arrangements conducive to the utmost secrecy.

4.   I imagine that course (a) above would not be favoured by H.M. Government in the absence of an international agreement on the subject.

5.   If course (b) is adopted it will be impossible to conceal for long the fact that this development is taking place.   Many interests are involved, and the need for constant consultation with my organization (which is the sole repository of the knowledge of atomic energy and atomic weapons derived from our war-time collaboration with the United States) would result in very many people, including scientists, knowing what was going on.

        Moreover, it would certainly not be long before the American authorities heard that we were developing the weapon "through the normal channels" and this might well seem to them another reason for reticence over technical matters, not only in the field of military uses of atomic energy but also in the general "know-how" of the production of fissile material.

6./

6.   If, for national or international reasons, the special arrangements referred to in 3(c) above are thought desirable, we are at present well placed to make them.   The Chief Superintendent of Armament Research (Dr. Penney) has been intimately concerned in the recent American trials and knows more than any other British scientist about the secrets of the American bomb.   He has the facilities for the necessary research and development which could be "camouflaged" as "Basic High Explosive Research" (a subject for which he is actually responsible but on which no work is in fact being done).   His responsibilities are at present to the Army side of the Ministry of Supply, but by special arrangements with the head of that Department he could be made responsible also to me for this particular work and I would arrange the necessary contacts with my organization in such a way as to secure the maximum secrecy.   Only about five or six senior officials outside my own organization need know of this arrangement.

7.   I have already discussed this matter with the Chiefs of Staff, who authorised me to say that they are in agreement with me in strongly recommending the special arrangements outlined in paragraph 6 above. If these were adopted, the Chiefs of Staff would see to it that security was not prejudiced by enquiries from the Service Departments.   (The Chairman of the Defence Research Committee would of course be informed).

8.   I therefore ask for direction on two points: first, whether research and development work on atomic weapons is to be undertaken; and if so, whether the arrangements outlined in paragraph 6 above are to be adopted.

C.P.A.E.

Ministry of Supply.
31st December, 1946.

Portal's was a powerful steer not just on the need for a clear-cut decision, but also on the super-secret route he proposed to implement a 'yes' if it was forthcoming. He preferred the latter route because of the lack of agreement at the United Nations on international control *and* the need to keep Washington in the dark about Britain's nuclear intentions for fear it would reinforce US resistance on technical, atomic-related matters. Dr William Penney, a British member of the Manhattan Project, had a good deal of 'the secrets of the American bomb' in his head and would be the man, under suitable cover, to lead the scientific side of the project if it were approved.

Attlee acted swiftly, but he did not take Portal's paper to the existing Atomic Energy Committee, GEN 75. Instead he set up GEN 163, a bespoke ministerial group which met but once. It is significant that GEN 163 did not include the dissenters from the economic departments, Dalton and Cripps (though when bomb-related business reverted to GEN 75, they were included).

Before the meeting, Sir Edward Bridges, Secretary of the Cabinet, briefed Attlee on the state-of-play on possible international atomic agreement and the thinking of Bernard Baruch, leader of the US delegation to the United Nations Atomic Energy Commission. (Margaret Gowing wrote of the 75-year-old Baruch, 'his determination to introduce from the outset subjects which were bound to terrify the Russians—such as the abolition of the [UN] Security Council veto when atomic issues were discussed—made the co-operation, which was unlikely, quite impossible, while his general behaviour added a slightly farcical note to the proceedings. Even the British suspected that some members of Baruch's team were determined that the United States should neither give up atomic weapons nor give the know-how to Russia.'[28])

Sir Edward Bridges, Cabinet Secretary: co-ordinator of the decision to make a British Atomic Bomb, 1946–47.

7. 'Research on Atomic Weapons': Bridges to Attlee, 7 January 1947.

TNA, PRO, PREM 8/911

TOP SECRET

PRIME MINISTER

RESEARCH ON ATOMIC WEAPONS

Note for Meeting of Ministers to be held at
No. 10 Downing Street on
WEDNESDAY, 8TH JANUARY, 1947 at 3 p.m.

The Memorandum by Lord Portal circulated by the
Minister of Supply (GEN.163/1) asks for directions on two
points:-

   (1) Whether research and development work on
       atomic weapons is to be undertaken.

   (2) If so, whether special arrangements conducive
       to secrecy (outlined in paragraph 6 of the
       Memorandum) are to be adopted.

As Lord Portal says in paragraph 4 of his Memorandum,
His Majesty's Government will presumably not wish to refrain
from developing atomic weapons, unless this is prohibited by
an international agreement to which they are parties.

It should be noted that recommendation 3(a) of
the Report of the Atomic Energy Commission (the draft text
of which was circulated as GEN.75/50) proposed (last sentence
of page 6 of the paper) that "The exclusive right to carry
on atomic research for destructive purposes should be vested
in the international authority".

Our representative on the Commission has supported
Mr. Baruch's proposals as a general statement of principles,
the detailed working out of which would require further
discussion by the Commission. Ministers may feel that when
the Commission comes to discuss the matter it will be found
difficult to secure in practice that the international
authority should have the exclusive right to conduct research
on atomic weapons.

In the first place it seems hardly possible to
prevent individual governments carrying on research in
secret. Each government would naturally feel that it would
be too dangerous to refrain from such research and to rely
upon the prohibition being observed by others. Moreover,
the fact that such research is to be undertaken by the
international authority must surely mean that it will be
carried out as a joint enterprise by scientists seconded by
a number of individual governments. Are these scientists
to be prohibited from communicating to their governments the
results of the research work in which they engage ? It
seems too much to suppose that such a prohibition would be
observed in all cases. If no such prohibition is imposed,
then to say that only the international authority may engage
in research into atomic weapons seems to mean no more than
that the results of such research must be made available to
all governments. This was not the intention of the authors
of the proposal. They argued that the authority must be in
the forefront of development in order to detect illicit
research by individual governments. They could not, so it
was argued, suppress activities the nature of which they did
not fully understand. The fallacy seems to lie in supposing
that there can be an antithesis between the international

/authority

7. (cont.)

authority, which is to exercise control and the individual governments which are to be subject to it. Taken collectively the controllers and the controlled are identical.

In further discussions, therefore, of the Baruch proposals it seems desirable that our representatives should call attention to the difficulty of giving practical effect to any prohibition of research into atomic weapons. If this is so it seems inevitable that we should undertake such research in this country.

On the second point raised, namely the arrangements to be adopted for carrying on research, the proposal made in Lord Portal's Memorandum seems right on grounds not only of secrecy, but also of efficiency. It seems reasonable that the Chief Superintendent of Armament Research, Dr.Penney, should be responsible to Lord Portal for research on atomic weapons, rather than to the Controller of Supplies (Munitions).

EEB

7TH JANUARY, 1947

8. Minutes of the meeting of GEN 163, Atomic Energy, 8 January 1947; Confidential Annex.

TNA, PRO, CAB 130/16

DOCUMENT IS THE PROPERTY OF HIS BRITANNIC MAJESTY'S GOVERNMENT

241

The circulation of this paper has been strictly limited.

It is issued for the personal use of................*C. L.*................

SECRET

Copy No. *11*

GEN.163/1st Meeting

CABINET

ATOMIC ENERGY

NOTE of a Meeting of Ministers held at
No. 10, Downing Street, S.W.1., on
WEDNESDAY, 8TH JANUARY, 1947 at 3 p.m.

PRESENT:

The Rt. Hon. C.R. Attlee, M.P.,
Prime Minister (In the Chair)

The Rt. Hon. Herbert Morrison,   The Rt. Hon. E. Bevin, M.P.,
M.P., Lord President of   Secretary of State for
the Council   Foreign Affairs

The Rt. Hon. Viscount Addison,   The Rt. Hon. A.V. Alexander,
Secretary of State for   C.H., M.P.,
Dominion Affairs   Minister of Defence

The Rt. Hon. J. Wilmot, M.P.,
Minister of Supply and
Aircraft Production

THE FOLLOWING WERE ALSO PRESENT:

Sir Edward Bridges,   Viscount Portal of Hungerford,
Permanent Secretary,   Ministry of Supply
Treasury

Mr. Nevile Butler,   Mr. Gorell Barnes,
Foreign Office   10, Downing Street

SECRETARY:

Mr. D.H.F. Rickett

Fission : 1940–53   55

8. (cont.)

1. RESEARCH IN ATOMIC WEAPONS

   THE MEETING had before them a Memorandum by the
Minister of Supply covering a Note by the Controller of
Production (Atomic Energy), (GEN. 163/1).

   A record of the discussion and of the conclusions
reached on this subject is contained in a Confidential
Annex to these Minutes. (See also CAB 104/255)
attached

2. DISCUSSIONS ON INTERNATIONAL CONTROL

   THE FOREIGN SECRETARY gave a brief account of
recent discussions in New York on the international
control of atomic energy.   The Baruch Plan had been
accepted in principle with two abstentions, but many
details of the scheme remained to be discussed.   It
was important that the powers to be given to the
international authority should not be such as to cripple
the development of atomic energy in this country for
industrial purposes.   We could not afford to be dependent
on other countries in that field.   Progress was rapid
and new technical developments were taking place.   He
was not clear what was the significance of Mr. Baruch's
resignation, but it might be the result of some difference
of opinion with the State Department.

TOP SECRET   Copy No 4.

GEN.163/1st Meeting

MEETING OF MINISTERS

CONFIDENTIAL ANNEX. MINUTE 1

(8th January, 1947 - 3.0 p.m.)

RESEARCH IN ATOMIC WEAPONS

    The Meeting had before them a Memorandum by the Minister of Supply covering a Note by the Controller of Production (Atomic Energy), (GEN.163/1) asking for directions on two points:-

    (a) Whether research and development work on atomic weapons was to be undertaken;

    (b) If so, whether special arrangements conducive to secrecy (outlined in paragraph 6 of the Memorandum) should be adopted.

    LORD PORTAL said that so far as he was aware, no decision had yet been taken to proceed with the development of atomic weapons. He had discussed the matter with the Chiefs of Staff who were naturally anxious that we should not be without this weapon if others possessed it. About three years' work would be needed to solve the problems of nuclear physics and engineering involved in developing the bomb mechanism. If this matter were handled through the ordinary agencies responsible for weapon development, the result would inevitably be that a large number of persons in the Service Departments and in the Ministry of Supply would be made aware of what was being done. The alternative would be to make special arrangements whereby research could be carried on by the Chief Superintendent of Armament Research (Dr. Penney). He would set up a special section at Woolwich, the work of which would be described as "basic high explosive research". He would be responsible for this work to Lord Portal, who would arrange for the necessary contacts with the Atomic Energy Department and with the Chiefs of Staff in such a way as to ensure the maximum secrecy.

    THE FOREIGN SECRETARY said that in his view it was important that we should press on with the study of all aspects of atomic energy. We could not afford to acquiesce in an American monopoly of this new development. Other countries also might well develop atomic weapons. Unless therefore an effective international system could be developed under which the production and use of the weapon would be prohibited, we must develop it ourselves.

-1-

8. (cont.)

THE MINISTER OF DEFENCE agreed and said that in his view the arrangements suggested by Lord Portal should be effective in securing the greatest possible secrecy.

THE MINISTER OF SUPPLY said that a considerable amount of work would have to be done, particularly on the engineering side. In two years' time, the staff of all grades which would be employed would amount to about 180 people.

THE MEETING:-

(1) Agreed that research and development work on atomic weapons should be undertaken:

(2) Approved the special arrangements for this purpose, outlined in paragraph 6 of the Memorandum circulated by the Minister of Supply (GEN.163/1).

Cabinet Office, S.W.1.,

10TH JANUARY, 1947.

-2-

The lack of expectation about genuine international control around the Cabinet Table when GEN 163 met on the afternoon of 8 January 1947 is indicated by Attlee and his colleagues taking the decision to make a British atomic bomb *before* they turned to the state of the negotiations at the United Nations.

After Portal had outlined his proposals, Bevin spoke strongly in favour of Britain going it alone. Unless an effective system of international control was forthcoming, the UK must have its own weapon: 'We could not afford to acquiesce in an American monopoly of this new development. Other countries also might well develop atomic weapons.' Once again, it is US factors, if the minutes are an indication, that provided the primary motive power for the British decision to become a nuclear power, as much if not more than the possibility of other nations, primarily the Soviet Union, acquiring the same status. The great power impulse took pride of place over cold war anxieties.

Urged on by A. V. Alexander, the Minister of Defence, GEN 163 opted for the practice of 'super secrecy' for the atomic weapon's programme. The developing cold war, however, was an increasing conditioner both of the need for secrecy and of the politico-military-intelligence atmosphere in 1947 Whitehall. The Joint Intelligence Committee's all-source analyses of the Soviet 'threat' made increasingly anxious reading for their Whitehall customers.

THIS DOCUMENT IS THE PROPERTY OF HIS BRITANNIC MAJESTY'S GOVERNMENT

SECRET   Copy No. 6 9

J.I.C. (47) 7/2.   Final.
6th August, 1947

Circulated for the consideration of the Chiefs of Staff

CHIEFS OF STAFF COMMITTEE

Joint Intelligence Sub-Committee

SOVIET INTERESTS, INTENTIONS AND CAPABILITIES—GENERAL

REPORT BY THE JOINT INTELLIGENCE SUB-COMMITTEE

ANNEX

THIS Annex, which has been approved by the Joint Intelligence Sub-Committee, contains the material referred to in the conclusions of the Report, entitled as above (J.I.C. (47) 7/1 (O). Final).

(Signed)   P. GLEADELL.

Ministry of Defence, S.W. 1,
  6th August, 1947.

33947   *a*

PART I

FUNDAMENTAL PRINCIPLES IN THE OUTLOOK OF THE SOVIET LEADERS

General

The policy of the Soviet Union can only be understood if it is realised that she is not merely, like Nazi Germany, a totalitarian dictatorship engaged in power politics, but a unique and abnormal member of international society inspired by a dynamic ideology, with a strong international appeal.

The Fundamental Long-Term Principle

2. The fundamental factor which determines the Soviet view of the outside world is the belief that the capitalist system contains the seeds of its own decay and is bound eventually to be replaced by Communism of the Soviet type throughout the world. Meanwhile the Soviet leaders believe that it is their task to direct and hasten this inevitable process. This belief is the long-term principle underlying the outlook of the Soviet leaders, and all the other objectives of Soviet policy, including even the immediate search for security, must be regarded as subsidiary and derived from it.

Corollaries of this Principle

3. There are four corollaries of this fundamental belief in the ultimate triumph of Communism which must now be considered.

4. In the first place, it results in the conviction that the capitalist Powers, on their side, are likely to resort to arms against the Soviet Union in the hope of arresting the progress of world Communism and their own inevitable decay, and that therefore a clash involving the use of force must sooner or later be expected between the capitalist and communist worlds. Hence the Soviet Union is obsessed, meanwhile, with the idea that she is surrounded by hostile capitalist Powers and can never overlook the risk of renewed intervention against her on the analogy of 1919. This is the main ideological basis of the Soviet Union's preoccupation with security.

5. Secondly, the Soviet leaders believe that the decay of the capitalist world will be largely due to the imperialistic rivalries and conflicts which, according to Marxist doctrine, are a normal feature of the capitalist system. They will consider it to the interest of the Soviet Union to play on these differences and exploit them to the utmost. It also follows that the Soviet Union must be strong enough to look after herself if involved in a war between rival capitalist Powers; so the Soviet leaders have here a further motive in their search for security.

6. Thirdly, the Soviet leaders do not believe that it is possible for communist and capitalist States to co-exist in any normal manner. For them, the only " one world " which could exist would be an entirely communist one and, until this is achieved, there are bound to be two worlds, and very sharply divided worlds at that. The Soviet leaders, in fact, regard a state of constant friction and tension as the only normal relationship which can exist between communist and capitalist societies. No consciousness of her own temporary weakness and no concessions by the outside world will lead the Soviet Union to abandon this conviction. For tactical reasons, however, the Soviet leaders will not wish to advertise this conviction in present circumstances, and have in fact found it expedient to deny it by expressing a belief in the possibility that the two worlds can co-exist and engage in " healthy competition " with each other.

7. Fourthly, the conception of the inevitable decline of capitalism will inspire the Soviet leaders with a belief that in their dealings with the outer world time is on their side, and that they need only wait until the process of decay has made further headway. This feeling that time is on their side will be reinforced by their consciousness of the present weakened state of their economy, and of the long-term nature of their ambitious projects for its reconstruction and further development. These two considerations will both lead them to believe that it will be in their interests to avoid an early outbreak of a major war.

33947 B

9. (cont.)

The Immediate Aim

8. It follows from the above analysis that the Soviet leaders' long-term belief regarding the nature of the world conflict of ideologies leads straight to their immediate aim, which is to ensure by all possible means the security of the Soviet Union. In this preoccupation with security, the Soviet leaders have been influenced by old motive forces in Russian history altogether independent of Marxist belief. In the past, Russia has suffered severely from the lack of natural defensive frontiers to protect her from the incursions of hostile peoples from beyond her borders. Her frontiers have tended in consequence to change with the ebb and flow of Russian success in war; and since defence in depth has been Russia's natural method of wearing down foreign invaders, she has always tended to push out her frontiers as far as possible whenever she has been in a position to do so.

9. Having thus summarised the fundamental principles underlying the outlook of the Soviet leaders, we now consider Russian capabilities, before examining the combined effects of the principles and the material factors as manifested in present Soviet policy.

PART II

CAPABILITIES

A.—Economic Potential

Backwardness in Development

10. Throughout her history Russia has been a poor and ill-developed country by western European standards and has repeatedly paid for this backwardness by having to endure invasion. Effective measures directed towards increasing her economic strength only began as recently as 1928 with the First Five-Year Plan, and Russia is still in the early stages of her industrial revolution. Enormous areas of her territory remain unexploited and even unexplored.

11. As a result of the ravages of war, Russian economic development has not only been retarded but has retrogressed and by the end of 1946 industrial production in the devastated areas had not reached half pre-war level. She is in many respects technically backward and she suffers from a lack of skilled craftsmen, particularly in the engineering industries. Railway transport was still a serious bottleneck on the eve of the last war and since then over a quarter of the network has been very seriously damaged. Good roads are confined almost entirely to the neighbourhood of the larger towns, except for a few specially-constructed military highways.

Basic Strength

12. The basic strength of Russia lies in her immense expanse of contiguous territory containing practically every raw material of consequence and in her great and rapidly-expanding resources of man-power. Her population, which is approaching 200 million, is predominantly young; in 1939, 45 per cent. of the total population were under 20, and although these classes must have suffered heavily in the war they compare with similar pre-war figures of 32 per cent. for Great Britain and 34 per cent. in the United States. The Russian 45 per cent. under 20 will, however, have shrunk to 35 per cent. by 1970, although the total population will probably by then have increased to 250 million.

13. Though little is known of her reserves of some of the rarer commodities essential for war production, there is so far no evidence that the Soviet Union lacks within her own borders an adequate material basis for the execution of her economic plans or, at any rate, for the maintenance and development of her internal economy. Given normal conditions of peace and average harvests she is, for example, self-supporting in food. Her reserves of timber are incalculable; she possesses about 20 per cent. of the world's coal deposits; and her proved and recoverable reserves of crude oil in 1946 were estimated to amount to 9 per cent. of the world total.

14. Russia's reserves of raw materials, however, are still a potential rather than an actual source of strength. In terms of capital assets and current productive capacity she has still a long way to go before she can compare in these respects with the United States, who will herself not remain static at her present stage of development. In 1946 comparative production in basic items was as follows :—

	U.S.S.R.	United States	United Kingdom
Steel (millions of tons) ...	14	61·6	12·7
Coal (millions of tons) ...	168	524·8	189
Oil (millions of tons) ...	21·7	248	...
Motor Vehicles	132,000	3,096,000	365,000
	(90 per cent. lorries)	(30 per cent. lorries)	(40 per cent. lorries)

Distribution of Industrial Development

15. A concurrent feature of the programme of economic expansion on which the Soviet Union has embarked is the shift in the centre of gravity of her main industrial areas to the Eastward. New industrial areas are being developed

33947   B 2

9. (cont.)

Navy

52. *General.*—The Russians have declared that they intend building a large ocean-going Navy and a considerable fleet of merchant ships. During the recent war their losses in warships and merchant ships were considerable, and the building programme will therefore have to be a big one. The fulfilment of such a programme will be handicapped not only by the damage inflicted on the shipyards and the current economic difficulties in the country, but also by the obstacles which the Navy are likely to meet in the allocation of priorities *vis-à-vis* the demands of the Army and Air Force, whose influence predominates in Service policy.

53. *Shipbuilding.*—During the war shipyards on the Black Sea were very severely damaged and the important yards on the banks of the Neva at Leningrad suffered, but less heavily, from bombing and shelling. Construction of warships heavier than destroyers has in consequence been put back for a considerable period in these yards. Apart from the recently constructed yard at Molotovsk on the White Sea, only the smaller Far Eastern yards, where vessels up to and including cruiser displacement can be built, have remained comparatively unaffected.

54. The Soviet capacity for building submarines has been less seriously affected by the war. The Soviet Navy has acquired much German material and technical assistance, both in the construction of prefabricated submarines, and in the production of new types with high under-water speed. The Russians are proceeding with the development of a German type of high-speed submarine, which, if successful, may develop an under-water speed of the order of 24 knots. This would present a serious problem to our anti-submarine forces and necessitate a complete revision of our present anti-submarine tactics, but it is unlikely that significant numbers of this type will be produced before 1950 at the earliest.

55. The rebuilding and expansion of the Soviet merchant fleet can only be achieved by extraordinary efforts, and progress in the initial stages must be slow. The expressed intention to build a large merchant fleet would therefore take years to put into effect, and could only be carried out at the expense of the projected Soviet warship building programme.

56. *Weapons—*

(a) *Guns.*—The main armament of the modern Russian-built cruisers consists of 7·1-inch guns in triple mountings, with a maximum range of 30,000 yards. The turrets appear to be well designed and workmanlike. Heavy high-angle armament in cruisers and destroyers is normally the 5·1-inch high-angle/low-angle gun, and standard light high-angle armament in all ships is the 1·46-inch Bofors gun. The Russians are aware of the principles and method of employment of variable-time fuses, but we do not know whether these have yet been produced.

(b) *Torpedoes.*—It is believed that the Russians have obtained full details of the latest German types, including the electrically-controlled torpedo used from submarines. It can be assumed therefore that these types will be put into production in due course.

(c) *Mine Warfare.*—German mining technique is known to the Russians, and they may be expected to improve on the known German type mines. They have been told how to sweep all types of German mines and are therefore capable of producing the necessary equipment to deal with any mines which operate on German principles.

(d) *Anti-Submarine Equipment.*—The Russians have been supplied with most of the British and American anti-submarine equipment in current use in the late war, and have obtained much additional knowledge on this form of warfare through their intelligence organisation. Their production of equipment should therefore be of reasonably modern standard.

Special Weapons

57. *Atomic Bombs.*—The manufacture of atomic bombs demands not only a high standard of scientific knowledge and the availability of certain materials, but also the application, on a very large scale, of difficult industrial techniques.

It is the latter which will probably provide the greatest difficulty for the Soviet Union, but at the present time it is believed that she is also suffering from a serious shortage of uranium. This shortage is likely to continue until she can evolve methods of extracting this material from her comparatively large supplies of low-grade ores, or alternatively until a supply of appreciable quantities of high-grade ore is found within her own territory.

58. By January 1952, the Soviet Union's stock of bombs is unlikely to exceed 5, though it may possibly reach 25. By the end of 1956 the stock may be from 40–60, unless an increase in the rate of output is made possible by the discovery of a large supply of high-grade ore.

59. It has been estimated* that some 30–120 atomic bombs *accurately* delivered by the U.S.S.R. might cause the collapse of the United Kingdom without invasion. (The number of bombs required to cause a similar collapse in the United States would probably be somewhat greater than for this country, but the problem of landing them accurately in the United States at the ranges involved is much greater.)

60. A large number of factors must be considered before it is possible to arrive at even a rough estimate of the number of atomic bombs which the Soviet Union would need to possess, before being in a position to deliver 30–120 bombs accurately in the United Kingdom. These factors include the accuracy and the vulnerability of the vehicle of delivery, the range, the size and density of the selected target areas, and the efficiency of passive and active counter-measures. On balance, we consider it reasonable to estimate that the Soviet Union would not be ready to deliver an attack on the United Kingdom, which might be expected to cause collapse, until she possessed between 60–240 atomic bombs.

61. On this assumption, the Soviet Union would not be capable of achieving a decisive result by atomic warfare, even against the United Kingdom alone, before 1957 at the earliest.

62. *Biological Weapons.*—The production of biological agents depends on materials which are readily available throughout the world, and the processes of manufacture do not require the same standard and quantity of engineering and scientific effort as the processes necessary for producing atomic bombs. While it would be difficult rapidly to expand the production of atomic bombs at short notice, there would be relatively much less difficulty in rapidly expanding the production of biological weapons. On the basis of our present knowledge, it seems probable that the atomic bomb will remain the most potent destructive weapon within the foreseeable future, but that biological warfare will be a close second.

63. Although we have no evidence on which to base a reliable estimate of when the Soviet Union may be ready to use biological weapons on a big scale, it seems probable that her production can be equal to, or greater than, that of any other Power by 1951. Furthermore, the slower her own estimated rate of production of atomic bombs, the more likely is she to seek to hasten her preparedness for using biological weapons.

64. *Chemical Warfare.*—The Russians are likely to be as well prepared to wage chemical warfare, both in offence and in defence, as any other Power, after 1948. Until then, the Western Allies will hold the advantage of possessing considerable stocks of the German nerve gas, Tabun, but will not yet have begun production of this or of the more toxic nerve gases. By contrast the Soviet Government could, if this were their policy, produce and build up stocks of Tabun after 1948, or of the other two more toxic types, Soman and Sarin, after 1951.

65. *Guided Missiles.*—Numerous reports indicate that the Russians are exploiting captured German data on guided missiles and utilising experienced German technicians. Neither firm production figures nor details of the factories involved are available and the following estimates are therefore highly conjectural.

66. It is likely that any guided missiles produced by the Russians up to 1951 will be similar to those which have already been produced, namely, the German V1 and V2. Alternatively, it is possible that, after five years of experiment and development, the Soviet Union may have perfected improved types for production in and after 1951 on a monthly scale of about 3,500 flying bombs

---

* T.W.C. (46) 15 (Final Revise) limited circulation.

33947

c 2

The August 1947 JIC assessment did not place a specific date upon the moment it expected the Soviet Union to become a nuclear power, but, paragraph 58 implies some point during 1951 (with 1957 as the likely date for a Russian atomic capability to achieve a decisive collapse of the UK if an attack came). Knowledge of Soviet weapons-of-mass-destruction capacities was the absolute top requirement placed on the British intelligence community in the late 1940s.

On 11 May 1948, the JIC circulated its priority list for the gathering of signals intelligence. All four 'Priority 1' targets were nuclear-related:

1. Development in the Soviet Union of atomic, biological and chemical methods of warfare (together with associated raw materials).
2. Development in the Soviet Union of scientific principles and inventions leading to new weapons, equipment or methods of warfare.
3. Strategic and tactical doctrines, state of training, armament and aircraft of: –
   (a) Soviet long-range bomber force.
   (b) Soviet metropolitan fighter defence force. . .
4. Development in the Soviet Union of guided weapons.[29]

The day after that requirements directive made its secret way to the JIC's SIGINT providers, the Attlee government gave Parliament a highly limited, almost *sotto* indication of its own atomic weapons policy using a planted Parliamentary Question (as we shall see in a moment). The motive for this was not a sudden urge towards open government on Attlee's part. It was entirely driven by practical requirements. Both civil servants and members of the Armed Forces, in the quite sizeable teams now involved on the bomb project, under the super-secret régime agreed by GEN 163, 'could not be given an inkling of the real nature of the job they were asked to do, to understand its importance and urgency.'[30] Attlee was briefed to this effect before the meeting of GEN 75 on 12 March 1948 which authorised the carefully guarded announcement.

TOP SECRET

PRIME MINISTER

<u>ATOMIC ENERGY COMMITTEE</u>

<u>Note for Meeting to be held on Friday, 12th March 1948,
at 3.15 p.m.</u>

A full attendance of Ministers is expected at the meeting
except for the Secretary of State for Commonwealth Relations
who will be represented by the Parliamentary Under-Secretary
of State.   Lord Portal of Hungerford and the Chiefs of Staff
have been invited for the first item on research on atomic
weapons.   It is understood that neither the Chief of the
Air Staff nor his deputy will be able to be present, but the
Chiefs of Staff have been considering the Minister of Supply's
memorandum and the Staff representatives present will be able
to express the combined view of the three Staffs.

1.   <u>RESEARCH ON ATOMIC WEAPONS</u>

The question was last considered in January 1947 when a
paper, GEN. 163, was circulated by the Minister of Supply.
The discussion at the Committee was recorded in a confidential
annex to GEN. 163/1st Meeting.   The annex was circulated only
to your office and the Minister of Supply.

The memorandum now circulated by the Minister of Supply
(A.E.(M)(48) 7) sets out the reasons why the extreme degree
of secrecy imposed in January 1947 on research activities on
atomic weapons is now becoming increasingly ineffective, as
well as being an impediment to progress and a possible source
of embarrassment.   The Minister therefore recommends a
limited relaxation of the existing secrecy to the degree set
out in paragraph 4 of the memorandum, which proposes that the
Government should announce that it is developing all types of
modern weapons, including atomic weapons.   The counter

–1–

10. (cont.)

arguments against this course are not set out in the memorandum but it is understood that the Minister of Defence has some doubts about the wisdom of an announcement like this at the present time, particularly in view of its possible effect on Soviet Russia. You will no doubt wish to ask him to develop his views at the meeting.

Paragraph 6 of the memorandum refers to consultation with the United States. In view of our general relations with the United States and with Canada on atomic energy questions, it is most important that the views of the United States and the Canadian Governments should be obtained before any announcement is made. (signed) J. S. Bhauni

Still Attlee kept discussion of the bomb away from the full Cabinet. Neither the Cabinet minutes for 6 May 1948[31] nor the recently released Cabinet Secretary's handwritten record of the meeting in his notebook for 1948[32] contain a whiff of it, even though the coming week's parliamentary business was item 1 on the agenda. Ten years later Attlee said of his decision to keep the bomb away from Cabinet to Professor John Mackintosh that 'I thought that some of them were not fit to be trusted with secrets of this kind.'[33]

Cripps, by now Chancellor of the Exchequer, had argued at the 12 March meeting of GEN 75 that an announcement in Parliament should be made as it was widely assumed that Britain was making atomic bombs and there was little point in trying to keep the fact secret.[34] The Minister of Defence, A. V. Alexander, duly made the announcement in the House of Commons on 12 May 1948.

Armed Forces
(Modern Weapons)

Mr George Jeger asked the Minister of Defence whether he is satisfied that adequate progress is being made in the development of the most modern types of weapon?

The Minister of Defence (Mr A. V. Alexander): Yes, sir. As was made clear in the Statement Relating to Defence, 1948 (Command 7327), research and developments continue to receive the highest priority in the defence field, and all types of modern weapons, including the atomic weapons, are being developed.

Mr Jeger: Can the Minister give any further information on the development of atomic weapons?

Mr Alexander: No, I do not think it would be in the public interest to do that.[35]

In the privacy of GEN 75, Bevin had repeated his view expressed in GEN 163 that secrecy was best for political reasons and he was concerned that a public announcement might cause difficulties with the United States.[36] Bevin need not have worried. Alexander's announcement caused no stir in Parliament. The press generally reported the parliamentary answer with little commentary or context (perhaps because of a new 'D' notice circulated by the Defence Press and Broadcasting Committee ahead of the announcement, requesting that no details be given of the development and production of the bomb or the location of the establishments where the work was being done[37]). Some of the country's highest quality media did not report Alexander's announcement at all (the *Financial Times*, *The Sunday Times*, *The Observer*, *The Economist* and *The New Statesman and Nation*, for example, were all silent on the bomb).[38]

Looking back on both Attlee's nuclear Cabinet committees and the more general public attitudes of the late 1940s, Sir Michael Quinlan described the decision, post-McMahon Act, to go it alone on the bomb was 'psychologically quite inevitable—it was an "of course" decision.' As for the country as a whole:

> For all our economic problems, we saw ourselves as one of the three great victors of the war. We still had global responsibilities. We still had quite a lot of Empire even if we knew the sun was setting on it. And given all that, it would have been enormously counter-identity, counter-cultural for us to do anything other than to decide to get into the [nuclear] business. . .[39]

The lack of fuss in Parliament and the press in May 1948 suggests that both Cripps and Quinlan were right.

Would the sense of urgency that could now be imparted fully to the nuclear workforce mean Britain would become the world's second atomic power? Within a few weeks of Alexander's parliamentary answer, the Soviets cut off the land and water routes from the western zones of Germany to the western sectors in Berlin, causing a considerable surge of anxiety about the prospect of a serious east–west confrontation and a rapid reappraisal of military and civil defence planning in Whitehall.[40] Intelligence on the likely date at which the Soviet Union would achieve atomic status was at an even greater premium.

On 23 July 1948, the Joint Intelligence Committee circulated an assessment of 'Russian Interests, Intentions and Capabilities' which contained a section on 'Special Weapons', i.e. weapons of mass destruction. The earliest the Soviet Union was expected to acquire atomic bomb status was January 1951. This estimate assumed Russian progress at a similar rate to the American and British projects. The technical difficulties and problems in acquiring sufficient uranium ores the Soviet Union was thought to be experiencing led the JIC to expect a delay in the production of the first Russian weapon of up to three years.

11. Joint Intelligence Committee report on 'Russian Interests, Intentions and Capabilities', JIC (48) 9 (0) Final, 23 July 1948.   TNA, PRO, CAB 158/3

THIS DOCUMENT IS THE PROPERTY OF HIS BRITANNIC MAJESTY'S GOVERNMENT

The circulation of this paper has been strictly limited. It is issued for the personal use of ....*Secretary's File*.........................

TOP SECRET   Copy No. 7 2

J.I.C. (48) 9 (O) Final *Circulated for the consideration of the Chiefs of Staff*
23rd July, 1948

CHIEFS OF STAFF COMMITTEE

Joint Intelligence Committee

RUSSIAN INTERESTS, INTENTIONS AND CAPABILITIES

REPORT BY THE JOINT INTELLIGENCE COMMITTEE

We have revised our previous report* entitled as above.

2. Our present report is divided into two parts. The first part (Annex I) consists of a small self-contained paper embodying the main conclusions of our examination. The second part (Annex II) is a detailed examination on which the first part is based.

Recommendations

3. We recommend that copies of this report be made available to all members of the Cabinet, the Commonwealth Governments, His Majesty's representatives in foreign countries, Commanders-in-Chief at home and abroad and to the American Chiefs of Staff, as an expression of the views of the Chiefs of Staff.

(Signed)   W. G. HAYTER.
E. W. L. LONGLEY-COOK.
C. D. PACKARD.
L. F. PENDRED.
K. W. D. STRONG.
P. SILLITOE.
D. BRUNT.

Ministry of Defence, S.W. 1.
23rd July, 1948.

* J.I.C. (47) 7 (O) Final.

35411

11. (cont.)

3

ANNEX I

RUSSIAN INTERESTS, INTENTIONS AND CAPABILITIES

1. What is Russia trying to do? How far is she capable of doing it? The present paper is intended to give the shortest answers that we can offer to these two fundamental questions.

2. We have not felt able, at this date, to assess the full implications of the recent open breach between the Cominform and the Yugoslav Government, and in particular the effect which the schism thus revealed will have on the relationship between the Soviet Government and Communist parties outside the Soviet Union. It is also too early to assess the effects of this development on Soviet policy in regard to the territories adjoining Yugoslavia, notably Austria, Trieste, Albania and Greece. Generally speaking, however, the circumstances of Tito's fall from grace bear out our view of the tight control which Russia normally expects to exert over Communist parties in other countries, and throw interesting light on the part played by the Cominform as an instrument of Russian policy.

3. It should be emphasised that in Russia's eyes the United Kingdom is still a capitalist and imperialist country, despite its Labour Government. In general the Soviet leaders are especially hostile to " reformist Socialism " of the British pattern, which they regard not only as an opponent to Communism, but also as a dangerous competitor for working-class support in many countries.

4. Our general appreciation is as follows: corresponding paragraphs in Annex II are shown in parenthesis.

Fundamental Principles

(a) The fundamental aim of the Soviet leaders is to hasten the elimination of capitalism from all parts of the world and to replace it with their own form of Communism. They envisage this process as being effected in the course of a revolutionary struggle lasting possibly for many years and assisted, should favourable conditions arise, by military action on the part of Soviet and satellite armed forces.

(b) The Soviet leaders are, however, also convinced that the capitalist world, aware of the growing strength of Communism, is likely eventually to resort to force in an attempt to avert its own collapse. This belief inspires the more immediate aim of Soviet policy, which is to ensure, by all possible means, the security of the Soviet Union. This aim is of short-term application, and is complementary to the long-term aim of establishing world Communism (paragraphs 1–10).

Capabilities

(c) It is unlikely that before 1957 the Soviet Union will be capable of supporting her armed forces entirely from the natural resources and industrial potential now under her control, in any major war, except one in which extensive operations are not prolonged. Nevertheless, if Russia wished to go to war, economic considerations would not in themselves be enough to prevent her from doing so if she felt confident of attaining her primary objectives rapidly.

(d) It is improbable that there is at present any economic objective outside the borders of the Soviet Union, or beyond her control, which she is likely to regard as essential for the fulfilment of her economic plans. The Soviet Union's economic condition appears therefore not to be, in itself, such as to impel her to use methods which might lead to a major war in order to acquire external economic resources (paragraphs 10–36).

(e) The Soviet land forces, with their close support aircraft, are sufficiently strong, at the present time, to achieve rapid and far-reaching successes against any likely combination of opposing land forces. In view of the present reduced effectiveness of the navies of the British Commonwealth, United States and the Western European Powers, the Soviet Union may appreciate that within the next few years her relative naval strength will be as great as it is ever likely to be, and that her naval situation is therefore in itself no additional deterrent against engaging in a major war. The strategic air situation, however,

35411　　　　　　　　　　　　　　　　　　　　　　　　　　　B 2

remains adverse to the Soviet Union in that she has at present no satisfactory answer either to atomic weapons or to strategic bomber attacks. She can thus not yet count upon a reasonable degree of immunity for her centres of population and industry from serious air attack. Her future readiness to embark upon a major war is likely therefore to be conditioned by considerations of her own air power in relation to that of probable opponents.

(f) As regards atomic weapons, we consider it unlikely that the Soviet Union will have enough atom bombs by the end of 1956 to defeat the United Kingdom by this means alone. Even though the Russians may take a different view about the number of bombs required for this purpose, the defeat of the United Kingdom would still leave them with the greater problem of defeating the United States, which such an attack on the United Kingdom would involve. It is a reasonable deduction that a realisation of her relative backwardness in atomic development may cause, or has already caused, the Soviet Union to hasten her preparedness to wage biological warfare; there are no raw material difficulties comparable to those for atomic development. We consider that the Russians could have biological weapons available in quantity some four or five years after a decision to allot first priority to such a project, but we have no means of assessing Russian intentions and present or future potential in this respect.

(g) Failing the early development of biological or other new weapons, to a point which she believed would ensure her rapid victory, the Soviet Union's economic situation is likely to be decisive in making her wish to avoid a protracted major war at any rate until 1957 (paragraphs 37–110).

Resultant Policy

(h) Against this background, the fundamental principles referred to in conclusion (a) above, namely the long-term struggle to establish Communism throughout the world, and the immediate search for security, manifest themselves in present Soviet policy in the simultaneous pursuit of five main objectives :—

First, a move towards increased strategic security by the establishment of a belt of subservient States around her frontiers, which could not, in any circumstances, be used as a base for attack on the Soviet Union.

Secondly, the restoration of Russian economy and its development to a point where it will rival and eventually outstrip that of the United States.

Third, the avoidance of armed conflict with the Anglo-American Powers, at least until circumstances are judged to be sufficiently favourable to the Soviet Union.

Fourth, the aggressive promotion of Communism throughout the capitalist world.

Fifth, an endeavour to weaken and disintegrate the capitalist world, starting at its weakest spots, both by political infiltration, leading to unrest, and by the fostering of nationalist movements and native unrest in the colonial territories of the capitalist Powers (paragraphs 111–129).

(i) As regards the methods which the Soviet leaders will use to put the above policy into effect, the Marxist doctrine regards a state of constant friction and struggle as only natural in the Soviet Union's relations with capitalist States, and prescribes a ruthless and completely callous attitude in the promotion of chaos in the outer world. It also teaches that, while the basis of Russian policy should remain unchanged, its tactics should be opportunist and flexible (paragraphs 130–133).

(j) The Soviet Union will make full use of all available means for the implementation of her policy, notably the Communist parties in foreign countries, and any other forces, such as disappointed nationalism, the interests of which may happen to fit in with her own.

(k) The Soviet Union's willingness to co-operate in international affairs is strictly limited to the direct furtherance of her own national and ideological interests, and she is only concerned in keeping the United

11. (cont.)

Nations, or other international organisations, in being so far as they serve these ends (paragraphs 134–168).

(*l*) The emergence of the United States as the Soviet Union's main rival in world affairs, and the recognition of United States superiority in war potential, particularly as regards the atomic bomb, are factors of decisive importance to the Soviet Union. It is probable, moreover, that, since Hiroshima, the possession of the atomic bomb by the United States has been one of the major factors in deterring the Soviet leaders from the pursuit of their fundamental aim by military, as opposed to " cold war," methods. The close co-operation between the United States and the British Commonwealth, the development of the European Recovery Programme, and of Western Union, are most disquieting to the Soviet leaders.

(*m*) Given the present balance of strength, the Soviet Union will wish her contest with the United States and the capitalist world generally to be played out in the conditions most favourable to herself; that is to say, on a basis of Communist penetration aided by economic distress, rather than on a basis of overt aggression; or, in other words, by " cold war " methods rather than by real war. Meanwhile the Soviet leaders will hope that changes in American public opinion or instability in the United States economy will have an adverse effect on the continuance of the present United States policy of opposition to Soviet expansion (paragraphs 169–174).

GENERAL ARRANGEMENT OF ANNEX II

11. (cont.)

be of reasonably modern standard since they will be assisted by many German technicians in this field.

(*e*) *Radar.*—The Russians are in possession of British and American ship-borne radar sets supplied under Lend-Lease. They have also acquired information on certain more modern sets through their intelligence service. In addition they have captured a large quantity of German radar equipment and are actively developing this with the help of German technicians. It is unlikely, however, that they will master radar control technique for some years yet.

(*f*) *Small Battle Units.*—The Russians are in possession of details of most German and Italian types of midget submarine and remote controlled explosive motor boats. They are at present actively engaged with German assistance on working out a production programme for both these types.

Special Weapons

54. *Atomic Bombs.*—The manufacture of atomic weapons demands not only a high standard of scientific knowledge and the application on a very large scale of difficult industrial techniques, but also the use of large quantities of uranium. The most reliable present estimate that can be made of Russian progress indicates that the limiting factor is their supplies of uranium. At the present time it is considered to be most misleading to attempt to forecast how much uranium will be available to any Russian project beyond January 1952 since this depends on two unpredictable factors :—

(*a*) the discovery within Russian-controlled territory of new high-grade deposits, which is believed to be unlikely, and

(*b*) the success the Russians will have in developing a practicable process for the large-scale extraction of the small percentages of uranium present in oil-shales, large deposits of which are available to them.

55. Existing estimates of the date when the Russians began their programme and of their ability to overcome the technological difficulties involved suggest that they may possibly produce their first atomic bomb by January 1951, and that their stockpile of bombs in January 1953 may be of the order of 6 to 22. Any subsequent production would be at the rate of 2 to 4 per year on existing knowledge of the ore supplies. These, however, will almost certainly alter considerably in the later 1950's.

56. These figures, however, are the maximum possible based on the assumption that the Russian effort will progress as rapidly as the American and British projects have done. Allowances for the probably slower progress of the Russian effort will almost certainly retard the first bomb by some three years.

57. On these assumptions it is improbable that the Soviet Union will have sufficient atom bombs by the end of 1956 to defeat the United Kingdom by this means alone. Even though the Russians may take a different view about the number of bombs required for this purpose, the defeat of the United Kingdom would still leave them with the greater problem of defeating the United States, which such an attack on the United Kingdom would involve. It is impossible at this juncture to add to this statement or to forecast the probable development in atomic weapons beyond 1956–57.

58. *Biological Weapons.*—We have no knowledge of Russian offensive biological warfare intentions, and are unable to assess her present or future potential in this respect. We must assume, however, that she possesses the necessary basic knowledge and that her ability to wage biological warfare will be limited only by the effort allotted to such a project and by the availability of the requisite means of delivery.

59. It is a reasonable deduction that a realisation of her relative backwardness in atomic development may cause, or already has caused, the Soviet Union to hasten her preparedness to wage biological warfare; there are no raw material difficulties (comparable to those for atomic development) and progress would depend essentially on the effort applied. We consider that the Russians could have biological weapons available in quantity some 4 or 5 years after a decision to allot first priority to such a project, but we have no information to indicate whether or not such a decision has been made or is contemplated.

60. *Chemical Warfare.*—We have no knowledge of any Russian intentions to initiate offensive chemical warfare. Russian chemical warfare research may have been stimulated by knowledge of German nerve-gas developments and it is possible that comparable but independent discoveries have been made. Russian progress in chemical warfare would depend essentially on the effort applied and

It was a very considerable shock, therefore, to both American and British intelligence when a specially equipped B-29 of the US Air Force on a weather flight over the North Pacific on 3 September discovered that Russia had exploded an atomic bomb somewhere in Soviet Asia over the past few days. In fact the explosion took place on the Kazakhstan steppes at the Semipalatinsk test-site on 29 August 1949.[41] The world in general was shocked when Truman broke the news in Washington on 23 September.

As the diplomat Sir Gladwyn Jebb, Chairman of the Official Committee on Communism (Overseas), told both his colleagues on this most secret body and the Imperial Defence College in February 1950, '[i]t is quite useless ... for us to minimise the great accretion of strength, both physical and psychological, which this achievement has conferred on the Soviet Union. It may well be that they would have produced the bomb in the long run, but however much assistance they may have had in the way of illicit information, the fact remains that the work of their scientists and specialised workers represents a technical achievement of which the best brains on this side did not believe the Russians to be capable. If they can do this, perhaps they can produce other things, such as fighters, bombers and rockets unexpectedly well and surprisingly fast,' Jebb concluded prophetically, adding portentously: 'The mechanized barbarian must never be underestimated if civilization is to endure.'[42]

How had the Soviet bomb been made so soon? British intelligence thought it knew a few weeks later when (thanks to Soviet intelligence signals decoded in the USA) it uncovered an atom spy at the heart of the British programme, Klaus Fuchs who had also been a leading theoretical physicist in the Manhattan project at Los Alamos. Dick White (who would later head both the Security Service, MI5, and the Secret Intelligence Service, MI6) was intimately involved with the Fuchs inquiry in 1949–50. Once Fuchs had confessed in late January 1950, White concluded, as he would later say, that Fuchs had given the Soviets '[n]othing less than the full design of the atomic bomb.'[43] He was the most damaging of the British and American atom spies. Between them, it has been suggested, they enabled Stalin to get his bomb 18 months sooner than if his scientists had worked unaided[44] i.e. at roughly the time predicted by the JIC in 1948. Fuchs himself, as his interrogation files show, was surprised at the speed with which the Russian bomb had been tested 'as he had been convinced that the information he had given could not have been applied so quickly and that the Russians would not have the engineering, design and construction facilities that would be needed to build large production plants in such a short time.'[45]

Britain would now be the world's third atomic power. Just how soon that might be—and at what financial cost—was carefully concealed from Parliament, the public and indeed from the Leader of the Opposition, Winston Churchill. Once restored to office in the autumn of 1951, Churchill was amazed by the amount Attlee had kept from Parliament and sought an explanation of how his predecessor had done it from Sir Edwards Bridges, by now Permanent Secretary to the Treasury.

12. Churchill/Bridges exchanges on the financing of the atomic bomb project, plus correspondence with Cherwell, December 1951.   TNA, PRO, PREM 11/297

PRIME MINISTER'S
PERSONAL MINUTE

SERIAL No. M.140⁴/51

SIR EDWARD BRIDGES

How was it that the £100 millions for atomic research and manufacture was provided without Parliament being informed? How was this very large sum accounted for? Pray let me have a one-page note on the position and on the sequence of events.

W.S.C.

8.12.51.

G. R.

PRIME MINISTER

TOP SECRET · 4

Atomic Energy Expenditure

1. The short answer to the first question in your M.140/51 is that expenditure on atomic energy is provided as part of the general expenditure on the Ministry of Supply Vote: and that this Vote does not show how much of the expenditure on research is for atomic energy, how much for aircraft and how much for guided missiles, etc.

2. The total expenditure on atomic energy since 1945 is shown in Annex A.

3. As to your next question, Annex B shows how the £31 millions which we expect to spend on atomic energy in 1951/2 is distributed under the various sub-heads of the Ministry of Supply Vote.

4. Since 1945 the Government has deliberately restricted the information in Estimates about defence and in particular about research and development. This policy, which was re-affirmed by Ministers, following reviews by the Joint Intelligence Committee and the Chiefs of Staff, in 1947, 1948, 1949 and 1950, applied to atomic energy equally with other defence research and development: indeed successive Defence White Papers have given a single total for all defence research development and production with the express purpose of concealing the expenditure on atomic energy.

5. Information about Atomic Energy has been given in confidence to N.A.T.O. and the Select Committee on Estimates. See Annex C.

EEB

Lord Cherwell

R. 12th December 1951

12. (cont.)

5

ANNEX A

TOTAL (NET) EXPENDITURE ON

ATOMIC ENERGY

	£
1946/47	4,782,000
1947/48	11,090,000
1948/49	17,026,000
1949/50	16,827,000
1950/51	23,214,000
1951/52	31,703,000 (a)

(a) Revised Estimate. Original Estimate
was £26,982,000

MINISTRY OF SUPPLY

ESTIMATE 1951/2[x]

(1) Ministry of Supply Subhead		(2) Total of Subhead	(3) Amount included in (2) devoted to Atomic Energy
		£	£
Subhead A	Salaries and Wages (H.Q.)	6,750,000	100,000
B1	Research & Development: Salaries and Wages at Research Estab.	17,500,000	5,387,000
B2	Research & Development: Stores, etc.	13,000,000	9,407,000
B3	Research & Development: Work by Industry, etc.	45,000,000	1,050,000
B4	Loan for Production of Uranium	1,000,000	2,500,000
C	Royal Ordnance Factories	30,000,000	150,000
E1	Armaments	28,000,000	85,000
E4	Mechanical Transport	55,000,000	30,000
F1	Clothing & Textiles	38,000,000	40,000
G2	Radiac Production	4,800,000	10,000
H1	Salaries & Wages, Inspection	6,800,000	350,000
K1	Capital Expenditure: Land and Buildings	1,300,000	94,000
L1-3	Works Services	24,450,000	10,631,000
M1	Capital Expenditure on plant, etc.	11,000,000	4,560,000
N1	Fuel, Water, etc.	3,250,000	1,405,000
N2	Travel & Subsistence	1,350,000	212,000
N5	Miscellaneous	400,000	1,000
			36,038,000
Z	Appropriations in Aid		4,336,000
			31,703,000

[x] As revised December 1951.

The figures in column 3 are not, of course, shown in the Estimate.

12. (cont.)

ANNEX C   •   7

<u>Disclosures of Information about Atomic Energy</u>

1.   Details of expenditure on works services, including
atomic energy projects, are given to the Public Accounts
Committee in a secret supplement to the annual Appropriation
Account.

2.   A global figure for atomic energy expenditure, actual
or estimated, has been given in secret to N.A.T.O. for the
years 1949-1954.   This was in connection with the assessment
of relative defence burdens and the figures were included, by
Ministerial direction, because the United States had included
atomic energy as defence expenditure.

3.   In June 1951 the Minister of Defence told the Chairman
of the Select Committee on Estimates that senior official
witnesses might have discretion to give the Estimates Committee
orally and in confidence unpublished information about defence
matters on the understanding that it would not be quoted.   This
discretion was not to extend to particularly secret subjects:
but it enabled the Estimates Committee to be given in confidence
the 1951-52 figure for total atomic energy expenditure as then
estimated.

13th December, 1951.

TOP SECRET

Dear Madge,

I enclose a file about Atomic Energy
Expenditure on which the Prime Minister
would like to have Lord Cherwell's views.
Would you please send the file back with
your reply?

Yours sincerely,
D. W. S. H.

J.R. Madge, Esq.,
Paymaster General's Office.

12. (cont.)

Tube alloys
2

·Prime Minister

    In my view it would in general be most undesirable
to publish details about expenditure on new projects of
importance to defence. I am therefore pleased that
it should be possible to wrap up such expenditure in the
Estimates so well. Concealment was certainly very
necessary at the inception of atomic energy work. And
frankly I am agreeably surprised that the Socialist
Government was sufficiently imaginative and patriotic
to risk the Parliamentary criticism to which this might
expose them.

    Now that most of our great atomic buildings are in
being or in course of construction, no doubt the Russians
have a pretty good idea of the scale of our effort in
this field, so that there would seem to be less reason
to conceal the broad facts of our expenditure on atomic
energy.

Take with me. (K.H.)

Cherwell.

R. 21st December, 1951

Bridges' reply indicated that if the revised estimate for the financial year 1951–52 were included, the cumulative cost of putting a Union Jack on top of it would be £104,642,000. He carefully stuck to the convention that the ministerial groups in which previous administrations took decisions are not divulged to current governments of a different political stripe, though he did reveal the degree to which Emmanuel Shinwell, Labour's Minister of Defence in 1951, had taken the Chairman of the House of Commons Estimates Committee into his confidence.

For Parliament and public no figure for the cost of the bomb was available. The breakdown of the current Ministry of Supply estimate for 1951–52 showed the greatest single element of deception was under heading B4, 'Loan for the production of Uranium'. The published estimate put this at £1m. The real figure was £2.5m.

Lord Cherwell had been appointed Paymaster General in 1951 and was Churchill's principal adviser on atomic energy both military and civil. Note his patronising attitude towards the patriotism of Attlee and his ministers. It was, in fact, Attlee's (or, perhaps more precisely, Bevin's bomb) that was nearing completion. But it fell to Churchill to authorise its testing in the Monte Bello Islands off the north-west coast of Australia. Churchill briefly flirted with the idea of Britain's possessing 'the art rather than the article' to save money. Cherwell swiftly talked him out of this and of his view that in forthcoming bilateral negotiations in Washington, he could talk Truman out of the McMahon Act.[46]

A wartime picture of Winston and the 'Prof.': Lord Cherwell on the far left; next to him Lord Portal.

On 14 December 1951 Churchill authorised the test.[47] On 18 February 1952 he told Parliament it would take place later in the year. It was exploded on 3 October 1952. Britain thereby became the world's third nuclear power. It had its 'certificate of grandeur.' But, less than a month later, the United States exploded the world's first thermonuclear device at Eniwetok in the Pacific. At 10.4 megatons, it was twice the power of *all* the explosives used in World War II. In terms of the UK's nuclear programme, it demonstrated that the new generation of weapons would be some thousand times more powerful than the bombs dropped on Japan or the device detonated in the Monte Bellos. The UK had caught up for a mere 28 days. On 7 November 1953 the Royal Air Force took delivery of its first operational 'Blue Danube' atomic bomb at RAF Wittering. At last, there *was* 'a bloody Union Jack on top of it'.

Sir William Penney returns to RAF Lyneham after overseeing Britain's first atomic test off north-west Australia, October 1952.

During his final premiership, Churchill became more and more preoccupied by the destructive power of the H-Bomb and devoted every ounce of his failing powers to seeking a summit to ease global tensions before the catastrophe of a thermonuclear war wrecked the world.[48] British intelligence knew that the 'first' Soviet 'H-Bomb test' on 12 August 1953 at Semipalatinsk[49] was a 'hybrid' device not a 'true' thermonuclear explosion, though, as the JIC put it in its February 1954 estimate of 'Soviet and Satellite War Potential, 1954–1958', the bomb 'contained a thermo-nuclear component' and that '[f]rom this it was evident that the Soviet Union has made remarkable technical progress in the production of ingredients for atomic weapons.'

A dummy Blue Danube '10,000 pound' bomb leaves a Valiant bomber during flight trials.

amended
Amended 2nd Ref 31/5.

THIS DOCUMENT IS THE PROPERTY OF HER BRITANNIC MAJESTY'S GOVERNMENT

Amended 3rd Ref 15/11

Circulated for the consideration of the Chiefs of Staff

The circulation of this paper has been strictly limited.   It is issued

for the personal use of .... *the Record*

TOP SECRET   Copy No. 6 0

J.I.C. (54) 3 (Final)
15th February, 1954

CHIEFS OF STAFF COMMITTEE
JOINT INTELLIGENCE COMMITTEE

———

SOVIET AND SATELLITE WAR POTENTIAL, 1954–1958

REPORT BY JOINT INTELLIGENCE COMMITTEE

Our estimate of Soviet and Satellite capabilities in the event of war in 1954–58 is at Annex.

2.   This report supersedes our previous study* of this subject.

(Signed)   P. H. DEAN.
             A. W. BUZZARD.
             V. BOUCHER.
             F. J. FRESSANGES.
             K. W. D. STRONG.
             C. Y. CARSTAIRS.
             H. S. YOUNG (Acting D.S.I.).

Ministry of Defence, S.W. 1,
15th February, 1954.

* J.I.C. (53) 14.

TOP SECRET

45697   B

Deductions

43. The Soviet Union is economically capable (unless the economy can be seriously disrupted by Allied air action) of waging a major war effectively for a considerable period. Certain economic weaknesses, however, would constitute one of the factors which might deter the Soviet leaders from precipitating a general war in the near future despite their immediate superiority in conventional arms and arms production. By 1958 the economic position will have been strengthened, but some of the weaknesses will not have been eliminated.

Scientific and Technical

Atomic Warfare

44. The Soviet atomic energy project is on a very large scale and has an over-riding priority.

45. Uranium is mined in the U.S.S.R. and the Satellites, a major contribution coming from Eastern Germany. The current rate of production is probably running roughly parallel with the rate of consumption.

46. Plutonium is produced in nuclear reactors and U_{235} is separated from natural uranium, possibly by more than one method.

47. The Soviet test explosions which have been detected fall into three series : —

    (*a*) A single test in August 1949, in which the fissile core was probably plutonium.

    (*b*) A series in September and October 1951. The nature of these is still slightly uncertain, but it may be stated fairly confidently that one employed a composite core of mixed U_{235} and plutonium.

    (*c*) The 1953 series, of which the first contained a thermo-nuclear component. The latter could probably be manufactured without great difficulty and without involving the use of " piles."

From this it is evident that the Soviet Union has made remarkable technical progress in the production of ingredients for atomic weapons.

Stocks and Production of Atomic Bombs

48. The U.S.S.R. is now manufacturing fissile material on a very large scale. If the Soviet stock of this material at mid-1954 were made up, according to conventional proportions, into strategic bombs, we think that it might produce between 250 and 400 bombs. Such bombs would have an energy release of between 20 and 100 kT and would weigh about 10,000 lbs. After mid-1954, Soviet stocks of fissile material available for bombs might increase at a rate sufficient to provide 100 new strategic bombs of the same type each year; but there is a considerable factor of uncertainty about this figure.

49. It is most unlikely, however, that the Russians would make up all their fissile material into the conventional type of strategic bomb described above. They are now in a position, if they wish, to incorporate a thermo-nuclear component in their strategic bombs and thus obtain a much more powerful explosion for the same expenditure of fissile material. Again, we are satisfied, from the progress that the Russians have made with atomic weapons, that they could now make up tactical bombs, if they so desired. Such bombs would have an energy release of 5 to 20 kT and might weigh as little as 1,000 lbs. We would also expect the Soviet choice of tactical weapons to include the artillery projectile. We estimate that the gun equipment for this would be based on German dual-recoil designs and would probably be initially of 280-mm. calibre. The Russians could also make a shallow-burst underwater atomic mine: there are many sea-board cities which would be particularly vulnerable to such a weapon. How the Soviet Union would in fact divide its considerable stock of fissile material between the various types of weapons would depend on Soviet intentions and Soviet intelligence on Western war plans.

Clandestine Delivery of Atomic Bombs

50. It would be technically possible to import the components of a bomb, in the guise of ordinary merchandise, in a number of cases, each of no great size, for subsequent assembly and detonation ashore; or to carry an atomic bomb as cargo in a merchant ship and detonate it in port. No instruments exist, or are in

TOP SECRET

13. (cont.)

sight, for the detection from a short distance of any component of an atomic bomb. The likelihood of the U.S.S.R. attempting such clandestine attacks is examined elsewhere.*

Future Developments in Atomic Energy

51. We have little information about Soviet hopes and intentions in the atomic energy field. We have usually assumed, and Soviet actions provide justification for this, that their first general aim was to build up a stockpile of atomic weapons sufficient to deter any group of nations contemplating war against them. However, Soviet statements, both in the United Nations and after the announcement by the West of the first Soviet test explosion, have frequently asserted that they preferred to use atomic energy as a source of power. It is clear that in a war with the West, atomic-powered submarines would be of great value to the Soviet Union, because of its geographical position. Thus, it is reasonable to suppose that they may be devoting effort to advanced reactors, particularly for propulsion and power generation, but of this we have had no evidence.

Biological Warfare

52. There is no evidence on Soviet progress in this field, but the available information points to the following as the most reasonable conclusions about the present position:—

    (a) We know of at least one group of medical scientists and technicians which may be engaged upon human B.W. research under the control of the Soviet Army. There may also be other such groups, as well as teams working on diseases of domestic animals and plants.

    (b) The Soviet Union could produce toxic substances from bacteria and from higher plants for use against man or animals, and is producing substances of the selective weed-killer type which could be used for crop destruction.

    (c) The Soviet Union is capable of employing sabotage methods, either directly against man, or by the introduction of diseases likely to spread among livestock or crops.

    (d) The Soviet Union should now have the basic theoretical knowledge, as well as the industrial know-how, to enable it to engage in bulk production of living pathogens (bacteria, viruses and fungi) for use on a strategic scale.

53. Soviet progress in the field of B.W. during the years 1954–58 cannot now be foreseen, but there is no particular reason to doubt that it will take place, probably along orthodox lines, similarly to that in the West.

Chemical Warfare

54. We have no evidence to show whether large-scale production of any chemical warfare agent is or is not in progress in the U.S.S.R. We consider, however, that, provided the necessary priorities were allocated:—

    (a) the Soviet Union could produce and stock standard agents on a large scale.

    (b) the Soviet Union could have started large-scale production of nerve gas during 1951. If so, they could have accumulated, by 1958, sufficient nerve gas weapons to sustain chemical warfare on a scale similar to that hitherto estimated for the standard agents alone.

55. We have no knowledge of recent Soviet developments in chemical warfare weapons, but we believe the Soviet Union to be capable of producing weapons with a performance comparable to our own.

Antibiotics

56. For treatment of casualties resulting from atomic, biological or chemical warfare, antibiotics are of first importance. At present antibiotics research and development are not so advanced in the Soviet Union as in the West. Soviet antibiotics production has, however, increased both in range and quality of products and in total output, permitting of some export to Satellite States. The Soviet Union should, during the years 1954–58, achieve a production level sufficiently high to enable them to compete with the effects to be expected from the use of weapons of mass destruction.

* J.I.C. (53) 85.

TOP SECRET

Nineteen Fifty Four was to be Britain's thermonuclear year when decisions had to be made about whether the UK could—or should—move to a new and immensely more destructive nuclear capacity. For Churchill, once he was told it was feasible and doable within the financial resources at Britain's disposal, it was, in Michael Quinlan's phrase, an 'of course' decision.

As Lord Plowden, the first Chairman of the Atomic Energy Commission (which had taken over executive responsibility for the UK nuclear weapons programme from the Ministry of Supply) recalled for the Radio 4 *A Bloody Union Jack on Top of It* programme,

> I went to see Churchill in his room in the House of Commons after lunch, and when I'd explained what the effort necessary would be, he paused for a time, and nodded his head, and said in that well-known voice of his, 'We must do it. It's the price we pay to sit at the top table.' And having said that, he got up and tied a little black ribbon round his eyes, and lay down on his bed in his room, and went to sleep.[50]

A great deal of Whitehall effort had gone into the making of Plowden's briefing; and a considerable political push on Churchill's part was needed to adjust the existing defence programme and to steer the H-bomb decision through his Cabinet committees and full Cabinet during the spring and summer of 1954.

In the cricketing argot then favoured in Whitehall, the key figure in priming both the technical and political pitches was the Secretary of the Cabinet, Sir Norman Brook, who convened a meeting for this purpose in his office on 12 March 1954.

THIS DOCUMENT IS THE PROPERTY OF HER BRITANNIC MAJESTY'S GOVERNMENT

The circulation of this paper has been strictly limited.

Gen 465. (1st)

It is issued for the personal use of...........................

TOP SECRET   Copy No. *18*

NOTE of a Meeting
held in Sir Norman Brook's Room, Cabinet Office, S.W.1.,
on Friday, 12th March, 1954, at 10.30 a.m.

PRESENT:

The Rt. Hon. Sir Norman Brook
(In the Chair)
Sir Edwin Plowden
Sir John Cockcroft
Sir William Penney
Sir Richard Powell
Sir Frederick Brundrett
General Sir Nevil Brownjohn

SIR NORMAN BROOK said that he had called this meeting as a
preliminary to a meeting on Friday, 19th March, to be attended by the Chiefs
of Staff. The purpose of that meeting would be to acquaint the Chiefs of
Staff with the latest available information concerning the development of the
hydrogen bomb by both the Americans and the Russians. He believed that
the development of this bomb had now reached a stage which required us to
re-assess first, our foreign policy and general strategy and, thereafter,
the "size and shape" of the Armed Forces, our civil defence policy and our
atomic weapons programme. He invited Sir William Penney to give an
account of his information on American and Russian development of the
hydrogen bomb, in the light of his recent visit to the United States.

SIR WILLIAM PENNEY said that at Eniwetok, in 1952, the Americans
had exploded a 14 megaton bomb. This had made a crater 1-mile wide and
175-ft. deep, and had produced a fire-ball $3\frac{1}{2}$-miles in diameter. These
details had recently been revealed in a public statement by Mr. Sterling Cole,
the Chairman of the Joint Congressional Atomic Energy Committee. The
Americans had now embarked on a series of six more test explosions of
bombs ranging from 100 kilotons to 10 megatons. All six of these bombs
were different in design, but they were so made that, if required, they could
be put into production quickly.

There were two forms of hydrogen bomb - a "hybrid" bomb and a
"true" hydrogen bomb. The "hybrid" bomb was something like the earlier
atomic bomb but "boosted" with lithium deuteride, of which 300 lbs. was
required for each bomb. The Russians had developed a "hybrid" bomb
of about 1 megaton in 1953. The "true" hydrogen bomb was a new departure:
it involved a series of chain-reactions which at the last stage produced
very fast neutrons; and in theory there was no limit to the size of
explosion which could be produced by a bomb of this type. Moreover, it
used uranium or thorium, not plutonium, as the main explosive element;
and was highly economical in its use of fissionable material. Its cost
was therefore relatively low (about £1.5 to £2 millions a bomb). It was
72-in. in diameter, 10 to 30-ft. in length, and weighed 7 to 8 tons. It
could be carried in a B.29 or B.36 aircraft, both of which types were now
obsolete, and in a B.52, an 8-jet bomber which was now coming into
production.

-1-

There was good reason to believe that the United States Strategic Air Force would rely on "true" hydrogen bombs by the end of 1954. "Hybrid" bombs of about 80 to 100 kilotons would be used by the United States Air Force for tactical purposes.

The Russians had already developed the "hybrid" bomb, and they were likely to develop the "true" hydrogen bomb before long. It should be possible to tell when the Russians did explode "true" hydrogen bombs from the magnitude of the explosions.

Sir William Penney said that a 5 megaton "true" hydrogen bomb would have the following effects. A bomb dropped on London and bursting on impact would produce a crater $\frac{3}{4}$-mile across and 150-ft. deep, and a fire-ball of $2\frac{1}{4}$-miles diameter. The blast from it would crush the Admiralty Citadel at a distance of 1 mile. Suburban houses would be wrecked at a distance of 3 miles from the explosion, and they would lose their roofs and be badly blasted at a distance of 7 miles. All habitations would catch fire over a circle of 2 miles radius from the burst.

A 1 megaton "hybrid" bomb would have the following effects. It would produce a crater 1,000-yds. across and 150-ft. deep; the Admiralty Citadel would be wrecked at a distance of 1,200-yds. from the point of burst, houses would be wrecked at 2 miles, and bad blast would be experienced at 4 miles.

In discussion the following points were made: -

(a) Whatever progress the Russians might make from now on in developing the hydrogen bomb, we should be justified in advising Ministers now that the Russians had already developed the material for an attack on this country, the intensity of which far exceeded our previous assumptions and the plans which we had based on them.

(b) Sir William Penney had said that by the end of this year the United States Strategic Air Force would rely on hydrogen bombs. But it was not clear whether the Americans now excluded the possibility of strategic bombing with conventional high explosive bombs. Up till now it had been thought that they were basing their plans for dropping atomic bombs on the "queen bee" method whereby a bomber carrying an atomic bomb would be accompanied by a large number of bombers carrying conventional bombs. They were thought to be still making conventional bombs, but it did not follow that they proposed to use them for strategic bombing. It was agreed that it would be valuable if the Chief of Air Staff could discover what change, if any, had taken place in American theory on the dropping of atomic bombs.

(c) SIR WILLIAM PENNEY said that there were now several plants on the east and west coasts of the United States, run by the United States Air Force, at which it was intended that bomber aircraft which had already been armed with bombs elsewhere would pick up the liquid hydrogen which was necessary to arm a hydrogen bomb. The range of aircraft at present available for carrying hydrogen bombs was 3,000 miles: this was not sufficient for an aircraft to take off from the United States, drop bombs on Russia and return to its base in the United States. The Americans might intend to re-fuel bomber aircraft in flight on the way to their target. Alternatively they might, for example, land for re-fuelling at a base in the United Kingdom on the way to the target and on the way back. He understood that at present the Americans did not intend to instal liquid hydrogen plants outside the United States.

-2-

14. (cont.)

This might be thought to reduce to some extent the dangers to us which had hitherto been supposed to arise from the location of United States atomic air bases in East Anglia. If they were to be used only for re-fuelling, they might not seem so provocative. On the other hand the Americans might, in the long term, want to establish their liquid hydrogen stations abroad as well as in the United States.

(d) Though the Russians were rapidly reducing the Western lead in atomic development, it was not certain that they were making the same progress in developing the means of delivering an atomic attack. They could bomb the United Kingdom, but not the United States (even by means of one-way missions), with TU.34 aircraft, which were the equivalent of the obsolete B.29. They had not yet developed jet engines of sufficient power to enable them to build bombers which could attack the United States. As they were lagging behind in the development of jet engines of the power required for heavy bombers, we should take special care to avoid the risk that British aircraft equipped with this type of engine might fall into their hands. It was proposed that Comet IIs, which were equipped with Avon engines, should be exported to France, Japan and Brazil this year. When this decision was taken, it had been thought sufficient that we should maintain our lead in the development of military types of aircraft. The present discussion suggested that it might now be necessary to apply a different criterion, viz., that we should deny the Russians any aircraft engines capable of powering a bomber which could carry a hydrogen bomb from Russian air bases to the United States. In any event, the highest priority should now be given to the obtaining of intelligence of the Russian capacity to deliver a long-range air attack.

(e) The United Kingdom atomic weapons programme was at present concentrated on three objects – the manufacture of 10 kiloton bombs, the stepping-up of 10 kiloton bombs to 30 kiloton bombs by means of improvements in design, and the production of smaller weapons to be carried in Javelin aircraft. The latest information about American and Russian development of the hydrogen bomb made it necessary to consider whether this programme needed modification, with particular regard to the serious shortage of skilled manpower, the money available and the security risks which might have to be faced if the programme were to be expanded.

(f) SIR NORMAN BROOK said that, before modification of the present atomic weapons programme was considered, we should need to get clear the fundamental issues of foreign policy and strategy which were raised by the latest developments. He had already suggested to the Prime Minister that it was necessary to re-assess, in the light of the new information about the hydrogen bomb, the following points:-

(i) The likelihood of war.

(ii) The form which war was most likely to take if it came.

(iii) The changes which would need to be made in the pattern of our defence arrangements, active and passive, in order to adjust them to meet the most likely contingency.

(iv) The extent to which we should ensure against the possibility that war might take some other form than that which now seemed most likely.

-3-

He had suggested that a small Ministerial Committee should be set up
to supervise such a re-assessment; and that, under the guidance of this
Committee, studies of the issues raised in (i) and (ii) should be undertaken
by the Chiefs of Staff in consultation with representatives of the Foreign
Office, while work on (iii) and (iv) was remitted to the Home Defence
Committee, who would in turn arrange for the Chiefs of Staff and officials
of the Civil Departments concerned to go into the resultant problems of
military and civil planning. He agreed that to these four issues should
be added a fifth, namely consideration of the bearing of this re-assessment
on our atomic weapons programme.

Cabinet Office, S. W. 1.

15TH MARCH, 1954.

-4-

Sir Norman Brook: Cabinet Secretary and co-ordinator of the thermonuclear rethink 1954–55.

The new Whitehall consensus, developed in response to the H-bomb era, is neatly encapsulated in this note as is, thanks to Penney's contribution, the physics of the leap from fission to fusion. It was plain the Russians would soon reach full thermonuclear status and all aspects of politico-military and civil defence planning would need to reflect the new reality, as would the configuration of the British Armed Forces.

From this meeting, and Brook's prospectus for the interlinking of decision-making processes, came the Chiefs of Staff's recommendation on the H-bomb, the Cabinet committee deliberations and the full Cabinet discussions from which eventually emerged the authorisation of a UK thermonuclear capability. The 1955 Strath inquiry into the consequences of a ten 10-megaton Soviet H-bomb attack on the UK, also flowed from the Brook group's March 1954 reappraisal.[51]

Before the decision to go thermonuclear could be taken, Whitehall's atomic community needed to ensure the ingredients would be available when, if so instructed, the Atomic Weapons Establishment at Aldermaston produced a viable design for what, in the dreadful jargon of the trade, became known as the 'physics package' for a British H-bomb. Churchill presided over a special Cabinet committee on Atomic Energy Development created for this purpose, GEN 464. At its meeting on 13 April 1954, Lord Salisbury, the Lord President (who in 1953 had replaced Cherwell as lead minister on the bomb), made the case for stockpiling thorium and heavy water without prejudging final ministerial decision-taking.

15. Note of a meeting of Ministers on Atomic Energy Development, GEN 464, 13 April 1954.   TNA, PRO, CAB 130/101

CABINET OFFICE
RECORD COPY   Copy No. 22

TOP SECRET

GEN. 464/1st Meeting

CABINET

NOTE of a Meeting of Ministers held
in the Prime Minister's Room, House of Commons, S.W.1., on

TUESDAY, 13TH APRIL, 1954,

at 6.45 p.m.

P R E S E N T :

The Rt. Hon. Sir Winston Churchill, M.P.,
Prime Minister

The Rt. Hon. Anthony Eden, M.P.,   The Most Hon. the Marquess of Salisbury,
Secretary of State for Foreign Affairs   Lord President of the Council

The Rt. Hon. R.A. Butler, M.P.,   The Rt. Hon. the Earl Alexander of
Chancellor of the Exchequer   Tunis, Minister of Defence

The Rt. Hon. Viscount Swinton,
Secretary of State for
Commonwealth Relations

The Rt. Hon. Sir Norman Brook .... Secretary

ATOMIC ENERGY DEVELOPMENT

THE LORD PRESIDENT said that he was not at this stage seeking authority to undertake research and development work on the hydrogen bomb. If, however, it were decided that we should make hydrogen bombs, we should need additional supplies of thorium and heavy water. Therefore, without pre-judging the major decision of policy, he was seeking authority to take two steps which would put us in a position to go forward with this project, if it were eventually decided that we should do so.

As regards thorium, the United States authorities were placing such large orders that, if we did not stake our claim to some supplies, American demands would exhaust the available capacity. He had therefore arranged, with Treasury approval, to notify United Kingdom requirements for thorium which would cost somewhere between £1 and £7 millions over the next three years.

As regards heavy water, he wished to revive the scheme discussed with the New Zealand Government in 1953 for building a heavy water plant in New Zealand as part of their programme for developing their power resources. This scheme had been abandoned because we had thought that we should not need heavy water for the industrial side of our atomic energy programme. If it were now revived, the New Zealand Government would have to re-arrange their programme of power development, and on this account it was necessary that a firm decision should be communicated to them before 21st April. He had no doubt that, if before then we gave the New Zealand Government a firm indication of our needs, they would be ready to revive the earlier scheme, which would involve us in expenditure of £1.8 millions over the next two years.

THE CHANCELLOR OF THE EXCHEQUER said that he favoured both these proposals and was ready to give the necessary financial sanction.

THE COMMONWEALTH SECRETARY said that, in communicating to the Prime Minister of New Zealand our decision on the heavy water project, he would wish to disclose that our new decision had been taken because of the possibility that we might decide to manufacture hydrogen bombs.   It would also be necessary, in his view, to assure the Prime Minister of New Zealand that we should not again abandon our proposed association with them in this part of their power development project, even if we should in the end find that we did not need heavy water for the manufacture of hydrogen bombs.
THE LORD PRESIDENT said that he accepted the Commonwealth Secretary's view on both these points.

THE PRIME MINISTER said that he would like to invite the Cabinet at an early date to decide in principle that hydrogen bombs should be made in the United Kingdom.   THE LORD PRESIDENT said that Sir William Penney was already considering what effect such a decision would have on the existing programme for the production of atomic weapons.   THE FOREIGN SECRETARY said that in this connection account should be taken of the tenatative suggestion, put to him informally by the United States Secretary of State during the last two days, that the United States Government might call for international agreement on a moratorium for hydrogen bomb experiments.
Mr. Dulles had indicated that, if such a moratorium was not to work to our disadvantage, the United States might have to consider whether they could either supply us with hydrogen bombs or with such technical information as would enable us to make them without further experiments.

The Meeting -

(1)   Endorsed the action taken by the Lord President, with the concurrence of the Chancellor of the Exchequer, to place orders for additional supplies of thorium.

(2)   Agreed that we should now revive the earlier project for building a heavy water plant in New Zealand as part of the New Zealand programme of power development; and invited the Commonwealth Secretary to arrange for this decision to be conveyed in a personal message to the Prime Minister of New Zealand.

(3)   Agreed that the Cabinet should at an early date consider whether the United Kingdom should embark on a programme of research, development and production of hydrogen bombs.

Cabinet Office, S.W.1.

15th April, 1954.

-2-

In summing up, Churchill 'said that he would like to invite the Cabinet at an early date to decide in principle that hydrogen bombs should be made in the United Kingdom' and the committee agreed. In constitutional terms, this outcome was of considerable significance. As we have seen, Churchill during World War II had kept the bomb away from Cabinet committees let alone the War Cabinet. Attlee had confined it to two Cabinet committees, GEN 75 and GEN 163. For the first time, a British prime minister was proposing that the full Cabinet should be allowed to take a hugely important nuclear weapons decision.

Towards the end of April, the members of Norman Brook's Cabinet committee, GEN 465, received a report they had specifically commissioned from the Joint Intelligence Committee on the Soviet Union's capacity to drop thermo-nuclear weapons on the UK. On 22 April 1954, the JIC reported that the Russians could 'now' deploy in large numbers 'manned aircraft . . . with picked crews' capable of dropping nuclear weapons within a range of 750 yards of their targets in 'visual conditions and 1500 yds. under blind bombing conditions'. As for ballistic missiles, British intelligence reckoned the Soviets would be able to deliver a 6-ton loaded missile by 1957–60, warning that '[w]ith a 2500 lbs. load, availability could be NOW.'[52]

Before the thermonuclear decision reached full Cabinet, the question had to slog its way through the Chiefs of Staff system and another special Cabinet committee under Churchill, the Committee on Defence Policy, *not* to be confused with the Cabinet's standing Defence Committee. At its meeting on 19 May 1954, the DPC wrestled with the problem of reducing expenditure while at the same time including the cost of developing the H-bomb within the defence programme.

16. Minutes of a meeting of the Cabinet's Defence Policy Committee, DP (54) (2nd meeting), 19 May 1954.
TNA, PRO, CAB 134/808

THIS DOCUMENT IS THE PROPERTY OF HER BRITANNIC MAJESTY'S GOVERNMENT

The circulation of this paper has been strictly limited.

It is issued for the personal use of.........................

TOP SECRET
Copy No. 33

D.P.(54) 2nd Meeting

CABINET

COMMITTEE ON DEFENCE POLICY

MINUTES of a Meeting of the Committee
held in the Prime Minister's Room,
House of Commons, S.W.1., on
WEDNESDAY, 19TH MAY, 1954 at 5.0 p.m.

PRESENT:

The Rt.Hon. Sir Winston Churchill, M.P.,
Prime Minister   (In the Chair)

The Most Hon. the Marquess   The Rt.Hon. Sir David
of Salisbury,   Maxwell-Fyfe, Q.C., M.P.,
Lord President of the   Secretary of State for the
Council   Home Department and
                                       Minister for Welsh Affairs

The Rt.Hon. R.A. Butler, M.P.,   The Rt.Hon. the Earl Alexander
Chancellor of the Exchequer   of Tunis, Minister of Defence

The Rt.Hon. Duncan Sandys, M.P.,
Minister of Supply

THE FOLLOWING WERE ALSO PRESENT:

The Rt.Hon. Selwyn-Lloyd,   The Rt.Hon. J.P.L. Thomas, M.P.,
Q.C., M.P., Minister of   First Lord of the Admiralty
State

The Rt.Hon. Anthony Head, M.P.,   The Rt.Hon. Lord de L'Isle and
Secretary of State for War   Dudley, Secretary of State
                                       for Air

Admiral of the Fleet,   Field Marshal Sir John Harding,
Sir Rhoderick McGrigor,   Chief of the Imperial General
First Sea Lord and   Staff
Chief of Naval Staff

Air Chief Marshal Sir William Dickson,
Chief of the Air Staff

SECRETARIAT:

Sir Norman Brook
General Sir Nevil Brownjohn

CONTENTS:

DEFENCE EXPENDITURE

DEFENCE EXPENDITURE

(Previous Reference: D.P.(54) 1st Meeting. Item 3)

The Committee had before them two memoranda by the Minister of Defence on Defence Expenditure (D.P.(54) 4 and 5).

THE MINISTER OF DEFENCE said that he fully accepted the need for a substantial reduction in the level of defence expenditure, and he believed that it would be possible to secure this. In his memorandum he had emphasised the magnitude of the reduction required by the Chancellor of the Exchequer, and had indicated certain directions in which major economies might be sought. He was, however, strongly of the opinion that, before taking decisions, the Committee should await the new study on Defence Policy which the Chiefs of Staff were preparing and expected to complete by the beginning of June. This paper by the Chiefs of Staff was likely to show that Ministers must make a fresh assessment of priorities as between our commitments in the Cold War and our preparations for Hot War. The paper on Russian capacity to produce and deliver thermo-nuclear weapons (D.P.(54) 3) suggested that the Russians would not be ready to attack the United States until 1960. Perhaps, therefore, it would be sound policy to accept the risk of reducing our preparations for major war. When the paper was available, the Committee would have to take bold and quick decisions.

THE FIRST SEA LORD said that the Chiefs of Staff were examining in detail the effect of the development of the hydrogen bomb on our strategic policy. Their report would be ready shortly; in the meantime they would prefer not to commit themselves.

THE CHANCELLOR OF THE EXCHEQUER said the Government were now publicly committed to reducing the level of defence expenditure. This commitment had been made, with the approval of his colleagues, in his Budget Speech; it was essential - and to the Government's credit that it should be honoured. He hoped that, pending consideration of the promised paper by the Chiefs of Staff, Departments would avoid entering into forward commitments which might subsequently have to be cancelled.

THE MINISTER OF SUPPLY agreed with the Chancellor of the Exchequer on the need for early decisions. The majority of major items of equipment took eighteen months to three years to mature, and delay in making decisions would make it more difficult to reduce expenditure.

He also agreed that there should be a re-assessment of priorities. In his view we should concentrate on providing the minimum forces required to meet our Commonwealth commitments, and to maintain our contribution to N.A.T.O., at the expense of other preparations for Hot War and air defence. Our ability to put up an effective defence against air attack was decreasing and we ought, therefore, to concentrate on measures calculated to prevent war rather than on measures of defence, which were rapidly becoming obsolete. We must have the power to retaliate. In particular, we should secure supplies of hydrogen bombs, from the United States or from our own production; and we should have enough bomber aircraft to carry the hydrogen bombs at our disposal. The next stage of development would be the ballistic rocket, against which there was no foreseeable form of defence. He had already informed the Committee of the United States suggestion that the two countries should collaborate in the development of long-range rockets, on the basis that we should concentrate on a rocket with a 1,500 mile range and the Americans on an inter-Continental rocket of longer range.

-1-

In discussion the following points were made:-

(a) Officials in the Ministry of Defence and Service Departments were already engaged in a study of the items of production which it would be possible to cut at short notice, with consequential reduction in expenditure in 1955.   This study should be ready at about the same time as the paper by the Chiefs of Staff.

(b) THE SECRETARY OF STATE FOR AIR said that the problem was how to devise means of securing economies in 1955 and 1956. He believed that it would be found that the cuts had to be made mainly in production programmes.   We should have to consider what items of equipment could be dispensed with altogether and what items could be deferred

(c) THE SECRETARY OF STATE FOR WAR questioned the possibility of reaching major decisions before the end of July.   The paper by the Chiefs of Staff would deal with policy in broad terms; the effects on the size and shape of the forces would then have to be examined in detail, and costed.   For the Army, the commitments of the moment presented the main dilemma: these already demanded more money and more men than the War Office could provide.

(d) THE FIRST LORD OF THE ADMIRALTY suggested that it would be valuable if the Foreign Office, Commonwealth Relations Office and Colonial Office could submit a review of our existing overseas commitments and a new appreciation of the contribution which other Commonwealth countries could make in meeting them.

(e) THE CHANCELLOR OF THE EXCHEQUER suggested that before a final decision on manufacture of the hydrogen bomb was taken, the Committee should have an opportunity to consider the type and size of the bomb to be produced.   THE CHIEF OF THE AIR STAFF said that a paper was now being prepared on this question, which would include consideration of the capital cost involved.

THE PRIME MINISTER, summing up the discussion, said that the difficulties of choice which lay before the Committee had been put boldly forward.   The problem was to decide what practical steps could be taken to effect the saving of £200 million a year, with the least risk of weakening our influence in the world, or endangering our security.   Influence depended on possession of force.   If the United States action were tempted to undertake a forestalling war, we could not hope to remain neutral.   Even if we could, such a war would in any event determine our fate.   We must avoid any action which would weaken our power to influence United States policy.   We must avoid anything which might be represented as a sweeping act of disarmament.   If, however, we were able to show that in a few years' time we should be possessed of great offensive power, and that we should be ready to take our part in a world struggle, he thought it would not be impossible to reconcile reductions in defence expenditure with the maintenance of our influence in world councils.   .

The Committee:-

Agreed to resume their discussion at a later meeting.

Cabinet Office, S.W.1.

20TH MAY, 1954.

-2-

Churchill's summing up is interesting for two reasons. First, the importance of the UK remaining a full (i.e. H-bomb possessing) nuclear power if it were to retain its political influence in Washington, especially if the United States 'were tempted to undertake a forestalling war' with the Soviet Union. Secondly, the acquisition of 'great offensive [i.e. thermonuclear] power' pre-echoed the Sandys Defence White Paper of 1957[53] in arguing that the nuclear deterrent would create the possibility of substantial reductions in conventional forces.

Before the DPC reached its final decision to recommend the manufacture of an H-bomb to the full Cabinet on 16 June, the Chiefs of Staff prepared a wide-ranging paper on future UK defence policy with a thermonuclear component (the bulk of which went to the full Cabinet in July as a Cabinet Paper, C (54) 249).

17. 'United Kingdom Defence Policy' briefing by the Chiefs of Staff for the Defence Policy Committee (and later, minus detail on the number of bombs planned, for the full Cabinet), 31 May 1954. C (54) 249. TNA, PRO, CAB 129/69

bin 24/7 8am 238

THIS DOCUMENT IS THE PROPERTY OF HER BRITANNIC MAJESTY'S GOVERNMENT

Printed for the Cabinet. July 1954

The circulation of this paper has been strictly limited. It is issued

for the personal use of ...... *Sir Norman Brook* ......

Copy No. **26**

C. (54) 249
23rd July, 1954

CABINET

———

UNITED KINGDOM DEFENCE POLICY

NOTE BY THE SECRETARY OF THE CABINET

I circulate, for the information of the Cabinet, the memorandum by the Chiefs of Staff on United Kingdom Defence Policy to which reference is made in paragraph 3 of the Report of the Committee on Defence Policy (C. (54) 250).

(Signed)   NORMAN BROOK.

Cabinet Office, S.W. 1,
22nd July, 1954.

46546A

17. (cont.)

UNITED KINGDOM DEFENCE POLICY

MEMORANDUM BY THE CHIEFS OF STAFF

I.—Introduction

We were invited by the Minister of Defence to review our defence policy in the light of changes in the political and military spheres which have taken place during the last two years. We were instructed in particular to take into account the rapid development of weapons of war which has resulted from the application of new scientific knowledge, both in the Western nations and Soviet Russia, and the need to reduce the present level of defence expenditure.

II.—Aim of United Kingdom Policy

2. More than ever the aim of United Kingdom policy must be to prevent war. To this end we must maintain and strengthen our position as a world Power so that Her Majesty's Government can exercise a powerful influence in the counsels of the world. Certain new factors affecting this aim are discussed in succeeding paragraphs.

III.—Weapon Developments

The Hydrogen Bomb

3. The world situation has been completely altered by recent progress in the development of nuclear weapons. The Americans have exploded a weapon approximately 1,500 times more powerful than the " nominal " atomic bomb and we have every reason to believe that they are now putting into production weapons of this order of power. There is no theoretical limit to the destructive power which can be achieved with the latest techniques.

4. The biggest Russian explosion to date is estimated to be about 50 times more powerful than the " nominal " bomb, but the Russians are expected to improve on this considerably in the near future. Although we believe them to be well behind the Americans at present, we must reckon that within one or two years they will have weapons of devastating power, even by American standards.

5. A provisional estimate of the effect of 10 bombs dropped one each on 10 selected cities in the United Kingdom indicates that, if they are of 100 times " nominal " power, the death roll would be 5 millions, and, if 1,000 times " nominal " power, 12 millions. It is therefore clear that a country which can equip itself with the means of delivery needs only a comparatively small stockpile of such weapons in order to be able to deliver a devastating attack on an enemy.

6. Another factor of immense significance is that these weapons can now be made with much smaller quantities of fissile materials than was originally thought. Thus the availability of fissile material is no longer a critical factor. The cost of producing these weapons should not be beyond our financial capabilities.

Means of Delivery from a Land Base

7. There are three possible means of delivering these weapons by air from a land base.

    (*a*) Manned aircraft.
    (*b*) Unmanned aircraft.
    (*c*) Ballistic rocket.

The unmanned aircraft is likely to be much more vulnerable than the other two; and, although the United States have three types under development, we do not think this means will be a primary method of delivery. For the other two, the question of range is critical and we therefore examine the cases of Russia *vis-à-vis* the United States and Russia *vis-à-vis* the United Kingdom separately.

46546   B

2

Russia vis-à-vis *the United States*

8. The United States has at present the great advantage of the use of advanced bases in Allied countries. For purposes of attack, therefore, she is closer to Russia than Russia is to her. The following table shows the dates by which we estimate either side could launch an effective attack on the other.

Method	By the United States	By Russia
Manned aircraft	Now	1958
Ballistic rocket	1965	1970

Russia vis-à-vis *the United Kingdom*

9. Here Russia is in a better position since it is she who has the use of advanced bases in Eastern Germany and satellite countries.

Method	By the United Kingdom	By Russia
Manned aircraft ...	On present forecasts we could have X bombs by 1959 and Y by 1960, if production were started now	1955
Ballistic rocket ...	Not before 1965	1960

Other Means of Delivery

10.—(*a*) *From aircraft carriers.*—The United States may develop the capacity to deliver these bombs from carrier-borne aircraft. The Russians have no aircraft carriers and show no sign of constructing any.

(*b*) *From submarines.*—It may be possible to develop ballistic rockets with hydrogen heads and with a limited range of about 400–500 miles for use from submarines. The rockets could be developed by both the United States or Russia within the next few years but the operational problems of despatch from an unstable platform are very difficult and may require much longer for solution.

(*c*) *Clandestine methods.*—We consider it improbable that the Russians would use merchant ships for this purpose but we cannot ignore this possibility or the use of submarines. The explosion of one of these bombs in a submarine in the comparatively shallow water of a port or harbour or their approaches would cover the surrounding district with radio-active material, cause heavy casualties and put the area out of action for a considerable period.

Defence

11. The main danger is from the air. The effect of these weapons is so devastating that no country could withstand the effect of more than a very few exploding on or near their target. Their power is so great that errors of even three miles are not particularly significant, against which guns are valueless and even the capabilities of fighter aircraft and guided missiles will be limited. In theory, it might be possible to develop, during the next ten years, an air defence system which would destroy a very high percentage of attacks by manned aircraft. It would consist of large numbers of supersonic fighters armed with air-to-air guided weapons supported by, and possibly eventually superseded by, long- and short-range ground-to-air guided missiles; the whole depending on a much elaborated Control and Reporting system. It is however unlikely for practical reasons that even a project of this magnitude and great cost could give the complete protection necessary against these weapons. Furthermore, except for the Control and Reporting component, the system would be valueless when the ballistic rocket threat develops, and even this component would itself be of no use until a method of active defence against the ballistic rocket had been developed. No such method is yet in sight.

Russian Air Defence

12. It is some consolation that Russia's air defence problem is even less hopeful of solution than our own. The advantage which she derives from her ability to disperse industry is off-set by the corresponding need to disperse the defence forces available to protect that industry. Her long frontiers and enormous areas of undeveloped territory make the provision of complete radar cover, backed by adequate defences, a formidable problem. There is no reason to

17. (cont.)

3

suppose that for many years to come the Soviet air defence system will be able to prevent jet bombers making shallow penetration raids by day and deep penetration raids by night, with relative immunity.

Smaller Nuclear Weapons

13. The United States have developed a large variety of weapons involving smaller nuclear components which have important applications in all types of operations. We must presume that Russia has done the same but the stockpile of the Western Powers must be much greater than that of Russia and would go some way towards redressing the balance of numerical superiority which the Soviet land forces will always enjoy.

14. A weapon of the V–1 type with a small nuclear head could be developed within the next few years. It is conceivable that Russia might use submarines to make sporadic attacks on cities on the American seaboard with such weapons.

Other Weapon Developments

15. Important new developments are in prospect in such fields as aircraft, guided weapons and electronics: but, except in so far as they are concerned with the delivery of the hydrogen weapon, their effects will not be relatively significant.

Deductions

16.—(*a*) Short of sacrificing our vital interests or principles, we must do everything possible to prevent global war which would inevitably entail the exposure of the United Kingdom to a devastating nuclear bombardment.

(*b*) The ability to wage war with the most up-to-date nuclear weapons will be the measure of military power in the future.

(*c*) Our scientific skill and technological capacity to produce the hydrogen weapon puts within our grasp the ability to be on terms with the United States and Russia.

IV.—Likely Form of a Future Global War

Possible Restrictions on Nuclear Warfare

17. We have given much thought to the highly speculative question whether, if global warfare should break out, there might initially be mutually acceptable restrictions on the use of nuclear weapons. We have come to the conclusion that, if war came in the next few years, the United States would insist on the immediate use of the full armoury of nuclear weapons with the object of dealing the Russians a quick knock-out blow. We must therefore plan on the assumption that, if war becomes global, nuclear bombardment will become general.

The Threat to the United Kingdom

18. The Russians will, we believe, appreciate that, apart from its importance as a strategic base, the United Kingdom is the major political target in Western Europe; and that the extinction of the United Kingdom would quickly lead to the disintegration of Western Europe and the break-up of the Commonwealth and would greatly strengthen the Soviet position in any negotiations which they might hope to open with the United States. We therefore consider that, whatever the Russians' ability to attack the United States—and for the next few years they are not likely to be able to deliver more than sporadic attacks—the United Kingdom will be the primary military target for initial attack in any future war, and will be subjected to devastating attack by a large part of the Russian bomber effort together with any ground-to-ground missile capacity which she may possess.

19. Our defence system within the foreseeable future will not be able to provide the complete protection necessary against air attack employing weapons of mass destruction. Though we can count on the allied strategic air forces being able to strike an immediate and crippling blow at the sources of attack and centres of control, we cannot be certain that this counter-offensive would be in time. Thus, if war did break out, we should have to expect that the United Kingdom would be devastated in the opening days to such an extent that it could no longer function as a main support area. Indeed, the real problem might well be one of mere physical survival.

46546

B 2

4

Progress of Global War

20. We can expect that, concurrently with strategic air operations, major attacks will be made by Soviet naval, land and amphibious forces, supported by part of the Soviet nuclear potential, against Western Europe and our sea communications. We must also expect offensive campaigns in other theatres. An attack by Russia against Western Europe would entail preparatory moves which should be detectable and thus afford us some period of warning. The scale and progress of these offensive operations will depend on how quickly the Allied strategic air forces could bring the full effect of their offensive to bear.

Deductions

21.—(a) If war becomes global, the employment of nuclear weapons will become general.

(b) It is of the utmost importance to the United Kingdom that the Allied strategic air forces should be capable of hitting back immediately without any limitation on targets or weapons.

(c) We must be prepared for the United Kingdom to receive such damage from nuclear bombardment in the opening days of a war that it cannot continue to function as a main support area. Our policy for the organisation, equipment and maintenance of our forces overseas and the provision of material reserves at home should be adjusted accordingly. Equally we must review our present plans for the organisation, equipment and employment of our reserve forces.

V.—Likelihood of War

22. Soviet Russia and China are at present employing the technique of subversion, backed by supply of arms and financial aid, as opposed to overt attack or invasion. They are being successful in this, and we believe that they are likely to continue to aim at extending the Communist sphere of influence by infiltration and disruption of the existing Governments of free countries. None the less, the danger of war remains because the fundamental aims of both sides are in conflict.

23. After examination of the intelligence material available, we have reached the following conclusions:—

(a) Russia is most unlikely to provoke war deliberately during the next few years, when the United States will be comparatively immune from Russian attack.

(b) The danger the United States might succumb to the temptation of precipitating a " forestalling " war cannot be disregarded. In view of the vulnerability of the United Kingdom we must use all our influence to prevent this.

(c) Careful judgment and restraint on the part of the Allies on a united basis will be needed to avoid the outbreak of a global war through accident or miscalculation resulting from an incident which precipitated or extended a local war.

(d) A possible danger is that China might reach a position where it would be difficult for her not to resist by force pressures resulting from United States policy. Such circumstances might lead to a local situation which might in turn lead to global war.

(e) Even when the Russians are able to attack North America effectively, the ability of the United States to deliver a crippling attack on Russia will remain a powerful deterrent to the Soviet Government.

(f) It is most probable that the present state of " cold war " will continue for a long time with periods of greater or less tension.

24. Our general conclusion is that, provided the Allies maintain their unity and military strength, global war is unlikely and should be avoidable particularly during the period of United States superiority. Therefore, in considering changes which might be made in our defence effort, we would be more justified in taking risks during the next four or five years, than at a later period. This means that during the next four or five years, the military means to exert our influence as a world power and to meet our " cold war " commitments must take priority over preparations for global war, wherever they conflict.

17. (cont.)

5

VI.—United Kingdom Strategic Policy

25. All that has been said leads to the over-riding conclusion that, short of sacrificing our vital interests or principles, our first aim must be to prevent global war. We must therefore strengthen our position and influence as a world power and maintain our alliance with the United States. To that end the objectives of our strategic policy should be:—

    (a) To possess the means of waging war with the most up-to-date nuclear weapons.

    (b) To play our part with the Commonwealth and our Allies in stopping and turning back the spread of Communism.

    (c) To preserve security and to develop stable government in our Colonial territories and overseas dependencies and to support our world-wide trade interests.

In the ensuing paragraphs we examine the minimum requirements which are involved.

Contribution to the Deterrent

26. *Nuclear.*—The nuclear threat is the main deterrent to war. Moreover, an immediate and overwhelming counter-offensive with the most powerful nuclear weapons offers the only hope of preventing the enemy from completely devastating this country. We must contribute to the deterrent by producing a stockpile of nuclear, including hydrogen, weapons and the means of delivering them.

27. *The North Atlantic Treaty Organisation.*—The maintenance of the political unity of the North Atlantic Treaty Organisation (N.A.T.O.) and the provision of a shield of land and air forces in Western Europe and of naval forces for the protection of Allied sea communications is an essential complement to the main deterrent. We are under an obligation to retain land and air forces on the Continent and to contribute to the naval and maritime air forces in the Atlantic, the Mediterranean and the Channel. Any large and precipitate reduction in the forces which we have allocated to the support of the N.A.T.O. would have a disastrous effect on the resolution of the Continental countries, particularly at this time when the stability of France is in question. We believe, however, that, from the military point of view, some reductions in all three Services could be justified now in those forces which, though allocated to the N.A.T.O., will not be available immediately on the outbreak of global war. Two factors would justify further reductions in our contribution to the land and air forces deployed in Europe. They are:—

    (a) a German contribution fully equipped and trained; and

    (b) the existence in Western Europe of a Allied stockpile of tactical nuclear weapons markedly superior to that of the Russians.

Containment of Communism

28. *Far East.*—The Far East is the present focus of Communist aggression. To ensure an effective defence of the area, we should do everything possible to promote the creation of a South-East Asia Defence Organisation, including the participation of Asian states. We should encourage the Commonwealth countries to join it and to support it with armed forces. Its creation would strengthen our position in the Far East generally. We should undoubtedly be expected to contribute United Kingdom forces to the support of the organisation; but, in view of the heavy burden we are shouldering in Malaya whereby we are already making a major contribution to the security of the whole area, we should do our utmost to ensure that our present commitment in South-East Asia is not increased. We should aim to withdraw our forces from Korea as soon as circumstances permit and to reduce our forces in Hong Kong to an internal security basis, relying on indirect means to prevent that place from being attacked.

29. *Middle East.*—In the Middle East we must maintain a semblance of military power in order to check the spread of Communism, to support our Treaty obligations, to protect our political and other vital interests in the area, and to provide the back-bone of a defence organisation. We should aim at achieving a settlement with Egypt which will allow us to withdraw our combatant forces from the Canal Zone and to re-deploy our forces in the Middle East according to plans already approved by the Cabinet.

46546   B 3

6

30. *Preservation of Security in Colonial Territories and Dependencies.*—The United Kingdom is at present ultimately responsible for maintaining the territorial integrity of, and internal security within, our Colonial territories and dependencies overseas. In order to quell subversive movements, we have had to send United Kingdom forces or reinforcements during the last few years to Malaya, Kenya and the Caribbean. Recently, for political reasons, a small detachment has had to be stationed at Sharjah. Although these commitments fall primarily on the Army, the other Services inevitably become involved. These commitments tend to grow and become permanent and result in uneconomic dispersion of our land, sea and air forces. Colonial Governments should be put in the way of providing the necessary police forces, intelligence services and local military forces to ensure internal security. The military responsibility of the United Kingdom should be limited to holding forces centrally, with air transport, to enable them to be despatched as reinforcements only in the event of a grave emergency. It is essential that Colonial Governments should progressively accept responsibility for their own internal security, and that existing United Kingdom commitments should be reduced to facilitate reduction in the size of the Army.

VII.—Financial Considerations

31. The Chancellor of the Exchequer has indicated that he wants expenditure on defence to be reduced to £1,500 millions annually and we recognise fully the absolute necessity for defence expenditure to be kept at a level compatible with a sound national economy. We are advised, however, that the above figure means a cut of at least one-eighth in our planned rate of defence expenditure and we are convinced that a reduction of this order cannot be effected by administrative economies or minor modifications to our plans. It can only be achieved by radical changes in defence policy, which will involve the taking of risks. Even then, if disorganisation, inefficiency, and waste are to be avoided, the reduction will have to be spread over a considerable period of time.

VIII.—Consideration of Possible Changes in Defence Policy and Plans in the Light of our New Strategic Concept

32. A small number of the latest nuclear weapons can achieve a devastating effect. Moreover, during the next decade, means of delivery against which there is no foreseeable defence will be developed These two factors are creating a new military situation which will reduce progressively the value of certain conventional war preparations and weapons. It is here that risks must be taken. The problem is to identify the precise weapons and preparations which we can abandon or scale down with the least risk to our world influence, security, and ability to conduct limited war. The solution will in many cases have to be based on judgment rather than fact. It will also be necessary for Her Majesty's Government to weigh the interests of economy against the maintenance of public morale at home, our prestige abroad and the cohesion and confidence of our Allies. The effect on the morale of the Services must also be taken into account.

33. We set out in the Annex to this memorandum the issues which we recommend that Ministers should consider, together with our preliminary views on the immediate action which might be taken to secure early savings in expenditure.

(Signed)   R. McGRIGOR.

J. HARDING.

W. F. DICKSON.

Ministry of Defence, S.W. 1,
31st May, 1954.

The Chiefs, pre-echoing the 1955 Strath Report, outlined the 12 million people (out of a total population of 46 million) who would be killed if ten 10-megaton H-bombs struck the UK and, like the Brook group before them, the degree to which this changed 'the world situation'. The paper incorporated the latest JIC estimates on the 'Likelihood of War'. While recognising the possibility of some compensating savings, the Chiefs pressed hard for a British H-bomb and the indispensability of the UK maintaining and strengthening 'our position as a world power so that Her Majesty's Government can exercise a powerful influence in the counsels of the world'.

The Chiefs drafted their own embellishment of Churchill's 'top table' rationale by arguing that '[t]he ability to wage war with the most up-to-date nuclear weapons will be the measure of military power in the future' and '[o]ur scientific skill and technological capacity to produce the hydrogen weapon puts within our grasp the ability to be on terms with the United States and Russia.'

At the DPC session on 16 June, which considered the Chiefs' paper, a confidential annex to the main minutes records that the meeting '[a]uthorised the Lord President [Salisbury] and the Minister of Supply [Duncan Sandys] to initiate a programme for the production of hydrogen bombs.'[54] It might be thought that the full Cabinet's endorsement would have been an 'of course' decision. It turned out not to be so. But the reasons were not related to any impulse towards unilateral disarmament.

It was Churchill's misfortune that the H-bomb question became entangled with wider Cabinet resentment about the very personal diplomacy in which (to his Foreign Secretary, Eden's, fury) he had engaged in during his recent visit to see President Eisenhower in Washington, and the telegram he despatched, from the Cunarder carrying him and Eden home, to the post-Stalin leadership in Moscow calling for a summit meeting. This particularly enraged his lead nuclear minister, Lord Salisbury, who had a well developed habit of threatening resignation.[55]

When the Cabinet met on 7 July 1954, there were several waves of emotion swirling around No. 10 when Churchill briefed them on the Defence Policy Committee's decision-taking and reprised his own and the Chiefs of Staff's argument for Britain's moving up to H-bomb status.

348.

THIS DOCUMENT IS THE PROPERTY OF HER BRITANNIC MAJESTY'S GOVERNMENT

Printed for the Cabinet. July 1954

SECRET

Copy No. 42

C.C. (54)

47th Conclusions

CABINET

CONCLUSIONS of a Meeting of the Cabinet held at 10 Downing Street, S.W.1, on Wednesday, 7th July, 1954, at 11·30 a.m.

Present:

The Right Hon. Sir WINSTON CHURCHILL, M.P., Prime Minister.

The Right Hon. ANTHONY EDEN, M.P., Secretary of State for Foreign Affairs.

The Most Hon. the MARQUESS OF SALISBURY, Lord President of the Council.

The Right Hon. LORD SIMONDS, Lord Chancellor.

The Right Hon. Sir DAVID MAXWELL FYFE, Q.C., M.P., Secretary of State for the Home Department and Minister for Welsh Affairs.

The Right Hon. R. A. BUTLER, M.P., Chancellor of the Exchequer.

The Right Hon. VISCOUNT WOOLTON, Chancellor of the Duchy of Lancaster and Minister of Materials.

The Right Hon. H. F. C. CROOKSHANK, M.P., Lord Privy Seal.

The Right Hon. the EARL ALEXANDER OF TUNIS, Minister of Defence.

The Right Hon. VISCOUNT SWINTON, Secretary of State for Commonwealth Relations.

The Right Hon. OLIVER LYTTELTON, M.P., Secretary of State for the Colonies.

The Right Hon. JAMES STUART, M.P., Secretary of State for Scotland.

The Right Hon. Sir WALTER MONCKTON, Q.C., M.P., Minister of Labour and National Service.

The Right Hon. HAROLD MACMILLAN, M.P., Minister of Housing and Local Government.

The Right Hon. FLORENCE HORSBRUGH, M.P., Minister of Education.

The Right Hon. GWILYM LLOYD-GEORGE, M.P., Minister of Food.

The following were also present:

The Right Hon. J. P. L. THOMAS, M.P., First Lord of the Admiralty (*Items 1–2*).

The Right Hon. ANTONY HEAD, M.P., Secretary of State for War (*Items 1–2*).

The Right Hon. LORD DE L'ISLE AND DUDLEY, Secretary of State for Air (*Items 1–2*).

The Right Hon. DUNCAN SANDYS, M.P., Minister of Supply (*Items 3–5*).

The Right Hon. A. T. LENNOX-BOYD, M.P., Minister of Transport and Civil Aviation (*Items 1–2*).

The Right Hon. D. HEATHCOAT AMORY, M.P., Minister of State, Board of Trade (*Item 3*).

The Right Hon. PATRICK BUCHAN-HEPBURN, M.P., Parliamentary Secretary, Treasury.

Field-Marshal Sir JOHN HARDING, Chief of the Imperial General Staff (*Items 1–2*).

Marshal of the Royal Air Force Sir WILLIAM DICKSON, Chief of the Air Staff (*Items 1–2*).

Vice-Admiral W. W. DAVIS, Vice-Chief of Naval Staff (*Items 1–2*).

The Right Hon. LORD CHERWELL (*Items 4–5*).

Secretariat:

The Right Hon. Sir NORMAN BROOK.

Mr. R. M. J. HARRIS.

47694—1

B

353.

which it would be very difficult for us to hold; and (ii) that we could not accept his arguments for excluding rolling mills from the list of items on which the embargo should be lifted, and were only agreeing to their exclusion in the interests of securing a settlement and on the understanding that Mr. Stassen would reconsider this question again before the end of the year.

Washington Talks.
(Previous Reference: C.C. (54) 44th Conclusions, Minute 1.)
Parliamentary Debate.

4. The Cabinet considered what steps would need to be taken to inform Parliament of the results of the discussions which the Prime Minister and the Foreign Secretary had held during their recent visit to Washington and Ottawa. If an immediate statement had to be made, it could add little to what had already been published in the press. On the other hand, no Government time was available for a debate on foreign affairs before the summer recess, and there was as yet no indication that the Opposition would wish to make one of their Supply Days available for this purpose. It was the general view of the Cabinet that in the circumstances the best course would be for the Prime Minister to make as full a statement as possible early in the following week.

During the course of the meeting the Chief Whip ascertained, at the Cabinet's request, that the Leader of the Opposition would be content if a statement were made in the House of Commons on 12th July.

The Cabinet—

(1) Took note that the Prime Minister would make a statement in the House of Commons on 12th July on the results of the visit which he and the Foreign Secretary had recently made to Washington and Ottawa.

(2) Authorised the Commonwealth Secretary to send advance copies of this statement to other Commonwealth Governments.

Anglo-Soviet Meeting.

The Cabinet were informed of a proposal that the Prime Minister might meet M. Malenkov, with a view to exploring the possibility of arranging a meeting of Heads of Governments of the United States, United Kingdom and Soviet Union.

The Cabinet's discussion on this proposal is recorded separately.

Atomic Energy. Weapons Programme.

5. *The Prime Minister* said that the Defence Policy Committee had approved, on 16th June, a proposal that our atomic weapons programme should be so adjusted as to allow for the production of hydrogen bombs in this country. His recent discussions in Washington and Ottawa had been conducted on the basis that we should produce hydrogen bombs. He therefore suggested that the Cabinet should now formally approve the proposal that hydrogen bombs should be produced in this country, and should endorse the preliminary action which had already been taken to this end.

The Prime Minister said that we could not expect to maintain our influence as a world Power unless we possessed the most up-to-date nuclear weapons. The primary aim of our policy was to prevent major war; and the possession of these weapons was now the main deterrent to a potential aggressor. He had no doubt that the best hope of preserving world peace was to make it clear to potential aggressors that they had no hope of shielding themselves from a crushing retaliatory use of atomic power. For this purpose the Western Powers must provide themselves, not only with a sufficient supply of up-to-date nuclear weapons, but also with a

355

multiplicity of bases from which a retaliatory attack could be launched. They must put themselves in a position to ensure that no surprise attack, however large, could wholly destroy their power of effective retaliation. These considerations, in his view, made it essential that we should manufacture hydrogen bombs in the United Kingdom so as to be able to make our contribution to this deterrent influence.

The Lord President said that he accepted the strategic argument outlined by the Prime Minister. Plans were now in preparation for the production of the hydrogen bomb in this country. If further scientists could be recruited, this additional production could be undertaken without serious disruption of the existing programme for the manufacture of atomic weapons. Some preliminary steps to this end had already been taken with the approval of the Defence Policy Committee.

The Lord Privy Seal said that the Cabinet had had no notice that this question was to be raised and he hoped they would not be asked to take a final decision on it until they had had more time to consider it.

The Cabinet—

Agreed to resume their discussion of this question at a later meeting.

Cabinet Office, S.W. 1.
7th July, 1954.

Dry Cabinet Office minute-taking drills prevented Norman Brook from capturing the ferment and the chaos of that meeting. Harold Macmillan's diary does just that. After several members of the Cabinet had voiced their anxieties about Churchill's approach to the Russian leadership without consulting them first, the Prime Minister dropped

> his second bomb. He told us that the decision had been taken to make the hydrogen bomb in England, and the preliminaries were in hand. Harry Crookshank [Lord Privy Seal] at once made a most vigorous protest at such a momentous decision being communicated to the Cabinet in so cavalier a way, and started to walk out of the room. We all did the same and the Cabinet broke up—if not in disorder—in somewhat ragged fashion.[56]

Norman Brook's handwritten note of that extraordinary Cabinet meeting also fails, unsurprisingly, to capture its jagged ending. What it does reveal, however, is the gloriously English metaphor Churchill used to persuade his Cabinet that they were faced with an 'of course' choice:

Atomic Weapons Programme

PM   Cab. must now decide whr we shd. go on with m'fure of H.bomb.

           Badge to R.Enclosure [the Royal Enclosure at Ascot Racecourse].

           Essential to m'tenance of deterrent. This, in turn, depends on multiplicity of bases—to offset—risk of effecting surprise attack. Must be able to make it clear to R. [Russia] that they can't stop effective retaliation. That is only sure foundation for peace. Power of effective reprisal must be assured. This makes it essential that we shd. make the H.bomb + play our part in this.

SAL   [Lord Salisbury] Accept strategic argument. We have reached concln. that we shd. make H.bomb as well as atomic. Taken preliminary steps. One diffy [difficulty] is scientific man-power.

           Can't say more at present.

PM   Will Cab. approve in principle? And endorse preliminary action taken.

HC   [Harry Crookshank] Wd. sooner have more time to reflect on this.

HM   [Harold Macmillan] Are we to make it—or put ourselves in a posn [position] to make it?[57]

The Cabinet resumed its discussion the following morning.

Cab 128/27.

35˙6

THIS DOCUMENT IS THE PROPERTY OF HER BRITANNIC MAJESTY'S GOVERNMENT

Printed for the Cabinet. July 1954

SECRET   Copy No. 48

.C.C. (54)
48th Conclusions

CABINET

*CONCLUSIONS of a Meeting of the Cabinet held at 10 Downing Street,
S.W.1, on Thursday, 8th July, 1954, at 11·30 a.m.*

Present:

The Right Hon. Sir WINSTON CHURCHILL, M.P., Prime Minister.

The Right Hon. ANTHONY EDEN, M.P., Secretary of State for Foreign Affairs.

The Most Hon. the MARQUESS OF SALISBURY, Lord President of the Council.

The Right Hon. LORD SIMONDS, Lord Chancellor.

The Right Hon. Sir DAVID MAXWELL FYFE, Q.C., M.P., Secretary of State for the Home Department and Minister for Welsh Affairs.

The Right Hon. R. A. BUTLER, M.P., Chancellor of the Exchequer.

The Right Hon. VISCOUNT WOOLTON, Chancellor of the Duchy of Lancaster and Minister of Materials.

The Right Hon. H. F. C. CROOKSHANK, M.P., Lord Privy Seal.

The Right Hon. the EARL ALEXANDER OF TUNIS, Minister of Defence.

The Right Hon. VISCOUNT SWINTON, Secretary of State for Commonwealth Relations.

The Right Hon. OLIVER LYTTELTON, M.P., Secretary of State for the Colonies.

The Right Hon. JAMES STUART, M.P., Secretary of State for Scotland.

The Right Hon. Sir WALTER MONCKTON, Q.C., M.P., Minister of Labour and National Service.

The Right Hon. HAROLD MACMILLAN, M.P., Minister of Housing and Local Government.

The Right Hon. Sir THOMAS DUGDALE, M.P., Minister of Agriculture and Fisheries.

The Right Hon. FLORENCE HORSBRUGH, M.P., Minister of Education.

The Right Hon. GWILYM LLOYD-GEORGE, M.P., Minister of Food.

The following were also present:

The Right Hon. J. P. L. THOMAS, M.P., First Lord of the Admiralty (*Item 1*).

The Right Hon. ANTONY HEAD, M.P., Secretary of State for War (*Item 1*).

The Right Hon. LORD DE L'ISLE AND DUDLEY, Secretary of State for Air (*Item 1*).

The Right Hon. DUNCAN SANDYS, M.P., Minister of Supply (*Items 2-6*).

The Right Hon. GEOFFREY LLOYD, M.P., Minister of Fuel and Power (*Item 7*).

The Right Hon A. T. LENNOX-BOYD, M.P., Minister of Transport and Civil Aviation (*Item 5*).

The Right Hon. PATRICK BUCHAN-HEPBURN, M.P., Parliamentary Secretary, Treasury.

Admiral of the Fleet Sir RHODERICK McGRIGOR, First Sea Lord and Chief of Naval Staff (*Item 1*).

Field-Marshal Sir JOHN HARDING, Chief of the Imperial General Staff (*Item 1*).

Marshal of the Royal Air Force Sir WILLIAM DICKSON, Chief of the Air Staff (*Item 1*).

Secretariat:
The Right Hon. Sir NORMAN BROOK.
Mr. R. M. J. HARRIS.
Mr. K. L. STOCK.

47694—2

19. (cont.)

4

was most undesirable that he should visit the Protectorate at this time, and the Governor of Aden had sought authority to exclude him from it. If such action were considered to be too provocative, arrangements might be made for Major Salah Salem to be met at the frontier and escorted from there to Aden either by aircraft or by motor transport.

The Cabinet agreed that steps should be taken to exclude Major Salah Salem from the Aden Protectorate, but that arrangements should also be made to escort him from the frontier to Aden in the event of his attempting to enter the Protectorate.

The Cabinet—

(4) Authorised the Colonial Secretary to take the necessary steps to ensure that Major Salah Salem was not at liberty to travel unescorted through the Aden Protectorate on his return journey from the Yemen to Egypt.

Atomic Energy.
Weapons
Programme.
(Previous
Reference.
C.C. (54) 47th
Conclusions,
Minute 5.)

2. The Cabinet resumed their discussion of the question whether our atomic weapons programme should be so adjusted as to allow for the production of thermo-nuclear bombs in this country.

The following were the main points raised in the discussion :—

(a) What additional financial commitment would be involved?

The Cabinet were informed that the *net* additional cost of adjusting the programme so as to allow for the production of thermo-nuclear bombs would not be very substantial. The capital cost should not exceed £10 millions, and the thermo-nuclear bombs would be made in lieu of atomic bombs at a relatively small additional production cost. Much of the material needed for the production of the new type of bomb would have been required for the production of atomic bombs, and there would be a substantial degree of flexibility in the programme, since atomic bombs could be converted into thermo-nuclear bombs. In terms of explosive power the thermo-nuclear bomb would be more economical than the atomic bomb.

(b) Might we not wish to prevent the manufacture of thermo-nuclear bombs in Western Europe, particularly in Germany? Would it be easier for us to prevent this if we ourselves refrained from producing these weapons? Some of our other defence preparations were already based on the assumption that we should not engage in major war except as an ally of the United States: could we not continue to rely on the United States to match Russia in thermo-nuclear weapons?

In reply it was pointed out that the strength of these arguments was weakened by the fact that we had already embarked on the production of atomic weapons. There was no sharp distinction in kind between atomic and thermo-nuclear weapons; and, as we were already engaged in the manufacture of this kind of weapon, it was unreasonable that we should deny ourselves the advantage of possessing the most up-to-date types. *The Foreign Secretary* said that our power to control the production of thermo-nuclear weapons in Western Europe would not in his view be weakened by the fact that we ourselves were making these weapons.

(c) Was it morally right that we should manufacture weapons with this vast destructive power? There was no doubt that a decision to make hydrogen bombs would offend the conscience of substantial numbers of people in this country. Evidence of this was to be found in the resolutions recently passed by the Methodist Conference in London.

In reply the point was again made that there was no difference in kind between atomic and thermo-nuclear weapons; and that, in so far as any moral principle was involved, it had already been breached by the decision of the Labour Government to make the atomic bomb. It was also argued that the moral issue would arise, not so much on the production of these weapons, but on the decision to use them; and that the resolution of the Methodist Conference was directed mainly against the use of atomic weapons. The further point was made that, if we were ready to accept the protection offered by United States use of thermo-nuclear weapons, no greater moral wrong was involved in making them ourselves.

(*d*) No country could claim to be a leading military Power unless it possessed the most up-to-date weapons; and the fact must be faced that, unless we possessed thermo-nuclear weapons, we should lose our influence and standing in world affairs. Strength in thermo-nuclear weapons would henceforward provide the most powerful deterrent to a potential aggressor; and it was our duty to make our contribution towards the building up of this deterrent influence. It was at least possible that the development of the hydrogen bomb would have the effect of reducing the risk of major war. At present some people thought that the greatest risk was that the United States might plunge the world into war, either through a misjudged intervention in Asia or in order to forestall an attack by Russia. Our best chance of preventing this was to maintain our influence with the United States Government; and they would certainly feel more respect for our views if we continued to play an effective part in building up the strength necessary to deter aggression than if we left it entirely to them to match and counter Russia's strength in thermo-nuclear weapons.

(*e*) Doubt was expressed about the feasibility of keeping secret, for any length of time, a decision to manufacture thermo-nuclear weapons in this country. It was therefore suggested that thought should be given to the question how a decision to manufacture these weapons could best be justified to public opinion in this country and abroad.

It emerged from the discussion that there was general support in the Cabinet for the proposal that thermo-nuclear bombs should be manufactured in this country. Some Ministers asked, however, that there should be a further opportunity for reflection before a final decision was taken. Meanwhile, it was agreed that there should be no interruption of the preliminary planning which had already been put in hand.

The Cabinet—

Agreed to resume their discussion of this question at a further meeting before the end of July.

Washington Talks. Anglo-Soviet Meeting. (Previous Reference: C.C. (54) 47th Conclusions, Minute 4.)

3. The Cabinet continued their discussion of the possibility of an Anglo-Soviet Meeting.

The Cabinet's discussion on this question is recorded separately.

Parliament.

4. The Cabinet were informed of the business to be taken in the House of Commons in the following week.

The Opposition had expressed the wish that foreign affairs should be debated, in Committee of Supply, on 14th July. It was now clear, however, that the Foreign Secretary would be obliged to return before then to the Geneva Conference. When they knew this the Opposition might suggest another subject for debate on that day. If, however, they still wished to hold a Foreign Affairs debate related mainly to the recent meeting in Washington, it might be convenient that the Prime Minister's statement on the Washington talks should be made

The printed Cabinet minutes have long intrigued historians because an unknown minister, familiar with the doings of the Methodist Conference, raised the question of morality and the impact of the H-bomb on the national conscience. Similarly, the possibility of relying on the US nuclear umbrella over western Europe was raised. Both arguments were rebutted rather peremptorily. There was 'no sharp distinction in kind between atomic and thermo-nuclear weapons' (which the Chiefs of Staff paper showed was not the case). And if morality was an issue, 'it had already been breached by the decision of the Labour Government to make the atomic bomb' (even if this were true, it did not—if morality were a factor—absolve those in the Cabinet Room on 8 July 1954 from their moral responsibility for manufacturing an immensely more powerful weapon). Brook's notebook solves the mystery of who said what:

C.48   8th July 1954

2. *Atomic Weapons Programme*

PM   Invite LPS [Lord Privy Seal, Harry Crookshank] to express his view on moral issue.

HC   What financial commitment is involved?

        Is it sensible for UK, alone in Europe, to do this when we know we shall not wage war w'out U.S. as Ally. Shd. we not leave U.S. and R. as sole manufacturers: and preserve our right to say no European power shd. make it so.

DS   [Duncan Sandys, Minister of Supply] Latter argument weakened by fact we are making the less efficient a. weapons.

AE   [Anthony Eden, Foreign Secretary] Have we not a duty to our people to possess best weapons.

RAB   [R.A.Butler, Chancellor of the Exchequer] On cost: cheaper per power developed than a. weapons.

DS   About 9/10ths of effort is required for going on with a. weapons. Much flexibility retained as between H. and A. bombs. Can convert A. into H.bombs.

HM   [Macmillan] Shock to be told, casually, tht. we were going to do this. A no [number] of us felt like that.

PM   Must take a decision in principle. Not necessarily to-day.

        Doesn't depend on technical detail

        Mainly a moral questn. c.f. Soper's [Revd. Donald Soper, President of the Methodist Conference 1953–54] statements as reported in Press to-day: D.Worker [the *Daily Worker*, newspaper of the Communist Party of Great Britain].[58]

        I advise in favour of manufacture—but don't minimise moral issue.

AE   Thought moral issue was decided by Labour Govt., when made a bomb. No difference in principle.

Possession of a. weapons is now measure of power + influence in world.

Believe tht. as its deterrent power is realised this may well make war less likely.

MF [Sir David Maxwell-Fyfe, Home Secretary] Agree with AE.

i.) Deterrent. We must make our contn [contribution] to that. More likely to prevent war than bring it on.

ii.) Anxiety lest US shd. start a war—out of choice or to forestall. Our best chance of restraining them is to retain their respect. More likely to do so, if we play our part in deterrent influence.

Sim [Lord Symonds, Lord Chancellor] morally, can't distinguish between a. + h. bombs.

We are ready to accept protn [protection] of US possession of these bombs. If so, can't be wrong to make them ourselves.

[At this point, several ministers indicated they agreed H-bomb should be made]

OL [Oliver Lyttleton, Colonial Secretary] Agree. Even in smaller wars, total reliance on US won't enable us to conduct independent f. [foreign] policy.

FH [Florence Horsburgh, Minster of Education] Agree with Sim [Symonds].

Was worried by spread of this into Europe, incldg [including] Germany. But don't dissent from decision to make this.

HC Wd. wish to reflect a little longer. HM. So would I

PM. Then can we bring it up in a week or so.

HM Cd. we have some guidance on our public line. We can't hope to keep it a secret for ever.

PM Resume at convenient day before end of July. Prelimy [preliminary] work to go ahd [ahead] meanwhile.

FH Abolition agreement—more easy if we were, or were not, making it.

AE Probably easier if we did make it.[59]

So ended the first ever proper debate on the bomb at a full Cabinet meeting.

As Churchill predicted, the Cabinet did give the final go ahead by the end of the month, on 26 July to be precise.[60]

July, 16, 1954.

Madam,

It is my duty to inform Your Majesty
that the Cabinet are considering whether
it would be right and advantageous for
this country to produce the hydrogen bomb,
and have meanwhile agreed to the continuation
of the preparatory work which has been going
on for the last few months. Your Majesty
will, I understand, be receiving the account
of the proceedings in the Cabinet at which
this matter was recently discussed. A final
decision is to be taken before the end of
the month.

There is very little doubt in my
mind what it will be.

The experts, such as Sir William Penney
and Sir John Cockcroft, are confident of
our ability to produce the bomb although it
will in all probability be some two years
before it is completed.

                    I remain, Madam, Your Majesty's
                        faithful and devoted
                            subject and servant,

                    Winston S. Churchill

But it took rather longer than the two years Churchill anticipated to achieve an H-bomb with a Union Jack on top of it (some 3¼ years). As the official historian of the project, Lorna Arnold, has pointed out, the 'months following the White Paper of February 1955[61] [which announced that Britain was making an H-bomb] were an anxious time for the Aldermaston theoreticians as they groped for solutions' on how to design and make it.[62]

Rapid advances in both American and Soviet nuclear technology (Russia tested its first 'true' H-bomb on 22 November 1955) *and* missile development left Britain struggling in the second half of the 1950s, rather exposing the Chiefs of Staff's argument in the spring of 1954 that merely by reaching a thermonuclear stage, the UK might acquire 'the ability to be on terms with the United States and Russia'.

The H-bomb programme, however, did enable the British government eventually to take what Macmillan called the 'great prize'[63] of restored nuclear weapons collaboration with the United States. Macmillan, thanks to the Christmas Island nuclear test series, OPERATION GRAPPLE, in the Pacific during the course of 1957, managed to acquire a ticket for entry not so much for the Royal Enclosure at Ascot (in which he liked to sit, toppered and tailed, at the races[64]) but for the White House Rose Garden in Washington. In fact, Macmillan shimmered in a few weeks *before* the UK achieved true thermonuclear status.

The first test in the South Pacific on 15 May 1957 had produced a thermonuclear explosion which yielded 300 kilotons, some 30 per cent of megaton standard which was the target.[65] Nevertheless, the world was told that Britain was now an H-bomb power.[66] A larger explosion, produced by an enhanced fission device, created a yield of between 700 and 800 kilotons on 31 May.[67] But the first real UK megaton H-bomb (codenamed GRAPPLE X and based on an improved version of the 15 May device) was not detonated until 8 November off Christmas Island. It achieved 1.8 megatons—75 times more power than the HURRICANE test off Australia just over five years before.[68]

Two weeks earlier in the White House, Eisenhower, to Macmillan's delight, had shown him a presidential directive authorising the resumption of Anglo-American technical talks about nuclear collaboration.[69] The shadow of McMahon was lifting. On 30 June 1958, the US Congress approved changes to the McMahon Act to permit technical talks between the two sides.[70] Two months later, the British and American nuclear weaponeers began discussions.[71] Designs and techniques were shared. Edward Teller, the formidable American physicist behind the Eniwetok test in 1952, told his UK interlocutors that after 12 years of disruption in Anglo-American collaboration, it was plain that the laws of physics operated on both sides of the Atlantic.[72] On 4 August the US and UK governments concluded an *Agreement for Co-operation on the Uses of Atomic Energy for Mutual Defence Purposes*. The 'great prize' was secured. It had profound and enduring consequences. As a briefing for the recently installed Prime Minister, Edward Heath, put it in September 1970,

Since 1958 we have had a deep and intimate exchange of information with the Americans on nuclear weapons technology, involving frequent exchanges of information and equipment between the Atomic Weapons Research Establishment at Aldermaston and the Americans Weapons Laboratories and occasional use of each others' facilities for specific purposes.[73]

And the 1958 Agreement remains the basis of the US-UK nuclear collaboration to this day.

GRAPPLE X was a home-grown UK device, as were the V-bombers designed to carry the British atomic and hydrogen bombs. Britain had, at considerable cost, managed to go it alone. But once collaboration was restored, superior American warhead designs began to eclipse the best Aldermaston could manage. When the YELLOW SUN Mark II H-bombs (the Mark I s were fission weapons) were fitted to the V-bombers at their Lincolnshire bases in the very early 1960s, it was a British version of the American Mark 28 design that comprised the warhead known as RED SNOW. In the late 1950s, both the Americans and the Russians were racing ahead in missile capability as well as warhead design. A considerable delivery gap was opening up between the two superpowers and a Britain still striving to keep its 'certificate of grandeur'.

A Yellow Sun Mark II beside a Victor bomber.

A Vulcan bomber carrying the Blue Steel stand-off missile.

A quartet of fully-armed Vulcans on quick reaction alert, ready to fly from RAF Waddington.

The V-bombers came on stream in considerable numbers in 1957 making Harold Macmillan the first truly nuclear-equipped Prime Minister. With anticipated advances in Soviet air defences, Whitehall's planners were seriously concerned in the late 1950s about the durability of the V-bomber/free-fall bomb combination. As Peter Nailor, a former Ministry of Defence official on the nuclear side, put it,

> you got quite unexpectedly fast technical breakthroughs in reliable solid-fuel rocket motors, the development of miniaturised components, both for warheads and for guidance and instrumental systems. And the pace of change was accelerating to an extent where a country like Britain was being forced to make technical choices with bewildering rapidity . . . could we, in fact, find something that would enhance and prolong the service life of the V-bombers, or would we have to make the switch straight away to something like land or sea-based missiles? That was an option which . . . as late as 1954–5 nobody thought would be an immediate problem. By 1957–8 it was already knocking on the door.[74]

The Blue Streak ground-launched rocket was intended to fill the gap with a stand-off missile, Blue Steel, to prolong the active life of the V-force. By the first months of 1960, this strategy was in trouble[75] and the Joint Intelligence Committee were warning of Soviet advances to come in the variety, quality and capability of Russia's nuclear forces.

THIS DOCUMENT IS THE PROPERTY OF HER BRITANNIC MAJESTY'S GOVERNMENT

The circulation of this paper has been strictly limited. It is issued

for the personal use of.. *C. L.*

TOP SECRET   Copy No. **48**

J.I.C. (60) 3 (Final)

1st March, 1960

CABINET

JOINT INTELLIGENCE COMMITTEE

SINO-SOVIET BLOC WAR POTENTIAL, 1960–64

REPORT BY THE JOINT INTELLIGENCE COMMITTEE

In the report at Annex we estimate the war potential of the Soviet Union, the Satellites, Communist China and associated countries for the period 1960–64.

2. This report supersedes our previous study (JIC (59) 3) of this subject.

(Signed) **P. H. DEAN,**
Chairman, on behalf of the Joint
Intelligence Committee.

Cabinet Office, S.W.1.

1st March, 1960.

21. (cont.)

22. *Defence Industries.*—The industrial backing she can afford her armed forces is quite inadequate for modern warfare on a large scale. In none of the defence industries is it likely that the scale of production has permitted the building up of strategic reserves. This applies especially to reserves of liquid fuels.

23. Considerable extensions and improvements to the rail system, scheduled to be effected during the Second Five-year Plan, will give much needed flexibility of operation and increased capacity. Growing traffic demands from a constantly expanding economy will, however, continue to strain the railway capacity during the period under revue.

24. *Aid from Russia.*—In a war during the period under review, Chinese operations would depend to a critical extent on imports of military material coming from or through the USSR by overland routes.

SECTION IV

SCIENTIFIC AND TECHNICAL

Part I.—Soviet Bloc

General

1. After 14 years of growth the Soviet atomic programme has reached the status of a major industry and there are signs that the breakneck expansion of earlier years has been moderated. We have found no new production site for six years: we have noted a regard for economy in certain fields not of direct military importance; and while we have yet to hear an unambiguous version of Khrushchev's suggestion that the production of fissile material would be curtailed, it seems likely that the suggestion implies a new attitude to this question, or, at least, a readiness to ~~work~~ LOOK at it in a new way.

Fissile Material Production

2. Feed materials are available to the Soviet programme in ample quantities. In particular, there is enough uranium in the Soviet *bloc* to provide for any foreseeable requirement. Even the loss of the Satellites would leave the Soviet Union with ample uranium inside its own borders, though its recovery might involve heavy new expenditure at the outset.

3. The fissile materials produced in the USSR are plutonium and U-235. The plutonium is made in plutonium-producing reactors, several of which are graphite-moderated and water-cooled. The U-235 is made in diffusion plants. In diffusion technique Soviet progress has been slow and laborious. They started in 1946 with a small and inefficient plant. Since then they have continued to build plants, still fairly small, but better each time. By now they are thought to have achieved both a big production of U-235 and a reasonable economy in the use of electric power. The Soviet Union also produces in quantity deuterium, lithium, and probably tritium.

Nuclear Weapons

4. Since the first explosion in August 1949, over 70 explosions have been detected in the Soviet Union.

5. The tests of weapons in the kiloton range show evidence of interest in ground, air and underwater bursts, and the pattern of testing is consistent with a programme of development of efficient warheads in a range of sizes and yields. The Soviet have made considerable progress in the design of light-weight kiloton warheads which would have application to tactical weapons systems as well as surface-to-air missiles. The most recent series (October 1958) included some tests in the 100–400-kiloton range, and these appear to have been aimed at obtaining a significant reduction of weight in that yield bracket.

6. Soviet testing of devices incorporating thermonuclear reactions started with their fourth test in August 1953 and have continued, interspersed with other tests, to date. Up to the announcement of cessation of testing at the end of March 1958, most of the megaton tests had been in the ½–2½-megaton range, the highest recorded just exceeding 4 megatons. The autumn 1958 series included one

shot of about 6 megatons and another of about 7 megatons. The principal aim in the whole of their programme of thermonuclear warhead development appears to have been to achieve higher yields and reduced weights. Economy in fissile material does not appear to have been a first consideration. A test of about 400 kilotons in October 1958 appears to have been an experiment in the design of a "clean" warhead. Although some success was achieved in this respect, it was much inferior in its other military characteristics to the other warheads discussed.

7. Until the autumn of 1957 most of the tests took place at a proving ground in Siberia. The exceptions were one in 1954 which appears to have been a demonstration of a standard weapon, possibly associated with a military exercise, a naval test in the Arctic in 1955, which may have been an underwater burst, and two other tests early in 1956 and early in 1957 which are believed to have been associated with the Kapustin Yar Guided Missile Range.

8. The Soviet tests in the autumn of 1957 and the spring of 1958 were divided between the Siberian proving ground and a new proving ground in the Arctic. Of the most recent tests (autumn 1958) two took place near the Kapustin Yar Guided Missile Range, the remainder in the Arctic. Since the autumn of 1957 all tests in the megaton range have taken place in the Arctic which suggests that the Siberian proving ground is not considered safe for the highest yield weapons. No other reason for the change of proving ground is immediately apparent.

9. To sum up, on the evidence available from these tests, we must assume that the Soviet could by now have stockpiled a variety of warheads ranging from a few kilotons to several megatons. Any or all of these types could be in the form of bombs for delivery by aircraft, but we must also assume that they are capable of designing or producing warheads for specialist purposes such as guided weapons of all types including those for air defence, ballistic missiles, land and sea mines, artillery shells and torpedoes. While some of these warheads can be common to more than one purpose, others would have to be designed and stockpiled for use with their own particular weapons systems. This variety in requirements not only covers a very wide range in yields, but also leads to a number of designs in which the efficient use of fissile material varies over quite wide limits.

10. Although we have approximate estimates of the Soviet stockpile of fissile material, we have no means of knowing how they propose to allocate it. It is apparent, therefore, that it is not possible to provide any single simple estimate of the Soviet stockpile of nuclear weapons. A detailed estimate can be given only in relation to a detailed set of assumptions.

11. With the assessed quantities of fissile material we can say that at the end of 1959 they could have made it up into slightly over 1,000 MT. weapons of $\frac{1}{2}$ to 8 MT. yield or about 3,000 weapons of less than 100 KT. yield. However we do not know what choice they have made between these extremes. We show below some of the possible stockpiles for the end of 1959. Throughout the examples the kiloton weapon of up to 100 KT. can be replaced by weapons of yield 100–500 KT. at the rate of two of the smaller for one of the larger weapons.

$\frac{1}{2}$–8 MT.	Up to 100 KT.
200	2,500
500	1,900
1,000	500

These stockpiles could be more than doubled by the end of 1964.

Storage of Nuclear Weapons

12. Nuclear weapons storage has been discovered at a number of Soviet LRAF, Tactical and Naval airfields ranging from the Arctic to the Crimea as well as in the Far East.

13. In addition to airfield nuclear weapons storage, a number of National Stockpile sites have been detected which might be intended for the storage of weapons for all Services.

There were multiple problems with Blue Streak (Blue Steel was a success and was fitted to the V-force in late 1962). The development costs of the land-based rocket were mounting fast; it was liquid-fuelled, rather than solid-fuelled, and took 15 minutes to prepare for firing; the US Ballistic Missile Early Warning System at RAF Fylingdales in North Yorkshire would, when operational, only provide a four-minute warning of attack.[76] On the recommendation of the Chiefs of Staff, Macmillan's Cabinet decided to cancel it on 13 April 1960.

SECRET

THIS DOCUMENT IS THE PROPERTY OF HER BRITANNIC MAJESTY'S GOVERNMENT

Printed for the Cabinet.   April 1960

C.C. (60)   Copy No. 34
26th Conclusions

CABINET

*CONCLUSIONS of a Meeting of the Cabinet held at 10 Downing Street, S.W.1,
on Wednesday, 13th April, 1960, at 10 a.m.*

Present:

The Right Hon. HAROLD MACMILLAN, M.P., Prime Minister

The Right Hon. R. A. BUTLER, M.P., Secretary of State for the Home Department

The Right Hon. VISCOUNT KILMUIR, Lord Chancellor

The Right Hon. D. HEATHCOAT AMORY, M.P., Chancellor of the Exchequer

The Right Hon. THE EARL OF HOME, Lord President of the Council and Secretary of State for Commonwealth Relations

The Right Hon. JOHN MACLAY, M.P., Secretary of State for Scotland

The Right Hon. VISCOUNT HAILSHAM, Q.C., Lord Privy Seal and Minister for Science

The Right Hon. HAROLD WATKINSON, M.P., Minister of Defence

The Right Hon. HENRY BROOKE, M.P., Minister of Housing and Local Government and Minister for Welsh Affairs

The Right Hon. Sir DAVID ECCLES, M.P., Minister of Education

The Right Hon. LORD MILLS, Paymaster-General

The Right Hon. EDWARD HEATH, M.P., Minister of Labour

Dr. The Right Hon. CHARLES HILL, M.P., Chancellor of the Duchy of Lancaster

The Right Hon. ERNEST MARPLES, M.P., Minister of Transport

The following were also present:

The Right Hon. LORD CARRINGTON, First Lord of the Admiralty (*Item 4*)

The Right Hon. THE EARL OF PERTH, Minister of State for Colonial Affairs (*Items 3–4*)

The Right Hon. JOHN PROFUMO, M.P., Minister of State for Foreign Affairs

Mr. F. J. ERROLL, M.P., Minister of State, Board of Trade (*Item 3*)

The Right Hon. SIR REGINALD MANNINGHAM-BULLER, Q.C., M.P., Attorney-General (*Item 4*)

The Right Hon. MARTIN REDMAYNE, M.P., Parliamentary Secretary, Treasury

Mr. J. B. GODBER, M.P., Joint Parliamentary Secretary, Ministry of Agriculture, Fisheries and Food (*Items 3–4*)

Secretariat:

The Right Hon. SIR NORMAN BROOK
Mr. F. A. BISHOP
Mr. M. REED

SECRET

57150—8   B

22. (cont.)

Nuclear Weapons.
(Previous Reference:
C.C. (60) 7th Conclusions, Minute 6.)
Blue Streak.

1. *The Prime Minister* said that the Defence Committee had for some time been considering what would be the best vehicle for delivering the United Kingdom contribution towards the nuclear deterrent when the Bomber Force ceased to be an effective means of delivery. Hitherto it had been assumed that this Force would be supplemented, and eventually replaced, by the static ballistic missile Blue Streak. In view of later technical developments, however, the Chiefs of Staff had advised that a static weapon of this kind would be excessively vulnerable and that our contribution to the nuclear deterrent, if it was to continue to be effective, must in future be based on some mobile means of delivery. The Prime Minister said that, during his recent visit to Washington, he had satisfied himself that we should be able in due course to obtain from the United States, on acceptable terms, supplies of one or other of the alternative types of mobile weapon, to be armed with a British warhead. In these circumstances the Defence Committee had decided that it would be wrong to proceed with the existing programme for the development of Blue Streak as a military weapon. There was a possibility that the Blue Streak programme could be adapted for the development of a rocket for use in space research; and this possibility would now be explored in detail in consultation with the firms concerned.

This decision was of close concern to the Australian Government in view of their expenditure on the range at Woomera. The Prime Minister of Australia had therefore been kept fully informed of the strategic arguments and he concurred in the view that Blue Streak should not be further developed as a military weapon.

It was proposed that this decision should be announced in the House of Commons by the Minister of Defence that afternoon.

The Cabinet—
Confirmed the decision that the further development of the ballistic missile Blue Streak as a military weapon should be abandoned.

Parliament.

2. The Cabinet were informed of the business to be taken in the House of Commons in the week after the Easter recess.

Economic Situation.
Balance of Payments.
(Previous Reference:
C.C. (60) 22nd Conclusions, Minute 4.)
Oversea Development.
(Previous Reference:
C.C. (60) 15th Conclusions, Minute 6.)

3. The Cabinet resumed their discussions of a memorandum by the Chancellor of the Exchequer (C. (60) 60) about the prospects for the balance of payments during 1960 and the scale of external expenditure in the period 1960–63. They also had before them a memorandum by the Chancellor of the Exchequer (C. (60) 61) covering a report by officials on oversea development policy.

The Chancellor of the Exchequer said that the latest information tended to confirm the forecast that the external monetary position was likely to deteriorate by about £200 millions in 1960. There was, however, some possibility that the continued increase in the rate of imports was beginning to moderate. Nevertheless there was a sombre prospect that the unfavourable trend in the balance of payments might continue for a number of years. On present policies it was most unlikely that over the next few years our surplus on current account would be enough to enable us to meet our capital commitments. In the long run we should have to relate our oversea commitments to the foreign exchange earning capacity of the economy.

If the economy were to proceed on its present course, the growth of exports might be restrained by the competing pull of the home market. It would be undesirable to reimpose physical controls on imports, even if it were possible to do so, because of the possibility of

To fill the gap left by the cancellation of Blue Streak, Macmillan negotiated with Eisenhower the purchase of Skybolt, a stand-off missile still under development in the US. As Harold Watkinson, Minister of Defence, told the Cabinet on 20 June 1960, there was 'no absolute certainty' that the system would work. But if it did, and it was fitted to the Mark 2 Vulcan bombers, it would sustain the effectiveness of the V-force into the later 1960s.

SECRET

THIS DOCUMENT IS THE PROPERTY OF HER BRITANNIC MAJESTY'S GOVERNMENT

Printed for the Cabinet. June 1960

C.C. (60)
35th Conclusions

Copy No. **36**

CABINET

———

CONCLUSIONS of a Meeting of the Cabinet held in the Prime Minister's Room, House of Commons, S.W.1, on Monday, 20th June, 1960, at 5·30 p.m.

Present:

The Right Hon. HAROLD MACMILLAN, M.P., Prime Minister

The Right Hon. R. A. BUTLER, M.P., Secretary of State for the Home Department

The Right Hon. SELWYN LLOYD, Q.C., M.P., Secretary of State for Foreign Affairs

The Right Hon. D. HEATHCOAT AMORY, M.P., Chancellor of the Exchequer

The Right Hon. The EARL OF HOME, Lord President of the Council and Secretary of State for Commonwealth Relations

The Right Hon. JOHN MACLAY, M.P., Secretary of State for Scotland

The Right Hon. DUNCAN SANDYS, M.P., Minister of Aviation

The Right Hon. HAROLD WATKINSON, M.P., Minister of Defence

The Right Hon. HENRY BROOKE, M.P., Minister of Housing and Local Government and Minister for Welsh Affairs

The Right Hon. Sir DAVID ECCLES, M.P., Minister of Education

The Right Hon. LORD MILLS, Paymaster-General

The Right Hon. JOHN HARE, M.P., Minister of Agriculture, Fisheries and Food

The Right Hon. ERNEST MARPLES, M.P., Minister of Transport

The following were also present:

The Right Hon. LORD CARRINGTON, First Lord of the Admiralty

The Right Hon. GEORGE WARD, M.P., Secretary of State for Air

The Right Hon. MARTIN REDMAYNE, M.P., Parliamentary Secretary, Treasury

Secretariat:

The Right Hon. Sir NORMAN BROOK
Mr. F. A. BISHOP
Mr. J. S. ORME

SECRET

58020—1

B

Nuclear Weapons

(Previous Reference: C.C. (60) 26th Conclusions, Minute 1)

SKYBOLT

The Cabinet had before them a note by the Minister of Defence (C. (60) 97) on the SKYBOLT missile.

The Minister of Defence said that, following the agreement in principle which the Prime Minister had reached with President Eisenhower in March, he had during his recent visit to Washington concluded a memorandum of understanding with the United States Secretary of Defence about SKYBOLT to give effect to our intention to order this weapon if it were successfully developed in a form suitable for the Mark 2 V-Bombers of Bomber Command. He now sought approval for the negotiation of a more detailed technical and financial agreement with the United States authorities.

There could as yet be no absolute certainty that SKYBOLT, which was not due to be tested as a complete weapon for about a year, would be successful and it must be recognised that the Americans would not develop it for our use alone. However, the United States authorities were confident that it would be effective and they attached importance to it both for their own Air Force and as a means of prolonging the effectiveness of our V-Bombers, which they recognised were an important part of the strategic nuclear deterrent. By acquiring 144 missiles, with spares and associated equipment, we should be able in the later 1960s to maintain with the Vulcan Mark 2 bombers a deterrent force equivalent to that previously planned for BLUE STREAK. The Victor Mark 2 bombers would not be adapted for SKYBOLT, but could be a complementary component of the deterrent with a developed version of the British powered-bomb BLUE STEEL, if necessary. It would be in our interests to respond without delay to the American desire to expedite the joint development of SKYBOLT, in order to ensure that it would be fully compatible with our requirements.

On present estimates, the cost of our requirement would be between £76 millions and £115 millions (depending on the unit cost of the missile), with a dollar content of up to £108 millions. We should have to ensure that the price would be based on the cost of production, without any contribution from us to the underlying development costs. We should only be committed to purchase if the price were on this basis and if the weapon was successful.

The Chancellor of the Exchequer said that, while he felt there was a danger that the bomber force itself might have become unduly vulnerable by the time SKYBOLT was available, he recognised that, if the weapon were successful, the proposals of the Minister of Defence might be the cheapest means of maintaining an effective contribution to the Western deterrent. It was not possible to foresee at this stage the burden that the dollar costs would ultimately involve, but if this proved excessive our policy might have to be reconsidered at a later stage.

Discussion showed that the Cabinet were in agreement with the course recommended by the Minister of Defence. They were informed that there was a promising prospect that the Vulcan Mark 2 aircraft would give longer service than originally planned; and that no need was foreseen at the present time to order additional replacement aircraft of this or another type, such as the VC-10, that would add to the cost of the programme.

The Cabinet—

(1) Approved the proposals in C. (60) 97.

(2) Invited the Foreign Secretary, in consultation with the other Ministers concerned, to arrange for instructions to be sent to Her Majesty's Ambassador in Washington for the conclusion of a technical and financial agreement with the United States Government on SKYBOLT.

SECRET

The nuclear arsenal of the Soviet Union in 1961 grew apace with the acquisition of monster thermonuclear weapons (the JIC rated one test at 58 megatons) and was pressing ahead with warheads for land, sea and air systems of all kinds.

24. Joint Intelligence Committee assessment of 'Sino-Soviet Bloc War Potential, 1962–66', JIC (62) 3 (Final), 16 February 1962. TNA, PRO, CAB 158/45, Part 1

Amended 3/4/62

J.I.C. (62) 3 (Final)
16th February, 1962

CABINET

JOINT INTELLIGENCE COMMITTEE

SINO-SOVIET BLOC WAR POTENTIAL, 1962–66

REPORT BY THE JOINT INTELLIGENCE COMMITTEE

In the report at Annex we estimate the war potential of the Soviet Union, the Satellites, Communist China and associated countries for the period 1962–66.

2. This report supersedes our previous study (J.I.C. (61) 3) of this subject.

(Signed)   HUGH STEPHENSON,
*Chairman, on behalf of the Joint
Intelligence Committee.*

Cabinet Office, S.W. 1,

16th February, 1962.

TOP SECRET

24. (cont.)

any numerical estimate of such submarines on this basis. Other evidence, however, is growing and the assessment yielded by this evidence is given in Section VIII. It is estimated that the Russians have had the theoretical technical capability for some time of producing a submarine propulsion unit and it must be assumed that they now have the capability of producing these units in some numbers. It is difficult at first sight to reconcile the *Lenin's* severe troubles with the current estimate of nuclear submarines given elsewhere. On the other hand, it is quite feasible that the *Lenin* reactor development programme was in no way associated with the submarine reactor programme and while the *Lenin* has met difficulties, the submarine reactors have been generally successful. This is the only hypothesis that fits the apparent facts.

52. *Aircraft Propulsion.*—References to Soviet development of nuclear-powered aircraft continue to be made in the Press, but we have no reliable information about any Soviet programme or actual progress in this field.

Nuclear Weapons

53. In the latter part of 1961, the Soviet Union conducted an intensive series of 45 nuclear tests. This raised to 119 the number of Soviet nuclear events detected by the West. Soviet tests have ranged in yield from the low kiloton to the massive explosion, in the latest series, the yield of which was assessed at about 58 megatons.

54. The available evidence on Soviet developments is not inconsistent with the general assumption that the Russians have proceeded along lines known to the West, although the West have never extended testing into the very high yield region covered in the latest Soviet series. It must now be assumed that Soviet nuclear weapon technology, with some exceptions, can be regarded as being on a par with that of the West. Evidence from the last test series suggests that the Russians have been concerned with the development of very high yield weapons, with improving yield-to-weight ratios and with improving the economy in fissile material of their warheads.

55. *Warheads in the Megaton Range.*—It must be recognised that the Russians can now stockpile warheads of very high yield. They are now capable of producing a 100-megaton warhead without further testing. Further, they can now produce lighter warheads in the lower megaton range, say, up to 5 megatons. The full implications of these advances will be known only after further study.

56. *Warheads in the Kiloton Range.*—The latest test series showed a continued interest in the development of fission warheads in a variety of weights and dimensions. Some of these developments show the expected improvement over those tested in 1958. Once again the implications of these advances will be clear only after further study.

57. *Warhead Production.*—As a result of their test series carried out since 1949, it must be assumed that the Soviet are capable of producing warheads for aircraft bombs, ballistic missiles, rockets, land and sea mines, artillery shells, torpedoes and depth charges.

58. *Weapon Stockpiles.*—Although we have approximate estimates of the Soviet stockpile of fissile material, we have no means of knowing how they propose to allocate it between different types of weapons. It is apparent, therefore, that it is not possible to provide any single simple estimate of the Soviet stockpile of nuclear weapons. A detailed estimate can be given only in relation to a detailed set of assumptions. In order to arrive at a simple and useful set of examples we have assumed two main classes of warheads: the $\frac{1}{2}$–8-megaton class, and the 1–100-kiloton class. With this assumption we find that at the end of 1961 the Soviet Union could have about 2,700 megaton warheads or over 5,000 kiloton warheads. We show below some of the possible stockpiles:

$\frac{1}{2}$–8 Megatons	Up to 100 Kilotons
300	4,800
600	4,300
1,200	3,400
2,000	2,000
2,500	800

At the expected rate of production of fissile material these stockpiles could be more than doubled by the end of 1966. Further increases would also be obtained by refabrication to the more economical designs developed in 1961.

TOP SECRET

59. *Storage of Nuclear Weapons.*—Nuclear weapons storage has been discovered at a number of Soviet LRAF, tactical and naval airfields ranging from the Arctic to the Crimea as well as in the Far East. In addition to airfields nuclear weapons storage, a number of national and regional stockpile sites have been detected. These might be intended for the storage of weapons for all services. There are also indications that facilities suitable for nuclear weapons storage exist at some satellite airfields, but at present there is no evidence that weapons are deployed outside the Soviet Union, although Khrushchev broadly hinted that there may be some in East Germany.

Biological Warfare

60. Only indirect information on the existence of any Soviet offensive BW plans has ever been received. Statements by various Soviet leaders have indicated that biological weapons would be included in the Soviet armoury in the event of a future world war. Civil Defence training includes defence again BW, and useful pamphlets cover this subject. At least half the adult population of the Soviet Union is estimated to have taken some kind of Civil Defence course.

61. From a study of Soviet achievements and progress in the medical sciences and related fields, as revealed in publications, the following deductions can be made:

(a) The Soviet Union has the necessary knowledge and technical capacity to mass-produce living pathogens or their toxic products for use in offensive BW on a strategic scale or by sabotage methods.

(b) The Soviet Union has the necessary skills and industrial capacity to produce medical supplies (including antibiotics, vaccines and serums) in quantities sufficient for defence against BW; and in this connexion their experience in the use of aerogenic and other means of mass immunisation for public health purposes would be of great value.

There is no reason to doubt that progress in the study of both offensive and defensive aspects of BW will be made in the Soviet Union during the years under review.

62. There is no evidence that the Soviet military forces are equipped to wage offensive biological warfare. The Soviet Union is, however, capable of developing and using various means of disseminating BW agents on a large scale such as (a) cluster bombs delivered from aircraft or from ballistic or cruise-type missiles; and (b) spraying from such vehicles at low level or from surface craft; such spraying could be carried out either overtly or covertly. In addition, the Soviet Union is capable of developing and using devices for small-scale covert dissemination by the individual saboteur. Although there is no indication that any of these possible methods of attack have been studied in the Soviet Union, there can be do doubt that cognisance will have been taken of relevant Western publications, and it is considered that effort will have been made to keep at least on a par with the West.

Chemical Warfare

63. *Research and Development.*—There is good evidence for the existence of a Soviet research and development programme on chemical warfare, including a large trials area for work on this subject. This programme probably includes not only work on the improvement of existing types of agent and on more efficient means of dissemination but also a search for new lethal and new incapacitating agents.

64. *Production of Agents.*—There is no firm evidence to show whether large-scale production of any chemical warfare agent is or is not in progress in the Soviet Union, but it is considered that the Soviet Union:

(a) could be producing standard agents on a large scale, and stocking them in bulk and as filled munitions;

(b) could have started production of G agents by 1951 and hence (even allowing for normal deterioration) could by now have accumulated considerable stocks (in bulk and as filled munitions);

(c) could have developed agents similar to the Western V agents and could by now have these in production.

It is not possible to put forward any useful tonnage figures for the probable annual rate of production or for the accumulated stocks of any CW agents, the information

The confidence of the US authorities in Skybolt as reported by Watkinson to the Cabinet was misplaced. A few weeks after the Cuban missile crisis, the Pentagon cancelled the weapon on 11 December 1962. As Robert McNamara, the US Secretary of Defence in the Kennedy Administration, expressed it to me many years later:

> Skybolt. It was an absolute pile of junk . . . the development of which had been paid for 100% by the US the British hadn't put it a dime. . . We had no obligation, or at least we thought we had no obligation, to produce a pile of junk for . . . an ill-defined but very real political requirement in Britain. So when we cancelled the weapon, all hell broke loose and the agenda for Nassau [the planned meeting in the Bahamas between Kennedy and Macmillan] was totally scrapped and we didn't talk about a damn thing at Nassau except Skybolt and what to do to replace it in the British inventory to permit them to replace their independent deterrent, which ultimately became Polaris.[77]

On the 18 December 1962, Macmillan flew to Nassau with Alec Home, Foreign Secretary, and Peter Thorneycroft, Defence Secretary, for what McNamara called 'a very, very, very difficult meeting', with President Kennedy and his team.[78] Macmillan kept his full Cabinet in touch with the negotiations through a spate of telegrams and his number two, Rab Butler, chaired a special Cabinet meeting to consider them on 21 December 1962.

President Kennedy greeted by Harold Macmillan and Lord Home (centre), Nassau, December 1962.

25. Cabinet Minutes, CC (62) 76th Conclusions, 21 December 1962.

TNA, PRO, CAB 128/36 Part 2

SECRET

THIS DOCUMENT IS THE PROPERTY OF HER BRITANNIC MAJESTY'S GOVERNMENT

Printed for the Cabinet. December 1962

C.C. (62)
76th Conclusions

Copy No. 37

CABINET
———

CONCLUSIONS of a Meeting of the Cabinet held at Admiralty House, S.W. 1, on Friday, 21st December, 1962, at 10 a.m.

Present:

The Right Hon. R. A. BUTLER, M.P., First Secretary of State (*in the Chair*)

The Right Hon. VISCOUNT HAILSHAM, Q.C., Lord President of the Council	The Right Hon. LORD DILHORNE, Lord Chancellor
The Right Hon. REGINALD MAUDLING, M.P., Chancellor of the Exchequer	The Right Hon. HENRY BROOKE, M.P., Secretary of State for the Home Department
The Right Hon. JOHN HARE, M.P., Minister of Labour	The Right Hon. EDWARD HEATH, M.P., Lord Privy Seal
The Right Hon. ERNEST MARPLES, M.P., Minister of Transport	The Right Hon. CHRISTOPHER SOAMES, M.P., Minister of Agriculture, Fisheries and Food
The Right Hon. FREDERICK ERROLL, M.P., President of the Board of Trade	The Right Hon. JOHN BOYD-CARPENTER, M.P., Chief Secretary to the Treasury and Paymaster General
The Right Hon. J. ENOCH POWELL, M.P., Minister of Health	The Right Hon. Sir EDWARD BOYLE, M.P., Minister of Education
The Right Hon. Sir KEITH JOSEPH, M.P., Minister of Housing and Local Government and Minister for Welsh Affairs	The Right Hon. WILLIAM DEEDES, M.P., Minister without Portfolio

The following were also present:

The Right Hon. LORD CARRINGTON, First Lord of the Admiralty	The Right Hon. JOHN PROFUMO, M.P., Secretary of State for War
The Right Hon. JULIAN AMERY, M.P., Minister of Aviation	The Right Hon. HUGH FRASER, M.P., Secretary of State for Air

The Right Hon. MARTIN REDMAYNE, M.P., Parliamentary Secretary, Treasury

———

Secretariat:

Mr. A. L. M. CARY
Mr. N. J. ABERCROMBIE

SECRET

1900—19

A

25. (cont.)

Bahamas Meeting, December 1962
(Previous Reference: C.C. (62) 75th Conclusions, Minute 1)

Nuclear Weapons
(Previous Reference: C.C. (60) 35th Conclusions)

*The Cabinet had before them four telegrams from the Prime Minister (Nassau telegrams Nos. Codel 16, 17, 18 and 24 of 20th December, 1962) on the action to be taken following the decision of the President of the United States to cancel plans for the development of the airborne ballistic missile SKYBOLT for use by the United States. The action proposed included the provision of POLARIS missiles to be carried in United Kingdom submarines. The Prime Minister had asked for the advice of the Cabinet on the question whether the terms of a proposed joint statement in his own name and that of the President were acceptable.

The First Secretary of State drew attention to the principal differences between the United States draft in telegram No. Codel 16 and the subsequent joint draft in telegram No. Codel 18 which had been elaborated in further discussion on 20th December and on which the advice of the Cabinet was now sought. It was clear that a great deal had been achieved by the Prime Minister and his colleagues in Nassau in persuading the President to move away from the original United States positions. Whereas the United States draft would have committed the United Kingdom Government to " an agreement to meet their NATO non-nuclear force goals at the agreed NATO standards ", the latest draft referred only to " agreement on the importance of increasing the effectiveness of their conventional forces ". Again, the latest draft included a new provision that our strategic nuclear forces would be used for " the international defence of the Western Alliance in all circumstances except where Her Majesty's Government may decide that the supreme national interests are at stake ". The Prime Minister had particularly directed attention (in telegram No. Codel 24) to these words, which had the effect of giving us the sole right of decision on the use of our strategic nuclear forces, and had asked whether the Cabinet endorsed the view, which he shared with the Foreign Secretary, the Commonwealth Secretary and the Minister of Defence, that these words could be publicly defended as maintaining an independent United Kingdom contribution to the nuclear deterrent.

The Cabinet accordingly considered first the wording of this passage in the statement. There was some doubt whether, as it stood, the exception would be generally interpreted as allowing Her Majesty's Government to use United Kingdom strategic forces in circumstances not involving the defence of the Western Alliance, or whether it would be taken to mean only that the Government could decline to use those forces in particular circumstances involving the interests of the Alliance. It was clear that the Prime Minister intended the exception to cover both cases. If he were free to make this interpretation public, with the consent of the President, this would safeguard the principle of independence; but there would be advantage in clarifying the terms of the statement and removing the ambiguity, if this could be done without jeopardising United States agreement to the other features of the arrangement proposed. This was especially important in view of Western European opinion. We might easily suffer from the growth of a suspicion that our military independnce was, or might be, less secure than, for example, that of the French. Again, as no early opportunity could be found for Parliamentary discussion of the joint statement, this was an additional reason for seeking to ensure that the terms of the statement itself were free from doubt. In any case some public explanation would be called for before Parliament reassembled. An alternative form of words was suggested, emphasising first the right of Her Majesty's Government to act in accordance with the supreme national interest, subject to which United Kingdom strategic nuclear forces would only be used in defence of the Alliance.

---

* Previously recorded in a Confidential Annex.

SECRET

While Ministers were agreed upon the value to this country of an arrangement by which we should eventually have within our own control a virtually indestructible second-strike deterrent weapon of proven capability, and with prospects of a long life, it was recognised that the conditions which the United States Government were stipulating represented a heavy price in money and otherwise.

The First Lord of the Admiralty informed the Cabinet that a force of POLARIS-firing nuclear submarines could be built for the Royal Navy in either of two ways. Four submarines each equipped with 16 missiles could be completed between early 1968 and 1970, providing a full deterrent during 1969; this was estimated to cost £220 million over a period of seven years, including the necessary missiles, but excluding the cost of research and development of a United Kingdom warhead. Alternatively, seven submarines each equipped with eight missiles could be completed over a period of 11 years, providing a full deterrent in the course of 1971, at a total cost of £290 million. In both cases it might be reasonable to reckon a saving of £100 million on SKYBOLT as offsetting the cost of the submarines: in the latter alternative of eight-missile submarines, these vessels would be able to perform the full military role of seven nuclear-powered submarines in the conventional fleet, in addition to their deterrent function. On this basis, the extra cost of the missile-firing capability of the seven submarines would be £95 million.

There was no mention in the telegrams under examination of any arrangement for hiring United States submarines, or otherwise bridging the gap which would occur in our deterrent forces after the V-bomber force armed with BLUE STEEL began to diminish in effectiveness in the latter half of the current decade. It thus appeared that expenditure on the V-bomber force might continue unabated during the period of construction of United Kingdom POLARIS-firing submarines. Furthermore, United States pressure for improvement in the effectiveness of conventional forces was likely to lead to increased United Kingdom expenditure.

In the absence of any reliable estimate of the total financial and economic consequences involved, *the Chancellor of the Exchequer* said that he must reserve his position about the implications for defence expenditure as a whole of a decision to accept a United Kingdom deterrent based on POLARIS.

In the course of further discussion, reference was made to the likelihood of public criticism of the Government's acceptance of a period of some years during which the possibility of effective action by United Kingdom strategic nuclear forces would be seriously diminished. Responsible opinion was also likely to take the point that the proposed arrangement included our acceptance of the idea of a multilateral strategic nuclear force for the North Atlantic Alliance, which was a new and untried concept. Coupled with insistence on the need to improve the effectiveness, which would be taken to mean the size, of our conventional forces in Europe, there was at least a possible risk that, before the time came when we were ready to accept POLARIS missiles for our submarines, the United States Administration would make use of alleged shortcomings in our policy towards the North Atlantic Alliance as an excuse for defaulting on their offer.

The Chief Secretary, Treasury, invited attention to the fact that the proposed joint statement appeared to exclude any consideration of the fitting of POLARIS missiles in surface ships. While this method would not have the advantages of submarine operation, and although any technical effort expended in this direction would mean a delay in the fulfilment of the submarine programme, surface ships could probably be made ready earlier and cheaper than submarines.

25. (cont.)

While the wording of the passage about conventional forces in telegram No. Codel 18 represented a very great improvement on the wording earlier proposed by the United States in telegram No. Codel 16, it could be further improved if the idea were introduced that the effectiveness of our conventional forces ought to be increased " on a world-wide basis ": without some such addition it would be widely misunderstood as necessarily implying an increase in the strength of the British Army of the Rhine, which would be very difficult to achieve. This passage of the proposed joint statement was also unsatisfactory in that it gave currency to a new (and probably unsound) United States strategic doctrine of a " nuclear shield " and a " non-nuclear sword ".

Summing up the discussion *the First Secretary of State* said that there seemed to be general agreement in the Cabinet that the Prime Minister and his colleagues deserved their full support for the largely successful efforts that they had made to evolve a satisfactory agreement with the United States Government. In conveying the sense of this feeling to the Prime Minister it would however be right to emphasise their view that the Government were being asked to pay a heavy price and that for this reason the independent role of Her Majesty's Government in the use of nuclear forces must be clearly and unambiguously expressed. The wording of the relevant passage in the joint statement could in their view be improved in order to make the Prime Minister's own interpretation of it plainer. On conventional forces, while the substance of the proposed joint statement was unexceptionable, certain changes of wording might be recommended to avoid subsequent difficulty in application. It would be necessary to inform the Prime Minister of the reservation which the Chancellor of the Exchequer had made. As there would be no opportunity to explain the new arrangement in Parliament for a month, it would be right to inform the Prime Minister of the views which had been expressed about the form which criticism of the arrangements might take in responsible quarters, and of the need for some earlier and fuller exposition of the Government's policy than would be conveyed by the statement itself.

The Cabinet—

(1) Agreed that the Prime Minister should be assured of their full support in his endeavours to secure a satisfactory statement.

(2) Agreed that the draft in telegram No. Codel 18, if interpreted on the lines of telegram No. Codel 24, safeguarded the essential principle of an independent United Kingdom contribution to the Western strategic nuclear deterrent, but that the wording as it stood was open to misinterpretation.

(3) Took note that the First Secretary of State would arrange for the Prime Minister to be advised of their views on this point, and of the other points made in their discussion.

Cabinet Office, S.W. 1,
  21st December, 1962.

The discussion turned on the degree to which UK independence as a nuclear power could be sustained through a Polaris purchase in both practical reality and political appearance. Surprisingly, this had not happened when the Cabinet discussed the procurement of Skybolt 2½ years earlier, which was the moment when abandoning a wholly UK made system was approved. (There is no evidence from the Cabinet minutes that ministers collectively knew the degree to which the Yellow Sun Mark II weapon was essentially a modified American design.) Macmillan's negotiation of a 'supreme national interests' clause was plainly crucial to the acceptability of the deal that morning in the Cabinet Room.

The French deterrent makes an appearance (and would do again in future discussions throughout the 1960s and 1970s), in this instance as a more independent capacity than the one Macmillan was proposing Britain should acquire. Lord Carrington, First Lord of the Admiralty, provided what turned out to be a pretty accurate forecast of the timing of a four-boat Royal Navy Polaris force and the stage at which it was likely to take over the primary deterrent role from the RAF Vulcans equipped with Blue Steel. The Treasury reserved its position on costs, but the full Cabinet authorised a telegram to the Bahamas assuring Macmillan 'of their full support' in his continuing negotiations. If ultimate success came at Nassau it would, as the Cabinet minutes indicated, produce for the UK 'a virtually indestructible second-strike deterrent weapon of proven capability, and with prospects of a long life', provided a future government did not abandon it before the system was ready or decommission it after the Polaris force had begun its patrols.

The deal was successfully struck at Nassau but it left Macmillan in a state of anxiety about its durability. After a characteristically broody Christmas at his country home, Birch Grove, Macmillan on Boxing Day 1962 minuted Home and Thorneycroft about possible fall-backs if Nassau unravelled, wondering 'if we were driven into a corner, [whether] we could either as a bluff or as a reality, make a Polaris missile perhaps of a simpler kind, ourselves from our own designs; how long would it take etc?'[79] And on New Year's Eve, he convened a special meeting of ministers and officials at Admiralty House (No. 10 was under repair) at which some of those anxieties surfaced as well as his fear (justified as it turned out) that the special Anglo-American nuclear relationship, made manifest once more at Nassau, might affect relationships with General de Gaulle to the point where the first British application to join the European Economic Community could be jeopardised, even though Kennedy was offering a 'similar' deal to the French.[80]

26. Record of the Prime Minister's Admiralty House meeting on Polaris, 31 December 1962. TNA, PRO, PREM 11/4147

Record of a meeting at Admiralty House at 6.00 p.m.
on Monday, December 31, 1962.

Present: The Prime Minister

      The Foreign Secretary

      The Minister of Defence

      The Lord Privy Seal

      Sir Pierson Dixon

      Lord Hood

      Mr. Bligh

The **Prime Minister** outlined the course of the discussions in the Bahamas which had led up to the agreement with the United States to supply us with Polaris missiles. He was anxious that the technical negotiations should be pushed ahead as soon as possible and that they should be kept on a naval and technical level so that political considerations need not be brought in. He also hoped it would be possible to settle quite quickly the financial arrangements which should include a down-payment for immediate delivery of one or two missiles. It was important that it was manifest that some equipment was actually crossing the Atlantic.

He hoped that the French Government would take some time before reaching a final decision on the American offer to them. There were many difficulties that would confront them if they were to accept the offer and it might be that we could help them in a number of ways. It might be useful to emphasise to the French that there was nothing in the Nassau Agreement which would prevent us making our own missiles either alone or jointly with some other country. It might also be useful to

29

26. (cont.)

emphasise to the French ~~that~~ the qualifying phrase 'guaranteed our
Sovereign rights' since the U.K. Government would alone judge
what constituted our supreme national interests.   It might
perhaps be explained that we did not foresee that we should
have to use this right in any except the most grave
circumstances.   If, for example, Indonesia threatened North
Borneo we would not necessarily wish to pose a direct threat
to ~~Prince~~ *President* Soekarno, but if as a result of our adopting
conventional methods of defending North-Borneo the Russians
threatened us direct as they had done in somewhat vague terms
at the time of Suez, then we might withdraw our Polaris force
from the joint forces to counter the threat from Khruschev.   That was the sort of
way - this was only an illustration - in which we might wish
to use our Polaris submarines independently.

The <u>Foreign Secretary</u> thought it was worth emphasising
three aspects of the Nassau Agreement:-

(a) We had been able to secure for the purpose of following
a strong and firm U.K. foreign policy the best system of an
independent national deterrent.   This might have a long life,
some 15 years or so, and was a guaranteed effective second
strike system;

(b) It was our own weapon and we would have independent control
over it;

(c) Our undertaking to assign some of our V-bomber force to
SACEUR might act to stop further discussion on M.R.B.M.s for
NATO.

The most difficult point of the Nassau Agreement lay in the
multilateral or multi-national concept.   It was doubtful
whether this could ever work out satisfactorily since there

30/

was not likely to be any strong credibility of political control.

The Minister of Defence added that there was no doubt that militarily the effectiveness of any system of imposing a deterrent lay in the second strike capacity. It was this which made Polaris such an outstanding weapon.

The Lord Privy Seal said that the Skybolt episode had brought before the public in a very clear manner the extent of our dependence on the United States. The same difficulty would be felt to apply to Polaris and until we actually had the missiles in our possession we would be at the mercy of the United States Government. For example, if there were some strong disagreement on important policy issues they might threaten to cancel the contract. In commenting on this, the Minister of Defence noted that we would not be able to afford starting from scratch to develop a reinsurance system of imposing the deterrent.

In the discussion on the possible French reactions to the offer, the Foreign Secretary said that the French Ambassador in London had expressed the view that the General would turn the offer down because he would not wish the French forces to be armed with anything that was made somewhere other than France. Sir Pierson Dixon The Ambassador thought this was likely to be the position. The General would be holding a Press Conference on January 10 and it was quite likely that he would then publicly state a view on the attitude of the French Government to the American offer.

The General was likely to be guided by two considerations; how far the acceptance of the offer would forward his plans for

31

26. (cont.)

French hegemony in Europe, and to what extent the American offer could be turned to French interests or whether it was in fact a further attempt by the Americans to secure the leadership of Europe.

The French would not be able to make any contribution to SACEUR's nuclear force to match the V-bomber offer, but it was well-known that *de Gaulle* thought NATO was a fraud and useless so it was not likely that he would fall in with this idea even if the French bombs and bombers were ready.

It was quite likely that de Gaulle still believed that the French should appear to look forward to constructing independently their own missiles and nuclear warheads. To some extent the General might therefore be interested in acquiring know-how and he might also be interested in co-operating over manufacturing the warheads. But it was very unlikely indeed that the General would enter into any arrangement of this sort as part of a deal – he would not pay anything for such assistance or an offer of help.

The <u>Prime Minister</u> commented that it was quite possible that de Gaulle did not realise all the complexities and complications of modern weapons and especially the great structure that lay beneath the successful deployment of the Polaris system with all the controls, communications etc. Moreover, the latest developments in the field of anti-ballistic missiles made the manufacture of an offensive warhead a very difficult and complicated business. It would be very helpful if the French sent a delegation, perhaps including M. Mesmer, to this country to have a talk about the technicalities.

The <u>Minister of Defence</u> thought it might help to point out to de Gaulle that the idea of putting some of our V-bombers into NATO was a British suggestion.   It was consistent with the French concept of the important powers really running NATO.   The <u>Foreign Secretary</u> added that a further advantage of this idea lay in its obscuring the true multilateral doctrine.   This cannot but please the French.

The <u>Prime Minister</u> thought it seemed likely that de Gaulle would turn the American offer down but hoped it would be possible to persuade him, were he to do so, to do it without contempt.   And not on the grounds that the American offer would not result in the French having an independent system but rather that France intended, should she wish to have such a system, to manufacture it herself.

At the end of the meeting the Minister of Defence and Lord Hood prepared a number of questions and answers which the Ambassador might use in talking to the French.   Copies of these have already been sent under separate cover to the Minister of Defence and Lord Hood and the Ambassador took the top copy with him to Paris.

J.B
·1·/63

Copies sent to
Lord Hood (FO)
M. Hockaday (Defence)
M. Samuel FO. 1/1

33/

The minutes of the meeting, far fuller than those normally produced for Cabinet or Cabinet committee discussions, contain an insight not only into Macmillan's worries about the deal, but also into what he envisaged as the kind of circumstances that might trigger the 'supreme national interests' clause of the Nassau Agreement. The Ambassador to Paris, Sir Pierson Dixon, accurately forecast de Gaulle's reaction to Kennedy's offer, prompting a rather patronising aside from Macmillan about de Gaulle's probably failing to realise the complexities that lay behind a sophisticated weapons system like Polaris.

In terms of the future politics of Polaris, it's noteworthy that Macmillan was already aware that 'the latest developments in the field of anti-ballistic missiles made the manufacture of an offensive warhead a very difficult and complicated business.' Of special interest, too, is the view strongly expressed by Ted Heath (who, as Lord Privy Seal, was the lead minister in Britain's negotiations for entry into the EEC),

> that the Skybolt episode had brought before the public in a very clear manner the extent of our dependence on the United States. The same difficulty would be felt to apply to Polaris and until we actually had the missiles in our possession we would be at the mercy of the United States Government.

This stressing of Britain's nuclear dependence was very similar to the line Harold Wilson would take as Leader of the Opposition to the Nassau Agreement (as we shall see).

Two days later, Dixon despatched from Paris a very timely leak of a telegram from Herve Alphand, the French Ambassador in Washington, about his conversations with Kennedy about the nature of the deals on offer to de Gaulle and Macmillan. Kennedy cited Suez 1956 and the threatened Iraqi invasion of Kuwait in 1961 as the kind of episodes where Soviet threats to the UK (or France and the UK in the Suez case) might activate the 'supreme national interests' formula. On 3 January, Macmillan's Foreign Affairs Private Secretary, Philip de Zulueta, alerted Macmillan to the importance of Dixon's telegram.

27. Telegram from Sir Pierson Dixon in Paris to the Foreign Office, 2 January 1963.

TNA, PRO, PREM 11/4147

Prime Minister
This is an important
Telegram.

SECRET

FROM PARIS TO FOREIGN OFFICE

Cypher/OTP

FOREIGN OFFICE (SECRET) AND
WHITEHALL (SECRET) DISTRIBUTION

Sir P. Dixon

No.3   D.7.39 p.m. January 2,1963
January 2,1963   R.7.54 p.m. January 2,1963

SECRET

Addressed to Foreign Office telegram No.3 of January 2.
Repeated for information to: Washington
                and Saving to: Bonn   UKDEL N.A.T.O.

Nassau Agreement.

The Directeur des Pactes (de la Grandville) at the Quai
d'Orsay showed the Head of Chancery today in strict confidence
a telegram from M. Alphand, reporting a long "tete-à-tete"
conversation about the Nassau Agreement which he had had with
President Kennedy on board his yacht on December 29.   The
following are the main points.

2.   The President had emphasized that the main purpose of his
initiative was to help Britain and France to develop effective
atomic forces which would be available for the defence of the
Western Alliance as a whole, but which could also be used
individually in case British or French "intérets superieurs"
were threatened.   The President also hoped in this way to find
a formula which would discourage the other N.A.T.O. Powers
from seeking to create their own national nuclear forces.   From
his point of view the Nassau offer was an "opening", a kind
of framework which he sincerely hoped that the French Government
would now be prepared to examine carefully and discuss.

3.   The President confirmed that the right of Britain or France
unilaterally to decide to use their Polaris forces in the event
that their supreme national interests were at stake should be
assured without equivocation.   Thus the crews of their submarines
would be composed entirely of British and French nationals,
and the submarines would be capable of acting independently without
recourse to "foreign radio-electronic systems".   (On the latter
point the President emphatically denied a recent report from
the Times correspondent in Washington which implied that the
Polaris submarines would, in practice, have to be subject to
United States communication controls).   The President then
cited Suez or Kuwait as examples of how the "supreme interests"
formula might be invoked.   If some action on the part of the

/British

SECRET 34

27. (cont.)

Paris telegram No.3 to Foreign Office.

-2-

British or the French, not directly affecting the United States,
led to the Russians threatening either country with missiles, they
would be in a position to decide to use their own Polaris
missiles against, say, Moscow or Kiev.

4. British or French acceptance of the Polaris system would
in no way limit their right to develop other nuclear systems
which would not, therefore, come within the Nassau Agreement;
but they would find it extremely costly to develop and maintain
two effective long-term nuclear systems.

5. The conditions for operating a multilateral force, whether
on an Atlantic or a European basis, would have to be worked out.
There were difficult questions relating to command and the
modalities for taking decisions. But the President considered
it very important to calm the suspicions of the other N.A.T.O.
Powers, in particular Germany, and to give them the feeling that
there would be a nuclear force at their disposal and a European
finger on its use. He believed that if the three nuclear powers
could put forward some proposal on the lines of the Nassau
Agreement, this could help considerably in preventing the proliferation
of nuclear weapons.

6. The President recognized that France's situation was not the
same as Britain's. While the French had maintained their complete independence, they were less advanced than the British.
It was difficult to say at this stage whether, and when, French
industry would be able to make the thermo-nuclear warheads and
to adapt them to Polaris missiles and to the submarines which
would carry them.

7. The President had ended the conversation with a final plea
that the French Government should not take up a definite position
before there had been a thorough discussion of the American offer
and before its implications, strategic, political and financial,
had been fully considered.

8. In concluding his telegram, M. Alphand estimated that there
was now a possibility that United States policy, which had hitherto
been negative as regards nuclear cooperation with the French,
would develop in a more positive way.

 Foreign Office please pass to Washington 1 and Saving to Bonn 2.

[Repeated as requested]

VVVVV   SECRET

That evening (3 January 1963), Macmillan led a discussion within the full Cabinet of the Nassau deal. He kept the anxieties he had expressed in his Boxing Day minute and his New Year's Eve meeting away from his colleagues. Instead, he embedded the detail of the negotiation in a grand sweep of British nuclear history and a philosophical disquisition on the mutation of nuclear independence into interdependence.

SECRET

THIS DOCUMENT IS THE PROPERTY OF HER BRITANNIC MAJESTY'S GOVERNMENT

Printed for the Cabinet.   January 1963

C.C. (63)

2nd Conclusions

Copy No. **37**

CABINET

CONCLUSIONS of a Meeting of the Cabinet held at Admiralty House, S.W.1, on Thursday, 3rd January, 1963, at 5 p.m.

Present:

The Right Hon. HAROLD MACMILLAN, M.P., Prime Minister

The Right Hon. THE EARL OF HOME, Secretary of State for Foreign Affairs	The Right Hon. VISCOUNT HAILSHAM, Q.C., Lord President of the Council and Minister for Science
The Right Hon. LORD DILHORNE, Lord Chancellor	The Right Hon. REGINALD MAUDLING, M.P., Chancellor of the Exchequer
The Right Hon. IAIN MACLEOD, M.P., Chancellor of the Duchy of Lancaster	The Right Hon. PETER THORNEYCROFT, M.P., Minister of Defence
The Right Hon. JOHN HARE, M.P., Minister of Labour	The Right Hon. EDWARD HEATH, M.P., Lord Privy Seal
The Right Hon. ERNEST MARPLES, M.P., Minister of Transport	The Right Hon. JOHN BOYD-CARPENTER, M.P., Chief Secretary to the Treasury and Paymaster General
The Right Hon. MICHAEL NOBLE, M.P., Secretary of State for Scotland	The Right Hon. J. ENOCH POWELL, M.P., Minister of Health
The Right Hon. Sir EDWARD BOYLE, M.P., Minister of Education	The Right Hon. WILLIAM DEEDES, M.P., Minister without Portfolio

The following were also present:

The Right Hon. LORD CARRINGTON, First Lord of the Admiralty (*Item 1*)	The Right Hon. JOHN PROFUMO, M.P., Secretary of State for War (*Item 1*)
The Right Hon. JULIAN AMERY, M.P., Minister of Aviation (*Item 1*)	The Right Hon. HUGH FRASER, M.P., Secretary of State for Air (*Item 1*)
THE MARQUESS OF LANSDOWNE, Minister of State for Colonial Affairs	The Right Hon. MARTIN REDMAYNE, M.P., Parliamentary Secretary, Treasury

Secretariat:

Sir BURKE TREND

Mr. J. H. WADDELL

Mr. N. J. ABERCROMBIE

2180—2

SECRET

A

Bahamas Meeting, December 1962
(Previous Reference: C.C. (62) 76th Conclusions)

*1. *The Prime Minister* said that a current appraisal of the outcome of his discussions with the President of the United States in Nassau in December must be related to the international situation as a whole. There were some grounds for supposing that the prospect of a *détente* in relations between the West and the Soviet Union might be improving. The Soviet Government were momentarily less confident of their standing in the world, more preoccupied with domestic difficulties and more seriously disturbed by their theoretical dispute with the Chinese Communists than at any time in the last few years. Among the Communist Satellite countries the beginnings of independence in Poland and the growing weakness of Eastern Germany were additional factors making for a greater measure of flexibility in the foreign relations of the *bloc*. On the other hand, the Western Alliance was itself showing signs of strain. The intransigence of Germany and the unilateral character of French policy were considerable obstacles in the way of progress towards international agreement on disarmament and on Berlin. As a result there were symptoms of growing impatience and anxiety on the part of the United States Government, who felt that they were being asked to shoulder a heavy burden of responsibility and expenditure, while lacking any effective control over the policies of the alliance as a whole. It was against this background that the Nassau discussions had to be considered.

Those discussions, in which he had been joined by the Foreign Secretary, the Commonwealth Secretary and the Minister of Defence, had covered a wide range of topics; but they had necessarily concentrated mainly on the issues arising from the decision of the United States Government to abandon development of the airborne ballistic missile SKYBOLT for their own forces. Some sections of public opinion in the United Kingdom were disposed to take the view that this decision was intended to compel us finally to surrender any independent strategic nuclear capability. This was one indication of the current strains in the Western Alliance. The present United States Administration included hardly any of the men who had been associated with this country in the Second World War; and many of President Kennedy's advisers were inclined to indulge an inflated conception of the material power at the disposal of their Government. The natural reaction of the other members of the alliance, which was perhaps particularly evident in this country, was apt to take the form of suspicion of United States motives and policies. Nevertheless, it was certain that the decision to discontinue development of SKYBOLT was genuinely based on the fact that the United States Government had available, in POLARIS and MINUTEMAN, alternative deterrent systems of proved reliability, which made it unnecessary for them to continue a very expensive programme offering no certain prospect of a real improvement in the defence of the hemisphere. But the Administration would find it difficult to explain and defend the decision to their own people: it would entail writing off a large sum of past investment and it had already aroused the hostility of the powerful interests, both military and industrial, which had been engaged in the project. It was wholly unrealistic to suppose that the United States Government would expose themselves to immediate political risks of this order merely for the purpose of depriving the United Kingdom Government of an independent nuclear capability several years hence; and public opinion in this country must be convinced of the falsity of such a hypothesis.

President Kennedy had first suggested that the United States and the United Kingdom should share, on a basis of equality, the cost of continuing the development of the weapon and that we should

---

* Previously recorded in a Confidential Annex.

SECRET

thereafter place such production orders as we saw fit. But from our own point of view this would have been an open-ended commitment; and we should have found it difficult to exercise effective control over development carried out in the United States. He had no doubt that it would have been wrong to accept this proposal.

Before considering alternative deterrent systems, however, he had felt bound to consider once again whether it was right for this country to seek to continue to make an independent contribution to the Western strategic nuclear deterrent. The nuclear weapon had been invented originally by British scientists and we had made considerable progress, both before and after the amendment of the McMahon Act, in its development. But the gradual introduction of Soviet defence systems posed new problems; and the elaboration of modern systems of guidance and delivery implied that the development of an effective deterrent would become progressively more sophisticated and expensive. There was, therefore, little attraction in a policy of complete independence in this respect. Nevertheless, there were several compelling reasons for seeking to preserve a measure of independence as regards control over our nuclear deterrent.

In the first place, the Western Alliance would cease to be a free association if the whole of its advanced scientific and technological capacity in this respect were vested in one member. Second, we ought to ensure that we should always be able to react appropriately to a Soviet nuclear threat to this country, even if the United States, for whatever reason, were disinclined to support us. Third, a Soviet nuclear threat, to which there was no United Kingdom counter-threat, would render all our conventional forces ineffectual. Finally, if this country abandoned the attempt to maintain an independent nuclear deterrent, it would be unable to exercise any effective influence in the attempts, which would eventually have to be made, to achieve some international agreement to limit nuclear armaments. For all these reasons he and his colleagues had been convinced that the policy of a United Kingdom strategic nuclear deterrent capability should be continued; and they had welcomed the Cabinet's endorsement of this view.

He had therefore decided to press the United States Government to supply us with the seaborne ballistic missile POLARIS, instead of SKYBOLT. This weapon, which had a high degree of indestructibility, could be used in a second strike role and was independent of fixed installations on land, was particularly well suited to our requirements. The United States Government, however, regarded POLARIS as different in kind from SKYBOLT, particularly as it would extent the effectiveness and credibility of the United Kingdom deterrent for an almost indefinite period in the future. Moreover, they were anxious to find some means of sharing with the rest of the Western Alliance some of the responsibility involved in the possession of such weapons and therefore attached considerable importance to their being placed under some form of multilateral control. This concept was not wholly realistic since, even if it contributed to dissuading Germany from attempting to develop a nuclear capability, it was unlikely to be acceptable to the present French Government. Nevertheless, it was necessary to go some way towards meeting the United States stipulation that the United Kingdom must agree to commit POLARIS in some way to the alliance as a condition of United States agreement to supply the weapon. The Prime Minister had insisted, however, that any such arrangement must correspond to the basis on which our forces had been contributed to the Allied Command in France at the beginning of the Second World War, *i.e.*, with the explicit provision that they would remain subject to the ultimate authority of Her Majesty's Ministers in the United Kingdom and could be withdrawn in the last resort if the supreme interests of the country required it. This proposal was eventually accepted by the United States Government

SECRET

and was incorporated in the joint statement issued at the end of the conference. It would be criticised in this country from two opposing points of view, both as derogating from the concept of a wholly independent national deterrent and as falling short of complete integration with the rest of the alliance. In fact, however, it represented a realistic compromise, in present circumstances, between independence and interdependence; and if, as might well be the case, the development of a multilateral system proved impossible, our own situation would be unchanged, except in so far as we should have acquired, in POLARIS, a more effective weapon than SKYBOLT.

In discussion the Cabinet endorsed the Nassau Agreement and congratulated the Prime Minister and his colleagues on the successful outcome of the discussions. The following main points were made:

(a) There was no reason to suppose that the United States Government would not honour their undertaking to supply us with POLARIS weapons; and no real possibility of insuring against this improbable risk. But it would be desirable, if possible, to secure an earnest of fulfilment in the shape of actual weapons or detailed designs, if necessary by some measure of advance payment. Such an arrangement could be examined in the course of technical discussions between the Royal Navy and the United States Navy which were due to start in a few days' time.

(b) The elimination of SKYBOLT implied that from about 1965 until the availability of POLARIS-firing submarines between 1968 and 1970 the deterrent power of our nuclear forces would no longer be as effective, and therefore as credible, as we had previously assumed. The introduction of the TSR-2 aircraft during this period would help to remedy this deficiency; and other steps might be taken to improve the performance of Bomber Command aircraft and their weapons.

(c) The introduction of the POLARIS weapon implied heavy additional expenditure in the latter part of the present decade. This would inevitably involve even more drastic curtailment of other defence expenditure than had previously been contemplated, if defence was not to absorb an excessive share of national resources.

(d) It would be necessary to consider carefully the exact wording of any written undertaking to commit our POLARIS weapons to a multilateral force. For the same reason we should avoid any precise definition of the circumstances in which the supreme national interest might require us to withdraw them.

(e) Although French policy might make it unrealistic to suppose that any considerable progress towards an effective multilateral force could be realised in the near future, the industrial and technological resources of Europe were sufficiently powerful to allow us to assume that the concept might ultimately be practicable. Its implications deserved further study.

The Cabinet—

(1) Took note, with approval, of the arrangements recorded in the joint statement of 21st December, 1962, by the Prime Minister and the President of the United States, on Nuclear Defence Systems.

(2) Invited the Minister of Defence to examine, as a matter of urgency, further measures to improve the effectiveness of United Kingdom nuclear forces between 1965 and 1970.

(3) Invited the Minister of Defence to arrange to explore the possibility of obtaining POLARIS weapons or designs from the United States Government in return for advance payment.

Macmillan had a penchant for using history to ease his Cabinet through a policy shift, and the meeting in Admiralty House that Thursday evening in January 1963 was a classic example. The history was not always entirely accurate. Even allowing fully for the enormous contribution of Frisch and Peierls and the path to a bomb mapped out by the Maud Committee, it was a touch stark to declare that the 'nuclear weapon had been invented originally by British scientists.' Turning the concept, the physics and the mathematics into a bomb required engineering skills of a high order which it took the US-dominated Manhattan Project to provide. It was, however, absolutely true that UK scientists and engineers 'had made considerable progress' in the years when collaboration was cut off. The slide from independence to interdependence was well managed, no doubt delivered in that slightly world-weary and regretful tone that Macmillan often adopted:

> But the gradual introduction of Soviet defence systems posed new problems; and the elaboration of modern systems of guidance and delivery implied that the development of an effective deterrent would become progressively more sophisticated and expensive. There was, therefore, little attraction in a policy of complete independence in this respect. Nevertheless, there were several compelling reasons for seeking to preserve a measure of independence as regards control over our nuclear deterrent.

The chief reasons for carrying on?

1. US monopoly (though France not mentioned here) undesirable with NATO.
2. UK must have a deterrent defence if home base threatened and the US 'were disinclined to support us.'
3. If Russia threatened a nuclear-free UK, conventional defence would be 'ineffectual'.
4. Without a bomb, UK would be without real influence in future arms limitation talks.

The minutes indicate no flurry of dissent as there had been in Churchill's H-bomb Cabinet of 8 July 1954.

Other points worth noting include the UK's dislike of any kind of proposed multilateral NATO nuclear force as a means of dissuading West Germany to seek a capability of its own. The Cabinet was also told of a likely period between 1965 and 1970 when the deterrent would weaken as the V-bombers became less effective and the Polaris submarines were constructed (the TSR-2 aircraft, intended partly to fill this gap, was cancelled by the incoming Labour government).

Point (a) of the discussion induced an intriguing sentence:

> There was no reason to suppose that the United States Government would not honour their undertaking to supply us with POLARIS weapons [no hint of Macmillan's anxieties here]; and no real possibility of insuring against this improbable risk.

This last point was fleshed-out in detail later that month by the report which went to Macmillan and his inner group of Polaris-related ministers (not to the full Cabinet).

S E C R E T

MINISTER OF DEFENCE   See IRBMs - PG.S.

In his minute to you of December 26th the Prime Minister asked whether "If we were driven into a corner we could, either as a bluff or as a reality, make a POLARIS missile, perhaps of a simpler kind, ourselves from our own designs; how long it would take etc?".

You will remember that I advised you at the briefing meeting before you went to Nassau that it was within our capability to develop a British sea-launched or air-launched ballistic missile within about ten years and at a cost which would be comparable to other weapon systems on which we are engaged. I gave the same advice to our colleagues at the Cabinet meetings of December 21st (CC(62)76th Mtg.) and January 3rd (CC(63) 2nd Mtg.). I have now had the deterrent systems which we might develop studied as carefully as has been possible in the time. I attach a note giving details.

There are four possible systems which we could develop on our own. These are:-

1.   An air-launched ballistic missile

This would be similar to SKYBOLT. It would have a simpler guidance system, involving limitations on the routing of the aircraft, but the re-entry vehicle could contain penetration aids. It would take eight or nine years to develop and would cost about £175 million.

2.   A sea-launched ballistic missile

This would be similar in most respects to the POLARIS A2, but penetration aids could be included in it. This would take about ten years to develop and would cost not less than £200 million.

3.   An air-launched cruise type weapon

This would take about eight years to develop and would cost about £125 million.

4.   Two versions (a short range and a longer range) of a land based ballistic missile

These would be derived from the BLACK KNIGHT. The shorter range version would take 7 or 8 years to develop and would cost about £80 million. The longer range version would take 9 or 10 years and would cost about £120 million.

/The

29. (cont.)

The air and sea launched ballistic missiles would constitute a fully valid deterrent according to the criteria laid down by the BNDSC. The air-launched cruise type weapon would be rather short in range and to some degree vulnerable to interception. The land based ballistic missiles would be vulnerable to pre-emptive attack, though less so perhaps than has sometimes been stated.

The calculations with regard to the feasibility, timescale and cost of these projects have been carried out by scientists in our Establishments in collaboration with the Headquarters of the Ministry. They thus contain a substantial margin for contingency. To give fully considered estimates, however, it would be necessary to make project studies with industry. Short of undertaking such studies I think these calculations are as accurate as any that can be made in the time.

In the case of the air launched cruise type weapon and the land based missiles, the calculations can claim a considerable degree of accuracy. Where the former is concerned we have the experience of full feasibility studies made against the QR.1182 and of developing Blue Steel. Where the latter are concerned, we have several years practical experience of using and firing BLACK KNIGHT and of developing BLUE STREAK as a weapon.

The calculations of the air launched ballistic missile should also be reasonably accurate given our detailed monitoring, over nearly three years, of the SKYBOLT project in the United States.

Our experience in the case of submarine launched missiles is much more limited and the margin or error in our calculations on this score must accordingly be larger. As a cross check on our submarine launched missile, however, it may be relevant to note the French say that it will cost them about £300 million to produce a POLARIS-type missile by 1970. It would seem natural, given our greater experience in these matters, that it would cost us rather less than it would cost them.

To undertake research and development on one of these systems would naturally impose some strain on our resources, particularly intramural ones. So far as concerns extramural resources, the teams which have worked on BLOODHOUND, THUNDERBIRD, RED TOP, BLUE STEEL, AND BLUE WATER, have already or are soon to become spare. I do not think, therefore, that we would have any great difficulty in accommodating such a project as far as industry is concerned. Some intra-mural activities might have to be sacrificed, but I am assured that we could find the necessary intra-mural staff. There would be no question of any serious disruption of the existing programme though we might have to defer an early start on, for example, the third generation S.A.C.W.

42

/From

From the point of view of this Ministry, I would
naturally have preferred that we should have decided to
develop our own weapon rather than buy American.
This would have lessened the complaints of our guided
weapons industry faced as it is with the prospect of
redundancy. It would also have assured us of control
of the production of our deterrent system and so fully
guaranteed its independence. Most important of all
it would have given us the technological base from
which to develop the new weapons systems which will
no doubt be needed as and when the POLARIS becomes
obsolete. But of course we must now explore the
possibilities of the NASSAU arrangements and I recognise
that at the moment a British project is not in question.
There is, however, always the danger that for one reason
or another the POLARIS may still be denied to us.
Against this eventuality it seems important to be
clear in our own minds what we could do if we should
in the Prime Minister's words "be driven into a corner".

I think our colleagues on the Defence Committee
ought to know the position, but you may feel that these
calculations should first be examined by your people in
conjunction with mine.

I am copying this minute to the recipients of the
Prime Minister's minute of 26th December.

15th January, 1963.

29. (cont.)

MINISTER OF AVIATION

flag X

    I have carefully considered your minute
of 15th January about British alternatives to
Polaris. Clearly a lot of work has gone into
the preparation of these proposals, and they
would provide a useful starting point for more
detailed study should we have to face a go-it-
alone situation.

2.   I entirely agree with you, however, that
we cannot consider a British project at this
point in time, nor do I think that we should
carry out now the further studies in
consultation with industry that would be
needed to evaluate the merits and obstacles
in the alternatives that you pose. I would
prefer to leave these proposals on the record,
at least until we are clear how the Polaris
plan is likely to work out.

3.   I am sending copies of this minute to the
Prime Minister, the First Lord and the
Secretary of State for Air.

PETER THORNEYCROFT

28th January, 1963.

44

Macmillan was right in the Cabinet discussion of 3 January 1963 to anticipate that what he called his 'compromise ... between independence and interdependence' would be criticised as 'derogating from the concept of a wholly independent national deterrent and as falling short of complete integration with the rest of the alliance'.

This was very much Harold Wilson's line after he became Leader of the Labour Party following the death of Hugh Gaitskell on 18 January 1963. It was enshrined in Labour's manifesto for the October 1964 general election. Under the heading 'Tory nuclear pretence', Labour's *The New Britain* claimed:

> The Nassau agreement to buy Polaris know-how and Polaris missiles from the USA will add nothing to the deterrent strength of the western alliance, and it will mean utter dependence on the US for their supply. Nor is it true that all this costly defence expenditure will produce an 'independent British deterrent'. It will not be independent and it will not be British and it will not deter. Its possession will impress neither friend nor potential foe.
>
> Moreover, Britain's insistence on this nuclear pretence carries with it grave dangers of encouraging the spread of nuclear weapons to countries not possessing them, including Germany.
>
> The Government bases its policy on the assumption that Britain must be prepared to go it alone without her allies in an all-out thermo-nuclear war with the Soviet Union, involving the obliteration of our people. By constantly reiterating this appalling assumption the Government is undermining the alliance on which our security now depends.[81]

The manifesto went on to pledge that: 'We shall propose the re-negotiation of the Nassau agreement.'[82]

'The Government' at this stage was headed by Sir Alec Douglas-Home. Many years later, he told me he never expected Wilson, despite that pledge, would abandon Polaris:

> I had always found, in dealing with Harold Wilson on security matters, that he was reliable in terms of the national interest. And so in spite of the manifesto, in spite of what he said during the election campaign, I didn't think he'd be able to bring himself to cancel it when he understood the facts. There are quite a lot of facts the leader of the opposition doesn't have. When he got into government I thought he would carry on the programme, so it didn't worry me unduly.[83]

In 1995, after Home's death, a file reached The National Archives that helped explain his lack of worry about the durability of Polaris under Labour. It was a note in the Downing Street papers of the Douglas-Home premiership of a confidential meeting the Shadow Defence Secretary, Denis Healey, had had with the real Defence Secretary, Peter Thorneycroft, on 3 February 1964. Healey tried out on Thorneycroft the idea of pooling the British Polaris submarines with US ones as a NATO-assigned Atlantic Nuclear Force.[84]

Less than a month after winning the 1964 general election with the slimmest of majorities, Wilson convened an ad hoc Cabinet committee, MISC 16, under the title 'Atlantic Nuclear Force'. It was the smallest Cabinet committee in the history of UK nuclear policy-making so far, consisting of Wilson, his Foreign Secretary, Patrick Gordon Walker and his Defence Secretary, Healey.

72

TOP SECRET

Copy No............. 8

MISC. 16/1st Meeting

CABINET

ATLANTIC NUCLEAR FORCE

MEETING of Ministers held at
10, Downing Street, S.W.1., on
WEDNESDAY, 11th NOVEMBER 1964 at 12 Noon

PRESENT:

The Rt. Hon. Harold Wilson, M.P.,
Prime Minister

The Rt. Hon.   The Rt. Hon.
  Patrick Gordon Walker,   Denis Healey, M.P.,
  Secretary of State for   Secretary of State
  Foreign Affairs   for Defence

SECRETARIAT:

Sir Burke Trend
Mr. P. Rogers

SUBJECT:

ATLANTIC NUCLEAR FORCE

TOP SECRET

ATLANTIC NUCLEAR FORCE

The Meeting had before them a minute by the Secretary of the Cabinet covering a paper by officials (MISC.11/2 (Final)) which examined proposals for an Atlantic Nuclear Force.

In discussion there was general agreement that the proposals outlined in the paper presented a possible basis for discussions, in the first instance with the United States and German Governments and subsequently with other North Atlantic Treaty Organisation (NATO) powers. The proposals should not be considered as an alternative to the various schemes for a multilateral force (M.L.F.) which were currently under discussion. They should rather be considered as proposals which should lead to a reconstruction of the Alliance in accordance with present strategic and political requirements.

In initiating such proposals, the United Kingdom Government might in the first instance offer to make available to the proposed Force planned or existing United Kingdom nuclear forces, which would be juridically committed but without any form of physical restraint through a permissive link or electronic lock. However such a device, which might be produced by the United States Government in another year or so, could in any event be circumvented and its acceptance in subsequent negotiation would not mean that we could not regain independent control of our nuclear forces should, for example, the NATO Alliance dissolve. It should also be our initial position that we would not participate in any mixed-manned force. In negotiation however we might envisage the commitment of our nuclear forces under some form of physical veto through an electronic lock together with some form of participation in a mixed-manned force on a substantially smaller scale than anything which had so far been proposed in the present discussions on the M.L.F.

The nuclear forces which we might offer to commit in accordance with these proposals would be a part of the V-bomber force (the remainder being retained under United Kingdom control solely for use in a conventional role outside the NATO area) together with three POLARIS submarines. The three submarines would represent the minimum force which would be acceptable to us in the event of the dissolution of the NATO Alliance. It should also be borne in mind that even five POLARIS submarines would not represent a nuclear force adequate for a world-wide role, but would only meet the requirements of the European theatre. The provision of three submarines alone would not make it possible to guarantee that there would always be one United Kingdom submarine on station, but since it would be a part of the agreement that an equivalent number of United States submarines would be committed to the Force, sufficient coverage would be provided. Our own three submarines, which would cost some £6-700 million over a period of some ten years for capital cost and maintenance, would represent the commitment of forty eight POLARIS missiles to the Atlantic nuclear force or 25 per cent of the M.L.F. at present under discussion. Quite apart, therefore, from the force represented by the assignment of some of our V-bombers, this would involve a greater participation in the force than we were at present being asked to undertake. In considering the justification for

-1-

30. (cont.)

United Kingdom POLARIS submarines it should be borne in mind that their acquisition would, after the end of service of the V-bomber Force, be our only means of access to United States technology in the field of nuclear missiles.

In return for a commitment of this order we should seek substantial concessions. As a preliminary there should be a clear statement by the United States Government that they would in no circumstances be willing to abandon their veto on the use of nuclear weapons committed to the Force. Such a veto would be guaranteed by the presence of a United States contingent in the mixed-manned component of the Force better than by any permissive link which might be devised. The major concessions should include a revision of NATO strategy to accord with existing strategic needs. This might release a substantial number of our forces at present committed to Europe. We should also seek agreement to a renewed approach to the Soviet Union on a measure of disarmament in Europe. This would not be a matter of disengagement by the United States or United Kingdom, but would involve a thinning out of conventional forces which might under these proposals be more acceptable to the German Government than hitherto, since it would be accompanied by their participation in the control of nuclear forces and they might accept this as giving them greater security. Any measure of disarmament in Europe would have to be subject to verification, but this might not represent such a serious technical or political problem as measures which involved physical verification on Soviet territory itself. Finally we should seek a greater participation by NATO powers, including guarantees by the United States Government, in fulfilment of our commitments outside NATO, since these were in the general Western interest. In pursuing these discussions, regard must be had to the attitude of the French Government and to that end it would be advantageous if an early announcement could be made that the Prime Minister would be willing to visit France for discussions with General de Gaulle early in 1965.

The Meeting then discussed other issues which should be studied at the forthcoming Ministerial meeting at Chequers on 21st November.

The Meeting was informed that the official studies which would then be available to Ministers would, in addition to the paper before the Meeting, include a study of the burden on the United Kingdom economy imposed by defence expenditure, a study of our major regional defence commitments and a paper listing the areas in which functional economies might be sought in defence expenditure. It was suggested that the latter might include a study of the possibilities of combined defence production with the United States and that the views of the Chief Scientific Adviser on this should be available to the Chequers Meeting. It would also be helpful if the Minister of Aviation could participate in discussion of this aspect. It would be necessary in this connection for the Ministry of Defence to study further, after the Chequers Meeting, the type of equipment likely to be required for the kind of war which might have to be fought outside the NATO area.

–2–

75
END

The Meeting -

(1)   Invited the Foreign Secretary to be guided by
       the views expressed in MISC. 11/2 (Final), and
       by the points that had emerged in discussion,
       in his forthcoming talks with the German
       Foreign Minister, Herr Schröder

(2)   Agreed to give further consideration to these
       issues at the forthcoming discussion at
       Chequers.

(3)   Took note that the Prime Minister would arrange
       for the Minister of Aviation to participate
       in that discussion.

(4)   Invited the Foreign Secretary to indicate the
       topics which were likely to be covered at the
       subsequent discussions with the President of
       the United States on the occasion of the
       Prime Minister's visit.

(5)   Took note that the Prime Minister would arrange
       for consideration to be given to the
       possibility of an early announcement of his
       willingness to visit France early in 1965 for
       discussions with General de Gaulle.

(6)   Instructed the Secretaries to consult the
       Chief Scientific Adviser on the possibilities
       of economies in defence expenditure through
       the sharing of production with the United
       States.

Cabinet Office, S.W.1.

11th November, 1964.

-3-

Denis Healey later explained to me the thoughts that lay behind the meeting of MISC 16 in No. 10 on Armistice Day 1964 which decided to continue with the Polaris programme:

> The basic reason was that the deal which Macmillan had got out of Kennedy was a very good one. It was a very cheap system for the capability it offered. We'd already got one boat nearly complete and another was on the stocks. So the saving from cancellation would have been minimal, and given the uncertainties—the Cuban missile crisis was only a year or two behind us, the memory of Hungary [1956] was still in our minds, Khrushchev had been deposed the day before the British poll, the Chinese had just exploded their bomb the same day—we felt, on the whole, it was wise to continue with it.[85]

The minutes of MISC 16 avoid using the 'supreme national interests' phrase negotiated by Macmillan at Nassau. But the notion is there is a different guise:

> The three [Polaris] submarines would represent the minimum force which would be acceptable to us in the event of the dissolution of the NATO alliance.

Another point was somewhat at variance with the impression left by the manifesto pledge.

> In considering the justification for United Kingdom POLARIS submarines it should be borne in mind that their acquisition would, after the end of service of the V-bomber Force, be our only means of access to United States technology in the field of nuclear missiles.

This was a theme Harold Wilson himself stressed in a radio interview with me in 1985 which, in its way, echoed some of the 1954 arguments for keeping in the nuclear weapons business as a means of restraining the USA. 'I never believed,' Wilson said,

> we had a really independent deterrent. On the other hand, I didn't want to be in the position of having to subordinate ourselves to the Americans when they, at a certain point, would say 'We're going to use it,' or something of that kind—though in fact, I doubt if anyone expected it ever to be used. It wasn't that we wanted to get into a nuclear club, or anything of that kind. We wanted to learn a lot about the nuclear thing, and so on. We might need to restrain the Americans, if we learnt about new things that could happen of a devastating character.[86]

Two factors now confronted Wilson and his inner nuclear duo: how to sell the continuation of Polaris to a wider group of ministers and, eventually, the full Cabinet; plus how big should the UK Polaris force be—three, four or five boats? Between Cabinet committee meetings, Healey was briefed by the Ministry of Defence's Chief Scientific Adviser, Sir Solly Zuckerman.

TOP SECRET. Copy No. 11 of 12 copies
Reference............SZ/.793/.64............ 28

SECRETARY OF STATE

I have read the papers which have been prepared in answer to your question about the size of the POLARIS programme, and have thought it worthwhile to restate some of the propositions which have come up, against the background of what I discern emerging as a general policy. To some extent what I say here supplements the short note I sent you on the M.L.F.:-

a. Unless we can decrease the size of our NATO burden, few, if any, resources now going into defence are likely to be liberated for use in other sectors of the economy.

b. A decrease in our NATO burden is dependent on the achievement of an understanding with the Russians -, as well as with our allies - which would permit of a "thinning-out" in Western Europe. I use the term "thinning-out" to comprehend such difficult matters as a reduction in forces, zonal de-nuclearisation, non-dissemination, etc. Needless to say, an understanding with the Russians is also vital to the peace of the world. In order to reach this goal, the West can afford to surrender more than a little without endangering its security.

c. If the implementation of an M.L.F. concept were to mean the development of new nuclear delivery systems (or platforms) either additional to those already in existence or to those planned and publicised, the Russians would be discouraged from agreeing to any part of a process of "thinning-out". The construction of surface POLARIS vessels would thus run counter to any pacific policy - unless each new surface vessel were counter-balanced by the withdrawal or destruction of a corresponding number of existing delivery systems (how one would equate different kinds of delivery systems is by no means easy to see).

d. We have to find some way of satisfying West German nuclear aspirations without exacerbating the arms race. Since nuclear weapons can be regarded as having a greater political than military significance, this might be done if the Germans were to be given a voice equal to our own in the control and command of the NATO nuclear armoury. The essential thing is to bring them into the share of the control. Manning of the weapons systems by which nuclear warheads would be delivered, given the state of deterrence were to break down, is of lesser importance. Our readiness to assign unreservedly to NATO our existing and planned nuclear forces and to share their control within NATO with the Germans could, therefore, be a most powerful political lever. Such an undertaking could help both, the Germans and the Americans out of the present impasse. It would, however, have little purpose for us unless it were made conditional on the Americans carrying the Germans with them in a genuine approach to the Russians to accelerate by whatever means possible the process of détente. It should prove a powerful enough lever, too, to extract from the Americans undertakings in the field of co-operative research, development and production, at least comparable with those which they have now arranged with the Germans.

• 18-75

TOP SECRET

/e.

31. (cont.)

    e.   We should argue against multi-national manning of
units which cannot be sub-divided physically. Were
the Western Alliance to fall asunder, the question
of physical possession of mixed-manned delivery
systems could become an acute menace to peace.

    f.   Our 'V' bomber force is far less impressive as a
lever through which we could exercise our influence
than is our potential fleet of POLARIS submarines.
Obviously political judgment rather than mathematical
calculation is going to decide just how big a lever
we need have in our hands. My own belief is that to
be meaningful as a political weapon our POLARIS fleet
should certainly not be effectively smaller than the
proposed French strategic long-range systems, and
should also be large enough to impress the Americans
that what we would be ready to "hand over" to NATO
was a force which assured a reasonable second strike
capability if operated on its own. In my view, this
means five and at the least four boats; three boats
would not provide an assured second strike capability.
It may be that the existence of other strike systems,
e.g. the T.S.R.2, could, however, be used to compensate
for any departure from the "ideal" figure of a five-
boat POLARIS force.

2.   In saying all this I do not question for one second the
further proposition that, whatever the size of the POLARIS fleet
we might offer to NATO, it would never be deployed except in
co-operation with at least a corresponding number of U.S. POLARIS
submarines. Nor is my argument for a POLARIS fleet of more than
three ships based on the concept that we need to assure ourselves
against the danger that NATO might one day dissolve, and that we
should make certain that we could withdraw for national use a
coherent force which could be shown to have a second strike
capability and which could be paraded as an independent nuclear
force. My argument is directed entirely to the question of what
would constitute a nuclear lever of sufficient size which we
could wield effectively for the political purposes of helping
arrest the disruption of NATO on the one hand, and contributing
to further progress in the lessening of East-West tension on the
other.

18th November, 1964.

Healey used Zuckerman's material in the brief he prepared for MISC 17, the Prime Minister's larger Cabinet committee on the wider defence review the new government was undertaking. The Atlantic Nuclear Force idea (which never materialised) was presented as a desirable alternative to the MLF [Multi Lateral Force] for a NATO, mixed-manned surface nuclear fleet which was under discussion in Washington and Brussels. Healey also mentions the size of the Polaris force the UK would need for itself if NATO broke up.

TOP SECRET   Copy No. ....28....

MISC. 17/7

20th November, 1964

ATLANTIC NUCLEAR FORCE

THE SIZE OF THE BRITISH POLARIS FORCE

Memorandum by the Ministry of Defence

1.   By contributing a British Polaris force to an Atlantic Nuclear Force (A.N.F.) we should hope to avoid having to contribute to the proposed mixed-manned surface-ship force and would seek easements in the wider field of our Defence burdens as a whole.

2.   Before considering the wider proposal for an A.N.F., it is necessary to decide whether our Polaris contribution should be five, four or three boats.

3.   This paper takes no account of the nuclear capacity of our planned forces other than the Polaris boats, especially that of the TSR-2 force. This force could well provide a useful complementary insurance to the Polaris force.

4.   The main considerations are –

    (a)   What number is required for an adequate contribution to an Atlantic Nuclear Force?

    (b)   What number is required for minimal nuclear deterrent which would revert to national control in the event of the break-up of the NATO Alliance?

    (c)   What number if any, additional to (a), do we need to retain under national control for long term purposes outside the NATO area?

Present Position

5.   Planning has hitherto been based on the construction of a total force of five boats. It has been publicly declared that this force will become operational during the period 1968 to 1970 and that under the Nassau Agreement, the five boats will be assigned to NATO. Construction has already begun on the four boats, although only the keels of the first two have yet been laid. No firm order has yet been given to the contractor for the fifth boat; but if the production cycle is not to be upset a decision must be given by January, 1965.

–1–

TOP SECRET

6.   Weapon and fire control equipment for five boats has
been ordered, together with a similar set of equipment for
the R.N. POLARIS School; and a part set of equipment has also
been ordered as a contingency reserve.   The first twenty
missiles are about to be ordered from the U.S.A.

7.   The estimated capital cost of the five boat force has been
assessed at £406 million; in addition, the 1964 Costings
assumed that there would be running costs of about
£25 million a year from 1970/71.

Basic Considerations

8.   Five Boats

(a)   A five-boat force will permit a minimum of
two boats (32 missiles) to be kept on station
at all times and allow a margin to cover
unforeseen accidents, delays in the refit
programme and, in the worst case, a loss
at sea.

(b)   The destructive capacity of 32 missiles is
comparable to that of the present V-bomber
force and would, in the early 1970's at
least, ensure the destruction of some
20 major Soviet cities.   The Joint Intelligence
Committee consider that this would, in Soviet eyes,
undoubtedly represent an unacceptable level of
damage – and thus a credible deterrent.

9.   Four Boats

(a)   With four boats it would be possible to guarantee
to keep only one boat (16 missiles) on station at
all times.   There would be periods (approximately
35 weeks in each year) when the number at sea could
be increased to two.   On the other hand, there
would also be periods of about 17 weeks in each
year when there was no second boat either at sea
or at short notice to fire.

(b)   A force of this size would allow some margin for
unforeseen contingencies – but not much.   Any
unscheduled delays in the refit programme, which
is in any case based on unproven calculations,
would increase the periods when only one boat
could be kept on station.

(c)   The estimated capital cost of a four boat force
would be £366 million; in addition, there would
be about £21 million a year running costs from
1970/71.   There would be some cancellation
charges in this country, and the United Kingdom/
United States sales agreement would have to be re-
negotiated to cover the lower requirement of seven
less missiles and one less weapon system (capital
cost of the weapon system, about £6 million).

-2-

TOP SECRET

32. (cont.)

10. Three Boats

 (a) With three boats it would be possible barring
      accidents and extended refit delays, to keep one
      boat (16 missiles) on station for nearly all the
      time.   Even in the best case there would, however,
      be periods lasting some four weeks every four and a
      quarter years when no submarine would be available for
      deployment.   On the other hand, there would be
      periods, if all went well, when two boats could
      be on station.

 (b) A force of this size would allow no margin for
      unforeseen contingencies - which over the total
      life of the force (some twenty years) are almost
      certain to occur.   Any cycle for three submarines
      would be inflexible during periods lasting 16 to
      20 weeks every 14 to 15 months, during which any
      delay in refit or work-up would result in further
      periods when no submarine could be deployed on
      patrol.

 (c) The estimated capital cost of a three boat force
      would be £321 million;   in addition, there would be
      about £17 million a year running costs from 1970/71.
      There would be a cancellation charge for the fourth
      submarine;   there might also be United States
      charges for the cancellation of the two surplus
      Polaris weapons systems.

The Choice

11. The factors affecting the questions posed at (a) and (b)
in paragraph 4 above are as follows -

 (a) From the strictly military point of view a force
      of five boats would be best.   Moreover, it would
      enable the United Kingdom to make a major con-
      tribution to the proposed A.N.F. and provide a
      more powerful lever, than any smaller number, with
      which to bargain for the political and military
      quid-pro-quos we desire.   If matched by a United
      States contribution of the same size, it would
      provide a strong case against creating a shipborne
      force.   Finally, a force of this size would also
      provide an effective national deterrent in the
      event of the break-up of NATO.

 (b) Similar considerations would apply to a four-boat
      force.   It would be militarily acceptable.   The
      only difference would be that we should be offering
      to the A.N.F. a force of smaller size than we
      have already promised to NATO.   It is a matter for
      political judgment how far this would prejudice
      our negotiating position.

-3-

TOP SECRET

(c) A force of three United Kingdom boats, assuming
it proved feasible to link them for operating and
targetting purposes with a similar force of
United States submarines (i.e., six in all), would
represent in military terms an adequate contribution to the proposed A.N.F.   It is also possible
to argue that a United Kingdom force of this size,
could be regarded as a minimal deterrent for
national purposes - but only just.   However, a
force of this size -

(i) would weaken our case for arguing that
the shipborne force was unnecessary;

(ii) would be a contribution substantially lower
than we have already offered to N.TO.   This
would make it extremely difficult to demand
major concessions in return.   Our allies would
be highly suspicious of our motives and the
whole plan might fall to the ground as a
result.

12.   As regards the question at (c) in paragraph 4 above, the
British Polaris force is planned only in relation to the
U.S.S.R.   For purposes outside the NATO area our plans
provide for certain carrier-borne and airborne tactical
nuclear weapon systems.   There are at present no plans for
using the Polaris force except against Russia.

19th November, 1964

-4-

Notice Healey's words under 'present position'.

> Construction has already begun on the four boats, although only the keels of the first two have yet been laid. No firm order has yet been given to the contractor for the fifth boat; but if the production cycle is not to be upset, a decision must be given by January, 1965.

In his memoirs, Denis Healey is very revealing about the politics of those keels:

> The navy told me that, though the hulls of two Polaris submarines were already laid down and long-lead items had been ordered for two more, it would still be possible to convert them into hunter-killer submarines at no additional cost... When I gave Wilson and Gordon Walker this unexpected news they asked me not to let the other members of the Cabinet know; Wilson wanted to justify continuing the Polaris programme on the grounds that it was 'past the point of no return'. I did not demur.[87]

When MISC 17 met at Chequers over the weekend of 21–22 November 1964, it supported the idea of an Atlantic Nuclear Force and the justification for continuing with the construction of the Polaris submarines—'of the five submarines which had been planned, two were at an advanced stage of development and short of scrapping them it would be impracticable not to complete them.'

15

The circulation of this paper has been strictly limited.

It is issued for the personal use of .... *c/c* __ __

TOP SECRET   Copy No............**25**......

MISC. 17/3rd Meeting

CABINET

DEFENCE POLICY

Minutes of a Meeting held at Chequers on
SATURDAY, 21st NOVEMBER, 1964, at 5.30 p.m.

PRESENT:

The Rt. Hon. Harold Wilson, M.P.,
Prime Minister

The Rt. Hon.
George Brown, M.P.,
First Secretary of State
and Secretary of State for
Economic Affairs

The Rt. Hon.
Patrick Gordon Walker,
Secretary of State for
Foreign Affairs

The Rt. Hon.
James Callaghan, M.P.,
Chancellor of the Exchequer

The Rt. Hon.
Denis Healey, M.P.,
Secretary of State for
Defence

The Rt. Hon.
Arthur Bottomley, M.P.,
Secretary of State for
Commonwealth Relations

The Rt. Hon.
Frederick Mulley, M.P.,
Deputy Secretary of State
for Defence and Minister
of Defence for the Army

The Rt. Hon.
George Wigg, M.P.,
Paymaster General

Admiral of the Fleet,
The Earl Mountbatten
of Burma, Chief of the
Defence Staff

Admiral Sir David Luce,
Chief of the Naval Staff
and First Sea Lord

General Sir Richard Hull,
Chief of the General Staff,

Air Chief Marshal
Sir Charles Elworthy,
Chief of the Air Staff

Brigadier J.H. Gibbon,
Ministry of Defence

–i–

TOP SECRET

33. (cont.)

Sir William Armstrong,
  Treasury

Sir Harold Caccia,
  Foreign Office

Sir Henry Hardman,
  Ministry of Defence

Sir Solly Zuckerman,
  Ministry of Defence

Sir Saville Garner,
  Commonwealth Relations
  Office

Sir Richard Way,
  Ministry of Aviation

SECRETARIAT:

Sir Burke Trend
Mr. P. Rogers
Mr. D.S. Laskey
Air Vice Marshal J.H. Lapsley

SUBJECT

ATLANTIC NUCLEAR FORCE

-11-

ATLANTIC NUCLEAR FORCE

THE FOREIGN SECRETARY said that in his discussions about the nuclear policy of the Alliance in Washington and in Bonn and with the Italian and Belgian Foreign Ministers, he had spoken in general terms and without commitment. Reactions had been more favourable than might have been expected. There seemed to be more flexibility in the United States and German positions, particularly about timing, and there was also a general desire for British participation in any arrangement. At the same time the degree of United States and German commitment to the mixed-manned surface fleet should not be under-estimated. He had made it clear that such a fleet, if it were the only proposal for dealing with the German problem and with the question of nuclear sharing within the Alliance, was not acceptable and that the United Kingdom could not take part in it.

He suggested that we should have three long-term objectives in mind. We must try to prevent a Franco-German nuclear alliance which would result in the establishment of a European nuclear force. We should also try to prevent a special alliance between the United States and Germany; this might not be a serious danger, but could not be excluded. Thirdly, a place must be left for France.

The proposals for an Atlantic Nuclear Force (A.N.F.) might contain the following elements –

(i)   Britain would commit all her nuclear weapons to the Force so long as the Alliance lasted, though they would revert to national control if the Alliance should disintegrate. A question which would have to be considered was whether we should withhold some of the V-bombers for use outside the NATO area whether in a conventional or a nuclear role.

(ii) The United States would commit an equal force of Polaris submarines. Both the British and United States Polaris submarines should be nationally manned and not mixed-manned.

(iii) We should oppose the mixed-manned surface fleet and should suggest that any mixed-manned element should take a different form. There would however be heavy pressure for a surface fleet and if we had to accept its establishment we should try to keep it small and decline to make a British contribution.

(iv) The Atlantic Nuclear Force should be integrated with the main United States strategic forces and we should seek to obtain an increasing share in the control of United States weapons not formally committed to NATO.

(v)   We should oppose any European clause which would imply the possibility of the Force reverting to purely European control.

–1–

33. (cont.)

    (vi)   In the controlling Authority there should be formal equality between member countries, particularly between the Germans and ourselves. Without this a demand was likely to grow in Germany for national control of nuclear weapons.

    (vii) Although the Germans would press for the Force to come under the command of SACEUR we should try to ensure that it would be under an independent command, since it was wrong that SACEUR should have control over strategic nuclear weapons.

    (viii) It was important that the treaty or agreement constituting the A.N.F. should provide for the non-proliferation of nuclear weapons by the nuclear powers and for the non-acquisition of such weapons by the non-nuclear powers.

In presenting our proposals in Washington we should stress the size of the contribution which we should be offering. Our bargaining position would be strong since we could decline to contribute to an A.N.F. and stand on the present position. We should seek to obtain a review of NATO strategy which would lead to a reduction of United Kingdom forces in Europe. It would be desirable that this should be achieved by an agreement with the Russians for a general reduction of forces in Europe, though the approach to this would have to be handled with care in view of the susceptibilities of our allies.

In discussion there was general agreement with the line suggested by the Foreign Secretary. In particular it was agreed that we should try to prevent the establishment of a mixed-manned surface fleet and if it became clear that this aim was impossible we must insist that the United States would undertake publicly to maintain a veto on the use of the fleet. We should also resist pressure for any United Kingdom contribution to the fleet. It was also agreed that we should seek to present our proposals in as positive a form as possible and emphasise that they were designed to strengthen NATO, to move towards a reduction in East-West tension and to contribute to non-dissemination of nuclear weapons.

The following additional points were made –

(a) We had offered to contribute the Canberra squadrons in Cyprus with nuclear capacity to CENTO, and had also declared the carrier forces with nuclear capacity to SEATO. These undertakings must be considered in relation to any offer we might make to the A.N.F. If we undertook to give up our nuclear capacity outside the NATO area this could only be on the understanding that the United States would undertake to assume these commitments. This was a matter which would have to be worked out in the course of the negotiations.

-2-

(b) Our bargaining position would depend to a large extent on the size of the contribution we could make and on the degree to which we should commit our contribution without reservation to the proposed Force.   This consideration must also be judged against the need to retain forces for use outside the NATO area.

(c) The argument that the A.N.F. should come under the command of SACEUR was partly due to the mistaken theory that SACEUR should have sufficient strategic nuclear weapons to deal with all the Soviet missiles targetted against Western Europe.   The British and American Chiefs of Staff were agreed that this was not necessary for the effectiveness of the deterrent.

(d) It would be necessary to discuss with the United States the question of the "permissive link" (P.L).   If no such device were fitted to the Polaris missiles in the mixed-manned surface fleet, maximum security against possible misuse could only be obtained if a significant proportion of the crew of each ship was American.   We should also need to consider to what extent the permissive link would affect control over British Polaris submarines assigned to the Force, and our power to recover them if the Alliance came to an end.

Cabinet Office, S.W.1.

23rd November, 1964

-3-

33. (cont.)

2 0

The circulation of this paper has been strictly limited.

It is issued for the personal use of _____ C/C . _____ _

TOP SECRET   Copy No. _____ 25

MISC. 17/4th Meeting

CABINET

DEFENCE POLICY
_____

Minutes of a Meeting held at Chequers on
SUNDAY, 22nd NOVEMBER, 1964, at 10.30 a.m.

PRESENT:

The Rt. Hon. Harold Wilson, M.P.,
Prime Minister

The Rt. Hon. George Brown, M.P., First Secretary of State and Secretary of State for Economic Affairs	The Rt. Hon. Patrick Gordon Walker, Secretary of State for Foreign Affairs
The Rt. Hon. Herbert Bowden, M.P., Lord President of the Council (from 12 noon)	The Rt. Hon. James Callaghan, M.P., Chancellor of the Exchequer
The Rt. Hon. Denis Healey, M.P., Secretary of State for Defence	The Rt. Hon. Arthur Bottomley, M.P., Secretary of State for Commonwealth Relations
The Rt. Hon. Roy Jenkins, M.P., Minister of Aviation	The Rt. Hon. Frederick Mulley, M.P., Deputy Secretary of State for Defence and Minister of Defence for the Army
The Rt. Hon. George Wigg, M.P., Paymaster General	Lord Chalfont, Minister of State for Foreign Affairs
Admiral of the Fleet, The Earl Mountbatten of Burma, Chief of the Defence Staff	Admiral Sir David Luce, Chief of the Naval Staff and First Sea Lord
General Sir Richard Hull, Chief of the General Staff	Air Chief Marshal Sir Charles Elworthy, Chief of the Air Staff

-i-

Brigadier J.H. Gibbon,
    Ministry of Defence

Sir William Armstrong,
    Treasury

Sir Harold Caccia,
    Foreign Office

Sir Henry Hardman,
    Ministry of Defence

Sir Solly Zuckerman,
    Ministry of Defence

Sir Saville Garner,
    Commonwealth Relations
    Office

Sir Richard Way,
    Ministry of Aviation

SECRETARIAT:

Sir Burke Trend
Mr. P. Rogers
Mr. D.S. Laskey
Air Vice Marshal J.H. Lapsley

S U B J E C T

PHYSICAL CONTROLS FOR NUCLEAR FORCES
COMMITMENT TO THE ATLANTIC NUCLEAR FORCE
CONTROL SYSTEM FOR THE ATLANTIC NUCLEAR FORCE
AIMS IN WASHINGTON TALKS

-ii-

33. (cont.)

PHYSICAL CONTROLS FOR NUCLEAR FORCES

The Chief Scientific Adviser informed the meeting of various approaches that were being explored in order to secure the physical control of nuclear forces, including what he knew about various types of Permissive Action Links (PAL). He went on to say that if the British Polaris force was purely national no PAL need be fitted to the weapon system, and security of control would rest entirely on the discipline of the Commanding Officer and his team, as was the case in the United States Polaris force. In this case, the British force would be in no way dependent on the United States; authority to fire would rest with the Prime Minister, and would be exercised through direct national communications channels with the Commanders of the submarines.

If our Polaris forces were contributed as part of a larger A.N.F. it was conceivable that the fitting of a PAL system could be avoided. However, if the United States or any of our other Allies insisted on part of the force being fitted with PAL, it was probable that there would be pressure for all the component sections of the force, including the British submarines, to be similarly fitted.

The Americans were greatly concerned with the need to develop a satisfactory PAL system for the mixed manned surface fleet, and the United States Joint Chiefs of Staff had stated an operational requirement for an entirely foolproof PAL system for this purpose.

Three methods were under examination. The first of these, the inhibition of the launching system, had been rejected as being too easy to decouple clandestinely. The second was the inhibition of the navigational system, but this too had certain disadvantages, and efforts were now being concentrated on the development of a device which would inhibit the warhead detonator, and destroy the mechanism if tampered with. This would be an extension of the system, already fitted to United States free fall weapons allocated to NATO Air Force in Europe, other than those of United States and United Kingdom, in which a numerical code was dialled into the warhead rather like dialling a telephone number. Until this code was correctly dialled the warhead would not become live; the code was normally dialled into the warhead on the ground by the United States custodial officer, but in certain aircraft the capability was also fitted of dialling the code in flight from the cockpit.

A numbers code of this type could be shared between several nations. For instance, in a nine figure code, three separate countries might each have three figures, so that the weapon could not be activated until all three had released their section of the code. This system could, to some extent, be over-ridden by the authority holding and issuing the code.

−1−

Since we were responsible for the manufacture of our own Polaris warheads, the same could presumably apply to us. In the mixed-manned surface fleet the United States, as the basic authority, would, of course, know the whole code, but the United States personnel on the ship would not necessarily have this information.

Information should be available shortly on which method would finally be chosen by the United States for control of the weapons of the mixed-manned surface fleet.

If a submarine were manned nationally, the only foolproof PAL system would be one which inhibited the warhead and included a self-destruction device.

COMMITMENT TO THE ATLANTIC NUCLEAR FORCE

The Meeting then discussed the form which our commitment to the proposed Atlantic Nuclear Force (A.N.F.) might take, under the three aspects of V-bombers, Polaris submarines and the control system of the Force.

THE PRIME MINISTER said that we should approach the negotiations on the basis that we would maintain our present nuclear capability in the various theatres unless and until this could be replaced by something more satisfactory in the form of joint control. We should not contemplate withdrawal and leaving a nuclear vacuum. If we considered accepting joint control in respect of NATO nuclear forces we should in principle be willing to consider accepting similar joint control in respect of nuclear forces committed to CENTO and SEATO.

V-Bombers

All the V-bombers were equipped to carry nuclear bombs, but if we were to commit bombers juridically to the A.N.F. by withdrawing the supreme national interest clause we should have to exclude some part of the force if only because it was required for a conventional bombing role outside the NATO area. This was essential to the maintenance of our position in the Middle and Far East. Further consideration would be required of the way in which this could be done without making it to appear that we retained an independent nuclear capacity. We might on this account have to consider whether the nuclear warheads should embody some form of permissive action link.

-2-

33. (cont.)

Polaris submarines

The Meeting were informed that of the five submarines which had been planned, two were at an advanced stage of development and short of scrapping it would be impracticable not to complete them. The construction of a further two was well advanced, but nothing but the so called "long lead" items and the weapon system was yet on order for the fifth. No firm order had yet been given to the contractor for the submarine itself but if the production cycle were not to be upset a decision must be given by January 1965. The cost of additional submarines after the first three was an additional capital cost of £45 million for the fourth submarine and £40 million for the fifth submarine with additional annual running costs of £4 million a year for each.

The extent of our bargaining power with the United States and the European powers concerned with the creation of the A.N.F. would depend on the size and efficiency of the nuclear forces which we proposed to contribute. We had to consider both what the other countries concerned would wish to obtain as a constituent part of the force and therefore the price they would be prepared to pay for it, and further how much importance they would attach to our abandoning independent control of any given size of force. From both points of view the larger the size of the force which we were prepared to commit without the supreme national interest clause, the larger the price that we might expect to obtain but this was subject to the limitation that if our contribution were of such a size as to give us too large a share of the force at its present level, our allies might then feel called upon to increase the forces which they devoted to it in order to achieve a comparable quota and this could lead to pressure for a larger mixed-manned surface fleet. In considering the balance of issues we should bear in mind that each Polaris submarine carried sixteen missiles as compared with eight on each ship of the proposed mixed-manned surface fleet. A United Kingdom contribution of three submarines would commit forty eight missiles or one quarter of the proposed fleet total of 200 missiles. This would equal $2\frac{1}{2}$ times the contribution of 10 per cent which was at present proposed for the United Kingdom. Four United Kingdom submarines would represent a contribution of one-third of the total. On the assumption that our contribution of submarines was matched by a United States contribution, a six submarine fleet would commit 96 missiles and an eight submarine fleet 128 missiles or nearly the minimum delivery strength of the proposed M.L.F. These numbers must however be abated to the extent that the lengthier process of refitting meant that the submarines would spend a shorter time on station than ships of the surface fleet and there would therefore be a corresponding diminution of the proportionate contribution represented by the missiles of a submarine force.

-3-

TOP SECRET

The Meeting then considered the size of the Polaris submarine force which we should seek to commit to the A.N.F. in the light of these considerations. There was general agreement that a commitment of two submarines would be inadequate to achieve our objectives, while a commitment of five submarines was unnecessarily high and would, apart from the serious financial and economic objections, risk stimulating an increase of the contribution which our allies sought to make on the lines which had already been discussed.

There was considerable support for the view that a force of three submarines would be appropriate in that it would represent the contribution best calculated to achieve our political objectives in negotiation and would effect the maximum saving for the United Kingdom economy. There were, moreover, strong political reasons in favour of a United Kingdom force of this size, in that since it would not represent a creditable independent deterrent, it would make it apparent that we had abandoned any idea of regaining independent national control at any time in the future and had committed ourselves irrevocably to an international force. While this admittedly did not provide full national insurance should NATO break up, not only did the latter seem most improbable, but even if it were to happen we could not hope to maintain our national security alone, but should be bound to seek the negotiation of alternative alliances.

On the other hand it was argued there were strong reasons in favour of four submarines. A contribution to the A.N.F. of this size might prove inadequate as a basis for demanding major concessions in return. A force of three gave no margin in the case of an accident which might at any time put one submarine out of action for at least a substantial period and such a reduction of our forces would be unacceptable in view of the consequent reduction of our influence in the A.N.F. Furthermore, it was essential that we should bear in mind the morale of the men in the force. Unlike other sections of the armed forces in peace time, the submarines would operate throughout at a war-time level of maintenance. This could only be achieved with very high morale and in the knowledge that national importance was attached to the maintenance of one submarine always on station. A force of three submarines would not enable us to achieve this and the sense of national purpose would therefore suffer. From these points of view and bearing in mind that it would be impracticable operationally, and unacceptable to the United States, for us later to acquire one of their Polaris submarines, there were strong arguments in favour of buying a fourth submarine and maintaining it as a reserve against mishaps to an operational force of three. It was also relevant that the economy affected by cancelling the order for the fourth submarine would be abated by substantial cancellation charges. Furthermore the possibility of our possessing a force of four submarines would affect the price which other nations would be prepared to pay to prevent our acquisition of an independent nuclear force. At the outset of the negotiations we should retain the prospect of a fourth submarine and ascertain reactions to this. We might conclude with agreement to a force of three, which would not preclude our considering the acquisition of a fourth solely as a reserve.

-4-

TOP SECRET

MISC 17 had been persuaded. Would the full Cabinet be? Sir Burke Trend, the Cabinet Secretary, prepared a steering brief for the Cabinet meeting of 26 November 1964. He suggested Wilson indicate that the Polaris force would be four boats (rather than the five planned by the previous Conservatives governments of Macmillan and Douglas-Home). Such a decision, given the boats' allocation to an Atlantic Nuclear Force, 'will not affect the basic principle of our proposal to abandon our independent nuclear deterrent.'

E.R. ANF

Defence Org. 9
ALF Parl.

TOP SECRET

PRIME MINISTER
_____

      You may wish to inform the Cabinet of the upshot of the
Chequers Meeting on Defence Policy. I attach a note, from which
you can select as much as you wish to say.

      If we deal with this subject under the "Oversea Affairs"
item, you may wish to begin that item with some reference to
today's events in relation to sterling. This would provide a
very appropriate "lead in" to the report on defence policy and
the Chequers discussions.

R / 25th November, 1964

E.R.

TOP SECRET

Defence Policy

As the Cabinet know, we have started our review of defence policy. I should like to put before you what we propose as a result of the Chequers meeting and to outline the policy which, subject to discussion this morning and the approval of the Cabinet, the Foreign Secretary, the Secretary of State for Defence and I propose to put forward when we go to Washington next week.

We first considered the burden of defence upon our economy, both in relation to what we wish to achieve at home and in relation to the influence which we seek abroad. Some reduction of the burden is essential not only for the first purpose but also for the second, since our economic strength is as important to our oversea influence as our military power. But it is clear that no substantial reduction of defence expenditure is possible without a drastic review both of the commitments which we seek to discharge and the capabilities (i.e. the weapons systems) which we intend to maintain. Our existing forces, costly though they are, are stretched to the limit by our commitments. It is very relevant that we are trying to discharge a world-wide role on the basis of defence expenditure not much greater than that of France and Germany, whose commitments are almost entirely European; whereas the only other Power which fulfils a global role (the United States) spends about ten times as much on defence as we do. On the other hand, it would not accord either with our own interests or with the interests of the Western world for us to withdraw from any of our defence roles until something better can be put in their place. We took this as the starting point of our policy.

There are three main issues, none of which can be considered in isolation. They are -

(i) Our oversea commitments, in Europe, the Middle East and the Far East, to which we are bound by a series of treaties and from which in any case our withdrawal would have unforeseeable, and - at least in the Middle East - possibly dangerous, consequences.

-1-

(ii) The nature and cost of our weapons systems, which must be considered in relation to the differing roles which our forces have to carry out in the three oversea theatres. We must re-examine these weapons systems in relation both to the industrial consequences for this country if we changed to a policy of buying them abroad and to the balance of advantage between the saving on budgetary cost and the additional expenditure in foreign exchange.

(iii) Our nuclear forces, particularly in relation to the M. L. F., to which we have firmly declared our opposition.

In all this we cannot act in isolation and our freedom of manoeuvre is in many respects limited by the need to make changes in agreement with our allies. This will be a long process - of which the forthcoming Washington talks will only be a start.

We propose at the outset of these talks to make clear, bluntly if need be, our need to relate our defence expenditure to our resources; and we shall therefore seek to promote a new approach to the problem of nuclear forces. If the Cabinet agree, we shall propose the creation of an Atlantic Nuclear Force, to which we would commit, irrevocably so long as NATO existed, our strategic nuclear forces. There will be important related questions about the size of our Polaris fleet (probably 4 submarines) and about the extent to which we should retain control of some part of the V-bomber force for our Middle and Far Eastern roles. But these will not affect the basic principle of our proposal to abandon our independent nuclear deterrent. We shall seek an equivalent American contribution to the force; and we shall restate our opposition to the present proposals for a mixed-manned surface fleet. The Atlantic Nuclear Force might, however, have to include a mixed-manned component. This might be based on the mixed-manning of part of the Air Force and of land-based missiles. There will undoubtedly be heavy pressure for a mixed-manned surface fleet in addition; but, if we have to accept its creation, we shall still seek to keep it, and our contribution to it, as small as possible.

The control of this force will raise a number of difficulties. We shall try to make it an absolute condition that the United States will retain their veto over the use of its nuclear armament and that we also shall have a similar veto. We shall also try to stipulate that both we and the United States shall also have a veto on any change in the control arrangements themselves. On the other hand we must concede that in the controlling authority there should be formal equality between member countries, in order to contain European demands, and particularly possible German demands, for national control of nuclear weapons. We shall also seek agreement that the force should be integrated with the main United States

-2-

34. (cont.)

strategic forces, in order that we and other members of the Alliance may gradually acquire some influence on the control of the United States weapons not formally committed to NATO. In addition we shall try to ensure that the Treaty establishing the force should provide for the non-acquisition of nuclear weapons by existing non-nuclear Powers. In all these proposals it will be necessary to keep the way open for French participation, even if General de Gaulle is at present unwilling to take part; and also to bear in mind the effect of the project on East-West relations. In particular, we hope that there may develop from our initiative some agreement with the Soviet Union for arms control and a mutual thinning out of forces in Europe.

We believe that these proposals are valuable both militarily (since they make more strategic sense than the M.L.F.) and politically (since they offer some prospect of containing German nuclear aspirations). But we must at the same time seek concessions by our allies in return for the very considerable contribution which we shall make to the proposed Force, particularly by accepting a position of no more than parity with Germany within the Alliance. The main recompense which we must seek is some relief from the burdens which we carry in Europe in order that, if we continue to discharge our extra-European commitments, our total defence burden may nevertheless be reduced.

But we agreed at Chequers that we must also make a direct attempt to reduce the extra-European burden by means of a stringent review of our oversea policy and commitments and of the weapons systems which those commitments entail. It will take some months to complete such a review; but it should be possible to reach early decisions about the future of some of the particularly costly projects such as the T.S.R.2 - at least in time for the spring White Paper on Defence Policy.

The Cabinet will of course be consulted at all the appropriate stages, in the light of the Washington discussions and before there is any question of decisions being taken on the longer-term review.

25th November, 1964

-3-

TNA, PRO, CAB 128/39

70

SECRET

**THIS DOCUMENT IS THE PROPERTY OF
HER BRITANNIC MAJESTY'S GOVERNMENT**

Printed for the Cabinet. November 1964

C.C. (64)   Copy No. **36**

11th Conclusions

CABINET

———

*CONCLUSIONS of a Meeting of the Cabinet held at 10 Downing
Street, S.W.1, on Thursday, 26th November, 1964, at 10.30 a.m.*

Present:

The Right Hon. HAROLD WILSON, M.P., Prime Minister

The Right Hon. GEORGE BROWN, M.P., First Secretary of State and Secretary of State for Economic Affairs

The Right Hon. PATRICK GORDON WALKER, Secretary of State for Foreign Affairs

The Right Hon. HERBERT BOWDEN, M.P., Lord President of the Council

The Right Hon. LORD GARDINER, Lord Chancellor

The Right Hon. JAMES CALLAGHAN, M.P., Chancellor of the Exchequer

The Right Hon. DENIS HEALEY, M.P., Secretary of State for Defence

The Right Hon. Sir FRANK SOSKICE, Q.C., M.P., Secretary of State for the Home Department

The Right Hon. ARTHUR BOTTOMLEY, M.P., Secretary of State for Commonwealth Relations

The Right Hon. WILLIAM ROSS, M.P., Secretary of State for Scotland

The Right Hon. JAMES GRIFFITHS, M.P., Secretary of State for Wales

The Right Hon. ANTHONY GREENWOOD, M.P., Secretary of State for the Colonies

The Right Hon. DOUGLAS JAY, M.P., President of the Board of Trade

The Right Hon. THE EARL OF LONGFORD, Lord Privy Seal

The Right Hon. MICHAEL STEWART, M.P., Secretary of State for Education and Science

The Right Hon. RICHARD CROSSMAN, M.P., Minister of Housing and Local Government

The Right Hon. DOUGLAS HOUGHTON, M.P., Chancellor of the Duchy of Lancaster

The Right Hon. R. J. GUNTER, M.P., Minister of Labour

The Right Hon. FRANK COUSINS, Minister of Technology

The Right Hon. FRED PEART, M.P., Minister of Agriculture, Fisheries and Food

The Right Hon. FREDERICK LEE, M.P., Minister of Power

The Right Hon. TOM FRASER, M.P., Minister of Transport

The Right Hon. BARBARA CASTLE, M.P., Minister of Overseas Development

The following were also present:

Mr. JOHN DIAMOND, M.P., Chief Secretary, Treasury (*Item 6*)

The Right Hon. EDWARD SHORT, M.P., Parliamentary Secretary, Treasury

———

Secretariat:
Sir BURKE TREND
Mr. P. ROGERS
Miss J. J. NUNN

SECRET

5510—5   A

35. (cont.)

that in any public discussion of the Government's proposals to nationalise the iron and steel industry Ministers should emphasise the contribution which this measure would make to the expansion of exports rather than the political commitment which it would discharge.

The Prime Minister invited all Ministers to be guided, in any public statements which they might make in the near future, by the main considerations which had emerged from the discussion and to ensure that junior Ministers were similarly advised.

**Oversea
Affairs**

The Congo

(Previous
Reference:
C.C. (64) 9th
Conclusions,
Minute 3)

4. *The Foreign Secretary* said that the recent proposal by the Belgian and United States Governments to attempt to rescue the Europeans who were held as hostages by the rebel Congolese forces in Stanleyville had confronted us with a difficult choice. If we were seen to contribute to the operation by placing facilities on Ascension Island at the disposal of the United States aircraft conveying the Belgian paratroops concerned, we ran the risk that we might provoke the rebel forces to massacre the hostages forthwith and, by appearing to support the Government of M. Tshombe, might alienate opinion in other African countries. On the other hand, if we refused to assist the Belgian and United States Governments, we might be held partially responsible for any disaster which overtook the hostages. In these circumstances the obligation to try to save human life was clearly paramount; and we had therefore agreed that the aircraft engaged in the rescue operation should be given staging facilities on Ascension Island. This had undoubtedly contributed to the success of the operation; and many lives had been saved. In particular, all United Kingdom subjects, with one possible exception, had been rescued. The fact that a number of non-Europeans had also been saved and that we were now seeking to ensure that relief supplies would be provided for the Africans who had suffered during the attack on Stanleyville might moderate to some extent the sharp political criticism of our action which had been expressed by most African countries, with the exception of Nigeria.

The Belgian force were now engaged in a secondary rescue operation elsewhere in the Congo; but thereafter they would be withdrawn and should have returned to Belgium by the beginning of the following week. The humanitarian purpose of the operation would, by then, have been achieved as far as was possible; but an unknown number of Europeans, living in isolated parts of the Congo, would inevitably remain unaccounted for.

**Defence and
Oversea Policy**

*5. *The Prime Minister* said that the Ministers primarily concerned had now completed, under his chairmanship, an initial review of our defence and oversea commitments, which had been directed to considering both our global defence policy in the longer

---

* Previously recorded as a Confidential Annex.

SECRET

term and the more immediate issue of the proposals which we might put forward, during the forthcoming discussions in Washington, for reinforcing the interdependence of the member countries of the North Atlantic Alliance in relation to nuclear weapons.

The United Kingdom was attempting to discharge three major defence roles—a commitment to the defence of Europe under the North Atlantic Treaty Organisation (NATO); the role of a nuclear power, which the Government had inherited from their predecessors; and the maintenance of a world-wide military presence, based on our oversea commitments. The resultant burden on our economy made it impossible for us to sustain all three roles indefinitely; and it would be necessary for the Cabinet to consider on a subsequent occasion, when more detailed proposals had been formulated for the purpose, both a revision of the scale of our oversea commitments and the possibility of effecting corresponding reductions in the relevant weapons systems, particularly certain very costly aviation projects. The scope for economies would be conditioned partly by the fact that it was desirable, both in principle and as a means of maintaining the Commonwealth connection, that we should continue to play a significant military role in the Mediterranean and east of Suez and partly by the fact that we might nevertheless be unable, for local political reasons, to retain indefinitely the oversea bases on which our ability to discharge that role at present depended.

For these reasons it would be necessary to make it clear to the United States Government, at the outset of the forthcoming discussions in Washington, that we should henceforward be compelled to relate our defence expenditure more closely to our resources. As regards the European theatre we should not be able to ignore the momentum which the scheme for a mixed-manned surface fleet had now acquired. But this scheme, inasmuch as it would increase the nuclear potential at the disposal of NATO, was strategically unnecessary and economically unwelcome. We must therefore continue to oppose it; but we should do so more effectively by putting forward constructive alternative proposals, which would be directed to the same end as the mixed-manned surface fleet, *i.e.*, the containment of the aspirations of the non-nuclear members of NATO, but would seek to achieve this end without any increase in the nuclear armament of the Alliance. For this purpose we should propose the creation of an Atlantic Nuclear Force (A.N.F.), to which we would commit irrevocably, so long as NATO existed, our V-bomber force assigned to Europe and such Polaris submarines as we might construct. The precise number of these submarines would be for further consideration; but it was relevant to a decision that the construction of some of them was already sufficiently advanced to make it unrealistic to cancel the orders. On the other hand the number to be retained would be smaller than the number which the previous Government had envisaged and would be such as to make it clear that we no longer contemplated the maintenance of an independent nuclear force. We should look to the United States Government to commit an equivalent number of submarines to the proposed A.N.F.

SECRET

SECRET

In addition the force might include a mixed-manned component, to which the non-nuclear Powers could contribute; this might be constituted by the mixed-manning of V-bomber squadrons and land-based missiles.

The control of the A.N.F. would raise difficult problems; but it would be essential to make it clear that it would operate in close co-operation with the command system of NATO and that both the United States and the United Kingdom Governments would possess a veto not only on its use but also on any change in the method of control. It seemed unlikely that the French Government would participate in the project at the outset; but it would be desirable to leave the way open for them to do so later.

Although the fact that one element in the force would be contributed by the United Kingdom and that we should retain a veto on its use would imply that the non-nuclear Powers would still not obtain precise equality with us, our surrender of our right to independent nuclear action should go far to meet their susceptibilities; and we might hope to obtain, in return, general agreement to a new initiative for a relaxation of East-West tension. We must also use such bargaining power as our proposal afforded us to dispose of the existing project for a mixed-manned surface fleet. Initially, we should continue to oppose the creation of such a fleet at all. We might find it impossible to sustain that position; but, if so, the Cabinet would have to consider the nature and extent of any contribution which we might have to make to the fleet.

We must also seek, as part of our new initiative, to obtain fresh undertakings not only by the nuclear Powers not to disseminate nuclear weapons but also by the non-nuclear Powers not to acquire such weapons; and we must try progressively to extend the scope of these undertakings.

Finally, we must endeavour, through the A.N.F., to ensure that we and the other members of NATO would be brought into closer consultation on the use of United States nuclear weapons not only within the NATO area but also elsewhere in the world.

The Foreign Secretary said that it would be one of the main political objectives of the discussions to prevent a nuclear alliance between the United States and Western Germany and to keep the way open for a subsequent French Government to join the force. We should have to bear in mind in this connection the German reaction to the recent speech by General de Gaulle at Strasbourg. This had caused some division of opinion within the German Government but had also, for that reason, made them less insistent on an early decision on the proposals for a mixed-manned surface fleet.

The Secretary of State for Defence said that, whereas the proposals for a mixed-manned surface fleet involved the diversion of men and money to the creation of an additional and unnecessary nuclear force, our own project for an A.N.F. was directed to solving the political problem in Europe by establishing joint control of nuclear weapons which already existed. This would require a readiness on our part to commit to the new force both our V-bomber force, which would be operational until about 1970, and the Polaris submarines,

SECRET

which would be operational until about the end of the 1970s. It would be impracticable to look further at present. In return for this contribution we should seek some reduction in the extent of our commitment to ground defence in NATO, together with a measure of assistance in our main role of peace-keeping overseas. As regards the number of Polaris submarines to be constructed, two were already relatively far advanced, while contracts for another two had been placed and work on the prefabrication of essential parts had been taken a considerable way. No contract had yet been placed for the fifth submarine; but work on the so-called " long lead " items had started. The necessary steps were being taken to ensure that we should not be faced with further unnecessary expenditure on this vessel.

In discussion there was general agreement with the proposals put forward by the Prime Minister as the basis on which negotiations in Washington should begin. The following main points were made:

(a) The commitment of our nuclear forces to the A.N.F. would imply that the French Government would enjoy a degree of independent control over their *force de frappe* which we should have surrendered in relation to our own deterrent. There was considerable doubt, however, whether the *force de frappe* would in fact constitute a credible independent deterrent by the time it became operational.

(b) The Chiefs of Staff had endorsed the A.N.F. project in principle from the military point of view.

(c) The size of the reduction to be made in the programme of Polaris submarines could be determined only in the light of a further detailed examination of the requirement, with due allowance for a margin of insurance against accidental damage to one of the vessels. It would also be for consideration, in the light of the negotiations in connection with the A.N.F., how far we should continue research and development in relation to nuclear weapons.

The Cabinet—

(1) Took note, with approval, of the Prime Minister's statement about the project for the creation of an Atlantic Nuclear Force.

(2) Agreed that the proposals outlined in discussion should be put forward on behalf of the United Kingdom Government at the forthcoming discussions with the United States Government in Washington.

Pensions of Ministers and Members of Parliament

(Previous Reference: C.C. (64) 8th Conclusions, Minute 3)

6. The Cabinet considered a memorandum by the Lord President of the Council (C. (64) 17) on the pensions of Ministers and Members of Parliament and other related matters.

The Lord President recalled that the Cabinet had invited him to arrange for a Committee of Ministers under his chairmanship to examine the contributory pension scheme for Members of Parliament recommended by the Lawrence Committee, the position of Ministers in the House of Lords in relation to the daily attendance allowance

By cutting back on the Conservatives' planned force and by assigning the boats to an Atlantic Nuclear Force, Wilson told the Cabinet, the Government would 'make it clear that we no longer contemplated the maintenance of an independent nuclear force.' During discussion, it was pointed out by an un-named minister, that de Gaulle's nuclear *force de frappe* would be independent in a way that the UK's nuclear capability would not. But there was 'considerable doubt, however, whether the *force de frappe* would in fact constitute a credible deterrent by the time it became operational'. Wilson had got his policy through. However disguised, 'a bloody Union Jack' would remain on the bomb for decades to come unless circumstances intervened.

All that remained to be decided was the number of Polaris submarines. This the Cabinet's Defence and Overseas Policy Committee did two months later, following a Ministry of Defence recommendation that it should be four.

Harold Wilson and Denis Healey (left): sustainers of the Bomb, 1964–65.

CONFIDENTIAL

(THIS DOCUMENT IS THE PROPERTY OF HER BRITANNIC MAJESTY'S GOVERNMENT)
- -

O.P.D.(65)4   COPY NO. 61

12th January, 1965.

CABINET

DEFENCE AND OVERSEA POLICY COMMITTEE

POLARIS SUBMARINE BUILDING PROGRAMME

Memorandum by the Secretary of State for Defence

    I circulate herewith the text of a minute which I sent
to the Prime Minister on 6th January, 1965.

    The Prime Minister wishes to discuss this question at
an early meeting of the Committee.

                               D.W.H.

Ministry of Defence
S.W.1.

12th January, 1965.

CONFIDENTIAL

CONFIDENTIAL

PRIME MINISTER
<u></u>

<u>THE POLARIS SUBMARINE BUILDING PROGRAMME</u>

As you know, we have four Polaris submarines building, two at Vickers and two at Cammell Lairds. Vickers are now claiming that uncertainty about our intentions in respect of this programme is making things difficult. The latest computer run on the network schedule for the first boat forecasts a slippage of seven weeks, and until our intentions are more specific than at present it is hard to bring pressure on Vickers to maintain the rate of building called for by this compactly scheduled programme.

2. It is, I think, abundantly clear that we have decided to construct a Polaris submarine force of some kind as a corner-stone of our proposals for an Atlantic Nuclear Force. I think it is also clear that the Force must consist of at least three boats; even with three it is not possible to maintain one boat at sea for all of the time.

3. Equally, we have not specifically decided to rescind the decision of our predecessors that there should be five boats. Certain long lead items for the fifth boat have been ordered, and further orders to the value of about £400,000 against a running contract are due to be placed by Vickers over the next two months for items which are relevant only to the fifth boat. If we are not going to have a fifth boat we might as well say so now and save this expenditure.

4. For reasons which were explained in detail at our meeting at Chequers, and in your preparations for your talks in Washington, a fleet of four boats is preferable for many reasons to a fleet of three. Furthermore, the larger our national contribution to the Atlantic Nuclear Force the greater our chance of securing a significant American contribution of submarines, and of eliminating or reducing the mixed-manned surface fleet component.

/Since

CONFIDENTIAL

Since the fourth submarine is already under construction, cancellation at this stage would involve the payment of cancellation charges and nugatory expenditure. The fourth submarine is not due to be completed until 1969 so that there is no need to take an immediate decision upon whether it should join the operational fleet or be put in moth-balls.

5. I propose that we should take, and announce, a decision to complete the four submarines already building but to cancel the proposal for a fifth boat.

6. I am sending copies of this minute to our colleagues on the Defence and Oversea Policy Committee and to the Secretary of the Cabinet.

(Signed) Denis Healey

6th January, 1965.

TOP SECRET

**THIS DOCUMENT IS THE PROPERTY OF
HER BRITANNIC MAJESTY'S GOVERNMENT**

Printed for the Cabinet. January 1965

The circulation of this paper has been strictly limited. It is issued

for the personal use of...................................... *c/c* ....

Copy No. **25**

O.P.D. (65)
5th Meeting

CABINET

Defence and Oversea Policy Committee

*MINUTES of a Meeting held at 10 Downing Street, S.W.1, on
Friday, 29th January, 1965, at 10 a.m.*

Present:

The Right Hon. HAROLD WILSON, M.P., Prime Minister

The Right Hon. GEORGE BROWN, M.P., First Secretary of State and Secretary of State for Economic Affairs	The Right Hon. JAMES CALLAGHAN, M.P., Chancellor of the Exchequer
The Right Hon. MICHAEL STEWART, M.P., Secretary of State for Foreign Affairs	The Right Hon. DENIS HEALEY, M.P., Secretary of State for Defence
The Right Hon. Sir FRANK SOSKICE, Q.C., M.P., Secretary of State for the Home Department	The Right Hon. ARTHUR BOTTOMLEY, M.P., Secretary of State for Commonwealth Relations

The following were also present:

The Right Hon. THE EARL OF LONGFORD, Lord Privy Seal	The Right Hon. R. J. GUNTER, M.P., Minister of Labour (*Item 2*)
The Right Hon. FRANK COUSINS, M.P., Minister of Technology (*Item 2*)	The Right Hon. ROY JENKINS, M.P., Minister of Aviation
The Right Hon. FREDERICK MULLEY, M.P., Deputy Secretary of State for Defence and Minister of Defence for the Army	The Right Hon. GEORGE WIGG, M.P., Paymaster General
Mr. CHRISTOPHER MAYHEW, M.P., Minister of Defence for the Navy (*Item 1*)	Mr. GEORGE DARLING, M.P., Minister of State, Board of Trade
Admiral of the Fleet THE EARL MOUNTBATTEN OF BURMA, Chief of the Defence Staff	Admiral Sir DAVID LUCE, Chief of the Naval Staff and First Sea Lord
General Sir RICHARD HULL, Chief of the General Staff	Air Chief Marshal Sir CHARLES ELWORTHY, Chief of the Air Staff

Sir SOLLY ZUCKERMAN, Ministry of
Defence (*Item 2*)

TOP SECRET

1. Polaris submarines

The Committee considered memoranda by the Secretary of State for Defence (O.P.D. (65) 4 and 6) and by the Chancellor of the Exchequer (O.P.D. (65) 3) about the Polaris submarine building programme.

The Secretary of State for Defence said that the Defence Programme of the previous Administration provided for five Polaris submarines. Of these four were under construction. The hulls of two had been laid and the fabrication of parts of the remaining two was well advanced. No order had yet been placed for the fifth, though some work had been done on long-lead items for it. Broadly, the capital cost of each submarine was £40 million and the running cost £4 million a year. If the fifth submarine were cancelled there would be a negligible saving in the immediate future but relatively small cancellation charges. If the fourth submarine were cancelled there would be a saving of approximately £39 million, less substantial cancellation charges.

A fleet of four boats was for many reasons preferable to one of three. The larger our national contribution to the Atlantic Nuclear Force (A.N.F.) the greater the prospect of securing a United States contribution of submarines and of reducing the size of the mixed-manned surface fleet. From the point of view of the Navy Department a force of five submarines would be preferable if we had to station one in the Far East, since to do this with a force of four would require a depot ship unless we could rely on United States logistic support. Nevertheless, a force of four would meet our basic operational needs, whereas a force of only three would mean that every two years there would be a period when none would be on station. Such a force would not therefore constitute a credible deterrent if the negotiations for the creation of the A.N.F. were to fail or if subsequently the North Atlantic Treaty Organisation were to break up. Furthermore, contribution of four to the A.N.F. might facilitate our negotiations for a reduction of our forces stationed in Germany. The possibility of an accident which would put one of the submarines out of commission at any time reinforced the need, which could not be met by acquiring a fourth boat solely to hold in reserve. This was impracticable, since the nuclear reactor needed continuous attention. Nor would a submarine without the nuclear reactor in it be of any value as a reserve, since it would take some two years to install the reactor should the need arise. A decision to cancel the fourth submarine now would be irreversible, since the United States components could not subsequently be fitted into the United States construction programme and the cost of construction in the United Kingdom would be prohibitive. He therefore recommended that a decision should be taken to complete the four submarines now under construction and to cancel the fifth. If that were agreed, it would be possible for the nuclear Hunter/Killer submarine programme to be resumed with the order of one boat in mid-1965. The net financial saving in that event in 1965–66 would be of the order of £0·75 million. It would be desirable to announce the resumption of the programme at the same time as the decision on the size of the Polaris force.

4 **TOP SECRET**

Before any announcement could be made it would however be necessary to renegotiate the Polaris Sales Agreement with the United States Government. His preliminary discussions with the United States Secretary of State for Defence, Mr. MacNamara, suggested that this would not present serious difficulties.

The Chancellor of the Exchequer said that he agreed with the proposal not to proceed with the fifth boat. In view of the overriding need for major savings on the defence budget and since it did not appear that it would materially impair our negotiating position on the A.N.F. he considered that the fourth boat should also be cancelled.

In discussion it was argued that the strong financial arguments for reducing the force to three submarines were reinforced by political considerations. Not only would this more clearly demonstrate the Government's policy of not retaining an independent nuclear deterrent since a force of this size would not be credible as such but such a contribution to the A.N.F. might be politically more acceptable to the other countries concerned. It was, however, the general view that these arguments were outweighed by the other political and defence considerations. We could not yet assume that our proposals for an A.N.F. would succeed and our negotiating position would be strongly reinforced by our possession of a force of four submarines. Furthermore, the development of a nuclear bomb by the Peoples' Republic of China and the possible need for the Western Alliance to provide nuclear cover for India might well call for the stationing of a Polaris submarine in the Far East.

In further discussion the following points were also made:

(*a*) From the point of view of cost effectiveness the additional annual expenditure of £4 million on the fourth submarine was amply justified. This would enable an average of 85 submarine patrol weeks a year to be maintained as compared with 50 with a force of three. With more than four there was a decline in cost effectiveness.

(*b*) If an accident were to put one of the submarines out of commission a force of two would not constitute a sufficiently effective contribution to the A.N.F.

(*c*) Despite the shortages of skilled manpower in the armed forces a force of four boats would not involve serious personnel problems. Indeed, the strain on the personnel concerned of seeking to maintain one submarine always on station from a force of three would be harmful to morale.

Summing up the discussion *the Prime Minister* said that there was general agreement that the balance of argument was in favour of a force of four submarines, having regard particularly to the weakness of our position if one out of a force of three were involved in an accident. It was however necessary that the cost should be met within the total defence budget which it was the Government's aim to attain. It would be necessary in the first instance to negotiate with the United States Government an amendment of the Polaris Sales Agreement before any public statement was made. The terms of such a statement would require further consultation between the

TOP SECRET

In its manifesto for the March 1966 general election, *Time for Decision*, Labour took credit for its proposal of an Atlantic Nuclear Force and declared it 'stands by its pledge to internationalise our strategic nuclear forces.'[88] In the early autumn of that year, Wilson rejigged his nuclear decision-taking machinery by bringing military and civil atomic matters under a single, standing Ministerial Committee on Nuclear Policy, PN. It was to this committee that Healey reported on 3 August 1967 the terms under which the Royal Navy's Polaris submarines would be assigned to NATO.

THIS DOCUMENT IS THE PROPERTY OF HER BRITANNIC MAJESTY'S GOVERNMENT

The circulation of this paper has been strictly limited.
It is issued for the personal use of...................

TOP SECRET

Copy No. **14**

PN(66) 1st Meeting

CABINET

MINISTERIAL COMMITTEE ON NUCLEAR POLICY

MINUTES of a Meeting held at
10, Downing Street, S.W.1, on
WEDNESDAY, 28th SEPTEMBER, 1966 at 11.30 a.m.

PRESENT:

The Rt. Hon. Harold Wilson, MP,
Prime Minister

The Rt. Hon. George Brown, MP,
Secretary of State for
Foreign Affairs

The Rt. Hon. Michael Stewart, MP,
First Secretary of State and
Secretary of State for
Economic Affairs

The Rt. Hon. Denis Healey, MP,
Secretary of State for Defence

The Rt. Hon. Anthony Wedgwood Benn, MP,
Minister of Technology

THE FOLLOWING WERE ALSO PRESENT:

Mr. Niall MacDermot, QC, MP,
Financial Secretary, Treasury

Sir Solly Zuckerman,
Cabinet Office

SECRETARIAT:

Sir Burke Trend
Mr. D.S. Laskey

S U B J E C T:

NUCLEAR POLICY

TOP SECRET

TOP SECRET

NUCLEAR POLICY

THE PRIME MINISTER said that the military and civil aspects of nuclear policy were becoming increasingly interrelated; he had therefore decided to establish a new Ministerial Committee on Nuclear Policy to provide a focus of discussion and to enable a comprehensive and consistent view to be taken of all issues involved before major decisions of policy were reached. At the official level there were at present two main Committees: the Nuclear Requirements for Defence Committee, which reported to the Defence and Oversea Policy Committee, and the Atomic Energy (Official) Committee, which had no clear point of Ministerial reference. The new Ministerial Committee would consider the major issues affecting nuclear policy, whether in the military or the civilian field. Responsibility in nuclear matters was shared by a number of Departments but it had always been recognised that the Prime Minister himself carried a rather special responsibility in this field and the new Committee would therefore be under his chairmanship.

There was one urgent matter for consideration arising from Sir Solly Zuckerman's visit to Moscow and the indication that Soviet technicians would be prepared to take part in technical talks with ourselves and the Americans about the identification of underground nuclear explosions. This was an important development in Soviet policy which the Foreign Secretary would wish to discuss with the United States Secretary of State during his forthcoming visit to New York and Washington.

THE FOREIGN SECRETARY said that in his discussions in Washington he hoped to elucidate the attitude of the United States Government; it was not clear whether the American insistence on the need for on site inspection was due to their conviction that this was essential to detect violation of a comprehensive test ban treaty, or whether they were really concerned to continue underground tests. If the United States attitude to the suggestion of technical talks with ourselves and the Russians was favourable Sir Solly Zuckerman who would be in Washington could pursue the matter with the American scientists. He also hoped that his discussions with the United States Secretary of State would help to clarify the United States attitude on the wider question of the United Kingdom retaining a nuclear defence capability.

-1-

TOP SECRET

38. (cont.)

In discussion there was general agreement that a new Ministerial Committee on nuclear policy would fill a valuable role. It was also agreed that the Foreign Secretary should conduct his discussions with the United States Government on the lines he had proposed. It was often said that we could no longer count on United States co-operation in nuclear defence matters unless we retained a nuclear weapons capability. It was not clear, however, whether this represented the settled policy of the United States Administration, and particularly of the President himself. In view of the President's concern with the position of the Federal German Government he might be disposed to welcome a reduction of the United Kingdom's nuclear defence capability. In this connection our policy in regard to the Polaris submarine fleet and its deployment in the Atlantic or East of Suez might well be relevant.

Summing up the discussion THE PRIME MINISTER said that he would take steps to constitute a Ministerial Committee on nuclear policy on the lines he had proposed. It would also be necessary to consider the arrangements to be made at the official level, where it would be appropriate that Sir Solly Zuckerman should have a co-ordinating responsibility. In the light of the Foreign Secretary's discussions in Washington the Ministerial Committee would need to consider the whole range of issues affecting our future nuclear defence policy, including the deployment of the Polaris fleet.

The Committee –

(1) Took note that the Prime Minister would arrange for the establishment of a Ministerial Committee on nuclear policy and for appropriate arrangements to be made for the consideration of nuclear matters at the official level.

(2) Agreed that in the light of the Foreign Secretary's forthcoming discussions in Washington the Ministerial Committee would need to consider the issues affecting future nuclear defence policy.

Cabinet Office, S.W.1,

    29th September, 1966

Copy No. 7 of 25 Copies

MINISTRY OF DEFENCE

MAIN BUILDING, WHITEHALL, LONDON, S.W.1 *Enclosure*

TELEPHONE WHITEHALL 7022

SECRET

MO. 26/10/6

CABINET OFFICE

A 88854

- 3 AUG 1967

FILING INSTRUCTIONS
FILE No. 31911

PRIME MINISTER

       I was invited by the Ministerial Committee on Nuclear Policy in January*, in consultation with the Foreign Secretary to inform the authorities of the North Atlantic Treaty Organisation of our intention to assign the POLARIS submarines to NATO in terms which would retain ultimate United Kingdom control and which would not prevent the removal of the force from NATO command and its redeployment East of Suez from 1972 onwards, if that course were later to commend itself.

2.   As a result, SACEUR has been given a firm assurance that, in accordance with the Nassau Agreement, our POLARIS missiles will be assigned to him as soon as the first submarine becomes operational, i.e. in 1968. Ultimate United Kingdom control of the POLARIS force will not be affected, since control of the firing chain will remain in UK hands; in particular, no submarine commander will be authorised to fire the POLARIS weapons without the Prime Minister's specific authority. The reference to the Nassau Agreement ensures that the position in relation to our ability to re-deploy the submarines if we should ever wish to do so is not affected, since this would, in any case, require the re-negotiation of the Nassau Agreement.

3.   It is now necessary to settle the detailed terms of assignment of the UK POLARIS force. For this purpose, the missiles and the submarines must be treated separately. Although the missiles must be assigned to SACEUR, like the V-bombers which they will replace, the submarines themselves cannot be assigned to SACEUR unless they operate in the Mediterranean,

/which

*PN 1st Meeting, 1967.

SECRET

- 2 -

which is the only sea area under SACEUR's control
(the Baltic is not suitable for POLARIS operations).
There are a number of disadvantages in operating in
the Mediterranean, including the distance from the
Faslane base which would reduce the availability of
the submarines on patrol, and the difficulty of
safeguarding operations there after other British
Naval Forces have been withdrawn from the area. For
these reasons our submarines should operate in the
Atlantic, where they would have to be assigned to
SACLANT.

4.   Separate terms of assignment of the missiles
to SACEUR and of the submarines to SACLANT have therefore been drawn up; these are at Annex A and Annex B
respectively. The condition in paragraph 3b of
Annex B is necessary to safeguard US information to
the UK which cannot be released to other nations,
and corresponds to the arrangements which the
Americans have made to ensure that the actual
operational control of the POLARIS submarines which
they have assigned to NATO remains in national hands.

5.   These draft terms of assignment have been
discussed and agreed informally with SACEUR, SACLANT
and the American Department of Defense. Since we are
concerned with the interpretation of our obligation
to the United States under the Nassau Agreement, we
must now formally consult the United States Government
and I propose, subject to the concurrence of the
Foreign Secretary, that this should be done by the
Foreign Secretary. I should be grateful if you and
the other members of the Nuclear Policy Committee,
to whom I am copying this minute, would confirm that
you are content with the terms of assignment and the
proposed approach to the United States Government.

/6. By acting ..

SECRET

-3-

6.   By acting in this way we shall not be committing ourselves any more than we are already committed by the terms of the Nassau Agreement, which would have to be re-negotiated if, for example, we decided later to deploy POLARIS East of Suez. There is no need to seek any publicity about the terms of assignment of the missiles and submarines in Parliament or the Press: we should simply confirm in answer to enquiries that, as planned from the start, the POLARIS force will be committed to NATO when it becomes operational.

7.   I am sending copies of this minute to the Foreign Secretary, First Secretary of State and Secretary of State for Economic Affairs, Chancellor of the Exchequer, Commonwealth Secretary, Minister of Technology and Sir Burke Trend.

3rd August, 1967

SECRET

DRAFT MEMORANDUM TO SACEUR
ASSIGNMENT OF UK POLARIS MISSILES

In a memorandum dated 23rd May, 1963, Her Majesty's Government assigned to you the UK V-bomber forces in implementation of paragraph 6 of the Nassau Communique dated 21st December, 1962.

2. By the terms of paragraph 8 of the Nassau Communique, Her Majesty's Government undertook to assign and target in the same way British POLARIS forces developed under the Nassau plan; and you were informed on 13th January, 1967, of Her Majesty's Government's intention, in accordance with the Nassau Communique, to assign the missiles of the UK POLARIS force to you, as soon as the force becomes operational.

3. Her Majesty's Government therefore now assign to you, in accordance with paragraph 8 of the Nassau Communique, all the missiles of the UK POLARIS force, for targetting planning, state of readiness, co-ordination and execution of strikes in accordance with your nuclear strike plan; with effect from (the dates on which the submarines deploying these missiles first achieve an emergency operating capability).

4. Her Majesty's Government has, however, decided, for military and other reasons, that the submarines should operate in the Atlantic area. Subject to the assignment to you of the missiles in accordance with the preceding paragraph, the submarines themselves will be earmarked in the terms of a separate memorandum as part of the UK naval forces to be assigned to SACLANT in emergency.

5. The logistics and support of the assigned missiles and submarines will remain a national responsibility.

SECRET

DRAFT MEMORANDUM TO SACLANT

ASSIGNMENT OF UK POLARIS SUBMARINES

In accordance with paragraph 8 of the Nassau Communique dated 21st December, 1962, Her Majesty's Government have in a separate memorandum assigned to SACEUR all the missiles of the UK POLARIS force, for targetting planning, state of readiness, co-ordination and execution of strikes in accordance with his nuclear strike plan, with effect from (the dates on which the submarines first achieve an emergency operating capability).

2.   For military and other reasons, however, Her Majesty's Government have decided that the submarines should operate in the Atlantic area.   In order therefore to implement paragraph 8 of the Nassau Communique in respect of the submarines, Her Majesty's Government have earmarked them for assignment to you in emergency.

3.   This assignment, which will be in Category A, will be subject to the following conditions:

    a.   The missiles of the force must be available
          at all times for SACEUR's nuclear strike plan,
          in accordance with paragraph 1 above.

    b.   You are requested to issue instructions that
          during the whole period of assignment up to and
          including missile operations, the operational
          command and control of the submarines is to be
          delegated to CINCEASTLANT: after missile
          operations are completed, you will be free to
          dispose of the submarines as SSNs as you think
          fit.

    c.   The logistics and support of the submarines,
          as well as of the missiles assigned to SACEUR,
          will remain a national responsibility.

The terms of the assignment were fully in accord with the deal Macmillan had negotiated with Kennedy at Nassau. When *HMS Resolution* became operational in 1968, it would be assigned to the Supreme Allied Commander Europe. But the '[u]ltimate United Kingdom control of the POLARIS force' was not affected and 'no submarine commander will be authorised to fire the POLARIS weapons without the Prime Minister's special authority.' Tactfully, Healey suggested there was 'no need to seek any publicity about the terms of the assignment of the missiles in Parliament or the Press.' In effect, there was now a *de facto*, if unannounced, political bipartisanship on Polaris as it is hard to see how a Conservative government, had it been in office, would have assigned Polaris differently once it neared deployment stage.

The perilous position of the British economy, following the devaluation of the pound on 18 November 1967, caused the future of Polaris to be reopened. The question of its cost, in straitened public spending circumstances, had become bound up with the question of improving the warhead given the expected deployment of anti-ballistic missiles in the Soviet Union. The problem that Macmillan had anticipated during his New Year's Eve meeting in December 1962 was, five years on, very much on the horizon. Could and should the Royal Navy's Polaris missiles be made capable of penetrating an ABM screen around Moscow—a question that became known as the 'Moscow Criterion'?

MOSCOW CRITERION  1967–77

The future of Polaris became genuinely uncertain in the last weeks of 1967 when the urgency of an existing defence review was heightened by the substantial economic and spending crisis associated with the devaluation of the pound. Indeed, two of Whitehall's economic departments—the Treasury and the Department of Economic Affairs—made a serious attempt to kill off the programme altogether, not just to curb future improvements to the system designed to penetrate any ABM defences the Soviet Union might construct. Given the lack of agreement between departmental views at official level (which did not commit their ministers), the Cabinet Secretary, Sir Burke Trend, circulated what amounted to a green paper to Wilson's PN committee.

A test firing of a Royal Navy Polaris A3 missile.

40. 'British Nuclear Weapons Policy', report by the Defence Review Working Party, PN (67) 6, 1 December 1967.   TNA, PRO, CAB 134/3120

TOP SECRET

Copy No. **24**

PN(67) 6

1st December 1967

CABINET

MINISTERIAL COMMITTEE ON NUCLEAR POLICY

BRITISH NUCLEAR WEAPONS POLICY

Note by the Secretaries

Attached for the consideration of the Committee is a report by the Official Committee on Defence and Oversea Policy, covering a report by the Defence Review Working Party, on British nuclear weapons policy. The departmental views expressed in this report on the various policy questions requiring decision are without commitment for the Ministers concerned.

(Signed)   BURKE TREND
             E.M. ROSE
             H.L. LAWRENCE-WILSON
             R. PRESS

Cabinet Office, S.W.1.
1st December 1967

TOP SECRET

TOP SECRET

~~DRAFT COVER NOTE~~

The attached report by the Defence Review Working Party sets out the main facts and arguments bearing on the questions about our nuclear weapons policy raised in the Prime Minister's minute of 24th July (Annex I). We have the following comments on the very important policy issues that are involved.

2. This is the first occasion on which Ministers collectively have had the opportunity of considering nuclear weapons policy as a whole, including its effect on the Atomic Weapons Research Establishment (AWRE) at Aldermaston. The principal questions upon which Ministerial decisions are required (see paragraph 66 of the report) are –

(a) Is the implication in the July Statement on Defence that we are to retain Polaris through the 1970s to be confirmed? Or should we plan to give up the weapon system, along with other British nuclear weapons, earlier than this and, if so, how much earlier? The arguments bearing on this question are in paragraphs 21 and 33 and paragraph 37 of the report.

(b) If it were decided to plan on the basis of abandoning Polaris before the end of the 1970s should we plan to retain other British nuclear weapons even if Polaris is abandoned? The arguments bearing on this are in paragraphs 34 to 36 and 38-40.

(c) If it is decided to retain Polaris should we –
   (i) retain it unmodified?
   (ii) seek to improve it, given the general arguments set out in paragraphs 43-48 of the paper, the particular point of the ability of AWRE to maintain existing weapons, (paragraphs 38-40 and paragraph 52), the views of the Chief Scientific Adviser to the Government (paragraphs 22-24 below ~~and Annex VII to the report~~) and the response to these views by the oversea Departments and the Ministries of Defence and Technology (paragraphs 25-27 below)?
   (iii) if we seek to improve it, is there any general guidance to be given before the amount of improvement to be undertaken is further investigated (paragraphs 49 to 51)?

(d) Should we give ourselves the option to deploy Polaris east of Suez (paragraphs 53 to 63), and

(e) if so, should we do so on a basis that would enable us to deploy Polaris East of Suez at the earliest possible date (1972) or at some date after 1972, given three years' notice? (paragraph 64)?

These questions follow the order of the points brought out by the Prime Minister in his minute referred to above.

–i–

TOP SECRET

40. (cont.)

3.   There is no agreement between Departments on the main question, whether we should maintain our nuclear capability or abandon it as quickly as possible.   Nor is there agreement on whether, if the balance of advantage were seen by Ministers to lie in retaining Polaris, it would be worthwhile to go to the expense of improving it.   We are, however, agreed in doubting whether there is adequate advantage, now or in the immediate future, in going for the half-way house of retaining the rest of our nuclear capability while giving up Polaris.

4.   Apart from the need to maintain AWRE simply in order to maintain existing nuclear weapons (see paragraph 2(c)(ii) above), a relevant consideration in this connection and generally in the decisions that need to be taken is the risk that, as explained in paragraphs 38-40 and 52 of the report, Aldermaston may cease to be viable in the absence of a definite programme of design and development work.

5.   All the figures of dollar expenditures in the report and later in this cover note were incorporated before devaluation took place.   ~~The capital~~ "The capital cost of the existing Polaris programme will increase by £3.5 million in total and the running costs by about £1½ million a year. The cost of improvement would go up by £0.3-£5.0 million depending on the option taken."

concerned, for and against our continuing with a nuclear weapons programme with or without improving Polaris, with a final section on the case for and against deploying Polaris East of Suez - on which the Committee is also divided.

The Case for Retention of our Present Nuclear Capability

7.   In the view of the defence and oversea Departments, we should retain our nuclear weapons, including Polaris.   Decisions on our nuclear weapons capability cannot properly be taken in isolation from our foreign and defence policy as a whole.   As a result of the Defence Review, the Defence Expenditure Studies and the Supplementary Statement on Defence Policy, we have a defence policy, and a strategy with force plans to match, up to the mid-1970s.   A major assumption underlying this strategy and these force plans, which affects both our national defence capability and the contribution that we make to our alliances, has been that we shall retain Polaris as a credible deterrent system, together with our other nuclear weapons, throughout this period and beyond.   Indeed, the July Supplementary Statement on Defence (Cmnd. 3357) stated that "The Polaris force will be Britain's contribution to the strategic nuclear deterrent of the West".

-ii-

8.   To abandon British nuclear weapons at this time would present great difficulties for our policy.   The United States would interpret it as meaning that a major ally was further reducing its defence capability at a particularly awkward time.   Europe would regard it as leaving France as the only nuclear power in Western Europe and our chance of shaping Europe and European Atlantic relations in the way we want would be prejudiced.   Abandonment would be unwelcome to our European Allies other than France who would exploit it for her own ends.   The Supplementary Statement on Defence Policy 1967 stated that "we must continue to make a substantial contribution to NATO's forces".   Abandoning our nuclear capability would be seen as a sharp break with this policy, would cast doubt on our reliability as an ally, and might have an effect on our political standing and influence.   Some Europeans want to keep open the possibility of having some form of European nuclear deterrent.   In practical terms Europe has the technological skill and the financial capability to produce a credible deterrent.   It is not necessary to accept this as an aim to recognise that it would be against our interests and those of the Atlantic Alliance for these aspirations to become centred solely on the French nuclear capability.   Indeed from the general foreign policy point of view, there is a grave disadvantage in leaving France at this moment in General de Gaulle's foreign policy as the sole nuclear power in Europe.

9.   At present it is not easy to foresee the precise circumstances in which Europe, or we ourselves, would have need of a nuclear deterrent against the Soviet Union.   Such a situation implies for example, an unwillingness by the United States to risk a confrontation with the Soviet Union on a European issue, or doubts in either the Soviet Union or Europe about the reality in the longer term of total reliance on immediate United States nuclear support.   For various reasons the United States attitude to Europe has recently undergone a substantial change.   It is possible to imagine this process continuing and to envisage a situation in which Europe alone was under pressure from the Soviet Union, even if for only a short time.   The retention by the United Kingdom of a deterrent nuclear capability gives us the ability to use our strategic nuclear weapons independently in the last resort.   The prospect of our doing so may appear remote.   But the Soviet Union will always lack complete assurance about what we might do in a situation of last resort: so long as we, or Europe, possess strategic nuclear weapons, her policy and planning must be based on the assumption that we could take a decision which would be critical in terms of destruction (and therefore of the world balance of power) to her, whether or not the United States also became involved.

-iii-

10. This position is not affected by suggestions that a deterrent has no validity unless there is a "degree of symmetry" between the offensive and defensive nuclear capabilities of the two opposing sides. The fact that the two super-powers have an over-sufficiency of nuclear armaments does not mean that another strategic nuclear power will be unable to exert influence on both of them, provided it has a credible force capable of causing significant destruction.

11. Circumstances might arise in the future in which the political advantages to be gained by abandoning our nuclear capability would make it right to consider a consequent reshaping of our foreign and defence policy accordingly, but this is the wrong point in time at which to do this, both in terms of our policy towards Europe, and in particular our application to enter the Common Market, and of our position in the world generally, especially at a time when we are withdrawing forces from the Far East. Damage to our negotiating position on disarmament might flow from so doing and until we are clearer about the outcome of non-proliferation negotiations in practice as distinct from theory, we should not forgo the political influence with the United States and our other allies afforded by the possession of strategic nuclear weapons, or place ourselves in a position of vulnerability in relation to even medium-sized powers. Although the United States do not attach overriding importance to the military value of the British nuclear capability as part of the Western deterrent against the Soviet Union, abandonment of British nuclear weapons now would be unwelcome to them, in particular because of its European consequences, including the effect in NATO. Abandonment would also lose the United Kingdom the privileged access (albeit declining) which we now enjoy to American military and technical knowledge in the nuclear field.

12. For these reasons the Foreign Office, the Ministry of Defence, the Commonwealth Office and the Ministry of Technology consider that we should retain our planned nuclear capability including Polaris. The Foreign Office, Ministry of Defence and Commonwealth Office consider for the reasons set out below that it would not be sufficient merely to retain Polaris but that, because of the ABM threat, the weapons system should be improved, the precise extent of the improvement requiring further examination. The Ministry of Technology point out that the Atomic Energy Authority's advice about the situation at Aldermaston (paragraph 15 below) implies that an improvement programme will be necessary if we are to be sure we can retain even our currently-planned capability. The Board of Trade, while not fully endorsing the detailed argumentation set out in the

preceding paragraphs, agree that it would be desirable to retain our capability including Polaris, on the broad grounds that we already have it, that it is comparatively cheap to maintain, that it has political value and that to dispose of it would weaken our political position, particularly in Europe. They do not believe that its value would be materially enhanced by improving the Polaris weapons system, but would support improvement if this is necessary in order to retain staff at AWRE for the maintenance of the weapons system during its operational life.

The Case for Improving Polaris

13. The United Kingdom Polaris deterrent has been planned to have a capability, with three submarines on station, to threaten simultaneous destruction to thirty major cities in Western Russia, and we have hitherto considered this to constitute a deterrent credible in political and military terms. The advent of ABM defences in Russia, whatever may eventually prove to be the scale and thickness of their deployment, will reduce the amount of damage that our Polaris force can be expected to inflict. If, therefore, nothing is done to improve Polaris, we shall deliberately be allowing the threat which we can pose to decline. The fact that we are doing this despite our ability to avoid or minimise this decline will become known to our allies including the United States and to our own forces and will be apparent to the Soviet Union. This will inevitably cast doubts on the credibility of our deterrent. We can, if we wish, and this too will become known, improve Polaris to an extent that will leave its threat to the Soviet Union, and therefore its credibility, only marginally reduced even if their present defensive capability were completed and extended to cover the whole of Western Russia. The Soviet Union would than have to increase those defences more than ten-fold to reduce our Polaris threat below ten major cities.

14. The Overseas Departments and Ministry of Defence fully share the concern of the Economic Departments with the magnitude of the economic tasks which face this country. In this context it should be noted that the cost of maintaining our nuclear capability, including a full hardening of Polaris to make it effective against the foreseen ABM threat, can be contained within planned defence budgets and is small in relation to the capital investment which would otherwise be wasted. The savings that would result from abandoning our nuclear capability would amount to little more than about $1-1\frac{1}{2}$ per cent of the Defence Budget (see paragraph 42 of the Working Party's report). It is, of course, true that any major weapons system requires improvement during the long life that one is entitled to

--v--

40. (cont.)

expect from the heavy capital investment that the system requires. As a
result of the large scale experimental work which has been undertaken in
the United States, and of the theoretical studies undertaken in the United
Kingdom, the chance is reduced that some entirely new ABM techniques will
emerge that would require major modification to Polaris. So far as
redundant scientific resources are concerned significant numbers of the
highly skilled weapon technologists might flow into the "brain drain" in
the absence of any constructive plans for their future employment. Furthermore, if it were to be decided to drop our nuclear capability, either now
or in the near future, it would be necessary to re-examine comprehensively
both our overseas and defence policies and the forces needed to make them
effective. As regards our force requirements, we should either have to
increase substantially our conventional capability (we should be under
pressure, particularly in NATO, to maintain the general level of our
contribution by undertaking a larger share of other tasks) at a cost
which could be greater than continuing with our nuclear programme; or
decline sharply in political and military influence, both nationally and
within our Alliances. Since the continued military and political credibility of Polaris is an essential element in its value to us, the Foreign
Office, Ministry of Defence and Commonwealth Office believe that the need
to improve it to meet the ABM threat should be accepted, but that a more
detailed examination should be made of what minimum degree of improvement
is essential.

15. If the decision were to be to retain Polaris a consideration relevant
to whether or not we should also harden at least the warhead is explained
in paragraphs 38 to 40 of the report; the Atomic Energy Authority warn
us that Aldermaston may cease to be viable in the absence of scientifically
challenging work, such as the hardening of Polaris, with the consequence
that our nuclear capability as a whole would be put at risk. Whether and
in what timescale this might happen is a matter of judgement about the
likely behaviour of key staff at the establishment and about the likelihood
of our being confronted by difficult problems with any warheads that we
decide to retain. The considered view of the Authority is that in the
absence of major problems arising on nuclear weapons, key staff would in
fact drift away to an extent which would endanger our nuclear capability
as a whole. But it is not possible to forecast by what date this would
happen. Production of our nuclear weapons is at a stage at which the
emergence during production of further problems calling for major R and D
is becoming unlikely. But such problems may well arise in the maintenance
and refurbishing stage, though their extent and seriousness cannot be
foreseen; and key staff are unlikely to remain simply for such an uncertain

–vi–

prospect of stimulating work. The Ministry of Technology are in favour of retaining a nuclear capability (including Polaris) and, in the light of the foregoing advice, favour a hardening programme as offering the best and most realistic prospect of assuring the maintenance of that capability by retaining those staff essential to it.

16. Should Ministers decide in favour of retaining our nuclear capability and improving Polaris, all Departments are agreed that it will be necessary to make further investigations into the detailed alternatives (outlined in paragraph 49 of the Working Party's Report) which are open to us on the scale, method and cost of improvements before decisions are taken. In this connection the extent of the new information from the Americans that will be required under each of the alternatives and the conditions which they may attach to the release of such information will be important. A Presidential determination would be needed before additional nuclear information could be provided. The most advanced form of hardening the warhead only covered by paragraph 49(c) of the report and the alternative courses set out in paragraph 49(a) and (b) would require additional United States information. The most limited form of hardening of the Polaris warhead under paragraph 49(c) of the report could probably be achieved without further United States information (but at increased costs from £2 million to £5–£7 million), although we should need the use of their underground test facilities for any one of the proposed hardening options; if, however, it were to prove that we did need fresh information for this course, the United States attitude to providing it might be that it did not represent sufficient firmness of purpose on our part to ensure continuing United States/United Kingdom nuclear co-operation beyond the term of our present agreement which can be ended unilaterally after December 1969. This assessment of the likely United States attitude is based on discussions that have taken place with its officials; whether the United States Administration would adopt this attitude if an approach was made at the political level can be discovered only by making such an approach.

The Case against Retention and Improvement

17. The Treasury and the DEA do not find it possible to believe that the United Kingdom could or would confront the USSR with our nuclear capability independently of the USA. In conjunction with the USA our capability would be an insignificant addition . The Soviet Union would not believe that we would be willing to contemplate the total annihilation which would be the result of using our nuclear weapons against them. These Departments find the circumstances

–vii–

40. (cont.)

postulated by the overseas Departments for its hypothetical value so unreal as to make continued expenditure on it unnecessary and wasteful; nor do they consider it realistic to contemplate the creation of a future European nuclear capability which would be relevant in comparison with those of the USSR and the USA. Since only the United States and the Soviet Union have the capability of mutual self-destruction and the resources for effective anti-ballistic missile (ABM) defences, **they** conclude that the United Kingdom, whether in isolation or as part of a European capability, could never achieve a relevant capability in the context of that of the Soviet Union. They also see no grounds for maintaining a United Kingdom nuclear capability solely on the argument that we should be able to match other countries which have achieved a secondary nuclear capability or may do so in the future.

18. In the view of the Treasury and the Department of Economic Affairs, since we have already decided that we shall not develop or acquire a successor to Polaris (thereby setting a term to our participation in strategic nuclear deterrence) the right course is to abandon the whole of our nuclear capability as quickly as possible. The process of abandonment will take time; so the sooner a decision is reached the better. Given our difficult economic situation, the capability is a misuse of the resources that it will consume. Unless a decision is taken now to eliminate it, we shall not merely fail to make the substantial savings that are possible in currently planned expenditure but, as in the case of all other weapons systems, we might also be led into still more expenditure over the years to match further developments in defensive systems and to provide development work to keep AWRE viable. Given the scale and speed of the United States/ Soviet Union nuclear arms race, no one can say how soon further updating will be required if we continue in the race. It would be of great significance to the national economy to reduce planned expenditure by upwards of £300 million over the next decade, to rule out the prospect of any further pre-emption of resources on nuclear weapons, and to bring about the progressive redeployment of scarce and highly-skilled manpower.

19. As regards the suggestion that we should need to increase our conventional capability if we ceased to be a nuclear power, there are no convincing illustrations of the likely circumstances in which possession of the capability would be to the national advantage; and at no time during the Defence Expenditure Studies was it claimed that the planned level of conventional forces depended on our retaining a nuclear capability. Therefore, if it were decided that we should give up our nuclear capability, it does not necessarily follow that there would be need for increases in our planned conventional forces, even if economic and financial considerations would permit this.

-viii-

20. If it were decided that it was impracticable in present circumstances to abandon Polaris, there is no case for further expenditure on improving a weapon system which is basically irrelevant. As to the thesis that without the technical challenge which improvement would represent the key staff needed to maintain our nuclear armoury would start to leave AWRE, this process might well take some time and a situation of this sort could in any event present itself by about 1975, when the improvement would have been accomplished; we should then be likely to be called upon to devote still further resources to continued nuclear development in order even to maintain our existing nuclear weapons, whether or not such work were also then claimed to be necessary for the improvement of Polaris. We could only avoid this possibility by ceasing to spend money now.

21. The views of these Departments are set against the background of their concern with the magnitude of the economic tasks facing this country, and with the degree to which continued economic weakness affects the credibility, in political terms, of much of our foreign and defence policy. They believe that we must rely more, for our influence in the world, on the soundness of our economy and less on military presence or deterrent threat.

The Views of the Chief Scientific Adviser to the Government

22. The Chief Scientific Adviser's views and conclusions are set out in PN(67) 7. He accepts the basic technical facts that have already been established by experiment and which relate to ABM systems, i.e. that x-rays can damage the capsules of incoming warheads and their contents and that missiles can be accurately guided. But he does not believe that these facts do more than provide a theoretical basis for an ABM system. He also disputes the practical and strategic value of proposals for hardening our Polaris warheads. Since ABM defence would be a highly complex system about whose effectiveness there could be no assurance one way or another, and because the system is highly vulnerable operationally, he does not accept that the Soviet Union would ever rely on their ABM system to destroy all our weapons, even if they were unhardened. He believes that to achieve any increase in the credibility of our strategic forces in the eyes of the Russians, would require not just hardening but an increase in the size of our strike forces and, logically, our entry into the ABM race.

40. (cont.)

23. From the point of view of the strategic value of the proposals to harden Polaris and particularly having regard to the relative strength of Soviet and United Kingdom forces, the Chief Scientific Adviser believes that the Russian attitude to us would remain the same, whether our attacking weapons are hardened or left as at present planned. He believes that the extent of their reaction in terms of ABM defence would be unaffected by whether or not we decide to spend £40 million on the hardening proposals in the attached report. The issue of hardening does not arise with respect to any other possible deployment of our nuclear forces; it rests squarely on whether the United Kingdom should plan for an independent nuclear strike against the Soviet Union.

24. The Chief Scientific Adviser takes the view that the weight of strategic, technical and economic argument is against spending any more on our Polaris force than the sum already committed. He does not accept that the future of AWRE depends on the question of elaborating our Polaris warheads to include penetration aids (their interest lies primarily in hardening the warhead itself). He suggests an impartial enquiry on the future of AWRE even if immediate abandonment of our strategic nuclear forces is impracticable (paragraph 24 of PN(67) 7).

25. The overseas Departments and the Ministry of Defence do not accept all the arguments put forward by the Scientific Adviser to the Government but they only wish to comment briefly at this stage. First, no British Government has ever based its policy on a pre-emptive first strike against the Soviet Union. Indeed, neither the United States nor the Soviet Union could sustain a claim for first strike being a sensible basis for planning. Possession of Polaris gives us a force which is invulnerable to pre-emptive strikes and a capacity which, though small by American and Soviet standards, poses a threat to at least 30 Soviet cities. It seems difficult to argue that such a threat can be ignored, particularly if we show our determination to maintain its ability to penetrate. We have no requirement for parity in offensive and defensive weapons with the super powers; we are concerned with deterrence and the risk of escalation and not with fighting a war. The Soviet Union may not have absolute faith in the effectiveness of their ABM system but they must obviously regard it as having some value. It is logical to assume that as time goes on they will improve it. In military and scientific terms a Polaris improvement programme, including penetration aids, can be quantified and shown to have an effect of such significance against an ABM system that the Soviet Union must take it into account in forming their view of credibility. There is certainly no logic in the view that to achieve an increase in credibility we must increase our strike forces and enter the ABM race as the same objective can be achieved at much less cost by an improvement programme.

-x-

26. These Departments agree with the Scientific Adviser that it is impossible to quantify scientifically the precise moment at which it might be appropriate to give up our Polaris weapons, and agree that this problem is essentially one of political judgment (see paragraph 8). The publicly stated view of Ministers is that if we were to give up our nuclear capability we should seek to obtain the best possible return for it; it is the opinion of those Departments that we should still seek to keep Polaris as effective a weapon as possible for this purpose in order to maintain its value in any such exchange, even though they accept that this should not be an overriding consideration. They also agree in principle with a proposal for an inquiry into the staff requirement at AWRE for military purposes, if necessary in parallel with an examination of alternative programmes for hardening Polaris.

27. The Ministry of Technology endorse the view of the Atomic Energy Authority (AEA) that the full programme of improvement set out in paragraph 49(a) and part of 49(c) of the Working Party report offers the best prospect of work of sufficient interest to keep AWRE viable until 1975. That is because implicit in that proposal is a substantial redesign of the warhead; this would be a major task which should be quite sufficient to retain the relatively small number of key staff on whose expertise the Establishment depends. The two lesser programmes of improvement set out in paragraph 49(b) and part of (c) of the Report, based mainly as they are on United States technology, would admittedly be less sure of maintaining the viability of AWRE and would do so for lesser periods, but this of course has to be weighed against their smaller cost. As for the suggestion that key staff would not be persuaded "to remain in an Establishment on the basis of hand-to-mouth decisions"...... a firm programme lasting until 1975 gives more assurance than AWRE staff have had for some little time and certainly more assurance that staff in many defence establishments are accustomed to. As regards the suggested enquiry into the staff levels at AWRE and the possibility of diversification, the Ministry of Technology agree that this would be desirable and will discuss with the AEA and Ministry of Defence how it should be mounted at the appropriate time. An essential preliminary to such an enquiry would be a decision on whether or not to improve Polaris.

Summary

28. We are unable to make agreed recommendations on the question set out in paragraph 2 above, except that we are agreed in doubting whether there is adequate advantage in retaining the rest of our nuclear capability

40. (cont.)

while abandoning Polaris (see paragraph 3 above). On the main questions
whether we should retain a nuclear weapons programme, and, if so, whether
we should improve Polaris, the Committee are divided. The Treasury and
the Department of Economic Affairs consider that Polaris should be
abandoned at once, or, if it is to be retained, that there should be no
improvement. The Board of Trade and the Chief Scientific Adviser to the
Government consider that we should retain Polaris, but not improve it.
The Foreign Office, Commonwealth Office, and Ministry of Defence consider
that we should retain our nuclear capability and improve Polaris. The
Ministry of Technology agree that we should retain Polaris and draw
attention to the fact that the AEA's advice about the situation at AWRE
implies that an improvement programme will be necessary if we are to be
sure we can retain even our currently-planned capability.

Deployment East of Suez

29. Finally, there is the question whether we should provide ourselves
with a capability to deploy Polaris East of Suez. On this question the
Treasury and the Department of Economic Affairs do not consider that we
should give ourselves this capability, even if it is decided to retain
Polaris. They believe that the whole trend of our policy is away from
involvement in the Far East and that, apart from this, our publicly
expressed intention to provide sophisticated support for our friends and
allies in the Far East did not cover a nuclear capability in the form of
Polaris. The other Departments point out that the Prime Minister in his
talks with President Johnson in June this year indicated that the United
Kingdom Government had been considering whether there would be merit in
transferring our Polaris submarines East of Suez. They consider that, if
we decide to retain Polaris, it would be right, given the small additional
cost involved, to keep the East of Suez option open by building the
necessary capability into the submarine depot ship and buying some
equipment from the United States. However, they consider that it would
be sufficient to aim at having this capability at three years' notice,
thus keeping our immediate commitment down to £2 million.

It is interesting that Sir Solly Zuckerman, by this time Chief Scientific Adviser to the Government, distanced himself from the views of his old department (the Ministry of Defence) about the need to improve Polaris and the indispensability of such a programme to sustain the human and technical capacities of the Atomic Weapons Research Establishment at Aldermaston. It is worth noting, too, the degree to which France (and the undesirability of leaving it the only European nuclear weapons power) is used as an argument for sustaining a British capability. No sign now of the view that de Gaulle's deterrent would not amount to a viable system. The PN committee took the document at its meeting of 5 December 1967.

41. Minutes of a meeting of the PN Committee, PN (67) 4th meeting, 5 December 1967.

TNA, PRO, CAB 134/3120

PN(67) 4th Meeting

CABINET

MINISTERIAL COMMITTEE ON NUCLEAR POLICY

MINUTES of a Meeting held at
No. 10 Downing Street, S.W.1. on
TUESDAY, 5th DECEMBER 1967 at 9.45 a.m.

PRESENT:

The Rt. Hon. Harold Wilson, MP,
Prime Minister

The Rt. Hon. George Brown, MP,
Secretary of State for
Foreign Affairs

The Rt. Hon. Michael Stewart, MP,
First Secretary of State

The Rt. Hon. Roy Jenkins, MP,
Chancellor of the Exchequer

The Rt. Hon. Denis Healey, MP,
Secretary of State for Defence

The Rt. Hon. George Thomson, MP,
Secretary of State for
Commonwealth Affairs

The Rt. Hon. Anthony Wedgwood Benn, MP,
Minister of Technology

SECRETARIAT:

Sir Burke Trend
Mr. E.M. Rose
Mr. H.L. Lawrence-Wilson
Dr. R. Press

S U B J E C T:

BRITISH NUCLEAR WEAPONS POLICY

TOP SECRET

TOP SECRET

TOP SECRET

BRITISH NUCLEAR WEAPONS POLICY

The Committee considered a report on **British** nuclear weapons policy by the Defence and Oversea Policy (Official) Committee (PN(67) 6) covering a report by the Defence Review Working Party and a note on the same subject by the Chief Scientific Adviser to the Government (PN(67) 7).

THE DEFENCE SECRETARY said that the four main issues raised by the memoranda before the Committee were whether we should complete and maintain Polaris in an operational state; what if anything we should do, in view of the threats from anti-ballistic missiles (ABM), to improve the effectiveness of our Polaris missiles; the future of the Atomic Weapons Research Establishment (AWRE); and finally, what if anything we should do to give ourselves the capability of deploying Polaris East of Suez. He suggested that each of these issues required separate discussion.

On the question whether we should complete and maintain Polaris, there was a case for giving up the weapons system if this would make a major contribution to avoiding further proliferation of nuclear weapons. At present, however, no international agreement to this end was in sight. Nor did it seem likely that those nations, such as Israel or India, who were the most likely to become additional nuclear powers in the next few years, would be influenced in their policy in this respect if we were to abandon Polaris. From the economic viewpoint we had already spent or committed 90 per cent of the capital cost of the system and beyond the next two years its running costs alone would have to be paid. The full costs of our nuclear programme would then decline to some £30 to £40 millions annually which was about 2 per cent of the Defence Budget; Polaris was in fact among the most cost-effective of our contributions to the North Atlantic Treaty Organisation (NATO) and, if we had to replace this contribution in some other way, this would both be more expensive and involve an increased burden on the balance of payments. If we were to give up our nuclear capability and subsequently wished to restore it, this would be extremely expensive.

Very serious political consequences would be involved in abandoning Polaris. It would leave France as the only nuclear power in Western Europe at a time when she was moving further away from the NATO Alliance and planning to develop an inter-continental ballistic missile. Our other allies in Europe did not wish this to happen; they did not feel

—1—

TOP SECRET

41. (cont.)

that they could rely on the French deterrent which, in their view and unlike our own, did not add anything to the credibility of the Western deterrent as a whole for Europe. The military case for Polaris was not based on the concept of pre-emptive attack on the Soviet Union but on retaining a capability to deter her. Circumstances were conceivable in which the Soviet Union might wish to attack this country without also attacking the United States and, given the deterrent philosophy of controlled response on which United States policy was based, might only be deterred from such an attack on our cities if we ourselves had the capability to inflict heavy damage on her. Finally, we had to take account of the fact that political and technical developments were making it increasingly likely that there would be further proliferation of nuclear weapons and that effective control and inspection would be impossible to achieve. For these reasons he considered that we should complete the Polaris programme and maintain the weapon system in an operational state.

The Committee first considered whether we should complete the planned Polaris programme and maintain the weapon system in an operational state. In discussion there was strong support for this. A time might come when worthwhile political advantage could be gained by abandoning our nuclear deterrent or by making arrangements within NATO for internationalising it on a European basis. But there was no sign of this at present. Although there had earlier been a suggestion that the United States might be willing to purchase our Polaris submarines and missiles, which would have economic advantages for us, their motive for doing this would be purely political since they did not need the submarines or missiles. Any such arrangement would make us completely dependent on the United States for defence against nuclear attack and would have serious political consequences. We should lose the ability to influence nuclear policy, and the polarisation of nuclear power in the United States and the Soviet Union would be accentuated as would the likelihood that the United States would become less committed to Europe. We should cease to have any influence with the Soviet Union, who would regard us as wholly a satellite of the United States. These political arguments were so strong as to outweigh completely the economic advantages that we would gain from abandoning Polaris.

On the other hand, it was argued that our present economic circumstances were such that neither the Defence Budget as a whole nor any particular part of it could be regarded as sacrosanct. There was a widely held view that, despite the reductions that had already been made, defence expenditure was still too high and expenditure on the

–2–

social services too low. If we could both avoid the running costs of
the Polaris system and sell the submarines and missiles to the United
States, this would be of great financial advantage to us. We should
not decide whether or not to retain the Polaris programme in isolation
from the rest of the defence programme; nor could we in any event
properly do so without first establishing how far the retention of the
existing programme would inevitably carry with it continuing expenditure
at AWRE and improvements in the Polaris system.

The Committee next considered whether, if we were to decide to
retain Polaris, we should also improve it.

THE DEFENCE SECRETARY said that unless an improvement programme
for Polaris was undertaken, it would soon become obvious publicly
that ABM systems would reduce the effectiveness of our Polaris and that,
although it would be relatively cheap for us to counter this threat
by hardening the system and incorporating penetration aids we had
decided not to do so. This would reduce the credibility of our Polaris
in the eyes of the world and forfeit its value as a bargaining
counter should the time come when we wished to gain advantage from
abandoning or internationalising it. There were a number of options at
costs varying between £2 million and £40 million and of varying
effectiveness, open to us for hardening the warhead and for penetration
aids. We should arrange for six months' study work to be carried out
at AWRE and at the Royal Aircraft Establishment, Farnborough, into the
possibility of hardening the warhead, the inclusion of penetration aids,
the costs and implications of the various alternatives and plan to reach
a decision in the light of these studies on which of them, if any, we
should adopt; this would fit the timetable on which the United States
were working for the completion of their development programme for
penetration aids for Polaris and for their decision whether or not to
produce these. In the meantime he would welcome an independent inquiry,
which might take three months, into the level of effort that was
required at AWRE to ensure the continued serviceability of our existing
nuclear weapons and to carry out the various alternative improvement
programmes for Polaris; it might be that economies would be possible
for example by concentrating work at present undertaken by AWRE and by
the Royal Ordnance factories at Burghfield and Cardiff.

-3-

41. (cont.)

In discussion it was recognised that support for the retention of Polaris did not necessarily involve support also for succeeding stages in updating Polaris. There was support for the view that we should undertake the studies proposed by the Defence Secretary; logically it would be right at this point in time to decide that hardening of the warhead was necessary. But there would be advantage in having more time in which to consider the matter. If we were to initiate the proposed studies, this would give the Defence Secretary a basis on which to explore with the United States Secretary for Defense, Mr. McNamara, what additional United States information would be made available to us on penetration aids. Without such a basis Mr. McNamara would be prevented by United States law from discussing the subject.

On the other hand it was argued that it would be wrong to defer a decision and thus remove the possibility of making early savings. We should recognise the improvement proposal as a step which would lead inevitably to further expensive measures to update Polaris in order to keep pace with threats to it; we should therefore decide now that Polaris should not be improved. Unhardened missiles were sufficient for our purposes and we should not attempt to keep pace with the Soviet Union or the United States. As regards an inquiry into the possibility of reducing the level of effort at AWRE on nuclear weapons, doubts were expressed whether such an enquiry was likely to produce useful results. If an inquiry was undertaken, however, it would be necessary for it to include an examination of the extent to which staff currently employed at AWRE on nuclear weapons work could usefully be redeployed; the key staff there were highly qualified specialists who might prefer to find employment in their own specialisation abroad, particularly in the United States, than to take up alternative work in this country. It would be desirable that those undertaking the enquiry should include someone with experience of economic problems and cost accounting.

THE PRIME MINISTER, summing up the discussion, said that further studies should be undertaken to clarify the requirements and costs of alternative programmes for hardening the Polaris warhead and of penetration aids for the system. In his forthcoming discussions with Mr. McNamara about the extent to which further United States information might be forthcoming about penetration aids for Polaris, the Defence Secretary could take the line that there had been no change in the planned

—4—

programme for Polaris. Our economic situation was, however, such that further reductions in planned defence expenditure might be needed and in these circumstances no particular element of the defence programme could be regarded as sacrosanct.

At the same time consideration should be given to possible terms of reference and membership for an inquiry into the minimum scale of effort that would be necessary at the Atomic Weapons Research Establishment, Aldermaston, and at related establishments, on the alternative hypotheses that we decided to retain the Polaris programme as already planned or that we undertook in addition a Polaris warhead hardening programme, with or without penetration aids. An inquiry of this kind should also examine the extent to which further diversification of work at Aldermaston would be feasible on each of these hypotheses.

The Committee should resume discussion on these issues, if possible, at a meeting before the end of the year.

The Committee —

(1) Agreed that further studies should be undertaken to clarify the requirements and costs of alternative programmes for hardening the Polaris warhead and of penetration aids for the Polaris system.

(2) Invited the Defence Secretary to be guided by the Prime Minister's summing up of their discussion in his forthcoming meeting with the United States Defence Secretary, Mr. McNamara.

(3) Took note that the Prime Minister would arrange for further consideration to be given to possible terms of reference and membership for an inquiry into the minimum scale of effort that would be necessary at the Atomic Weapons Research Establishment and at related establishments on the basis indicated in his summing up of their discussion.

(4) Agreed to resume their discussion at a meeting before the end of the year.

Cabinet Office, S.W.1.
  6th December 1967

-5-

The Defence Secretary, Denis Healey, linked three arguments: 90 per cent of the capital cost of Polaris was effectively already sunk in the project; the French were an unreliable ally and moving towards an ICBM capacity; as his officials' paper had argued, there were 'conceivable' circumstances in which the Soviet Union might attack the UK and not the USA. The possibility of selling the Royal Navy's Polaris boats to the US Navy was dismissed. Wilson's argument in retirement about the need to influence US nuclear policy was aired, as the economic arguments for abandoning Polaris crowded in.

Polaris improvement was taken separately from the desirability of keeping the system as planned in being, and its several uncertainties, technical and budgetary, were recognised as was the future of Aldermaston. The committee followed Wilson's summing up which accepted the continuation of the Polaris programme as planned, while calling for further studies of the need to improve Polaris and the capabilities of the Atomic Weapons Research Establishment.

Polaris surfaced during the Wilson Cabinet's protracted discussions in early 1968 of the public spending consequences of the sterling devaluation. Barbara Castle, the Minister of Transport and a keen nuclear disarmer, compared Healey's November 1964 arguments with his latest thinking in her diary entry for 12 January 1968:

> Denis admitted that it would have made economic sense to cancel Polaris when we came in, but argued that it wouldn't do so now. Ninety-five per cent of the cost was spent or committed. If we abandoned it, it wouldn't affect the spread of nuclear weapons. And to leave France now as the only nuclear power in Europe would be an 'act of stupendous irresponsibility'. I challenged his version of the facts. My recollection of the decision of 1964 (and no one challenged it) was that we had been told the cost of cancelling Polaris would be as great as keeping them on, so all we could do was abandon the fifth, which we readily did.[89]

Polaris would continue, but would the R and D establishment on which the UK's capacity to make warheads depended? Tony Benn, the Minister of Technology, in line with PN's instructions, commissioned a review of its future under Lord Kings Norton.

The Kings Norton Working Party recommended it should. Lord Rothschild dissented in a minority report which reflected his views and those of his friend, Sir Solly Zuckerman.

42. Lord Rothschild's 'Minority Report' dissenting from the findings of the Kings Norton Working Party on Atomic Weapons Establishments, 18 July 1968.

TNA, PRO, CAB 134/3121, Part 2

TOP SECRET ATOMIC   Ref: AWE Report

U.K. EYES ONLY   (Volume 2)

Copy No. 34 of 60 Copies
(Series A)

REPORT

TO THE MINISTER OF TECHNOLOGY AND

THE CHAIRMAN OF THE ATOMIC ENERGY AUTHORITY

BY THE

WORKING PARTY ON ATOMIC WEAPONS ESTABLISHMENTS

JULY 1968

CHAIRMAN: LORD KINGS NORTON

VOLUME 2

TOP SECRET ATOMIC
U.K. EYES ONLY

42. (cont.)

TOP SECRET

Note: This also appears
in Volume I Page 40

EYES ONLY

Copy 34 of 60 Copies
Page 1 of 9 Pages

APPENDIX XII

LETTER FROM LORD ROTHSCHILD TO THE CHAIRMAN OF THE WORKING PARTY

Dear Lord Kings Norton,

I greatly regret that I do not feel able to sign the Report of your Working Party, and would ask you to have appended to it a Minority Report, attached. My reasons for this decision are recorded in the Minutes of the Working Party's Meeting held on the 15th July. In this letter, therefore, I need only mention the important points which influenced me to come to this conclusion. These were:

(1) The signature of the Report implies endorsement of an open-ended financial commitment, first because one cannot predict with certainty the outcome of the R. & D. required by hypotheses (b) and (c)*, which were not explicitly rejected in the Working Party's Report. Secondly, because these hypotheses involve increased expenditure in the form of Trials and Development elsewhere than at Aldermaston.

(2) The Working Party has been informed that even if hypothesis(a), which can be described as "care and maintenance", is adopted, only insignificant economies can be achieved, because of the diversification activities needed to "keep the scientists happy". Even accepting the unique nature of the work, I believe this conclusion to be untenable.

(3) When you examined a draft of my Minority Report you said it went beyond your Working Party's Terms of Reference. I do not believe the Working Party can adequately and conscientiously discharge its duties without consideration of certain strategic issues involving counter-measures and counter-action, subjects which come within the Working Party's remit.

What is said above naturally does not imply that I disagree with all the Working Party's findings. I concur, for example, with the views expressed in the Report about the Outstations, given that the status quo is maintained, which I believe to be wrong.

Yours sincerely,

Rothschild

18th July, 1968

---

* See Terms of Reference

APPENDIX XIII

SERIES A

MINORITY REPORT BY LORD ROTHSCHILD

INTRODUCTION

(1)   The Kings Norton Committee has been asked questions about
Aldermaston and its two sub-stations, Foulness and Orfordness.   These
questions can be roughly formulated, or interpreted, as follows:

(1.1)   What would be the effect on Aldermaston's operating
budget of starting a new Polaris warhead R and D
programme?

(1.2)   What would be the effect on Aldermaston's operating
budget of starting an R and D programme to improve
the existing Polaris warhead, or of engaging only in
the care and maintenance of the existing nuclear weapons?

(1.3)   Can the expert staff necessary for the care and maintenance of the existing nuclear weapons be kept, and kept
satisfied, at Aldermaston in the absence of new or
"interesting" nuclear R and D projects?

(1.4)   Do the results of the Committee's inquiries suggest the
need for rationalisation of nuclear weapons work at
establishments other than at Aldermaston?

FINANCE

(2)   Except at Universities and certain other institutes of higher learning
R and D has a practical objective whose cost is relevant to that of the R and
D in support of it.   The operational cost of our Polaris submarines is about
£20m. per year.

(2.1)   The operating cost, including depreciation and interest, of
Aldermaston and its two sub-stations is £26m.   The operating cost,
£2.5m. per year, of Burghfield, which is 95% concerned with nuclear
weapons, must be added to this sum, making £28.5m. in 1968/69.   The
Director of Aldermaston claims, however, that £28.5m. per year is too
high because it includes the monitoring programme, £1.6m., and the
cost of "diversification" (defined in (2.3)), £5.4m.   This naturally pre-
supposes that if Aldermaston did not exist, monitoring and "diversification"
would continue to cost the sums mentioned above.

(2.2)   The total cost of our Polaris H-bomb capability is, therefore,
£48.5m. per year.   This is probably an under-estimate, if only because
75% of the operating cost of the Royal Ordnance Factory, Cardiff, £1.1m.
per year, is at present necessary for the Polaris H-bomb capability.
A further £2m. per year might be added for interest on the capital cost
of fissile material, bringing the total to about £52m. per year.

/(2.3)

42. (cont.)

(2.3)   The Director of Aldermaston stated that 25% of Aldermaston's operating cost was spent on R and D which was not connected with nuclear weapons, defined in this report as diversification. 1,700 people, out of a total of 6,175, are so occupied. It could, therefore, be maintained that only £18m. out of the £24m. per year, which Aldermaston itself costs, is spent on nuclear weapons. This would reduce the total annual expenditure referred to in (2.2) to about £46m. But this argument is said by the Director to be fallacious because the scientists, engineers and mathematicians engaged in diversification are from time to time needed by the nuclear weapons groups and cannot, therefore, be got rid of, if this were thought necessary or desirable. Moreover, in the absence of new or improved Polaris warhead R and D, the Director believes that diversification provides the stimulus and interest required to retain his experts who it is claimed must remain at Aldermaston even for a care and maintenance programme. The nuclear weapons part of Aldermaston therefore costs between £18m. and £24m.

(2.4)   The economies achieved by running down staff numbers at an R and D institute are invariably less than might superficially be expected. Assuming 6,000 people at Aldermaston and an annual operating expenditure of £24m., it might be thought that a staff reduction of 2,000 would reduce the annual operating expenditure to £16m. This is not the case: the expenditure would probably fall only to £21m. According to the Director, it will not be until 1973/74 that there will be a direct relationship between a given percentage cut in staff and the savings which might be expected. The Director also says that, even if Aldermaston merely has a care and maintenance programme, staff numbers can only be reduced from their present level of 6,175 to a little under 6,000 by 1970, with the following, relatively small savings:

	1968/69	1969/70	1970/71	1971/72	1972/73	1973/74
£M.	23.8	22.3	20.7	19.6	19.5	19.3

If the nuclear weapons groups alone were considered for staff reductions, which the Director considers undesirable, or even impossible, an even less realistic situation emerges. Halving the staff engaged exclusively on nuclear weapons would effect a saving of £3.5m. on £24m. Apart from being impossible to achieve, the result of such action would be to create a nuclear weapons R and D establishment in which just under half the staff were mainly engaged on work which had nothing to do with the subject for which the establishment allegedly existed.

(2.5)   These peculiar conclusions arise in part because only 40% of Aldermaston's operating cost can be attributed to the salaries, wages and superannuation of the staff. At a conventional R and D establishment, at any rate an industrial one, salaries and wages

/would

TOP SECRET ATOMIC

would take up 60-65%* of the total operating cost. This anomaly makes it difficult significantly to reduce the operating cost of Aldermaston. The Committee has expresed some doubts about the Aldermaston estimates given above. But in the absence of a whole-time enquiry lasting many months, it had no alternative to accepting the Director's statements.

THE PURPOSE AND NATURE OF HARDENING

(3)   The scale of cost and effort for hardening as a means of reducing the vulnerability of the Polaris warhead cannot be considered without some preliminary observations on the strategic context within which hardening is assumed to have some value.

(3.1) The Committee has been told that the Polaris missile is exclusively deployed for use against Russia. China is not under consideration; nor is any other country such as a unified Germany of the future.

(3.2) While the missiles are at present programmed for use against military targets (a highly debatable concept), changing computer tapes is all that is necessary for the missiles to be fired against Russian cities, of which at least one quarter would be very seriously damaged by the missiles successfully launched from two of our four submarines.

(3.3) It would be naive, if not foolhardy, to imagine that these facts are unknown to or unsuspected by Russia, and this makes it desirable to consider two forms of Russian defence against our nuclear deterrent.

(3.4) The first, which is but briefly discussed, is counter-attack, possibly before and more certainly after, any nuclear attack by the United Kingdom on Russia. Russian medium range ballistic missile launchers are known to be trained on targets in the United Kingdom. The following table shows that the United Kingdom can be effectively eliminated as a viable country by a mere ten nuclear bombs, one above London, with a yield of twenty megatons, and the rest with yields of one megaton each.

Town	Population (millions)	Survivors (millions)
London	7.9	2
Birmingham	1.1	0.7
Glasgow	1.0	0.6
Liverpool	0.7	0.4
Manchester	0.6	0.3
Leeds	0.5	0.2
Sheffield	0.5	0.1
Edinburgh	0.5	0.1
Bristol	0.4	0.1
Belfast	0.4	.0
	13.6	4.5 (60-70% dead)

/(3.5)

* Factors probably contributing to this difference are, first a higher superannuation charge at industrial R and D establishments, and, secondly, the absence at them of an interest charge on capital. But the identification of the precise causes would necessitate a more intensive study.

42. (cont.)

TOP SECRET ATOMIC

(3.5) The Committee has been told that Polaris or Polaris-type missiles do not have Union Jacks or Stars and Stripes on them. How, then, would Russia react if such a missile were fired by the U.S.A., for example, at Moscow? <u>Inter alia</u> she might well take retaliatory action against the United Kingdom, with the results indicated in the preceding paragraph. Whatever the United States may say or believe about the acceptability of megadeaths in the U.S.A., the effective elimination of the United Kingdom by a small number of H-bombs must raise very serious doubts about the desirability of our having Polaris missiles at all. If it is undesirable, there must equally be a strong case for demonstrating to the world that we have got rid of them. In such circumstances a Polaris or Polaris-type missile attack by the U.S.A. on Russia would not necessarily have the consequences on the United Kingdom referred to above. By the same token the possibility of Russian preventive action would be eliminated.

(3.6) The second form of Russian Defence against our Polaris missiles is their destruction, in outer space, by a nuclear explosion. There are four possible counter-measures which could be taken against this defence:

(a) Hardening of the three H-bombs in the existing Polaris warhead;

(b) Hardening plus substitution of Decoys for one of the three H-bombs;

(c) Modification of the H-bomb ejector system (explained later); and

(d) A new Polaris warhead containing five hardened H-bombs and Decoys (with a new ejector system) of some other combination of hardened H-bombs and Decoys (with a new ejector system). This last project is not further considered as it would clearly involve a major increase in expenditure about which the Committee has no quantitative information.

(3.6.1) Contrary to what seems often to be believed in Government circles, I have not been convinced that hardening would be of major counter-defensive value. The argument in favour of hardening is that the explosion of a Russian Hot Bomb in outer space would render useless our existing Polaris H-bombs if they were within 150 miles of the Hot Bomb explosion. The destruction or inactivation of our H-bombs would probably be caused by the intense X-rays, emitted for an infinitesimal time, by the exploding Hot Bomb. Hardening would or might neutralize this defensive measure, by reducing the destructive range, 150 miles, to 15 (3 megaton Hot Bomb). However, a senior Ministry of Defence official told the Committee that Russian technology was such as to enable their defence system to explode a nuclear weapon within about 1000 feet of an incoming H-bomb, at which range Hardening would be useless. The fact that this might be expensive or difficult to do under certain circumstances does not alter the conclusion that Hardening is by no means the panacea it is often claimed to be.

/(3.6.2)

(3.6.2) There is a further problem about Hardening: can one harden against all the types of "radiation" which might be produced by a Hot Bomb or analogous weapon? The answer must involve much R and D which would necessitate the installation of expensive equipment at Aldermaston ("Energy Dumpers") and, probably, an expensive trial in Nevada.

(3.6.3) Two sorts of Hardening may be envisaged: first, what is called a Sock, which probably does not present very serious technical problems but even with the trial which would be necessary, may not be very efficient; and, secondly, a more sophisticated system about which, at present, Aldermaston can only say that a decision to go into production or not will probably be reached in three years time. This, like all R and D projects, has but a finite and, at present, unknown probability of success. In such circumstances the cost of a project is very difficult to estimate. The R and D and trial mentioned in (3.6.2) would, of course, be minimum requirements.

(3.6.4) There are other doubts about the efficacy of Hardening. The Committee has been told that the probability of our firing Polaris missiles is in the neighbourhood of zero except when the U.S.A. engages in a nuclear war against Russia. Leaving aside the fact that our Polaris missile capacity is so much smaller than that of the U.S.A. ($\simeq$ 10%)* as to make it relatively insignificant, questions of saturating Russian Defences, damage to Russian radar installations, and radar blackouts caused by Russian defensive Hot Bombs or offensive American H-bombs become of great importance. The U.S.A. claims to be able to deliver a greater number of H-bombs against Russia than the number of Hot Bombs or analogous weapons which the Russians have. It follows that the U.K. only has to wait a few minutes for the road to be clear. But apart from this, it is scarcely credible that all American or, for that matter, British H-bombs will be destroyed or inactivated in outer space. If the U.S.A. does not deliberately cause a "radar blackout", the radiations from exploding Hot Bombs may produce it, in which case the Russians will be unable accurately to locate incoming missiles and, therefore, explode subsequent Hot Bombs in the right place in outer space. If one H-bomb explodes over or on Moscow, the effectiveness of the radar on which the Russian anti-ballistic missile system depends is likely to be reduced, in which case Hardening becomes an unnecessary luxury.

(3.6.5) The conclusion seems inescapable that Hardening is not worth the candle, even though it may make Defence against Polaris H-bombs somewhat more difficult and expensive, assuming Russia has not already taken the possibility of Hardening into consideration. Hardening would not, in itself, make defence impossible.

/DECOYS

---

* Quite apart from the land-based and aircraft nuclear deterrent systems of the U.S.A.

42. (cont.)

DECOYS

(4)   The advantages of substituting Decoys for one of the three H-bombs in the Polaris warhead is open to question.   If the Russians cannot discriminate by radar between an H-bomb and Decoys, they will simply treat the objects as H-bombs, just as they would in the case of the existing warhead.   If, as is technically feasible, they can discriminate between Decoys and an H-bomb, they will concentrate their defences on the two H-bombs.   The cost of U.K.-developed Decoys is, apparently, unknown at the present time.

MODIFIED EJECTOR SYSTEM

(5)   The existing Polaris warhead contains three H-bombs which, at a particular moment in the flight of the warhead, are tipped out or ejected and travel on somewhat different trajectories towards the same target.   A new ejector system could be developed, by RAE Farnborough or Lockheed, whereby the three H-bombs would be separated from each other by a greater distance in outer space. This, together with Hardening, would make defence against the Polaris H-bombs more difficult and expensive; but the effect would be quantitative rather than qualitative.   Moreover, the programme to develop the new ejector system would certainly add significantly to the cost of our Polaris missile capability.   More sophisticated ejector and propulsion systems, involving, for example, changes in H-bomb trajectories in outer space, have been considered.   But their development would cost far greater, but unknown, sums of money.   Such programmes would be open-ended commitments.

DIVERSIFICATION

(6)   As mentioned earlier, no less than 1,700 people, out of a total of 6,175, work at Aldermaston on subjects other than nuclear weapons.   300 out of the 880 professionals are engaged on diversification.   In 1968/69 this activity cost £5.4m., 22% of the total operating cost.

(6.1)   Diversification at Aldermaston can be classified as follows:

    (a)   Pilot plant for manufacture of fast reactor fuel assemblies of an experimental nature.

    (b)   Reactors and accelerators (i) to provide data for civil reactor programmes;

           (ii) for University students.

    (c)   Basic work on health, safety and criticality for other Atomic Energy Authority groups.

    (d)   Other work

/These

TOP SECRET ATOMIC

These activities, which in general are of limited relevance to Aldermaston H-bomb R and D and production, are said to be conveniently located at Aldermaston; but the illogicality of this statement, given the existence in the U.K., of other civil reactor centres, at least one of which, Harwell, is also engaged in diversification, is so obvious as to need no elaboration. The Director's point, however, still stands: that care and maintenance of existing Polaris missiles is not a conventional technical service activity, but one requiring the employment of specialists who will not be satisfied and, therefore, work well, nor even, probably, stay, unless they have more interesting and creative work than care and maintenance. How much is the country prepared to pay to keep these experts happy? 22% of the cost of the establishment? 34% of the professional staff? 28% of the manpower?

(6.2) It is a fact well known to research administrators that the retention of top class or highly specialised staff in a research, development, or technical service establishment necessitates the allocation of some free time to some members of the establishment to work on projects relevant to the main activities of the establishment, but of their own selection. While such activities may amount to 25% or more in the case of an individual and his assistants, the overall cost should not be more than 5-10% of the establishment's operating budget. In the case of Aldermaston, with an operating budget of £24m., diversification should, therefore, cost about £2m., to be compared with £5.4m. This implies that the total staff on diversification should be reduced from 1,700 to 630.

(6.3) It is assumed in what is said above that the Government does not wish to engage in diversification at Aldermaston just for the sake of diversification: there are cogent reasons, of which the following are a few examples, in support of this assumption: first, Harwell also engages in diversification. If the Government wishes to control a centre similar to those of Arthur D. Little, Stanford Research Institute, or the Battelle Institute, to undertake contract work for industry and/or Government Departments, such work should be concentrated at one centre; it is inefficient and extravagent to do the work partly at Aldermaston and partly at Harwell. Secondly, the rigorous security measures which are essential at Aldermaston, both against espionage and because of the dangerous materials handled, are inappropriate for an Institute of the Arthur D. Little type. Thirdly, the staff have been selected because of their ability to work on nuclear weapons or allied subjects. In spite of the obvious creativity of some staff members of Aldermaston, selection as a whole has been inappropriate for an establishment of the Arthur D. Little type. Fourthly, it would be ludicrous to expect the staff at Aldermaston, engaging as they do in some of the most dangerous and specialised work done anywhere in the world, to be as cost-conscious, if not profit-orientated, as is necessary when working for a semi-commercial research establishment.

/RELATIONSHIPS

42. (cont.)

RELATIONSHIPS WITH THE U.S.A.

7.   The Director of Aldermaston and his senior staff attach great importance to the special relationship which exists between them and their opposite numbers in the U.S.A.   The relationship is stimulating and, provided Aldermaston engages in new R and D, there is a probability that the U.S.A. will provide Aldermaston with information based on U.S. research and which is relevant to the new R and D in question.   Aldermaston may, therefore, expect to get information about Socks, Improved Socks, New Ejector systems and Decoys, if U.K. research is done on these subjects and there is a clear intention to apply the results of this research in weapon systems.   Perhaps some information would also be made available if we bought Socks, etc. in the U.S.A.   If, however, Aldermaston concentrates on the care and maintenance of existing nuclear weapons, new information from the U.S.A. will dry up.   Even if the information from the U.S.A. is as important as is claimed, its acquisition is of questionable importance in the light of what has been said in this Memorandum.   The Committee has not had an opportunity of examining in detail how much information has actually been obtained from the U.S.A., nor how valuable, albeit interesting, the information was.

CONCLUSIONS

(8)   Without a whole-time investigation which would take many months, the Committee has had to accept that putting Aldermaston on a care and maintenance basis appears to achieve negligible economies.

(8.1)   Hardening or the development of more sophisticated warheads will incur additional, open-ended expenditure.

(8.2)   No technical considerations have been advanced which lead to the conclusion that hardening or the development of more sophisticated war- heads would confer clear-cut and unequivocal advantages on the United Kingdom.   These two possibilities can, therefore, be dismissed, but, if only for the reasons given in (8), the need for Aldermaston's care and maintenance activity also needs reconsideration.

(8.3)   A decision to spend the very large sum of money required to maintain Aldermaston, apparently at about its present level, just for the care and maintenance of existing weapons, depends on a political decision about the strategic advantage, whether real or imaginary, of our having atomic weapons at all.

(8.4)   The closure of Aldermaston raises problems of re-deployment to which many objections will be made.   These objections are surmountable.

ROTHSCHILD

31st July, 1968

The Rothschild minority report is highly revealing of the technical options under consideration in 1968 for 'hardening' Polaris, but also of the argument (which he found unconvincing) that, as the UK and US Polaris 'missiles do not have Union Jacks or Stars and Stripes on them', the Russian radars would not be able to tell if an incoming missile was British or American. The conclusion being (though Rothschild's paper does not reflect this) that the UK's possessing a small amount of the best American kit was a way of locking the USA into the defence of western Europe.

Aldermaston survived, and continued to work on the options for Polaris improvement in view of intelligence reports of an ABM system, the GALOSH, under construction around Moscow.

TOP SECRET

THIS DOCUMENT IS THE PROPERTY OF HER BRITANNIC MAJESTY'S GOVERNMENT

The circulation of this paper has been strictly limited. It is issued

for the personal use of...C/L..........................

Copy No. **133**

JIC (A) (69) 3 (Final)
17th January, 1969

CABINET

JOINT INTELLIGENCE COMMITTEE

————

SOVIET BLOC WAR POTENTIAL, 1969–73

REPORT BY JOINT INTELLIGENCE COMMITTEE (A)

In the report at Annex we estimate the war potential of the Soviet Union and the non-Soviet Warsaw Pact countries for the period 1969–73.

2.   This report supersedes our previous study (JIC (68) 3) of this subject.

(Signed)   EDWARD PECK,
Chairman, Joint Intelligence Committee (A).

Cabinet Office, S.W.1,
    17th January, 1969

TOP SECRET

SECTION X

AIR AND CIVIL DEFENCE

Appendices:
M. Composition of Soviet *bloc* Air Forces
N. Performance of Soviet Aircraft
P. Soviet Air-to-Air Missiles
R. Soviet Land-based Defensive Missile Systems.

SOVIET DEFENCE AGAINST MISSILE AND AIR ATTACK

General
1. The Soviet leaders have continued to show their traditional pre-occupation with the security of their homeland. Although they believe that co-ordinated use of all branches of the armed forces is required to achieve victory in war, even in the nuclear age, they regard the Strategic Rocket Forces and the Air Defence Forces as being of prime importance. Thus they have devoted, and continue to devote, a high proportion of their military expenditure to the air and missile defence of their homeland and its armies, both directly through the maintenance of their own air and missile defence forces and, so far as air defence alone is concerned, through the support given by them to the other members of the Warsaw Pact.

2. Air defence of the Soviet *bloc* is mainly entrusted to three organisations, the most important of which is PVO Strany (Air Defence of the Homeland), which is an independent armed service of equal status with the Soviet Ground, Navy, Air and Strategic Rocket Forces. It has its own Commander-in-Chief who sits as a Deputy Minister of Defence on the Military Council. The other two organisations which assist PVO Strany in its mission are the air defence organisations of Soviet field armies with their associated Tactical Air Armies and the air defence organisation in Eastern Europe set up within the framework of the Warsaw Pact. Although the air defence of Non-Soviet Warsaw Pact (NSWP) countries is a national responsibility and the defence of Groups of Soviet Forces stationed outside the Soviet Union is the responsibility of the local Soviet Air Defence Commander, the air defence role of PVO Strany is closely co-ordinated with those of *bloc* national forces and Groups of Soviet Forces. In addition mention has been made of a force called "Anti-Missile Defence Troops of the USSR" (PRO) but its status is not yet clear.

Organisation
3. PVO Strany consists of an early warning and control organisation (RTV), a fighter arm (IAPVO), surface-to-air missiles (ZRV) and possibly air defence guns (ZAPVO). Within Russia PVO Strany also co-ordinates the activities of the Tactical Air Force air defence regiments and may exercise a similar degree of authority over other field force air defence units.

4. PVO Strany forces are grouped into 10 Air Defence Districts (ADDs) which are in turn divided into Zones, some of which are further divided into sectors. The air defences of the other members of the Warsaw Pact are organised as if each were a Soviet ADD and are thus in effect extensions of the Soviet system.

Ballistic missile early warning
5. HEN HOUSE radars which have been constructed in the Kola Peninsula and on the Baltic coast are now believed to be operational. Used in a ballistic missile early-warning system (BMEWS) role these radars should be capable of detecting and tracking practically any ballistic missile approaching north-western USSR if launched from the United States or intermediate areas. This system would provide about 14 minutes' warning to Moscow of attack from the United States or up to 17 minutes' of POLARIS missiles fired from extreme range from the intermediate area. This deployment could be extended to give warning of attack from other areas.

6. The Soviet Union has been active for many years in developing back-scatter HF radar. This system, Over the Horizon Radar (OTHR), may have been used to detect Western nuclear detonations and missile launchings; it is also potentially capable of detecting material targets at all (including very low) altitudes. These radars have not at this time been detected in an operational watch-keeping surveillance role.

Anti-ballistic missile systems

7. There is evidence that Soviet defensive policy includes an active defence against ballistic missiles of all types. This has been demonstrated by the continuance since 1956 of an extensive R and D programme based on the Sary Shagan Anti-Missile Test Centre (SSATC) and deployment activities taking place at Moscow and possibly elsewhere in the USSR. There is insufficient knowledge on which to base an estimate of the characteristics or capabilities of any ABM systems which have been developed but it has been possible to make preliminary assessments of the missile and radar equipment almost certainly associated with the programme and to examine the developing deployment pattern. An ABM system is being constructed around Moscow. Early warning for the system will be provided by the BMEWS (HEN HOUSE radars) located at Skrunda on the Baltic coast and at Olenegorsk in the Kola Peninsula. Long-range acquisition and early tracking will be provided by a large radar (DOG HOUSE) sited 35 miles south-west of Moscow. Final tracking and defensive missile control is believed to be provided by radars housed in sets of three domed buildings known as TRIADs under construction on at least six sites round Moscow at a radius of about 45 miles. The missile in the system is GALOSH (see Appendix R). The system is expected to provide Moscow with a limited defence against ICBM launched from the United States and POLARIS missiles launched from the intermediate area, approaching within the arc of the BMEWS.

Early warning of air attack

8. The Soviet early-warning and control radar system for a non-ballistic missile attack is based on about 6,000 radars deployed in various combinations at some 1,300 sites throughout the Soviet *bloc*. The approaches to all peripheral areas are covered by the high-powered static metric radar TALL KING. This equipment will give coverage out to 250 nm against a 1 square metre target, *e.g.*, a small aircraft or ASM, at 50,000 ft, extending to 500 nm at 250,000 ft. At low altitude normal line of sight limitations will apply. TALL KING deployment is supplemented by large numbers of shorter range mobile radars which operate over a wide range of frequencies. In addition, it is possible that the OTHR described in paragraph 6 above could come into service during the period and provide early warning of aircraft attack at all heights and at approximate ranges between 1,500 nm and 500 nm. The deployment of passive electronic or infra-red sensors, perhaps vehicle mounted, from which tracking data on low-flying aircraft could be derived is also possible, although the effective range of such devices could not extend beyond the frontiers of the Warsaw Pact countries.

9. The radar early-warning system provides overlapping radar cover at varying heights over almost the whole of the USSR and Eastern Europe, with the greatest coverage in peripheral areas and west of the Urals. Information is also obtained from a network of visual observers. Recent evidence has revealed that the Soviets have modified a Tu-114 CLEAT by the addition of a discus-shaped radar antenna on the dorsal surface of the fuselage. Used in the early-warning role aircraft of this type could extend land-based early warning by as much as 200 nm over sea areas. The NATO nickname for the modified Tu-114 is MOSS. (See also paragraph 28.) There are a number of small ships and five submarines equipped with early-warning radar which could also be deployed to extend coverage in certain sectors.

10. It is difficult to assess the raid reporting capacity of the early-warning system as a whole. At heights of 3,000 ft and above it should be capable of dealing with small numbers of intruding aircraft at any point on a narrow front, or a wave attack over a wide front. In areas where data link reporting has been introduced the capacity of the early-warning system will have been increased. The system does not, and probably never will, provide unbroken overlapping cover at low altitude (*i.e.,* the height band from ground level to 1,000 ft). However,

APPENDIX R

SOVIET LAND-BASED DEFENSIVE MISSILE SYSTEMS

Serial	System (i)	IOC (ii)	Missile (iii)	Altitude (ft) (iv)	Range (nm) (v)	Warhead (lb.) (vi)	Radar/Band (vii)	Guidance (viii)	Remarks (ix)
1	SA-1	Before 1960	GUILD	6,000–60,000	16–22	420 Blast frag.	YO-YO S band	Command	Obsolescent
2	SA-2	Before 1960	GUIDELINE Mk. 2	1,500/5,000–80,000	19	420 Blast frag.	FAN SONG A/B S Band	Command	Obsolescent in USSR
3	SA-2	1962?	GUIDELINE Mk. 3	1,000/3,000–85,000	27	420 Blast frag.	FAM SONG /CE C Band	Command	Low altitude limit depends on aircraft speed, radar mask angle, etc.
4	SA-3	1962–63	GOA	500/1,000 up to 45,000/50,000	10–15	150 Prob. blast frag.	LOW BLOW X Band	Command	Limited evidence for guidance
5	SA-4	1967?	GANEF	Maximum probably below about 50,000 No assessment of lower limit pending knowledge of radar system	About 30	About 450	—	Possibly command	No information on fire control equipment Field Army SAM
6	GRIFFON	—	GRIFFON	10,000–80,000	50–100	600–750 HE or nuclear	—	—	Operational deployment abandoned
7	SA-5	1968	—	—	—	—	—	—	Long Range SAM. Increasing evidence of deployment
8	SA-6	—	GAINFUL	Low medium altitude (up to 35,000 ft)	About 10	150/200	—	Possibly semi-active radar and/or command	No evidence of deployment No information on fire control equipment Field Army SAM
9	ABM	By 1970	GALOSH	200 nm	450	2,000 HE or nuclear	—	—	Probably for deployment around Moscow

The incoming Conservatives in June 1970 inherited the Aldermaston research on Polaris improvement commissioned by the Wilson government of 1966–70. Heath and his ministers faced a choice: to seek to buy the Poseidon missile, the US successor to Polaris, and to fit to it a British version of the American multiple independently targeted re-entry vehicle (or MIRV) system; or to go for a less advanced, non-MIRV system that the US code-named Antelope, which would use decoys to swamp the Russians' GALOSH defences.[90]

At the end of May 1972, the Strategic Arms Limitations Treaty signed in Moscow limited the USA and the USSR to 200 anti-ballistic missile launchers each to protect Washington and Moscow. Without such a cap, the effectiveness of the Royal Navy's Polaris force, even with the Super Antelope improvements, would have been drastically reduced by GALOSH systems around several leading Soviet cities.

Lord Carrington, the Defence Secretary, had commissioned a good deal of preparatory work within the Ministry of Defence. In January 1972, Carrington called for a study of a 'Poor Man's Deterrent'. In just over three months it was ready, drafted by a sub-group of the Long Term Working Party on the British Deterrent chaired by Sir Hermann Bondi, Chief Scientific Adviser to the Ministry of Defence.

Carrington was told that: 'With a boat load of unimproved Polaris missiles [which carried 16 of them] there would only be a very low probability of one missile penetrating Soviet ABM defences once its radar coverage cannot be outflanked.'[91] The report was sent to Carrington on 21 March 1972. Six days later it was discussed by the Chiefs of Staff with a number of other nuclear-related papers.

All the chiefs, bar one, stressed the importance of a strategic nuclear deterrent to the UK's overall defence posture. The exception was Field Marshal Sir Michael Carver, Chief of the General Staff. He was very critical of 'the rationale' for a continued UK capacity being 'a wish to avoid France being the only nuclear power in Europe', and he diminished the argument that Britain might, in some circumstances, have to stand alone in nuclear terms against the Soviet Union:

> In the case of an invasion of Western Europe, the USSR would always have to face the possibility of US intervention, and this would surely pose a real fear in Russian thinking. It was inconceivable that the Soviets would run even a small risk of inviting a strategic nuclear attack on themselves. . .
>
> He also doubted [the minutes continue] the credibility of an independent UK strategic nuclear deterrent, either in our own or in Soviet minds, because of its dependence on the political will to use such a last resort measure. If it were to be used when Europe was attacked it would represent the voice of a suicide; if used when Europe had been overrun or we ourselves were under attack, it would be a voice from the grave.[92]

Heath and his inner group of nuclear ministers (Douglas-Home, Foreign Secretary; Carrington, Defence Secretary; and Anthony Barber, Chancellor of the Exchequer) reached their decision-taking stage on Polaris improvement over a year later, just as a wide range of economic and industrial problems began seriously to stretch the government in the autumn of 1973. The Treasury, as always, had cost worries, but there was no ministerial equivalent of Michael Carver to argue against carrying on as a nuclear power.

Lord Carrington briefed Heath and his nuclear group on the choices facing them in a minute of 10 September 1973. The options were a fully-mirved Poseidon system; option M, a de-mirved Poseidon front-end which was still at the design stage in the US; or the UK-designed decoy-system known by this stage as Super Antelope. Carrington stressed the need for a swift decision if the effectiveness of Polaris was to be sustained throughout the late 1970s.

Copy No. 1

Page 1 of 4

MINISTRY OF DEFENCE   WHITEHALL   LONDON SW1A 2HB

TELEPHONE 01-930 7022

TOP SECRET

UK EYES B

MO 18/1/1

PRIME MINISTER

IMPROVEMENT OF STRATEGIC NUCLEAR DETERRENT

On 12th September we shall be resuming our discussion on the options for improving the nuclear deterrent.

2.   Discussions which the Chief of the Defence Staff had with Admiral Moorer in America on 23rd and 24th August suggested that it would be worthwhile :

   (a)   taking a further sounding with Dr. Kissinger on his personal estimate of the likelihood of now securing Congressional approval for fully MIRVed POSEIDON against the background of the American Defense Secretary's announcement on 17th August that the Russians have successfully demonstrated flight tests of a MIRV capability on at least two of their missiles;

   (b)   seeking further up-to-date information from US officials on the costs of both MIRVed POSEIDON and Option M; and on the possibility of spreading the costs of a POSEIDON-based option more evenly than we had previously thought possible, thereby reducing the cost over the crucial early years.

3.   As to (a) above, HM Minister has reported (in Washington telegram No. 2711 of 31st August) that Dr. Kissinger's position remains (as stated by him to Sir Burke Trend on 30th July) that MIRVed POSEIDON would involve a quarrel with Congress which the Administration would not wish to take on, but that if HMG chose it the Administration would be disposed to be helpful; he estimates the chances of obtaining agreement at about 50/50, or at best 60/40. This can be read as marginally more optimistic than the assessment reported in paragraph 4 of my minute of 13th July; but I do not think we can regard it as sufficient to invalidate the view which I put to our meeting on 16th July, that the choice lies effectively between Option M and SUPER ANTELOPE.

/ 4. As

TOP SECRET   UK EYES B

TOP SECRET
U.K. EYES B

TOP SECRET

UK EYES B

- 2 -

4.   As to (b) above, discussions within the last week with US Navy officials on the latest costing of those elements which would be common to both MIRVed POSEIDON and Option M has suggested the attached revision of the estimated costs of SUPER ANTELOPE and Option M and their relationship to published Defence Budget targets and long term costing provisions.   The new assessment is substantially the same as the previous one.   So far as the calculations in my minute of 17th August are concerned the main effects are that :-

(a)   the differences between the 1973 Public Expenditure Report figures and the MOD bids (assuming Option II) referred to in paragraph 3 become £14m in 1974/75 and £50m in 1975/76.   The Option I differences stand;

(b)   the MOD Option II bid for 1976/77 shown in Annex A to my minute becomes £3567m: and the savings shown as required if Option II is chosen each rise by £6m.

In 1977/78 the MOD bid was in any case provisional and the change now required to the previous costings is comparatively small, so the figures for that year in Annex A can be assumed to stand.   Annex B therefore remains unchanged as an illustration of the military and industrial implications of the various levels of savings in 1977/78.

5.   Underlying this new assessment, however, are :-

(i)   a new assumption that we would purchase the inert re-entry bodies complete from America, instead of manufacturing substantial parts of them ourselves;

(ii)   no reduction in the uncertainty about the cost of developing and producing the new dispenser needed for Option M, which is the major area of technical risk in the project: we cannot begin to resolve this until we have asked for the Presidential determination needed for the release of the Mark III warhead for Option M.

6.   As I have said in my previous minutes, it is now urgent for us to reach a decision.   The later we reach a decision, the later will the necessary Congressional procedures (paragraph 2 of my minute of 13th July) be completed; and delay can be aggravated by Congressional recesses.   The cost of components of the Option M system, such as the non-nuclear parts of the warheads, will increase progressively as orders are delayed. We must start discussions with American officials very soon if we are to have any chance of meeting the dates for converting our submarines.   And whatever our decision the longer we delay, the longer will be the period in the later 1970s during which

/ the

TOP SECRET   UK EYES B

TOP SECRET   U.K. EYES B

44. (cont.)

TOP SECRET

U.K. EYES B

- 3 -

the credibility of our deterrent force will be degraded.
Funds will continue to be needed to keep SUPER ANTELOPE going;
my officials will be in touch with the Treasury about this.

7.   I am copying this minute to the Foreign & Commonwealth
Secretary, to the Chancellor of the Exchequer and to
Sir Burke Trend.

C

10th September 1973

IMPROVED STRATEGIC DETERRENT - FINANCIAL REQUIREMENTS AND BUDGETARY PROVISION

	73/4	74/5	75/6	76/7	77/8	78/9	79/80	80/1	81/2	82/3	83/4	TOTAL to 83/84	TOTAL to 93/94
TOTAL SYSTEM COSTS ESTIMATE (as before)													
1. Super Antelope	73	82	93	94	72	52	44	41	46	49	53	699	1179
2. Option M	59	76	118	126	121	108	73	58	47	40	37	863	1246
DEFENCE BUDGET PROVISION													
In Targets													
3. For 4 boat A3T force	40	45	53	58									
4. For "front end"	24	25	21	9									
In LTC 73													
5. For 4 boat A3T force					49	43	43	41	46	49	53		
6. For "front end"					22	20	15	5	2	1	1		
7. Total	64	70	74	67	71	63	58	46	48	49	53	663	
Difference													
Super Antelope (1 – 7)	9	12	19	27	1	-11	-14	-5	-2	0	0	36	
Option M (2-7)	-5	6	44	59	50	45	15	12	-1	-9	-16	200	

EXCESSES:

	Up to 76/7	Up to 82/3	Up to 83/4
SUPER ANTELOPE	67	36	36
OPTION M	104	216	200

TOP SECRET UK EYES B

The Cabinet Secretary, Burke Trend, supplemented Carrington's minute with a steering brief for Heath which raised the levels of dependence/independence in the technical choices ahead. Heath had made a substantial effort to engineer a nuclear weapons collaboration with France in the early 1970s.[93] But, Trend advised, this was not a realistic possibility for the improvement of Polaris, on which an urgent decision was needed as funding for Super Antelope was due to run out at the end of the month.

Lord Carrington (centre) with Edward Heath (who improved Polaris) and Margaret Thatcher (who replaced it with Trident).

45. Trend's brief for Heath on 'The Nuclear Deterrent', 11 September 1973.

TNA, PRO, PREM 15/2038

E.R.

Ref: A05090   TOP SECRET

Copy No. 1
of 5 copies

This is a copy. The original has been removed and retained under Section 3(4)

PRIME MINISTER

<u>The Nuclear Deterrent</u>

The most convenient way of opening tomorrow's discussion might be to deal with the issues involved in terms of the four basic objectives which we have adopted as our criteria at previous meetings and to try to compare, under each of these headings, the respective advantages and disadvantages of the options open to us.

2. But we must first decide how many options are available - 2 or 3? This means, in effect deciding whether we include, or finally exclude, the option of a fully-MIRVed POSEIDON. We have been encouraged to entertain this prospect once more by the latest exchanges between the CDS and his opposite number in Washington. But these were conducted at a professional level; and, when we asked Dr. Kissinger for a political assessment of our chances of securing a fully-MIRVed system, his answer remained as before - i.e. that we need not regard ourselves as debarred from asking for such a system; that, if we did so, the President would be "positive"; but that it would entail an argument with Congress in which the United States Administration were not anxious to involve themselves; and that the chances of obtaining Congressional agreement were perhaps only 50/50 or, at best, 60/40.

3. In these circumstances the Secretary of State for Defence concludes, in his minute of 10th September, that we should now rule out the option of a fully-MIRVed POSEIDON and that the choice before us lies effectively between Option M and SUPER ANTELOPE.

4. In deciding whether to accept this advice Ministers will need to weigh on the one hand, the risk of asking for a fully-MIRVed system and suffering a public rebuff, together with the fact that a system of this kind (if we secured it) would make us even more dependent upon the United States, against the considerations, on the other hand, that it would probably be cheaper than Option M, would be even more effective in operational terms and would ensure full compatibility with the United States system for the foreseeable future. They may decide that the balance inclines against the fully-MIRVed system and that the choice lies effectively therefore between Option M and SUPER ANTELOPE. But a decision of this kind entails certain consequences, which are indicated below.

-1-

45. (cont.)

TOP SECRET

5.   If we now try to evaluate the respective merits of Option M and
SUPER ANTELOPE in terms of our original four objectives, the picture
has not changed a great deal since the last discussion.   Thus -

(i)   Our first objective is to maintain the credibility of our
capacity to inflict an unacceptable level of damage on the
Soviet Union.   There can be little doubt that, by reference
to this criterion, Option M has the edge over SUPER
ANTELOPE.   This is probably clearer now than on any
previous occasion when we have discussed this subject,
since the latest disclosure that the Soviet Government
have successfully tested MIRV systems on some of their
ICBMs suggests that the chances of a successful outcome
to SALT II must be even more doubtful than hitherto.   If
so, we must reckon with the probability that the Soviet
Government will not observe SALT I for any longer than
it suits them and that their ABM system is accordingly
more, rather than less, likely to be upgraded in the
foreseeable future.   It follows that SUPER ANTELOPE may
not retain its credibility for very long.   It also follows
that, if it is United States policy - as we have repeatedly
been told by Washington - that the Soviet Government
should remain confronted with a credible nuclear capability
which would be an addition and an alternative to the United
States deterrent, the United States Government should be
correspondingly more willing to help us to realise Option M.

(ii)   Our second objective is to avoid prejudicing our conventional
contribution to NATO.   This raises the whole question of
defence expenditure, which has most recently been examined
in the minutes of 17th August and 10th September by the
Secretary of State for Defence, 30th August by the Foreign
and Commonwealth Secretary and 10th September by the
Chancellor of the Exchequer.

The annex to Lord Carrington's minute of 10th September
shows that the additional costs entailed by either SUPER
ANTELOPE or Option M, although not insignificant
(particularly in the years immediately ahead), are not,
quantitatively, very large.   Nor is the difference between

-2-

them particularly striking. Indeed, Option M would be
cheaper than SUPER ANTELOPE by £14 million in the
current financial year and £6 million in 1974-75, while in
the following 4 financial years the margin of additional
expenditure which it would entail would be only £25 million,
£32 million, £49 million and £56 million respectively.
These are orders of magnitude which it should be possible to
accommodate without too much difficulty in a programme of
defence expenditure <u>which was acceptable in other respects;</u>
and, if this was all that we had to reckon with, there can
surely be little doubt that the financial consideration should
not tip the balance against Option M if it is judged preferable
on other counts. But we face the additional complication that
the defence budget is <u>not</u> acceptable in other respects and
that in his minute of 10th September the Chancellor of the
Exchequer reiterates his view that the defence budget,
calculated as a percentage of GNP, should be reduced by not
less than 1 per cent below its current level of 5.5 per cent,
a reduction which should be achieved, if not by 1977-78, then
as soon thereafter as possible.
The implications of different possible levels of savings on the
defence budget, according to whether SUPER ANTELOPE or
Option M is preferred, are examined in the minute of
17th August by the Secretary of State for Defence.
Paragraph 6 of that minute indicates that a reduction in the
defence budget from 5.5 per cent to 4.5 per cent of GNP would
involve savings of some £600 million, and that these, in
Lord Carrington's view, could not be achieved "without
massive reductions in the size and capability of all 3 Services
in our contribution to NATO and in the overseas commitment
that we can sustain". It is clear from the Foreign and
Commonwealth Secretary's minute of 30th August that
Sir Alec Douglas-Home would see the gravest objection,
in terms of our foreign policy, to economies of this order.
Tomorrow's meeting is presumably not the occasion for an
examination of this major issue of policy. That must wait
upon the projected discussion between the Chancellor of the
Exchequer and the Secretary of State for Defence in the

-3-

45. (cont.)

E.R.

context of the PESC review. But if it is true, as suggested above, that the additional cost entailed by either Option M or SUPER ANTELOPE would be relatively trivial (amounting, in the case of the more expensive of the two options, to no more than about 0.2 per cent of GNP in the peak years 1976-77 and 1977-78), it would surely be unwise to allow the decision on so critical an issue as the future of the deterrent to be determined by financial considerations. It is a decision which should be taken on merits, in terms of the ultimate security of this country; and if, on these grounds, Option M is preferred, the relatively small additional expenditure involved should be found by one means or another.

The Secretary of State for Defence may reply that this would be merely to pre-empt to some extent the basic decision on the defence budget as a whole; and that it would be wrong to settle the nuclear component of that budget until the implications for the conventional component can be assessed in greater detail in the PESC context. But this is a chicken-and-egg argument; and I question whether it should prevail in so critical a matter as this. Other NATO countries have conventional forces, however reluctant they may be to pay for them; only we have an independent deterrent.

(iii) Our third objective is to retain an independent nuclear weapons technology of our own. It is true that, if we adopt Option M, we shall become dependent on the United States for the future maintenance of our deterrent unless we are prepared to keep an independent effort of our own in being in preparation for the third generation of missiles (and the second generation of submarines) in the mid-1990's. But we must also recognise that, if we do wish to maintain such a capability, neither Option M nor SUPER ANTELOPE will spare us the expenditure (perhaps £1,000 million to £1,250 million over the period 1975 to 1990) which will be entailed if we tackle this problem by ourselves (perhaps in association with the French). By contrast, this figure

-4-

might be reduced, perhaps to £800 million if we could continue to rely on help from the United States. And Option M would have the additional advantage of giving us more time in which to develop a successor system in the light of the degree of collaboration which the French were prepared to offer.

(iv)   Our fourth objective is to try to win the French back into some kind of European defence system by using, if possible, the bait of progressively closer nuclear collaboration. Here, we are no further forward than we were 3 months ago. We simply do not know the French intentions in this respect

✳ *Passage deleted and retained under Section 3(4)*
CMWayland, 2 Nov 2004

✳ I suspect that, for the purposes of our immediate decision, we must discount the possibility of ultimate French collaboration to a rather greater extent than we have done hitherto.

6.   Trying to strike a final balance between these conflicting considerations, I can only say that my own judgment inclines more positively than hitherto, in favour of Option M.

7.   Two further points:-

(a)   Even if a decision is taken in favour of Option M, it will be necessary to continue work on SUPER ANTELOPE (which is currently funded only until the end of September) until it is clear that the United States can supply the de-MIRVed system and that the cost will be close to the present estimate. The detailed arrangements could perhaps be settled direct between the Treasury and the Ministry of Defence.

(b)   You may also wish to consider at the meeting when it would be appropriate to inform the Cabinet about the decision and the nature and timing of any Parliamentary announcement. (If we decide for Option M, this would in any event presumably become public knowledge as a result of the reference of the Presidential determination to Congress.)

11th September, 1973   -5-

The meeting on 12 September 1973 extended the funding for Super Antelope, but deferred the final choice of system until further work was completed on defence expenditure as a whole. Heath indicated that 'the maintenance of a credible nuclear deterrent must be regarded as of very great importance in the wider political context.'

defence M2

THIS DOCUMENT IS THE PROPERTY OF HER BRITANNIC MAJESTY'S GOVERNMENT

The circulation of this paper has been strictly limited.
It is issued for the personal use of ...*Prime Minister*

TOP SECRET

Copy No. 1

M/17/2

14 September 1973

CABINET

THE UNITED KINGDOM NUCLEAR DETERRENT

MINUTES of a Meeting
held at 10 Downing Street on
WEDNESDAY 12 SEPTEMBER 1973 at 2.30 pm

PRESENT

The Rt Hon Edward Heath MP
Prime Minister

The Rt Hon Sir Alec Douglas-Home MP
Secretary of State for Foreign and
Commonwealth Affairs

The Rt Hon Anthony Barber MP
Chancellor of the Exchequer

The Rt Hon Lord Carrington
Secretary of State for Defence

SECRETARIAT

The Rt Hon Sir Burke Trend
Sir John Hunt
Mr J Roberts

SUBJECT

THE UNITED KINGDOM NUCLEAR DETERRENT

TOP SECRET

46. (cont.)

THE UNITED KINGDOM NUCLEAR DETERRENT
Previous Reference: Minutes of Meeting of Ministers held on 26 July 1973

The Meeting had before them minutes to the Prime Minister from the Secretary of State for Defence (MO 18/1/1 of 17 August), the Foreign and Commonwealth Secretary (PM/73/63 of 30 August) and the Chancellor of the Exchequer (of 10 September) about the effect for different levels of defence expenditure of a decision in favour of SUPER ANTELOPE or, alternatively, of Option M, together with a minute from the Secretary of State for Defence (MO 18/1/1 of 10 September) about recent discussions with United States officials on the choice between these two systems.

THE SECRETARY OF STATE FOR DEFENCE said that these discussions had resulted in only minor changes to the estimates of the cost of Option M. Similarly, the prospect of obtaining the Poseidon C3 missile system with a multiple independently targetted re-entry vehicle (MIRV) capability appeared to be substantially the same as when Ministers had discussed the subject on 26 July. There could be no certainty that the United States Administration would be able to obtain Congressional approval to supply fully MIRVed Poseidon if we were to ask for this; and an unsuccessful approach to Congress on this issue might well prejudice the prospect of our subsequently obtaining Option M.

In discussion it was suggested that a decision on the nuclear deterrent should not be made without taking account of the implications for our conventional capability and that this would necessarily raise the question of the level of future defence expenditure as a whole. The allocation of our resources to defence was high in relation both to our own economic capacity and to the corresponding burdens accepted by our European Allies. From the point of view of containing public expenditure and releasing capacity for exports it would be desirable, therefore, to reduce the proportion of the Gross National Product (GNP) which had recently been devoted to defence. On the other hand, if defence expenditure was held to the level recommended in the report of the Public Expenditure Survey Committee (and still more if the proportion of the GNP devoted to defence was to be reduced by 1 per cent), this would have far-reaching implications not only for our own conventional capability but possibly also for the future of the North Atlantic Treaty Organisation.

THE PRIME MINISTER, summing up the discussion, said that the maintenance of a credible nuclear deterrent must be regarded as of very great importance in the wider political context. But, before a decision could be made between the various options, further consideration would need to be given to the implications of possible changes in the level of defence expenditure as a whole. The Meeting would resume the discussion at an early date; and in the meantime arrangements should be made to enable work on SUPER ANTELOPE to continue.

The Meeting -

Took note, with approval, of the Prime Minister's summing up of their discussion.

Cabinet Office

14 September 1973

The Cabinet Secretaryship changed hands from Trend to Sir John Hunt between the meetings of Heath's inner group on the deterrent. In his 29 October 1973 brief for the Prime Minister, Hunt indicated that the balance had shifted in favour of Super Antelope, given likely Congressional difficulties if the UK asked the Nixon Administration for Option M. He warns Heath of the worsening public expenditure position (the Yom Kippur War had triggered a sharp rise in the price of oil).

E.R.

TOP SECRET

Ref. A05482

Copy No. **1** of **5** Copies

PRIME MINISTER

_____

Defence Expenditure

The purpose of tomorrow's meeting is to see whether sufficient progress can be made with the Chancellor and the Defence Secretary to facilitate the Cabinet's discussion of public expenditure on Wednesday. There is still a wide gap between the proposals of the Chancellor set out *See Econ. Pol* → in CP(73) 108 and those of the Defence Secretary in CP(73) 113.   The figures *June 1970 Pt.10* are complicated by the outstanding question of the choice of option for improving our strategic nuclear deterrent: but the time has probably now come to settle this and it would clear the way for a decision on the defence budget as a whole.

2.   The latest estimates for the cost of the two main nuclear options were set out in the Annex to the Defence Secretary's minute MO 18/1/1 of 10th September, which also showed that, in the years up to and including 1977-78, provision had been made in the existing Defence Budget Targets for only part of the cost of either option.   The Defence Secretary's proposal set out in the table in paragraph 1 of CP(73) 113 assumes that the extra cost of Polaris improvements (whichever option is selected) would be <u>additional</u>: the Chancellor assumes that these extra costs should be met from <u>within</u> the totals he has proposed.   The extent of the difference can be summarised as follows:-

	£ million			
	1974-75	1975-76	1976-77	1977-78
Difference between Chancellor's proposal and Defence Secretary's offer	–	20	75	100
Extra cost of Polaris + improvements	12(6)	19(44)	27(59)	1(50)
Total Difference +	12(6)	39(64)	102(134)	101(150)

+ Figures are for SUPER ANTELOPE.   Figures for Option M in brackets.

Polaris improvements

PS(73) 63 covering M(17)2

3.   At your meeting on 12th September, it was decided to defer a decision between the options for the nuclear deterrent, pending bilateral discussions between the Chancellor and the Defence Secretary on the Defence Budget as a whole.   There has been no major change since then in the operational,

-1-

technical and logistic arguments. On the financial side however the public expenditure position has become more serious. It could still be argued that it would be wrong to allow relatively short term financial considerations to determine the choice of system which is expected to provide such a fundamental part of our security for the next 20 years: but developments in Washington since September must raise very grave doubts about whether we could still rely on the Administration's ability to honour the offer of Option M (and must surely rule out any possibility of the President successfully obtaining Congressional agreement to supply fully-MIRVed Poseidon, the chances of which Kissinger, even in August, put at 50-50 or, at best, 60-40). Given the urgent need for a decision and the uncertainties about possible Congressional opposition to Option M, the balance of advantage seems to have swung perhaps decisively towards SUPER ANTELOPE.

4.   Whichever Option is selected, it will be necessary to consider:-

(a)   How and when to inform the Americans, who have been very patient and helpful over this issue and whose help we shall of course continue to need even if we decide for SUPER ANTELOPE.

(b)   What public and Parliamentary announcement should be made and when. If we decide on Option M, this will presumably become public as soon as a Presidential determination is referred to Congress. If we decide for SUPER ANTELOPE, there may be no need for any public statement before the Defence Debate in the spring.

Other Defence Expenditure

5.   A decision in favour of SUPER ANTELOPE would still leave a gap between the positions of the Chancellor and Defence Secretary on defence expenditure as a whole (paragraph 2 above). The critical year is likely to be 1976-77 in which the gap would amount to about £100 million - the published figure for 1977-78 would in any event be provisional. The Defence Secretary will argue that his offer would already entail a substantial cut back for all three Services: and he must certainly avoid any reductions which would genuinely weaken our commitment to NATO and encourage some of our European Allies to reduce their defence expenditure in advance of any results from the MBFR negotiations. Similarly any major equipment cancellation could be politically embarrassing. Nevertheless, there is reason to think that further economies could with difficulty be made which would enable an accommodation to be reached somewhere between the Chancellor's position and that of the Defence Secretary.

(John Hunt)

29th October, 1973

TOP SECRET

Copy No. 1

M/17/2

1 November 1973

CABINET

DEFENCE EXPENDITURE

MINUTES of a Meeting
held at 10 Downing Street on
TUESDAY 30 OCTOBER 1973 at 5.00 pm

PRESENT

The Rt Hon Edward Heath MP
Prime Minister

The Rt Hon Sir Alec Douglas-Home MP　　The Rt Hon Anthony Barber MP
Secretary of State for Foreign and　　　　Chancellor of the Exchequer
Commonwealth Affairs

The Rt Hon Lord Carrington
Secretary of State for Defence

SECRETARIAT

Sir John Hunt
Mr J Roberts

SUBJECT

DEFENCE EXPENDITURE

TOP SECRET

DEFENCE EXPENDITURE

The Meeting considered the question of future levels of defence expenditure in the light of the Chancellor of the Exchequer's memorandum to the Cabinet on Public Expenditure to 1977-78 (CP(73) 108) and the Secretary of State for Defence's memorandum on Defence Budget Targets (CP(73) 113).

See Econ. Pol. →
June 1970 Pt. 10 →

STRATEGIC NUCLEAR DETERRENT
Previous Reference: Minutes of Meeting of Ministers held on 12 September 1973

The Meeting was informed that, since Ministers had last discussed the future of the nuclear deterrent, the internal difficulties of the United States Administration called in question its ability to obtain the necessary Congressional support should we ask for Option M. The prospect of obtaining Poseidon with a Multiple Independently Targetted Re-entry Vehicle (MIRV) capability, which it had always been recognised would encounter more serious Congressional opposition, now seemed extremely remote. Furthermore, SUPER ANTELOPE, though less satisfactory than Option M in operational, technical and logistic terms, would constitute an adequate deterrent and would involve lower expenditure in the period up to and including 1977-78 as well as lower dollar expenditure. There must be some uncertainty at this stage about the cost of developing and producing the new dispenser which would be needed for Option M. If it were necessary to accommodate the whole of the cost of Option M as currently estimated within a defence budget at or below the level envisaged in the report of the Public Expenditure Survey Committee (PESC) this would entail extremely serious reductions in our conventional capability and in these circumstances it might be preferable from the purely military point of view not to proceed with improvements to our strategic nuclear deterrent. If we decided in favour of SUPER ANTELOPE, we should still need to rely on the assistance of the United States Administration in a number of important respects although to a much lesser extent than would be the case with Option M.

In further discussion, it was suggested that it we decided in favour of SUPER ANTELOPE the credibility of our position would be strengthened if we could secure the early agreement of the French Government to co-operate with us on a successor system. On the other hand it was pointed out that while the choice of SUPER ANTELOPE might facilitate such co-operation, the French Government might well be reluctant to commit themselves at this stage. There were uncertainties about the extent to which our obligations to the United States might inhibit us from co-operating with the French on warhead design and it would in any case be unwise at this stage to take steps which might preclude the possibility of co-operating on a successor system with both the French and United States Governments.

1

48. (cont.)

Summing up this part of the discussion THE PRIME MINISTER said that there was general agreement that the right course was to develop SUPER ANTELOPE. It would be necessary to inform the United States Administration of this decision and careful consideration would need to be given as to how and when this should best be done.

The Meeting –

1.   Took note with approval of the Prime Minister's summing up of this part of their discussion.

OTHER DEFENCE EXPENDITURE

THE SECRETARY OF STATE FOR DEFENCE recalled that the figure for the defence budget in 1976-77 published in the 1972 Public Expenditure White Paper had been provisional because it had not then been possible to agree on a firm figure; it did not therefore represent the full cost of fulfilling our current defence plans and commitments. To keep within the sum recommended by the Public Expenditure Survey Committee for 1976-77 would entail savings of £84 million in the current defence programme. The sort of measures which would be required were illustrated in the first part of Annex A to his memorandum, CP(73) 113. If in addition it was necessary to accommodate the extra cost of SUPER ANTELOPE within the PESC figure, further measures of the kind set out in Part 2 of Annex A would be required. Savings on this scale would have substantial industrial and operational implications and some of the measures would inevitably be politically embarrassing but he would be prepared to accept this position if this were necessary. The Chancellor's proposals for 1976-77 would however entail saving a further £75 million which could only be achieved by significant cuts in the front-line. It would, for example, be necessary to take such measures as the disbandment of the Amphibious Warfare Squadron including the associated helicopters, to disband five front-line regular Army units and 15 Territorial Army units and to abandon the RAF LYNX programme. The consequences would be very serious in terms of our own capability and of our relations with NATO where we had been urging our European Allies not to make unilateral cuts. He believed it would be wrong to decide now on measures of this gravity in the context of the Public Expenditure White Paper without the most careful examination of the military and political consequences. The Chancellor's proposal for 1977-78 would entail still more far reaching reductions. He believed the right course for 1977-78 would be to publish a provisional figure at the same level as he recommended for 1976-77; a firm figure for 1977-78 could then emerge from next year's Public Expenditure Survey in the light of the recommendations of the Working Party which the Chancellor of the Exchequer and he had established to examine the longer term defence programme.

2

THE CHANCELLOR OF THE EXCHEQUER said that it was essential for confidence that the yearly totals in this December's White Paper should not exceed in real terms those published last year. Even after very careful scrutiny of other parts of the public expenditure programme there were substantial excesses in forecast expenditure for each of the four years in question. It was difficult to see how this gap could be bridged. Against this background it was doubtful whether we could sustain defence expenditure at the level proposed by the Secretary of State for Defence.

Summing up a short discussion THE PRIME MINISTER said that there was still a significant gap between the level of defence expenditure proposed by the Chancellor of the Exchequer and the offer made by the Secretary of State for Defence. Difficult issues were involved and he would arrange for further consideration to be given to this problem at an early date.

The Meeting -

2.   Took note with approval of the Prime Minister's summing up of this part of their discussion.

Cabinet Office

1 November 1973

3

Heath's ministerial group plumped for Super Antelope to fill the gap until a successor system was procured to replace Polaris once its operational life was ended.* Interestingly, the possibility of collaborating with France on such a system was raised, though the restrictions placed in the US-UK 1958 agreement on third-party exchanges of nuclear know-how were stressed.

The decision to upgrade Polaris was due to be announced in the annual Defence White Paper in February 1974, but Heath's 'who rules?' snap-election[94] precluded this. Hunt briefed Heath on the possibility of announcing it by another means, such as the Conservatives' election manifesto, or of waiting until the result was in.

---

* When the Americans abandoned their Antelope programme and the UK decided to carry on alone, a new codename for the British project was needed. During the British Academy workshop in March 2007, Kevin Tebbit explained the genesis of Chevaline during his time as Lord Carrington's assistant private secretary:

> There was a day when Lord Carrington came into the office and said, 'We have decided we are going to do Super Antelope alone and so we had better rename it.' . . . I rang up the London Zoo and I said, 'I can't tell you why I want to ask you this question, but this is the Ministry of Defence. . . Can you imagine an animal that is like a large antelope? Do you have any on your list?' And they said, 'There is this South African creature called a Chevaline,' and I thought that sounded rather good.

So Chevaline it was—though this doesn't feature as the codename in the documents until the Labour administration was in office.

49. Hunt's brief for Heath on 'Super Antelope', 7 February 1974.

TNA, PRO, PREM 15/2038

E.R.

TOP SECRET   COPY NO 1 of 4 COPIES

Reference: A 06198

PRIME MINISTER

SUPER ANTELOPE

There is an awkward point which the Secretary of State for Defence and I would like to discuss with you either before or after the meeting of NI tomorrow morning.

2.   The decision to improve Polaris was due to be announced in the Defence White Paper next week: and the Ministry of Defence were all set to begin letting contracts immediately thereafter. But, due to the Dissolution, the White Paper cannot now come out until the next Parliament.

3.   I think there are two alternatives:-

   a.   To announce in some other way (eg in the manifesto) that, if returned, the Government intends to develop the Polaris system, and then to let the MOD proceed with letting contracts.

   b.   To defer both the announcement and the contracts until after the Election.

The hypothetical third choice of letting the contracts without an announcement would seem inadmissible during an election period.

4.   I think I am bound to recommend course b. It carries the penalty of a few weeks delay in developing the new system (which does not perhaps matter very much) and also inevitably a small risk of a leak from those who know the decision has been taken. For the latter reason, if you decide in favour of course b., I think you should send a message to President Nixon explaining why the White Paper cannot be published on the due date and asking him to do his best to ensure strict secrecy on the American side until after the Election.

JOHN HUNT

7 February 1974

TOP SECRET

TOP SECRET   NO. 2 of 2 copies DEFENCE

10 Downing Street
Whitehall

Sir John Hunt

     The Prime Minister has seen your minute
of 7 February reference A 06198 about Super
Antelope.

     The Prime Minister approves Course b.,
and agrees that a message should be sent to
President Nixon on the lines you suggest.
He **would be** grateful for a draft message.

R. T. ARMSTRONG

8 February, 1974.

TOP SECRET

As a result of Heath's decision to wait, Labour returned to power on 4 March 1974 in ignorance of just how far Polaris improvement had progressed. Labour's manifesto pledged defence cuts and participation in multilateral disarmament negotiations 'and as a first step will seek the removal of American Polaris bases from Great Britain.'[95] It was silent on the future of the UK Polaris force.

Labour swiftly authorised a defence review. As it progressed, the Joint Intelligence Committee reported that the Soviets' ABM system was probably undergoing an improvement.

TOP SECRET

THIS DOCUMENT IS THE PROPERTY OF HER BRITANNIC MAJESTY'S GOVERNMENT

Copy No. 109

JIC (A) (74) 3

13 June, 1974

CABINET

JOINT INTELLIGENCE COMMITTEE (A)

———

SOVIET BLOC WAR POTENTIAL, 1974

REPORT BY JOINT INTELLIGENCE COMMITTEE (A)

In the report at Annex we estimate the war potential of the Soviet Union and the non-Soviet Warsaw Pact countries.

2. This report supersedes our previous study (JIC (73) 3 (Final)) on this subject.

(*Signed*)   GEOFFREY ARTHUR,

Chairman, on behalf of
Joint Intelligence Committee (A).

Cabinet Office,
   4 February, 1974.

TOP SECRET

149225

Naval ballistic missiles

74. The SS-N-8, which has a range of 4,200 nm, has a form of stellar updating of missile position at one point in its flight. The requirement for this may well have arisen because of difficulty in determining accurately the submarine position at launch. There is no indication of MIRV or MRV development for the SS-N-8. The SS-NX-13 is a submarine-launched ballistic missile with a development in guidance technique which is of considerable potential significance. Its unique feature is that it carries a sensor that in some way detects and locates its target. After the missile has passed the highest point in its trajectory, the main motor is relit and a flight path correction is applied on the basis of information supplied by the sensor throughout most of its initial flight. A second smaller correction may also be applied just before re-entry into the atmosphere. It has been fired from a submarine to a range of 350 nm, and corrections of approximately 10 per cent of range in both Azimuth and range directions seem possible; evidence suggests that the missile's sensor uses passive radio techniques. The probable role for SS-NX-13 is as an anti-shipping weapon. [TOP SECRET]

75. More recently, test firings of an improved SS-N-6 (the Mod. 2), fitted with at least two RVs, have increased ranges up to 1,650 nm. This is the first Soviet naval ballistic missile to have been fired with more than one RV. [S]

Defensive missiles—SAM

76. Research and Development on Soviet surface-to-air missiles is probably directed at improving their performance in the face of a changing threat and remedying exploitable deficiences. Currently deployed Soviet SAM are vulnerable to ECM or IRCM techniques; they can be saturated by a sufficiently large number of targets; in some cases the missile can be outmanoeuvred; reaction times are long and may be exploited; system kill probabilities below 500 feet are generally low; and radar performance and missile range sometimes insufficient to provide protection against small fast targets. The USSR also currently lacks defence against Western tactical ballistic missile systems, *e.g.* LANCE. [S]

77. Developments to date indicate that the Russians are aware of their SAM systems deficiencies and are endeavouring to overcome them. Optical sights have been added to the fire control radar of the SA-2 system and, in good visibility, this enables an engagement to be initiated without emitting radar signals. In these circumstances the attacker is denied warning that he is becoming a SAM target. Optics can also give an increased ability to discriminate multiple jamming targets, and may improve system low altitude performance. There are indications that optics or electro-optics are being added to SA-3, SA-4 and SA-6. The performance of SA-5 is probably being upgraded to counter small fast targets such as the United States SRAM, either by direct engagement of the missile or by intercepting the parent aircraft before missile launch. [S]

78. There are two good candidates for new system development. The most probable is a short-range low-level system of the RAPIER or CROTALE type for use by ground forces. The employment of such a system would help to close the low-altitude gap over small defended areas. It is also possible that the Russians may develop an anti-tactical ballistic missile system (ATBM) or upgrade their current SA-4 or SA-6s to give them some capability in this direction. [S]

79. In the longer term (10–15 years) it is possible that laser damage weapons may assume an air defence role especially for the short-range low-altitude target. However, within the period under consideration laser semi-active homing developments of weapons such as SA-7 and the BRDM-2A1/2 SAM system could give such weapons a good all-round capability. [S]

Defensive missiles—ABM

80. There is evidence of a large and active ABM R & D programme at the Sary Shagan Range. It is not possible to say just how many ABM projects are under test or what their characteristics may be but there is evidence of testing

TOP SECRET

of at least one new missile and one new radar, and it is believed that the programme may include new fire control radars using phased array techniques. The first aim is thought to be the introduction of improvements to the deployed MOSCOW system and this may be the purpose of some of the new construction at Moscow.
[TOP SECRET]

81. In addition to the Moscow defences the SAL Treaty on ABM permits the Russians to deploy ABM defences at one selected ICBM complex. The problem of hard silo defence is different from that of population defence of a capital city. It is conjectured that the Russians may be developing an ABM system for ICBM silo defence based on employment of fire units (up to 18) deployed over the complex. There is, however, no evidence of Russian development of a true terminal defence system employing a missile having the acceleration, speed and agility of the United States SPRINT which permits missile launch to be delayed until atmospheric discrimination of the RV has occurred. In view of possible future threats which may include increased warhead hardening, MIRVs having additionally a terminal guidance phase, decoys and low trajectory to reduce warning time, it would be surprising if the Russians are not at least studying this solution.
[TOP SECRET]

82. The SAL Treaty permits the continuation of ABM R & D including the development of "exotic" systems not based on the conventional radar/missile concept, but whereas improvements to conventional systems can be deployed within the agreed numerical and geographical limitations of the treaty any proposal to deploy exotic systems must be referred to the consultative commission. We believe that Russian defence philosophy and the requirement to improve the effectiveness of the limited permitted deployment will dictate the need for continuation of a vigorous ABM programme to improve the quality of the defences. The emerging threat from CHINA may act as an additional spur.
[S]

Aerodynamic cruise missiles

83. We know little of recent Soviet detailed R and D on aerodynamic missiles but it is apparent that they consider such weapons as essential elements of their military arsenal. We suspect that development has continued over the whole spectrum of cruise missile application. There is evidence of a second generation of naval surface-to-surface cruise missiles for both short and medium ranges and similar developments in air launched missiles for use with current and possibly new bombers and fighters. There is no direct evidence of the development of pure body lift or ballistic air-launched weapons nor the application of sea-skimming techniques for missiles in the anti-shipping role. However, the latter technique is undoubtedly known to the Russians and is a design option which may be exploited in the period of this report.
[TOP SECRET]

Missile propellants

84. Whilst the current generation of missiles is apparently based on conventional combinations of fuel and oxidiser, both for cryogenic and storable systems, there has been an extensive programme of research and development into new and more energetic combinations. In particular there is evidence of a wide-ranging investigation of possible new rocket fuels and fuel additives, and of the considerable organisation to control and supervise the programme. The main interest continues to be in hydrazine, in finely divided hydrides of the light metals (lithium, beryllium, magnesium and aluminium), in various organo-boron derivatives and compounds of borohydrides with hydrazine. Considerable effort has been directed to the large-scale manufacture of hydrazine and of borohydrides.
[S]

85. The Russians appear to have had considerable success in avoiding combustion problems, and this may be attributed in part to extensive use of appropriate additives, which may include tetranitromethane, organo-boron compounds, or organo-metallics such as trialkyl-aluminium.
[S]

TOP SECRET

Labour's defence options were drafted by a Defence Studies Working Party which worked to a Defence Review Steering Committee, chaired by John Hunt. It produced three choices for Polaris: decommissioning; continuing with an unimproved system; or Super Antelope/Chevaline.

SECRET
SECRET

DSWP(P)51

DEFENCE STUDIES WORKING PARTY

FINAL DRAFT REPORT

Ministry of Defence
19 June 1974

SECRET
SECRET

98

XV OPTION G - NUCLEAR OPTIONS

137. In a separate more highly classified paper various ways in which savings in the nuclear programme might be achieved are fully examined. Justice cannot be done to this option in a paper classified 'Secret'; but a broad outline of the possible variations is set out below.

At the Critical Level

138. At the Critical level, (Option C), the only savings from the nuclear programme which could be contemplated from a military viewpoint would be cancellation of provision for possible future generation tactical weapons which would yield additional total savings in the LTC period of about £21m. The implications of this for the Royal Navy would be the deferment of an increased capability to destroy the more modern, fast, deep diving nuclear submarines.

Further Savings

139. Further more sweeping reductions (including manpower) in our nuclear capability have been considered, and are summarised in the following paragraphs. None is accepted from the military or political points of view; each would entail a radical change in UK defence policy, and seriously affect NATO strategy.

Reductions in the Strategic Deterrent (POLARIS)

140. There are two possibilities: to continue the existing force into the early 1990s, but not improve it so as to maintain its credibility as a national strategic deterrent; alternatively, to scrap the force altogether. The first alternative would save in practical terms a total of about £170m development, production and mining costs over the LTC period. The improvement project has been

81

140

52. (cont.)

under way since 1972/3 and some £50m has already been spent on it.
Cancellation of the project would mean that our Polaris missiles
could no longer be certain of penetrating Soviet ABM defences
throughout the existing life of the submarines; and, although our
ability to threaten undefended cities within range would remain,
our ultimate determination to go to the limit in confronting the
USSR would be in question and the main reason for possessing a
strategic deterrent negated. The British Polaris force is an
insurance against the worst situation, namely a break up of NATO
or the loss of credibility of the US guarantee. It is also
recognised in a number of Allied quarters as increasing the credibility
of the overall NATO deterrent by introducing a separate centre
of decision making in Europe. Its abandonment would leave France
as the only West European power with a strategic deterrent, and
would involve the abandonment of a major force (including capital
investment) that still has two-thirds of its life remaining. It is
unlikely that SSBN's could be redeployed effectively in other roles
e.g. as SSN's.

141. The second alternative - scrapping the force - would save
running costs averaging £50m a year and some marginal infrastructure
costs. It would also save improvement costs as indicated in
paragraph 140 above.

Cancellation of LANCE

142. The cancellation of the collaborative purchase of the US LANCE
surface to surface missile system would save at the most some £40m.
Loss of LANCE would mean that 1(BR) Corps would not possess a tactical
nuclear missile capability, which would severely strain the Alliance's
current flexible-response strategy; the gap would have to be filled

by the US or FRG. The purchase of LANCE is an important
collaborative venture within the Eurogroup and cancellation would
be likely to lead to considerable political repercussions, not
least in the sense that an opportunity to use standardisation to
maximum effect would have been lost.

Abandonment of UK tactical nuclear weapons for the RAF and RN

143. Initial savings would be £3m p.a., rising to £10m p.a. by
1983/4, making a total of £65m over the LTC period, subsumed
the £21m in paragraph 138 above. If RN tactical nuclear weapons
were given up, we would have to rely on the US to supply warheads
to ships; there may well be difficulties in their agreeing to this,
and its implementation in a Naval environment. Extra expense would
be incurred on modification of aircraft, and on custodial arrangements.
Total abandonment of Naval nuclear capability would yield only small
savings and would have serious operational consequences (e.g. we
would have no certain method of sinking modern nuclear submarines
using full evasive tactics). Some similar considerations apply to
the RAF: total abandonment of the RAF's nuclear strike role would
leave large gaps in SACEUR's GSP, and would significantly reduce the
option for selective release of nuclear weapons.

Total abandonment of all UK nuclear capability

144. Apart from the saving in Polaris running costs indicated above
averaging £50m a year, there would be savings in support and
infrastructure costs amounting to some £63m a year at the start
falling to about £44m a year by 1983/4. This would mean a loss of
10,000 jobs, including those in industry. (There would be a
residual charge of about £6m per annum on Defence Votes to cover
surveillance, safe disposal, nuclear fuel for SSNs, etc). Total

83

141

52. (cont.)

abandonment would thus yield around £1000m over the 10 year LTC period. But quite apart from the military consequences, it would severely affect our political influence and standing with both our allies and foes. Such a course of action is not judged to make military sense.

84

SECRET

THIS DOCUMENT IS THE PROPERTY OF HER BRITANNIC MAJESTY'S GOVERNMENT

MISC 16(74) 3rd Meeting   COPY NO   17

CABINET

DEFENCE REVIEW STEERING COMMITTEE

MINUTES of a Meeting held in
Sir John Hunt's Room, Cabinet Office
on FRIDAY 28 JUNE 1974 at 3.00 pm

PRESENT

Sir John Hunt
Secretary of the Cabinet
(In the Chair)

Sir Douglas Henley
Treasury

Sir Thomas Brimelow
Foreign and Commonwealth Office

Field Marshal Sir Michael Carver
Chief of the Defence Staff

Sir Michael Cary
Ministry of Defence

Mr A P Hockaday
Ministry of Defence

Lord Rothschild
Head of Central Policy Review
Staff

Mr H F T Smith
Cabinet Office

SECRETARIAT

Mr J Roberts
Mr N Bevan

SUBJECT

DEFENCE STUDIES WORKING PARTY - FINAL DRAFT REPORT

8

SECRET

52. (cont.)

SECRET

DEFENCE STUDIES WORKING PARTY - FINAL DRAFT REPORT
Previous Reference: MISC 16(74) 2nd Meeting

The Meeting resumed their discussion of the final draft report of the Defence Studies Working Party (DSWP) attached to MISC 16(74) 3. They also had before them a note by the Secretaries (MISC 16(74) 4) covering a provisional assessment of the military implications and costs of retaining certain overseas commitments and a further note by the Secretaries (MISC 16(74) 5) covering a re-assessment of the force levels which could be sustained at the First Level of expenditure ($4\frac{1}{2}$ per cent of Gross National Product by 1983/84).

THE CHIEF OF THE DEFENCE STAFF said that in the force structure represented by the Critical Level, although very serious reductions had been made in all three Services, our central contribution to NATO had so far as possible been preserved. The further reductions that would be required to reach the First Level could only be achieved by making serious inroads into this central contribution with the result that the credibility of NATO strategy could no longer be maintained.

In discussion it was noted that the definition of the Critical Level was based on military and strategic criteria and did not involve a political judgment of the point at which British reductions would initiate the progressive unravelling of NATO. But the British contribution, together with the American and German, formed the cornerstone of the Alliance and the political effects of reductions would need to be carefully assessed following consultation with our allies. It was recognised that there was a significant difference in the force contributions to NATO at the Critical Level and the First Level; but it was suggested that the financial difference between the two levels could be bridged either by a major reduction in our sea/air contribution or by eliminating our ability to reinforce the Northern Flank together with a series of further small reductions in our land/air contribution. Against this it was argued that a major reduction in our maritime forces could lead the Americans to concentrate their forces in the Western Atlantic in the initial stages of hostilities; the Northern Flank could be regarded as in the front line of the defence of the United Kingdom and it was the military judgment that further reductions in our forces of the sort proposed would undermine the credibility of NATO strategy.

1

9

In preliminary discussion of the future of our overseas commitments it was argued that the annual cost of a reduced presence could be of the order of £70 million. On the other hand if the Hong Kong Government could be persuaded to make a larger contribution to the costs of the garrison, and if Ministers were prepared to accept the political consequences of a major reduction in our presence at Gibraltar (the requirement for which depended principally on domestic political considerations and the attitude of the Gibraltarians), this figure could be reduced.

In further discussion the importance was emphasised of demonstrating that reductions in support had been achieved commensurate with those in the front line. This applied particularly to the size of the headquarters staff of the Ministry of Defence and of the intelligence establishment. It was noted that a 20-25 per cent reduction in headquarters staff had been assumed but it would be useful to know how we compared in this respect with other nations. It was suggested that some of our intelligence activities were more appropriately those of a world power; on the other hand, although some savings could be achieved by a complete withdrawal from our overseas commitments, these activities enabled us to obtain on a reciprocal basis intelligence information from the Americans the military and political value of which was incomparably greater than the costs of our own activities. Moreover the possible further savings in the field of support were not significant in the context of the financial difference between the Critical Level and the First Level.

THE CHAIRMAN, summing up the discussion, said that at their next meeting they would wish to resume their discussion of our non-NATO overseas commitments and to examine the scope for further savings in Research and Development, which was being studied by the DSWP. They would also wish to consider a first draft of their report to Ministers.

The Meeting —

1. Took note, with approval, of the Chairman's summing up of their discussion.

2. Instructed the Secretaries to circulate a draft report to Ministers for their consideration.

3. Invited the Ministry of Defence to obtain comparative data on the size of other nations' defence headquarters staffs.

Cabinet Office

1 July 1974

2

Decommissioning would save running costs of £50m a year. Not improving Polaris would mean the force was no longer 'an insurance against the worst situation, namely a break-up of NATO or the loss of credibility of the US guarantee'.

Hunt's steering committee, MISC 16, reported to the Cabinet's Defence and Oversea Policy Committee chaired by the Prime Minister, Harold Wilson.

53. MISC 16 report for Cabinet's Defence and Oversea Policy Committee, OPD (74) 23, 15 July 1974. TNA, PRO, CAB 148/145

SECRET

THIS DOCUMENT IS THE PROPERTY OF HER BRITANNIC MAJESTY'S GOVERNMENT

OPD(74)23
15 July 1974

COPY NO 51

CABINET

DEFENCE AND OVERSEA POLICY COMMITTEE

———

DEFENCE REVIEW

Note by the Secretaries

———

At their meeting on 4 April (OPD(74)3rd Meeting) the Committee instructed officials to review defence policies and priorities and to report to the Committee not later than July 1974. The review was to be undertaken by a Steering Committee with the following composition:—

> Secretary of the Cabinet (Chairman)
> Chief of the Defence Staff
> Permanent Secretary, Treasury
> Permanent Under Secretary of State, Foreign and Commonwealth Office
> Permanent Under Secretary of State, Ministry of Defence
> Lord Rothschild, Head of the Central Policy Review Staff

The attached report by the Steering Committee is circulated for the consideration of the Committee.

Signed JOHN HUNT
H F T SMITH
J ROBERTS

Cabinet Office
15 July 1974

SECRET

173

53. (cont.)

What would however be achieved is the avoidance of the heavy additional burden envisaged by present plans for the progressive re-equipment of the forces.   If Ministers were to endorse the broad level of forces and capabilities implied by the Critical Level this would not of course imply approval of every detail of force structure or of the equipment proposals (some of which are still at a very early stage) contained in the programme.   These would naturally be subject to detailed scrutiny as and when they arose, in accordance with the usual practice.

20. The nature of the judgements involved in the Critical Level and its implications are central to this review.   If these judgements are right any sizeable _further_ reductions in force levels, or in major weapon development and production, would leave serious gaps in the defence of the central land front in Europe, the Atlantic or the United Kingdom base, unless filled by our allies.   We believe that our allies, some of whom have already indicated that they do not accept our arguments about relative defence burdens, would not take on roles relinquished unilaterally by us.   The risk is that such action on our part would on the contrary initiate such reductions in other countries' defence efforts and commitments to NATO that the process of "unravelling" would ensue.   This implies that the cohesion of NATO is dependent on continuation of a major effort by the United Kingdom, even if this is disproportionate to our economic strength.

Strategic Nuclear Deterrent

21. Our strategic nuclear deterrent force consists of 4 nuclear powered submarines each equipped with 16 Polaris missiles with British warheads. There is always one boat on patrol and sometimes two. The boats have a service life of up to a further 20 years.   The running costs of the force average some £50 million a year over the LTC period.

22. The force is committed to NATO and would be available, subject to national political control, for use against targets assigned by SACEUR. Its significance however goes wider than the purely NATO context.   The force would also be available for national use in the event of a breakdown of NATO, or for use in support of the Alliance in the event of the loss of credibility - temporary or permanent - of the United States Strategic Nuclear Guarantee.   To provide an effective deterrent in either of these contexts the force must be capable of effectively

8

attacking particular targets which are specially defended, which is
not necessary in the NATO context when United States strategic
nuclear forces would also be employed. Both President Nixon and
Secretary Kissinger have on a number of occasions told us of the
importance they attach to our continued possession of a strategic
nuclear deterrent effective against any targets in the Soviet Union.
They believe that if a future United States Administration were
tempted to dilute its guarantees to NATO, our possession of such a
weapon could persuade them to maintain their commitment. The United
Kingdom force is recognised by them and also by a number of our other allies as
increasing the credibility of the overall NATO deterrent by introducing a second centre of decision-making in Europe. Its abandonment
would leave France as the only West European power with a strategic
deterrent.

23. Technical assessments have shown that if the force is to maintain
its credibility as a national strategic deterrent in the face of
expected improvements in Soviet defences, the penetration capability
of the missiles must be improved. This would not involve MIRVs.
The cost of effecting these improvements would amount to about
£170 million over the LTC period. A good deal of preliminary
work has been done (including the recent underground test) to keep
this option open, but the completion of development and production
of the improvements have not been authorised pending the outcome of
the defence review.

24. The programme of improvements has been included in the forces
required at the Critical Level and at the First and lower levels.

25. The remainder of the nuclear weapons programme is concerned with
the provision of tactical weapons. The savings from cutting these
parts of the programme would be small. If our forces were to have
no tactical nuclear capability, this would have serious consequences
for NATO strategy. The alternative of relying solely on using
United States weapons (under United States custodial arrangements)
would present practical problems, particularly for the Royal Navy,
and additional expense for the Royal Air Force.

MISC 16 stressed the keenness of the Nixon Administration for the UK's remaining a nuclear weapons power, and how its abandonment would leave France as the sole western European nuclear power. Polaris improvement was estimated to cost £170m over the long-term costing (i.e. 10-year) period.

Wilson began to prepare his Cabinet for Polaris improvement when asked on 27 June 1974 to explain the need for a recent test in Nevada (codenamed Fallon, it had taken place on 24 May). In a paper prepared for a Cabinet meeting on 1 August (though not shown to his colleagues until 12 September because of the pressure of pre-summer recess business at the 1 August meeting), Wilson said he, Healey (Chancellor of the Exchequer), Callaghan (Foreign Secretary) and Roy Mason (Defence Secretary) had decided on 5 April that the planned test, which they had inherited from the Heath Government, should go ahead. He implied that his inner nuclear group had decided to continue with Polaris improvement:

> We knew from technical assessment of all the available information on the nature and rate of development of Soviet anti-missile defence development that our missiles would have to be given better penetration capability if we wished to retain a credible deterrent. This could be done without so-called MIRVing, but it does involve some testing.

However, the future of the deterrent's existence, let alone its improvement, Wilson explained, remained an open question that would be considered as part of the defence review.

54. 'Nuclear Testing': note by the Prime Minister, C (74) 85, 31 July 1974.

TNA, PRO, CAB 129/178

THIS DOCUMENT IS THE PROPERTY OF HER BRITANNIC MAJESTY'S GOVERNMENT

The circulation of this paper has been strictly limited
It is issued for the personal use of.....*Bound Volume*

TOP   SECRET

Copy No.   26

C(74) 85

31 July 1974

CABINET

NUCLEAR TESTING

Note by the Prime Minister

1.   I was asked in Cabinet on 27 June (CC(74) 21st Conclusions, Minute 3) whether a paper could be prepared about the reason for holding the recent test in America and the way in which the decision was taken.   It was agreed that I would discuss the matter further with the Ministers most closely concerned and that there would then be a report to the Cabinet.

2.   The decision to hold the test was taken by the last Administration and the timetable was set.   We had to decide whether to interfere with the arrangements.   I discussed this on 5 April with the Foreign and Commonwealth Secretary, the Chancellor of the Exchequer and the Secretary of State for Defence and for the following reasons decided that the test should go ahead as planned.

3.   We knew from technical assessment of all the available information on the nature and rate of development of Soviet anti-missile defence development that our missiles would have to be given better penetration capability if we wished to retain a credible deterrent.   This could be done without so-called MIRVing, but it does involve some testing.

4.   Once the need for a test was established and accepted, the timing was governed by a tight logistic programme for modification of the missile and the need to fit it into the American test programme in Nevada - we having no underground test site of our own.   If we had decided not to allow this test to go ahead as planned, the slippage in time would have increased the cost in the event that, as a result of the defence review, it is decided to make this improvement.

5.   We also specifically agreed that the decision to hold this test was without prejudice to the policy decision of whether to retain our nuclear deterrent which would be taken in the context of the defence review.

1

TOP   SECRET

Moscow Criterion : 1967–77   299

54. (cont.)

6.   There is a long-standing convention that sensitive questions in the field of foreign affairs, defence matters and on s ecurity/intelligence are not necessarily brought before the Cabinet for decision. A small group of Ministers sometimes have to assume responsibility, although clearly policies (where these are involved) could not be pursued if it turned out that the Cabinet as a whole did not support them.

7.   The 1965 test was not discussed in Cabinet. The decision to hold the recent test was not a policy decision. A decision not to hold it would however have been a policy decision because it would have prejudiced the effective fulfilment, in terms of time and money, of one of the options which we may wish to take.

8.   As I have said there will be no need for a further British test before we decide, in the context of the defence review, on our future defence policy as a whole. If the strategic nuclear deterrent is then retained and if for exceptional reasons we felt unable on any future occasion to hold a Cabinet discussion in advance of a British test it would be my intention to inform the Cabinet as soon as possible after the test had taken place so that they would know the position before there was any publicity.

H W

10 Downing Street

31 July 1974

2

55. Confidential Annex to the Cabinet Minutes, C (74) 35th Conclusions, 12 September 1974.   TNA, PRO, CAB 128/55

CC(74) 35th Conclusions, Minute 5
Thursday 12 September 1974 at 10.30 am

NUCLEAR
TESTS

Previous
Reference:
CC(74) 21st
Conclusions,
Minute 3

THE PRIME MINISTER said that at their meeting on 27 June he had undertaken to consider, in consultation with the senior Ministers most immediately concerned, the procedures for authorising British nuclear tests, with particular regard to the security aspects, and to consider whether it would be reasonable to depart from precedent so that plans to hold any future tests could be discussed in Cabinet. He had done this and had prepared a note for the information of the Cabinet. It contained information of exceptional secrecy however and he had decided that it would not be right to circulate it to their offices. He had hoped to show it to them at the Cabinet on 1 August but the length of their discussion at that meeting had made it impossible. He would like the Cabinet to read it now.

Copies of C(74) 85 were then handed round and read, without comment, by all members of the Cabinet except the Secretary of State for Foreign and Commonwealth Affairs, the Secretary of State for the Environment, the Secretary of State for Energy and the Lord Privy Seal who were absent for this item. The copies were then withdrawn.

Cabinet Office

12 September 1974

So sensitive did Wilson deem nuclear matters that the Cabinet could only read the brief on the nuclear test in the Cabinet Room before handing it back to the Cabinet Secretary.

The 1974 Defence Review was constructed around a notion of a 'critical level' of provision which included the nuclear deterrent. If ministers wanted a lower level still of defence spending, they would have to consider the future of Polaris.

**56. Hunt and Roberts' brief for the OPD Committee, 'Defence Review—Critical Level',
13 September 1974.**   TNA, PRO, CAB 148/145

OPD(74) 33   COPY NO 50

13 September 1974

CABINET

DEFENCE AND OVERSEA POLICY COMMITTEE

——

DEFENCE REVIEW – CRITICAL LEVEL

Note by the Secretaries

At their meeting on 1 August (OPD(74) 13th Meeting) the Committee directed that a number of models of alternative force mixes should be designed within the total cost implied by the Critical Level. A presentation on the Critical Level and on alternative force mixes will be given on 18 September.

2.   The Critical Level reflects the judgement of the Chiefs of Staff on the minimum level of forces we need to contribute to NATO to preserve the continuing credibility of NATO strategy and to retain the confidence of our allies. It is described in more detail in paragraphs 16-20 of OPD(74) 23 and the level of forces involved is summarised in Annexes D, E and F. Paragraph 19 of OPD(74) 23 points out that "If Ministers were to endorse the broad level of forces and capabilities implied by the Critical Level this would not of course imply approval of every detail of force structure or of the equipment proposals (some of which are still at a very early stage) contained in the programme. These would naturally be subject to detailed scrutiny as and when they arose, in accordance with the usual practice."

3.   In the light of the Presentation Ministers will wish to consider –
    a.   whether they agree that if we are to provide an adequate contribution to meet NATO's military and political requirements there is no scope for significant reductions in the Critical Level as defined;
    b.   if the answer to the preceding question is 'no', in what area or areas should further reductions be sought:–
        i.   Strategic Nuclear Deterrent
        ii.   Central Region
        iii. Maritime
        iv.   United Kingdom Base
        v.   Reinforcement and Amphibious Forces

                                          Signed JOHN HUNT
                                                 J ROBERTS

Cabinet Office   241
13 September 1974   **SECRET**

57. Minutes of a meeting of the Defence and Oversea Policy Committee, OPD (74) 15th meeting, 18 September 1974.　　　　TNA, PRO, CAB 148/145

SECRET

THIS DOCUMENT IS THE PROPERTY OF HER BRITANNIC MAJESTY'S GOVERNMENT

OPD(74) 15th Meeting　　　　　　　　　　COPY NO　　50

CABINET

DEFENCE AND OVERSEA POLICY COMMITTEE

MINUTES of a Meeting held at
10 Downing Street on
WEDNESDAY 18 SEPTEMBER 1974 at 11.00 am

PRESENT

The Rt Hon Harold Wilson MP
Prime Minister

The Rt Hon Edward Short MP
Lord President of the Council

The Rt Hon James Callaghan MP
Secretary of State for Foreign
and Commonwealth Affairs

The Rt Hon Denis Healey MP
Chancellor of the Exchequer

The Rt Hon Roy Mason MP
Secretary of State for Defence

The Rt Hon Harold Lever MP
Chancellor of the Duchy
of Lancaster

THE FOLLOWING WERE ALSO PRESENT

Field Marshal Sir Michael Carver
Chief of the Defence Staff

Admiral Sir Edward Ashmore
Chief of Naval Staff
and First Sea Lord

Air Chief Marshal
Sir Andrew Humphrey
Chief of the Air Staff

Lieutenant General Sir David Fraser
Vice-Chief of the General Staff

Lord Rothschild
Head of Central Policy
Review Staff

SECRETARIAT

Sir John Hunt
Mr J Roberts
Brigadier N T Bagnall

SUBJECT

DEFENCE REVIEW

SECRET

SECRET

DEFENCE REVIEW

Previous Reference: OPD(74) 14th Meeting

The Committee had before them notes by the Secretaries on the Critical Level (OPD(74) 33) and on Non-NATO Commitments (OPD(74) 34).

THE CHANCELLOR OF THE EXCHEQUER said that he did not believe that a contribution to NATO of the size implied by the Critical Level was acceptable in public expenditure terms. It would involve an increase in the defence budget for 1975/76 in excess of the growth limit of $2\frac{3}{4}$ per cent in real terms which had been agreed for public expenditure generally and in 4 years time defence expenditure would still amount to 5 per cent of Gross National Product which was a higher percentage than that of either France or Germany. He believed that to continue to make a major contribution both to the allied forces in the Central Region and to the Eastern Atlantic and Channel Commands would be inconsistent with our economic situation. He was not persuaded that the maritime forces proposed at the Critical Level would be capable of carrying out the tasks assigned to them and if this was the case this was a further argument against them: a change in strategy was perhaps inevitable. The credibility of our force contribution must be judged in the light of political as well as military considerations. He believed that it would in any case be necessary to review the nature of the military problem facing NATO and the nature of the appropriate allied response in consultation with the United States and our European allies and this could materially affect the contribution we made. He could not agree that the cost of any non-NATO commitments which it might be decided to retain for wider political reasons should be additional to the cost of our NATO contribution.

In discussion other members of the Committee argued that the Critical Level would involve severe cuts in our military capability and in our contribution to NATO: and that it would be dangerous to reduce this contribution further. To do so could not only result in a lowering of the nuclear threshold but could seriously impair our relations with the United States and our European partners at a time when we needed their understanding and co-operation in the light of the financial and economic difficulties facing the Western World. Too much emphasis should not be placed on comparisons based on the percentage of Gross National Product devoted to defence by different countries.

57. (cont.)

We must recognise the point from which we were starting and the fact that our allies have come to expect us to make a significant military contribution and would react adversely if we tried to reduce this too far and too fast. The costs of maintaining certain residual non-NATO commitments had been estimated at about £70-80 million a year but this would be substantially reduced if it were possible (as the Committee had agreed would be their preferred course) to withdraw all our forces from Cyprus and to persuade the Hong Kong Government to contribute not less than three-quarters of the cost of the Hong Kong Garrison.

THE PRIME MINISTER, summing up the discussion, said that it would be necessary after the General Election to report to the Cabinet on the results of the Defence Review before international consultations were started. It was important that preparatory work should proceed if we were to maintain the aim of publishing the results of the Defence Review by the end of the year. Officials should prepare briefs for international consultation on the basis that our force contribution to NATO should be that defined in the Critical Level; that we should withdraw our forces wholly from Cyprus; that the Hong Kong Government would contribute not less than three-quarters of the cost of a reduced garrison in the Colony and that our other non-NATO and Mediterranean commitments should be reduced as proposed in OPD(74) 23 subject to the minimum necessary provision for the internal security and defence of the Falkland Islands and Belize so long as they remained dependent territories. Officials should also examine the implications of meeting the cost of our residual non-NATO and Mediterranean commitments for within the currently estimated cost of the Critical Level and this examination should cover the possibilities either that we might have to accept only a partial withdrawal from Cyprus or that the Hong Kong Government's contribution would not exceed half the cost of the garrison, or both. Further consideration should however also be given to the points made by the Chancellor of the Exchequer. In the light of these further studies the Committee would decide as soon as possible after the General Election what recommendations to make to the Cabinet.

> The Committee –
>
> Took note, with approval, of the Prime Minister's summing up of their discussion.

Cabinet Office
18 September 1974

2

At the OPD committee meeting on 18 September 1974, the Chancellor, Healey, pressed for cuts deeper than the 'critical level' but the discussion seems from the rather ambiguous minute to have decided not to lower 'the nuclear threshold'. Wilson's brief for the full Cabinet (as we shall see shortly) made it plain that the OPD Committee had indeed 'concluded that we should maintain our strategic nuclear deterrent' and that Polaris improvement would go ahead.

Another general election took place on 10 October, between the OPD discussion and the full Cabinet's discussion of the Defence Review the following month (Wilson was returned with an overall majority of three). This time Labour's manifesto contained a sentence on the future of the deterrent:

> We have renounced any intention of moving towards a new generation of strategic nuclear weapons.[96]

There was no whisper, however, of upgrading the existing generation.

In his 28 October 1974 Cabinet paper on the Defence Review, Wilson stressed that Polaris improvement would not involve 'a new generation of strategic weapons'.

58. 'Defence Review. Memorandum by the Prime Minister', C (74) 116, 28 October 1974.

TNA, PRO, CAB 129/179

SECRET

IS DOCUMENT IS THE PROPERTY OF HER BRITANNIC MAJESTY'S GOVERNMENT

C(74) 116

COPY NO 32

28 October 1974

CABINET

———

DEFENCE REVIEW

Memorandum by the Prime Minister

———

1.   The Defence and Oversea Policy Committee have completed their review of our defence commitments and capabilities, with the aim of determining the minimum essential level of our defences and the maximum savings on the defence budget.

2.   In recent years the defence budget has been subjected to a number of unplanned cuts which have been damaging to the efficiency and morale of the armed forces and economically wasteful.   Yet they have still left defence expenditure far too high in terms of what we can afford.   A stringent approach to defence expenditure, enabling us to get the best value for the money we spend, requires a planned programme over a number of years: and the Committee have concluded that we should make major reductions over a period of 10 years.

3.   In 1973-74 defence cost $5\frac{3}{4}$ per cent of GNP.   Cuts of nearly £350 million (1974 prices) imposed by our predecessors or forced upon us in the aftermath of the three-day week have already brought the figure down to $5\frac{1}{2}$ per cent of GNP for 1974-75.   Such cuts however are to some extent illusory since they have to be met partly by delaying rather than cancelling expenditure and thus build up problems for the future.   They have in fact complicated our task of achieving reductions over the next two or three years.

4.   The 1974 Long Term Costings show that to maintain and progressively re-equip forces of the present size would cost 6 per cent of GNP by 1978-79 and over $5\frac{1}{2}$ per cent of GNP by 1983-84: this is because successive generations of equipment necessary to match the greater sophistication of the equipment possessed by potential enemies inevitably cost more in real terms.   Savings can therefore only be made by reducing commitments and capabilities.   The Committee considered various models and have concluded that we can bring the figure down to $4\frac{1}{2}$ per cent of GNP by 1984, while maintaining a minimum essential level of defence.   In view of the distortion introduced by the unplanned cuts of £350 million, it will not be possible to avoid a modest rise in constant price terms over the next two years, but thereafter the figures will level off as the savings from the reductions in our commitments begin to show.

1

SECRET

d.　　Reducing the home based Army by 3, 000 men (the maximum cut consistent with our Northern Ireland commitment).

8.　　We would continue to contribute to NATO land and air forces in Germany and to naval and air forces in the Eastern Atlantic and Channel at a level consistent with NATO strategy.　We would be able to maintain the minimum forces necessary in the United Kingdom for home defence, including Northern Ireland, and for the reinforcement of BAOR in war.

9.　　The Committee concluded that we should maintain our strategic nuclear deterrent.　This is assigned to NATO and represents an insurance against the loss, temporarily or otherwise, of credibility of the United States strategic nuclear guarantee.　It would also be available for national use in the event of a breakdown of NATO.　If the force is to remain a credible deterrent in the face of advances in Russian anti-missile capability, some improvements need to be made to the missiles.　This would not involve Multiple Independently-Targetted Re-entry Vehicles or a new generation of strategic weapons, and in no way would conflict with the United States/USSR discussions on strategic arms limitations.　The cost of the Polaris force would be less than 2 per cent of the defence budget.

CONSULTATION

10.　　We have undertaken to consult our partners both in and outside NATO before reaching final decisions, and are indeed under formal obligation to do so in NATO.　The attitude of the Americans and the Germans will be crucial both in our discussions in NATO and in wider senses, and the first step is therefore to hold very confidential bilateral discussions with them. We should like to begin these right away.　We should then be ready in the third week of November to start the formal consultation process within NATO, and also to tell the non-NATO Governments affected.　Immediately prior to this we should make a statement in Parliament of our general intentions and the magnitude of the reductions proposed.　If we are to avoid arousing unnecessary hostility in NATO we must allow two months for the process of formal consultation.　We should then be able to publish a Defence White Paper giving the full details.

RECOMMENDATION

11.　　The Cabinet is invited to agree that we should enter into confidential bilateral discussions with the Americans and Germans forthwith on the basis set out above, and that subject to any further Ministerial consideration which their reaction may make necessary, we should make a statement in Parliament before beginning the NATO consultations and informing the non-NATO countries concerned.　The statement would of course be submitted to the Cabinet at the appropriate time.

H W

10 Downing Street

28 October 1974

4

SECRET

THIS DOCUMENT IS THE PROPERTY OF HER BRITANNIC MAJESTY'S GOVERNMENT

CC(74) 47th
Conclusions

COPY NO 84

CABINET

CONCLUSIONS of a Meeting of the Cabinet
held at 10 Downing Street on

WEDNESDAY 20 NOVEMBER 1974

at 10.00 am

PRESENT

The Rt Hon Harold Wilson MP
Prime Minister

The Rt Hon Edward Short MP Lord President of the Council	The Rt Hon James Callaghan MP Secretary of State for Foreign and Commonwealth Affairs
The Rt Hon Lord Elwyn-Jones Lord Chancellor	The Rt Hon Roy Jenkins MP Secretary of State for the Home Department
The Rt Hon Denis Healey MP Chancellor of the Exchequer	The Rt Hon Anthony Crosland MP Secretary of State for the Environment
The Rt Hon Michael Foot MP Secretary of State for Employment	The Rt Hon Eric Varley MP Secretary of State for Energy
The Rt Hon Shirley Williams MP Secretary of State for Prices and Consumer Protection	The Rt Hon Barbara Castle MP Secretary of State for Social Services
The Rt Hon Anthony Wedgwood Benn MP Secretary of State for Industry	The Rt Hon Peter Shore MP Secretary of State for Trade
The Rt Hon Roy Mason MP Secretary of State for Defence	The Rt Hon Reginald Prentice MP Secretary of State for Education and Science
The Rt Hon William Ross MP Secretary of State for Scotland	The Rt Hon John Morris QC MP Secretary of State for Wales

i

SECRET

The Rt Hon Merlyn Rees MP
Secretary of State for Northern Ireland

The Rt Hon Harold Lever MP
Chancellor of the Duchy of Lancaster

The Rt Hon Lord Shepherd
Lord Privy Seal

The Rt Hon Robert Mellish MP
Parliamentary Secretary, Treasury

The Rt Hon John Silkin MP
Minister for Planning and Local Government

SECRETARIAT

Sir John Hunt
Mr H F T Smith
Mr J Roberts

SUBJECT

DEFENCE REVIEW

ii

59. (cont.)

DEFENCE
REVIEW

Previous
Reference:
CC(74) 42nd
Conclusions,
Minute 1

The Cabinet resumed their discussion of the Defence Review.
Their discussion and the conclusions reached are recorded
separately.

Cabinet Office

20 November 1974

In discussion of the memorandum by the Central Policy Review Staff
(C(74) 132), it was noted that the employment implications of the
proposed reductions in the defence industries should, in general, be
manageable, though there would be problems for particular firms and
particular areas. Arms exports might take up some of the capacity
released by the reduced requirements of our own Services. It was
important that there should be consultations with both sides of industry
about the employment implications of the Defence Review in parallel
with the international consultations with our allies; this point should
be brought out in the proposed Parliamentary statement. Potentially
the most serious employment problem would be at Yarrows on
Clydeside if there were a major reduction in the frigate programme.
Decisions could not yet be taken on this question but it was important
that the situation should be clarified as soon as possible.

THE PRIME MINISTER said that if we were to retain the strategic
nuclear force it must be a credible deterrent. The improvements
necessary to ensure the continuing credibility of the present force
were relatively cheap; they would not involve either a new generation
of missiles or the introduction of Multiple Independently Targeted
Re-entry Vehicles. The essential question was whether to retain
the Polaris force or to reverse the policy followed in the past and
abandon it. The Defence and Oversea Policy Committee had
unanimously concluded that it should be retained. For our European
NATO allies it represented an insurance against a breakdown in the
credibility of the United States Strategic Nuclear Guarantee. If we
abandoned our deterrent France would be the only country in Europe
with a strategic nuclear capability and this was not committed to
NATO. Such a situation would be particularly disquieting to other
members of NATO and especially to the Germans. In normal times,
our possession of the nuclear deterrent gave us a unique entree to
United States thinking and the possibility of influencing this not only on
nuclear matters, including strategic arms limitation, but over a very
wide politico/strategic field. In times of tension, it provided us with
a unique opportunity to influence events both in Washington and Moscow
and counsel moderation. For this country it provided, in the worst
case, the best protection against the risk of nuclear attack or nuclear
blackmail. From his own knowledge of the Soviet leadership he was
satisfied that there was no question that our relations with the Soviet
Union would be improved if we were not a strategic nuclear power;
on the contrary, he believed that the Soviet Union valued the
contribution which our possession of the nuclear deterrent enabled us
to make to discussion in the arms limitation field. During the
recent bilateral discussions with the Americans Dr Kissinger and
Dr Schlesinger had reaffirmed the importance they attached to our
strategic nuclear contribution. Dr Kissinger had emphasised that the
existence of our Polaris force did not in any way hamper him in the
Strategic Arms Limitation Talks with the Soviet Union; on the
contrary, it was positively helpful.

59. (cont.)

In the course of a full discussion it was argued that, in addition to the strong views which some members of the Government Party held against the possession by us of nuclear weapons, a decision to improve the deterrent carried an implied intention to keep up with further developments in anti-missile technology and to replace the submarines in due course. It was questionable whether possession of the deterrent gave us a greater influence than we would enjoy if we abandoned it. It was also argued, however, that our influence as a nuclear power was real and would be no less important in the future than it had proved to be in the past. If we were to abandon the deterrent this would have a serious effect on our European NATO allies and would revive demands for a European nuclear force. Even with the proposed improvements, the cost of the Polaris force was less than 2 per cent of the defence budget; this was a small price to pay for the advantages it conferred.

(At this point the Prime Minister had to leave the meeting and the Lord President of the Council took the chair.)

In further discussion it was argued that the prospective spread of a nuclear capability among the smaller powers was a particularly disturbing development. We should seek to work for international agreement to reverse this trend and should be prepared to consider giving up our nuclear deterrent if by this means we could secure an effective agreement at a later stage, though nothing could be said about this intention now.

THE LORD PRESIDENT OF THE COUNCIL, summing up the discussion, said that the Cabinet had held a valuable and wide-ranging discussion of the international and domestic implications of the Defence Review. Their discussion of the nuclear deterrent in particular had been conducted with moderation and understanding of different shades of opinion. Agreement had now been reached on the outstanding points. It was clear that we would encounter very considerable American opposition to withdrawal from the SBAs in Cyprus and the Foreign and Commonwealth Secretary would be considering the terms of a reply to be sent to Dr Kissinger. Apart from this the proposals summarised in C(74) 116 would form the basis of the consultations with our allies and with both sides of industry. The next step would be to settle the statement to be made in Parliament on 3 December; this would be considered by the Cabinet on 25 November.

The Cabinet -

Took note, with approval, of the Lord President of the Council's summing up of their discussion.

Cabinet Office

21 November 1974

4

Wilson's argument for the UK carrying on as a nuclear power ranged very widely, embracing the customary 'insurance' case against a breakdown in the US 'nuclear guarantee'; the undesirability of France standing alone (which would particularly worry the West Germans); the 'unique entrée' the bomb gave the UK into US thinking; no evidence of an improved relationship with the Soviet Union if the UK disarmed; and, in the worst case, the bomb was Britain's 'best protection against the risk of nuclear attack or nuclear blackmail'.

Barbara Castle's record of the 20 November 1974 Cabinet meeting indicates that there was a whiff of the Campaign for Nuclear Disarmament in the Cabinet Room that morning, but no more:

> The main rub came over nuclear policy, on which Harold was clearly expecting trouble. He needn't have worried: Mike [Foot]'s comments were to be so muted as almost token. Harold prepared the way carefully by saying that, though we would keep Polaris and carry out certain improvements at a cost of £24 millions, there would be no 'Poseidonization and no MIRV'. The nuclear element represented less than 2 per cent of the defence budget but it gave us a 'unique entrée to US thinking' and it was important for our diplomatic influence for us to remain a nuclear power. Germany, for instance, would not like it if France were the only nuclear power in Europe. And he stressed that the policy was in line with the Manifesto and that the decision on it in the Defence and Overseas Policy Committee of the Cabinet had been unanimous.

Jim Callaghan, Mrs Castle recorded, backed Wilson playing the 'world influence' card. John Hunt's minute does not attribute views in the discussion that followed but the Castle diary does:

> Mike [Foot] came in almost hesitantly. He admitted Harold was trying to keep within the compromise of the Manifesto on this though we were committed to getting rid of the [American] nuclear bases [in Britain (which did not happen)]. 'We shall proceed to negotiate this within the overall disarmament talks,' Harold countered promptly. Mike then said that he remained of the view that we should rid ourselves of nuclear weapons, but recognised that he was in a minority and so would not press the matter. Peter [Shore] and Wedgie [Tony Benn] said nothing.

Mrs Castle tried her best, but to no avail:

> I was more emphatic than Mike. It was not only that I was a nuclear disarmer, I said, but I thought the decision was self-contradictory within the context of our own defence strategy. What we were saying was that we needed nuclear weapons in order to exercise influence, yet it tended to let them diminish in credibility by refusing to keep them up to date. This exercise in defence futility was not cheap. £24 million a year over ten years meant £240 million. . .
>   The debate then died away. Harold summed up cheerfully. . . The fact is that the spirit of the Campaign for Nuclear Disarmament no longer walks the land.[97]

At this point, in terms of Cabinet or Cabinet committee minutes, we go into the dark. For the Lord Chancellor, Lord Falconer, ruled at a British Academy/ National Archives conference on the first year of 'scholarship and the Freedom of Information Act' at the Academy on 11 February 2006, that such records could not be revealed until 30 years had elapsed, as under the old provisions of the Public Record Act, 1967. That position still holds.

However, in January 2007, a valuable assessment of the terms and updating of the 1958 US-UK Agreement on nuclear weapons information sharing was declassified as part of the 1976 archive of GEN 32 which examined possible contacts with France.

60. GEN 32 (76) 6, 'Nuclear Contacts with France' report, Annex D, 22 September 1976.

TNA, PRO, CAB 130/878

SECRET

THIS DOCUMENT IS THE PROPERTY OF HER BRITANNIC MAJESTY'S GOVERNMENT

GEN 32(76)6   COPY NO   7
22 September 1976   ~~126#~~

CABINET
NUCLEAR CONTACTS WITH FRANCE
———
REPORT
Note by the Chairman
———

The attached report is circulated in the form in which it has been
submitted to the Secretary of the Cabinet.

Signed   CLIVE ROSE

Cabinet Office
22 September 1976

SECRET

60. (cont.)

ANNEX D

UNITED STATES/UNITED KINGDOM AGREEMENTS
IN THE NUCLEAR FIELD

1.   There is a long history of United States/United Kingdom Agreements
in the nuclear field stretching back to the wartime days of collaboration
in the development of the first nuclear weapon.   These have governed the
co-operation between the two countries in various areas and to differing
degrees.   At present, co-operation in the defence field is almost
wholly determined by the Agreement for Co-operation on the Uses of
Atomic Energy for Mutual Defence Purposes which entered into force on
4 August 1958, and which has subsequently been amended in 1959, 1969,
1970 and 1974; it is known as the 1958 Defence Agreement.

2.   The purpose of the 1958 Defence Agreement is stated in Article 1:

> "While the United States and the United Kingdom are participating
> in an international arrangement for their mutual defence and
> security and making substantial and material contribution thereto,
> each Party will communicate to and exchange with the other Party
> information and will transfer materials and equipment in
> accordance with the provisions of the Agreement provided the
> communicating or transferring Party determines that such
> co-operation will promote and will not constitute an unreasonable
> risk to its defence and security".

The purpose of the Agreement has been well served over the past 18 years
by detailed collaboration on the design of nuclear weapons.   Classified
information exchanged under the Agreement has been concerned with all
aspects of nuclear weapon design, development and production to the
point where it is no longer possible to identify any specific item of
information now available in the United Kingdom as being of United States
or United Kingdom origin; all such information has to be treated as
originating jointly in the United States and the United Kingdom.   On the
materials and equipment front, there have been extensive transfers in
support of both the nuclear weapons and nuclear propulsion programmes.

3.   The constraints placed on the use which may be made of United States
information, materials and equipment within the United Kingdom are
spelled out in the Agreement in the following terms:

20

"Except as may be otherwise agreed for civil uses, the information communicated or exchanged, or the materials or equipment transferred, by either Party pursuant to this Agreement shall be used by the recipient Party exclusively for the preparation or implementation of defence plans in the mutual interests of the two countries." (Article V)

"Classified information, communicated or exchanged, and any materials or equipment transferred, pursuant to this Agreement shall not be communicated, exchanged or transferred by the recipient party or persons under its jurisdiction to any unauthorised persons or, except as provided in Article VII of this Agreement, beyond the jurisdiction of that Party." (Article VI)

"Neither Party shall communicate classified information or transfer or permit access to or use of materials, or equipment, made available to the other Party pursuant to this Agreement to any nation or national organisation unless

A /the recipient Party is informed that the other Party agrees_7 or

B /the recipient Party is informed by the other Party that the classified information concerned has already been communicated to the nation or international organisation in question or that access has already been permitted to materials or equipment for the nation or international organisation in question_7." (Article VII)

In short, classified information, materials and equipment made available to the United Kingdom by the United States under the 1958 Defence Agreement may be used only for defence purposes and may not be made available to third parties except by agreement with the United States. There have been no instances of the United Kingdom seeking United States agreement to exploiting co-operation under the Defence Agreement for civil or international purposes.

4.   These constraints apply in particular to all classified information passed under the 1958 Defence Agreement.   The fact that they apply specifically to naval nuclear propulsion information was confirmed in the exchange of correspondence in 1964 between Sir Solly Zuckerman, then Chief Scientific Adviser, Ministry of Defence, and Admiral Rickover. At that time, the United Kingdom accepted somewhat more onerous restrictions.   In respect of all United States originated propulsion information, even if unclassified, it was agreed that such information would be used only for naval propulsion purposes and would not be disclosed by any means to foreign nationals.   In respect of

60. (cont.)

United Kingdom originated naval propulsion information, it was agreed that such information would be classified in accordance with a Policy Guide which was drawn up by the United States and accepted by the United Kingdom. The broad outcome of this exchange of correspondence was that all technical naval propulsion information became special information not available for disclosure to third parties.

5. The 1965 Polaris Sales Agreement, under which the United States provided to the United Kingdom Polaris missiles (less warheads), equipment and supporting services is closely related to the 1958 Defence Agreement in as much as both Agreements are essential for the support of the United Kingdom's Strategic Deterrent Force. The Sales Agreement lays down that

> "The Government of the United Kingdom shall not, without the prior express consent of the Government of the United States, transfer, or permit access to, or use of, the missiles, equipment, services, or documents or information relating thereto which are provided by the Government of the United States under this Agreement, except to a United Kingdom officer, employee, national or firm engaged in the implementation of this Agreement." (Article XIV)

As with the Defence Agreement, United Kingdom co-operation with third parties on Polaris matters is subject to obtaining the prior agreement of the United States.

6. The specific question of the possibility of nuclear co-operation with France was raised in discussions between President Nixon and Prime Minister Wilson in August 1969, and this led to the so-called Mildenhall Agreement. The United Kingdom said that, in the event of an enquiry from the French we would

  a. make it clear that any bilateral co-operation would have
      i. to be developed within the context of our common membership of the Alliance and, where applicable, within the appropriate NATO Institutions; and
      ii. to be compatible with our various international obligations

  b. subject to a. express a willingness to enter into discussions

  c. keep the United States Government closely informed of any exchanges.

The United States replied that

> "If the French were to raise the question of nuclear
> co-operation between France and the United States, the
> substance of the American response would depend on what
> precisely had been proposed and on what the situation was
> at the time of the proposal. The American reply would
> also take into account the international obligations of the
> United States; its bilateral agreements, eg with the United
> Kingdom; the need to preserve the integrity of NATO; and the
> position of the Nuclear Planning Group. In any case the
> United States would keep the United Kingdom fully informed
> about any contacts with France."

Thus, the Mildenhall Agreement lays a specific obligation on both the
United States and the United Kingdom to consult with each other on any
question concerning possible co-operation by either country with France.

23

By this time Jim Callaghan was Prime Minister and in the throes of a severe sterling crisis which, in early December, led to the securing of a loan from the International Monetary Fund. At one point in the crisis, Sir Frank Cooper, Permanent Secretary at the Ministry of Defence, privately warned the Cabinet Secretary that cuts of more than £100m in the defence budget might put the Polaris deterrent itself (not just its improvement) at risk.[98] The Cabinet did agree defence cuts of £100m for 1977–78 and £200m for 1978–79 on 7 December 1976.[99] But Polaris and its improvement (by this time re-codenamed Chevaline—see note on page 278) survived.

Callaghan did not bring nuclear weapons matters before his full Cabinet. Its members knew neither the codename Chevaline, nor of its escalating costs and delay which meant it was not deployed in time to fill the late 1970s gap foreseen by Heath and his inner group in 1973. By the time Callaghan became Prime Minister its costs had reached £595m (the equivalent of £388m at 1972 prices). In 1977 it was revised upwards to £810m (£494m at 1972 prices).[100] In his retirement I asked Lord Callaghan if he had thought of cancelling Chevaline? 'When I came to office as Prime Minister,' he replied,

> I could then have said, 'Well, all right, we'd better cancel it.' But it's awfully difficult, unless you have the virtue of hindsight, when something is going on, has been going on for three or four years, and you're told, 'Oh, it's going to be pretty soon now, can we have another hundred million or fifty million?' to say 'No, put it all on one side,' to be so certain you're right that it's not going to succeed. In fact, it did succeed; but it did cost a lot more than everybody expected. And every time they called for a new tranche, I used to write 'agree' on the minute . . . because one always thought it was just around the corner.[101]

By the time Chevaline was disclosed to Parliament on 24 January 1980, Labour was out of office and its cost had risen to £1,000m (£530m in 1972 prices). Finally, in November 1982, the Ministry of Defence announced that Chevaline-improved Polaris missiles were operational at sea.

POLARIS TO TRIDENT   1978–2005

Chevaline had already left its scars, however, when Callaghan set up his Nuclear Policy Group in January 1978 to consider the possibility of an entirely new generation of nuclear weapons, despite the 1974 manifesto pledge. Knowledge of its existence was kept away from the full Cabinet and its membership consisted of Callaghan, Healey, David Owen (Foreign Secretary) and Fred Mulley (Defence Secretary).[102] Did Callaghan consider following the manifesto and allowing the deterrent to fade away as the Chevaline-improved Polaris reached the end of its operational life? 'No,' he told me,

> I never considered that. I considered that we ought certainly not to let it die out; that would have been ducking our responsibilities. I considered that we ought to have all the options in front of us and to take a decision on them. The option might have been, of course, not to go ahead with it— but that wouldn't have been a case of letting it die out, that would have been a case of taking a positive decision.[103]

Why had he begun the process as early as January 1978?

> It was believed, on expert advice, that the date at which the [Polaris] submarines would start to become obsolescent would be about 1990 to 1992. It was also believed that it would take about ten years to build them [a successor set of submarines]—as, indeed, proved to be the case. And so, in 1978, I took a decision that we'd better start examining this, knowing that we wouldn't have to take a decision in the lifetime of the government of which I was head, but expecting to have a decision, one way or the other, after a general election.[104]

The examination Callaghan was seeking was entrusted to a Nuclear Matters Working Party. Its task was divided into two parts: one on the technical choices from a group chaired by Sir Ronald Mason, Chief Scientific Adviser to the Ministry of Defence; a second on the politico-military factors chaired by the senior diplomat, Sir Antony Duff.

Sir Ronald was greatly affected by the Chevaline experience in terms of difficulty and cost:

> It left an indelible mark on my own mind, and that is the tremendous resources you have to call into play if you develop a major strategic programme unilaterally. I think that probably—consciously, rather than subconsciously—played a very considerable part in my approach to the government's request to look at strategic successor systems to Polaris. My feeling was that all opportunities for commonality—particularly, of course, with the United States—ought to be seen through before one really faced up again to an independent national programme.[105]

The compilers of Duff-Mason were aware that any successor system to Chevaline had to be substantially more advanced if the Moscow criterion were to be met. In the late 1970s, simulations and calculations suggested that even Chevaline-improved Polaris missiles would only have a 50 per cent probability of achieving the number of ABM-penetrations required to meet the Moscow damage criterion.

The politico-military section of Duff-Mason told ministers the capacity of a successor system to inflict unacceptable damage upon the Soviet Union could take three forms.

1. To destroy the command centres of the Soviet political and military systems (both above and below ground) inside the Moscow ring road and extra ones in the wider Moscow area.
2. To inflict a level of damage that would cause the breakdown of normal life in Moscow, Leningrad plus two more big cities.
3. To inflict breakdown on 10 big cities west of the Urals, including Leningrad, or lesser damage on 30 big targets (also including Leningrad).[106]

Not all the ministers on Callaghan's group accepted these 'unacceptable damage' criteria.

Two members of Callaghan's group of four took another lesson from Chevaline, as Denis Healey explained: 'David Owen and I both felt that the Chevaline programme was too expensive. We didn't need to be able to hit Moscow.'[107] They took the line Sir Solly Zuckerman had during the PN discussions in 1967. Zuckerman was by now a consultant in the Cabinet Office, and David Owen sought his help to run the option of sea-launched cruise missiles as a cheaper alternative to the latest Trident technology being developed in the US.

Owen's argument was that Sir Antony Duff, as chair of a Cabinet Office group, was 'no longer my man', so he was 'entitled to have somebody else [i.e. Zuckerman]' to help him prepare his alternative to what would become known as the Duff-Mason Report:

Jim Callaghan with Trident sceptic, David Owen (right).

I think Jim Callaghan knew perfectly well this was going on—and all credit to him; he thought it was a good idea to have a debate, he didn't resent this at all. He believed it was a major decision.[108]

Owen put in a 56-page paper to Callaghan's group for its meeting to consider Duff-Mason on 13 December 1978. Duff-Mason recommended Trident; Owen believes his and Zuckerman's paper 'totally demolished the Moscow Criteria.'[109]

Callaghan told the group that '[t]o give up our status as a nuclear weapon state would be a momentous step in British history' that would deprive the UK of influence and knowledge of US decision-taking.[110] Was the possibility of an alternative Anglo-French collaboration a serious option? 'Not very, at that stage,' said Owen.

> Probably we should have done. It was certainly something which I was talking to the French about. I opened a dialogue, with Jim Callaghan's full agreement, with my opposite number, Monsieur de Guiringaud, and we began to discuss nuclear questions. And there was a little bit of dialogue between the two ministries of defence. It was a glint in my eye, then, yes, but not fully developed. Their weapon system, at that stage, too, hadn't really become as effective as it has done since [Lord Owen was speaking in 1988].[111]

Callaghan's official biographer, Ken Morgan, reckons his subject kept nuclear weapons matters away from his full Cabinet in 1978 because of 'such ardent nuclear disarmers as Michael Foot and Tony Benn'.[112] Indeed, one heard at the time that the chief reason for the ministerial group not being a Cabinet committee was to spare the sensibilities of Callaghan's deputy, Foot.[113]

Callaghan later defended his decision to keep possible Polaris replacement to his group of four by arguing 'it was always traditional, and nothing new, for nuclear issues to be discussed in a small group' under both Labour and Conservative governments:

> It was because of the belief, I think expressly encouraged by the Ministry of Defence and by the Cabinet Office, that these matters were so sensitive and so secret that they ought to be kept to a small number of people; and that arose from our relationship with the United States, because they felt that they were giving us information that should not be conveyed to the French, although I believe that they did it themselves. . . But formally we weren't supposed to tell the French or the Germans or anybody else. So I think those are the reasons that that happened.[114]

A few weeks after the December 1978 meeting of his Nuclear Policy Group, Callaghan made sure that if a future British Cabinet opted for Trident, the Carter Administration would provide it under the terms of the 1958 Agreement. The crucial meeting between Prime Minister and President took place in a beach hut in the Caribbean:

> He was lying on his bed in his swimming trunks when I walked in—we all had grass huts or something equivalent [at the Guadeloupe summit], and I just walked across ten yards of grass, with the blue sea shimmering almost beneath our feet, and woke him up and said, 'Jimmy, before we resume tonight, on our next session, I want to have a word with you about the possible replacement of Polaris.'

And then I went on to explain that we hadn't taken any decision, that I was trying to find out all the information I could before we had to get to a decision. He was very forthcoming straightaway. He said he had no difficulty about transferring the technology, if we decided that we wanted it. . . I made it absolutely clear to him that we had taken no decision on this and would not take any decision on it for some time to come.[115]

In the end, it fell to Margaret Thatcher to lead her Cabinet to the decision to purchase Trident. If Callaghan had won the 1979 election, would he too have recommended Trident to his Cabinet?

It would have been my instinct. . . I probably would have come down that way. But I'm certainly not disposed to brush all the alternative arguments on one side.[116]

He was disposed, however, to make the Duff-Mason report available to Mrs Thatcher. As one of his last acts as Prime Minister in May 1979, he left instructions to this effect. Why?

Because it was a matter of national importance. I think it is very important that succeeding ministers and succeeding governments should not know about the political decisions of their predecessors—that is a principle I adhere to. But if one wishes to leave a note for his successor about a matter of the greatest national importance, then I think he is entitled to do so.[117]

As Mrs Thatcher said in her memoirs, '[w]e began to look at the options from almost the first days in government.'

By late September we had discarded the option of a successor force of air-launched cruise missiles because they would be too vulnerable to attack. The possibility of co-operation with France . . . was rejected for technological reasons. From an early stage the American Trident looked the most promising option.[118]

The 'we' in this case was Mrs Thatcher and her ad hoc Cabinet committee on Polaris replacement, MISC 7, which consisted of herself; Willie Whitelaw, Deputy Prime Minister and Home Secretary; Lord Carrington, Foreign Secretary; Geoffrey Howe, Chancellor of the Exchequer; and Francis Pym, Defence Secretary.[119]

On 6 December 1979, MISC 7 decided to opt for the Trident C4 missile.[120] Mrs Thatcher took the decision to full Cabinet for ratification on 15 July 1980 in something of a rush as it was feared that the *New York Times* was about to leak the story.[121]

As Lady Thatcher recalled:

In the summer of 1980 we thought that we had made our final decision on the independent nuclear deterrent. But it was not to be. President Reagan came into office in 1981 with a programme of modernizing US strategic nuclear forces, including Trident. On 24 August the new US Defence Secretary, Casper Weinberger, wrote to me to confirm that President Reagan had now decided to use the Trident II (D5) missile in the Trident submarines. The US Administration would make this missile available to us if we wished to buy it. On 1 October President Reagan formally told me of his decision.[122]

To accompany the announcement of the Trident decision, the Ministry of Defence published an Open Government Document entitled *The Future United Kingdom Deterrent Force*. Drafted by Michael Quinlan, its Deputy Secretary (Policy and Programmes), it strongly stressed the need for 'a second centre of decision-taking within NATO as part of the alliance's wider spectrum of deterrence. To achieve this,

> our force has to be visibly capable of posing a massive threat on its own. A force which could strike tellingly only if the United States also did so— which plainly relied, for example, on US assents to its use, or an attenuation or distraction of Soviet defences by United States forces—would not achieve the purpose. We need to convince Soviet leaders that even if they thought that at some critical point as a conflict developed the US would hold back, the British force could still inflict a blow so destructive that the penalty for aggression would have proved too high.[123]

In November 1981, MISC 7 resumed its discussions. In late January 1982, the MISC 7 decision to go for the D5 Trident missile went to the full Cabinet.[124]

This time there was a more substantial discussion. John Nott, now Defence Secretary, had protested on 15 July 1980 at the perfunctory nature of the Trident C5 procurement discussion:

> I was shocked that the Cabinet had neither been given any facts nor consulted on the issue. I protested. I said that I thought it was an unsatisfactory way of conducting the government's business, not least because this was a matter of fundamental national importance. I do not recall anyone else supporting me.
>
> The Prime Minister explained that it had happened in this way because the discussions had leaked out in Washington . . . and she had no choice but to announce it. The whole matter took up about ten minutes of Cabinet time.[125]

Nott was Trade Secretary when he made his protest. As Defence Secretary, he persuaded 'a somewhat reluctant Margaret Thatcher' that a more substantial Cabinet discussion was needed on Trident D5.

He had his way and the Cabinet met for the purpose in January 1982:

> Having obtained the permission of the Americans to pass on some very delicate information, we [Nott and the Chief of the Defence Staff, Sir Terry Lewin] explained to the Cabinet how much we knew about Soviet nuclear, biological and chemical capabilities, where their command and control bunkers were situated, and how the development of anti-ballistic missile defences bore down on the requirement for a credible deterrent. This was in an era when the extent of satellite photography and electronic and signal intelligence was not much known to those outside a small circle.

Nott concluded 'the briefing was worthwhile. My colleagues were fascinated; but the Chancellor [Sir Geoffrey Howe] had come down from a good lunch and slept during the briefing.'[126]

Between them, MISC 7 and Mrs Thatcher's full Cabinet ensured there would be 'a bloody Union Jack' on Trident into the 2020s unless a Labour Cabinet, with a disarmament-minded Prime Minister at its head, took power in the meantime. When Labour did return to power in 1997 under Tony Blair, its manifesto stated 'A new Labour government will retain Trident'[127] (the last Polaris patrol had ended the previous summer). Its manifesto for the 2005 general election declared 'We are . . . committed to retaining the independent nuclear deterrent. . .'[128] By this time, Tony Blair and his inner group on nuclear weapons policy had begun to prepare for the successor system to Trident D5.

Margaret Thatcher aboard the Polaris submarine, *HMS Resolution*, **August 1982.**

The Trident submarine *HMS Vanguard*, with the Polaris submarine *HMS Resolution* in its wake.

A Trident D5 missile being test-fired by *HMS Vanguard*, October 2005.

In January 2005, the Prime Minister's inner ministerial group on nuclear weapons met to agree increased funding for Aldermaston's human and physical capabilities to ensure it would be in a position to design warheads for a successor system to Trident D5 if the Cabinet should so decide.[129] Seven months later, the Defence Secretary John Reid announced in Parliament that an average of an additional £350m per annum would be invested in Aldermaston over three years.[130]

On 16 November 2005, the first meeting took place in the Cabinet Office of the Official Group on the Future of the Deterrent chaired by the Cabinet Secretary, Sir Gus O'Donnell. It met again on 14 December 2005 under the chairmanship of Sir Nigel Sheinwald, the Prime Minister's Foreign Policy Adviser. It met four more times between April and November 2006, preparing the options for consideration by Tony Blair's Ministerial Group on the Future of the Deterrent, which consisted of the Prime Minister; the Chancellor of the Exchequer, Gordon Brown; the Foreign Secretary, Margaret Beckett; the Defence Secretary, Des Browne and a mixture of officials drawn from the O'Donnell/Sheinwald group.[131]

The Prime Minister's group met twice—on 27 June 2006, for an interim discussion, and on 15 November 2006 for a final one.[132] The full Cabinet met for the first time on 23 November 2006 to consider possible future threats to the UK that might require the retention of nuclear weapons. On 4 December, without 'any dissenting voices', the Cabinet decided to authorise construction of a new generation of missile-carrying submarines to sustain the UK deterrent over the period 2020–2050.[133] That afternoon, the Government published a White Paper, *The Future of the United Kingdom's Nuclear Deterrent*.

Parliament was informed that

> We have . . . decided to maintain our nuclear deterrent by building a new class of submarines. . . A final decision on whether we require three or four submarines will be taken when we know more about their detailed design.
>
> We have also decided to participate in the US life extension programme for the Trident D5 missile, which will enable us to retain that missile in service until the early 2040s. Our existing nuclear warhead design will last into the 2020s. We do not yet have sufficient information to know whether it can, with some refurbishment, be extended beyond that point or whether we will need to develop a replacement warhead: a decision is likely to be necessary in the next Parliament.[134]

In a 'Foreword' to the White Paper, Tony Blair advanced a mix of reasons for the UK's remaining a nuclear power some 60 years on from Attlee's GEN 163 deciding to make it so.

We cannot predict the way the world will look in 30 or 50 years time. For now some of the old realities remain. Major countries, which pose no threat to the UK today, retain large arsenals some of which are being modernised or increased. None of the present recognised nuclear weapons states intends to renounce nuclear weapons, in the absence of an agreement to disarm multilaterally, and we cannot be sure that a major nuclear threat to our vital interests will not emerge over the longer term.

We also have to face new threats, particularly of regional powers developing nuclear weapons for the first time which present a threat to us. . . And we need to factor in the requirement to deter countries which might in the future seek to sponsor nuclear terrorism from their soil. . . We believe that an independent British nuclear deterrent is an essential part of our insurance against the uncertainties and risks of the future. . . I believe it is crucial that, for the foreseeable future, British Prime Ministers have the necessary assurance that no aggressor can escalate a crisis beyond UK control.[135]

In 2006, unlike 1980, the emphasis was much less on a second centre of decision-taking, and much more on national, rather than alliance, needs. The stress on an independent centre of decision-taking had a French tinge to it.

On 7 December 2006, Tony Blair and President George Bush exchanged letters arranging Britain's participation in Trident D5's 'life extension programme' under the terms of the 1958 agreement and the 1963 Polaris Sales Agreement while undertaking that 'any successor to the D5 system' will be compatible with UK submarine launch systems.[136]

Trident upgraders: Gordon Brown and Tony Blair.

61. The Bush-Blair exchange of letters, 7 December 2006.

1O DOWNING STREET
LONDON SW1A 2AA
www.pm.gov.uk

7 December 2006

THE PRIME MINISTER

Dear George,

The United Kingdom Government attaches great importance to the maintenance of its independent nuclear deterrent capability, both as a means of ensuring the security of the United Kingdom and our vital interests, and as an important element of our contribution and commitment to the North Atlantic Alliance.

We have therefore to set in train the steps necessary to maintain our current submarine-based nuclear deterrent system, replacing those elements – in particular the submarines – that will reach the end of their planned life by the 2020s.

Following the agreement reached in an exchange of letters between the United Kingdom and the United States Governments in 1982 under the framework of the 1963 Polaris Sales Agreement, our current Vanguard class submarines have carried the Trident II D5 missile since they began to enter service in 1994. We have decided that we will replace the Vanguard submarines with another class of submarines in the 2020s, and would like these submarines to continue to carry Trident II D5 missiles.

61. (cont.)

Accordingly, we wish to participate in the planned life extension programme for the Trident II D5 missile, which we understand is intended to extend the life of the missiles into the 2040s. We also seek assurance that, in support of those missiles, the United States will provide us, under the framework of the Polaris Sales Agreement, as amended for Trident, with sufficient equipment and supporting services to equip a force of new SSBNs. I propose that, as in the past, these matters be taken forward by the executive agencies of the two Governments to ensure mutually satisfactory solutions.

For the longer term, we need to be assured that we can, if we so choose, maintain a nuclear delivery system, with US assistance, for at least the remainder of the life of our successor submarine force. In this respect, the United Kingdom wishes to ensure that any successor to the D5 system is compatible with, or is capable of being made compatible with, the launch system for the D5 missile, which we will in the meantime be installing into our new submarines. We believe that there would be merit in the United Kingdom having the opportunity to participate, at an early stage, in any programme to replace the D5 missiles, or to discuss a further life extension – for UK purposes – of the D5 missile, to match the potential out of service date of our new submarines. I propose that, as in the past, close coordination should be maintained between the executive agencies of our two Governments in order to ensure the compatibility of equipment.

We wish also to maintain our cooperation under the 1958 Agreement for Cooperation on the Uses of Atomic energy for Mutual Defence Purposes ("Mutual Defence Agreement"). In addition, I believe that this programme has the potential to open up new opportunities for future cooperation and collaboration on other aspects of future submarine platforms, and we would wish our respective experts carefully to consider where this might be of mutual benefit.

As has been the case in the past with the Polaris force, and is currently the case with our Trident force, we intend that a future UK deterrent submarine force equipped with Trident, and any subsequent successor to Trident, will be assigned to the North Atlantic Treaty Organisation: and except where the United Kingdom Government may decide that supreme national interests are at stake, this successor force will be used for the purposes of international defence of the Atlantic Alliance in all circumstances.

yours ever,

Tony

The Honorable George W Bush

61. (cont.)

/ -

THE WHITE HOUSE
WASHINGTON

December 7, 2006

The Right Honorable
Tony Blair, M.P.
Prime Minister
London

Dear Prime Minister:

Thank you for your letter regarding modernizing your independent nuclear deterrent. The United States Government continues to attach great importance to the maintenance of an operationally independent nuclear deterrent capability by the United Kingdom and values the deep and long-standing cooperation between our two countries in this area.

The United States Government accordingly welcomes the steps outlined in your letter to maintain and modernize the U.K.'s capability in this area for the longer term. We also attach importance to, and welcome, your intention to continue to assign this force to NATO.

The 1958 Agreement for Cooperation on the Uses of Atomic Energy for Mutual Defense Purposes ("Mutual Defense Agreement") and the 1963 Polaris Sales Agreement have provided a strong, enduring basis for cooperation between our two countries. We believe that these two agreements, the terms of which are not affected by this exchange of letters, will continue to provide a solid basis for ensuring mutually satisfactory cooperation in those areas where you have requested assurances. I can reaffirm the U.S. commitment to support the missile system and associated equipment deployed by the United Kingdom under the terms of these agreements.

In this context, the United States fully supports and welcomes the intention of the United Kingdom to participate in the life-extension program for the Trident II D5 missile. We will work to ensure that the necessary components of the overall system are made available to the United Kingdom to support life-extended D5 missiles, under the framework of the Polaris Sales Agreement and the 1982 Exchange of Letters. I fully agree with your suggestion that, as in the past, these matters be taken forward by the executive agencies of our two governments to ensure mutually satisfactory solutions.

For the longer term, in accordance with your proposal and under the framework of the Polaris Sales Agreement and the 1982 Exchange of Letters, I would invite the United Kingdom to participate, at an early stage, in any program to replace the D5 missiles or to discuss a further life extension -- for your purposes -- of the D5 missile to match the potential out-of-service date of your new submarines. In this respect, any successor to the D5 system should be compatible with, or be capable of being made compatible with, the launch system for the D5 missile, which you will be installing into your new submarines. The United States will also ensure under the framework of the Polaris Sales Agreement and the 1982 Exchange of Letters that the United Kingdom has the option to sustain an effective nuclear delivery system for at least the life of your successor submarine force as was done with the Polaris system. Again, I agree with you that, as in the past, close coordination should be maintained between the executive agencies of our two governments in order to ensure compatibility of equipment.

I agree that we should maintain our cooperation under the 1958 Agreement for Cooperation on the Uses of Atomic Energy for Mutual Defense Purposes ("Mutual Defense Agreement"). I also concur in your proposal that our two countries should also explore the scope for cooperation and collaboration on other aspects of future submarine platforms. We recognize the importance of this potential collaboration and will work to ensure that further cooperation in this area can be deepened accordingly.

Sincerely,

George W. Bush

Downing Street published these letters on 19 December 2006.[137] On 14 March 2007, the House of Commons voted 409 to 161 to renew the Trident system (88 Labour MPs voted against). The gist of the Government's motion was

> That this House supports the Government's decisions, as set out in the White Paper The Future of the United Kingdom's Nuclear Deterrent (Cm 6994), to take the steps necessary to maintain the UK's minimum strategic nuclear deterrent beyond the life of the existing system and to take further steps towards meeting the UK's disarmament responsibilities under Article VI of the Non-Proliferation Treaty.

Earlier, the Government had defeated a motion to delay the decision by 413 to 167 (95 Labour MPs voted for the amendment).[138] Before the debate, Tony Blair said the vote would not 'bind' future parliaments, and that the House of Commons might debate and vote again when the contracts were about to be let for the new submarines between 2012 and 2014.[139]

The possibility of future votes had been stressed in a letter Margaret Beckett and Des Browne had sent to potential Labour dissenters on the morning of the vote. The note was principally directed at the proposers of the amendment, John Denham, Labour MP for Southampton Itchen, and Dr Alan Whitehead, Labour MP for Southampton Test.[140]

62. Beckett/Browne letter to dissenting Labour MPs, 14 March 2007.

**Foreign &
Commonwealth
Office**

SECRETARY OF STATE FOR DEFENCE

MSU 1/5/4

14 March 2007

Dear Alan,

We have seen the text of your proposed amendment to the Government motion for today's debate. The points you make on this important issue are serious and deserve a considered response.

The Government has made clear that we need to take a decision now to maintain our nuclear deterrent beyond the life of the existing system. The White Paper and the Prime Minister's statement to the House on 4 December 2006 explains that that decision needs to be made now because of the need to replace the submarines on which our deterrent is, and will continue to be, based. We believe that the strategic case for maintaining the deterrent has been made, and we have laid it out more fully than ever before, and it is for the House to decide whether to support that decision or not. Should there be a fundamental change for the better in the strategic environment and, in particular, significant further progress on non-proliferation and disarmament, it would obviously be right for future governments to look at this again, and they can, of course, do so.

Your amendment urges further consideration of the costs and design of the system, as well as of the strategic case. On the costs, our assessment is set out in detail in the White Paper. We will, of course, keep this under review to ensure the best possible value for money. As for the design, we have made clear that further decisions will be required, both on the number of new

Dr Alan Whitehead MP
House of Commons

62. (cont.)

submarines we will need in future to maintain our minimum strategic nuclear deterrent (4, as now, or 3), and on the detailed design and build. Those decisions will, of course, have an impact on cost.

Your amendment calls for development of our non-proliferation strategy, as recommended by the House of Commons Defence Select Committee. The Government's comprehensive strategy on non-proliferation and multilateral disarmament was set out in the White Paper, and in a speech by Kim Howells to the Conference on Disarmament in Geneva. We will take every opportunity to make further progress on this crucial issue. The Select Committee also urged us to set out a "stronger narrative" on the "commitment of the Government to achieve nuclear non-proliferation" and we will certainly respond to that along with the Select Committee's other recommendations.

Finally, your amendment would require the approval of the House "before main contracts are laid". The Government is, of course, committed to the fullest possible transparency of decision making on this. That is why, unlike previous decisions on the deterrent, we have set out in such detail the thinking behind our decision, in order to allow for public and Parliamentary debate ahead of the vote today.

Ultimately, we need to be clear about our decision, and to confirm to the British people, and to the rest of the world that we are not abandoning our deterrent. The Government believes that decision is in the best interests of the national security of the United Kingdom.

We have, as noted above, indicated that further decisions will be required on the precise design of the submarines and whether we need four or three to maintain the deterrent. The White Paper also notes that we will need to decide whether to renew or replace the warhead, whether to participate in any US programme to develop a successor to the D5 missile and, subsequently, whether to acquire such a successor. It will fall to future Governments and Parliaments to discuss the most appropriate form of Parliamentary scrutiny for these downstream decisions. In the meantime, we will ensure that there are regular reports to Parliament as the programme moves forward. We are sure that the Select Committee will maintain its regular scrutiny of these issues – we welcome this and will continue to offer our fullest cooperation.

We are copying this to those who have signed your proposed amendment.

Margaret Beckett

MARGARET BECKETT
Secretary of State for Foreign
and Commonwealth Affairs

DES BROWNE
Secretary of State for Defence

Even allowing for the possibility of a series of future votes, it seemed highly unlikely in the spring of 2007 that the upgrading of Trident would be halted in its tracks. It seemed highly probable, therefore, that the UK would be a nuclear weapons state for at least a century from the first atomic test of 1952 into the 2050s.

CONCLUSION

'From Hiroshima on August 6, 1945,' wrote Daniel Boorstin, the historian of discoverers, 'the world received the shocking discovery that man had opened the dark continent of the atom. Its mysteries would haunt the twentieth century.'[141] Its political, military and strategic consequences have haunted British Cabinets from that day to this. The question of the bomb has run like an irradiated thread through the history of high, bureaucratic, military and scientific politics for 60 years. It has been intimately bound up, too, with the history of official secrecy, parliamentary accountability, and governing styles of prime ministers from Churchill and Attlee to Blair and Brown, and an important sub-component of premiership—the nuclear aspect of the US-UK 'special relationship'.

As this is a book of explanation rather than advocacy, it is for the reader to judge, rather than for the author to declare, which factors trumped what at various times in the private debates in the Cabinet Room or Chiefs of Staff suite. What is especially interesting to observe is the shift in the blend of reasons for becoming and remaining a nuclear weapons state and for independence, and, later interdependence, in the pursuit of deterrence. Three other countries, in particular, were players in the British Cabinet Room over the sixty years—the United States, Russia and France. They still are, but of late they have been joined by a number of other nuclear or would-be nuclear states.

In human terms, the doctrine of unripe time (this is not the moment to disarm) and the consequent pursuit, as Michael Quinlan has put it, of 'a set of rationales to clothe that gut decision'[142] have undoubtedly been powerful shapers of private discussions in the most secret nuclearised parts of the state. Such factors are not unique to the making of nuclear weapons policy. As Alistair Cooke expressed it in a radio essay on 'Politics and the Human Animal' broadcast amid the embers of the Suez crisis in December 1956, one of the things that struck him most forcibly during his 'daily chore' of watching and listening to 'the chief actors on the political stage' is 'the ease with which a nation does something from instinct and justifies it by reason'.[143]

The shifts in international politics and the condition of the world have been both numerous, and, in many cases, unpredictable since Attlee sat down to write his memorandum for the GEN 75 Cabinet committee in late August 1945. Only one hugely important factor has held. No city, in Ronald Clark's phrase, has been 'put to the bomb'[144] since Nagasaki on 9 August 1945. Should that cease to be the case, the terms of the debate about nuclear deterrence will change the world over and not just in Britain.

APPENDIX

THE INTELLIGENCE ASPECTS

The Cold War was a classic intelligence conflict. As Michael Herman, a former intelligence professional turned-scholar put it six months before the fall of the Berlin Wall: 'Never before in peacetime have the relationships of competing power blocks been so influenced by intelligence assessments. Never before have the collection of intelligence and its denial to the adversary been such central features of an international rivalry.'[145] And from the beginning to the end of the 40–plus years of east-west confrontation, the collection of intelligence on what a 1948 list of signals intelligence requirements described as 'Development in the Soviet Union of atomic, biological and chemical methods of warfare (together with associated raw materials)'[146] remained the highest priority for the UK's secret agencies.

Yet with the exception of the period 1964–80, when intelligence (largely provided by the United States[147]) on likely—then actual—Soviet developments in ballistic missile defence in and around the Moscow region powerfully shaped the debate about the need to improve the penetrative power of the Royal Navy's Polaris warheads, intelligence (in its widest sense) played a lesser role in Cabinet and Cabinet committee discussions than political factors—such as, in Bevin's words in 1947, the need to prevent the United States possessing a nuclear monopoly; or in Churchill's 1954 metaphors, the need to retain our place at the 'top table' and our ticket to the 'Royal Enclosure' of the nuclear Ascot; or, from the early 1960s onwards under successive prime ministers of both major parties, not to allow France to become western Europe's sole nuclear state.

The Soviet bomb project gained an immense amount from the atomic spies run by Russian intelligence inside the Manhattan Project, from Klaus Fuchs especially. The British scientists at Los Alamos returned to Britain with the design of the Nagasaki plutonium bomb in their heads, whence it could not be extracted by the McMahon Act passed by the US Congress in 1946. Indeed, with Fuchs exposed and convicted in 1950, Cherwell told Churchill before the Monte Bello trial in 1952 that Penney

> is our chief—indeed our only—real expert in the construction of the bomb and I do not know what we should do without him. He played an outstanding part in designing the original American bombs at Los Alamos in the war and participated in the first tests.[148]

So clandestine intelligence was not an element in the manufacture of the first British atomic bomb. It was, however, of some use in the procurement of the first UK hydrogen bomb.

The so-called 'Modus Vivendi', concluded between the US and UK administrations in 1948 after the rupture in atomic collaboration caused by the McMahon Act, allowed for continued sharing of intelligence on other powers' (i.e. the Soviet Union's) nuclear tests.[149] This was of particular value to the UK thermo-nuclear project in 1955 when a joint US-UK project to garner and analyse the débris from the Russian tests of that year enabled the weaponeers in Aldermaston to reconstruct the ingredients of the Soviet Union's first 'true' H-bombs.[150]

During the crucial series of meetings and briefings on the H-bomb in 1954, the JIC's assessment of the current Russian capacity to wreck the UK with a nuclear attack was (as we have seen) of considerable importance.

Intelligence played its part, too, in the late 1950s and early 1960s, as successor systems to the V-bomber force absorbed a great deal of Whitehall time, in the debates about what constituted an effective UK deterrent, or, in bald terms, how many Soviet cities did Britain need to be able to ruin to exert a deterring effect on the men in the Kremlin. Harold Macmillan was the first truly nuclear-capable British Prime Minister. In 1958–59, the RAF operated a '30–40 cities' policy.[151] By the time Macmillan left office in 1963, this had been scaled down to 16 cities because of improvements in Soviet air defences.[152]

When Macmillan set off for Nassau to meet President Kennedy in the hope of securing the Polaris missile system, he was seeking a capability that would reach once more the 40-city threshold. This was based on a Joint Intelligence Committee assessment of January 1962,[153] which itself relied heavily on the so-called 'breakdown' studies produced by the Joint Inter-service Group for the Study of All-out Warfare (JIGSAW) of the point at which cities break down post nuclear attack. (The planners reckoned that 'About 30% destruction of a city renders the *whole* city population "ineffective"—i.e. wholly preoccupied with their own survival.'[154])

Yet only when the criticality of the 'Moscow Criterion' became a much debated topic in the mid to late 1960s and early 1970s did the intelligence input assume a truly central place in the story of Cabinets and the bomb. As Catherine Haddon's doctoral thesis will show,[155] western intelligence had its first substantial glimpse of what became the Soviet's GALOSH anti-ballistic missile system at a November 1964 military parade in Moscow. By late 1965/early 1966, the possibility of its deployment filled a growing place in the JIC's assessments of 'Soviet Bloc War Potential' up to 1970.[156] The Moscow criterion and associated intelligence dominated the nuclear weapons ministerial discussions of the second, third and fourth Wilson governments (1966–70 and 1974–76), as it did those of the Heath government which split them.

When Jim Callaghan's Ministerial Nuclear Policy Group was presented with the Duff-Mason Report on options for Polaris replacement in December 1978, the intelligence assumption on which it rested was that UK nuclear planning over the coming 30–40 years (i.e. up to 2020) need not be based on any nuclear threat except that posed by the Soviet Union.[157]

When Sir Gus O'Donnell's official group and, later, Tony Blair's ministerial group on the Future of the Deterrent began the meetings in 2005 which led to the December 2006 White Paper, the Joint Intelligence Committee prepared a paper on likely future nuclear threats to the UK.[158] Their assessment did not have the ring of confidence that underpinned their 1978 equivalent for the Duff-Mason and Callaghan groups. As the White Paper's summary put it:

It is not possible accurately to predict the global security environment over the next 20 to 50 years. On our current analyses, we cannot rule out the risk either that a major direct nuclear threat to the UK's vital interests will re-emerge or that new states will emerge that possess a more limited nuclear capability, but one that could pose a grave threat to our vital interests. Equally there is a risk that some countries might in future seek to sponsor nuclear terrorism from their soil. We must not allow such states to threaten our national security, or to deter us and the international community from taking the action required to maintain regional and global security.[159]

NOTES

1. Franciszek Draus (ed), *History, Truth, Liberty: Selected Writings of Raymond Aron* (University of Chicago Press, 1985), pp. 336–7. Aron's 'Max Weber and Modern Social Science' was published in 1959 as his introduction to an edition of two Weber lectures, 'Science as a Vocation' and 'Politics as a Vocation', both originally published in 1918–19.
2. *Statement on Defence*, Cmd 9391 (HMSO, 1955). See also Lorna Arnold, *Britain and the H-Bomb* (Palgrave, 2001), pp. 63–4.
3. Raymond Aron, *On War: Atomic Weapons and Global Diplomacy* (1956; published in Britain by Secker and Warburg, 1958), p. 46.
4. The National Archives, Public Record Office, PREM 11/565, 'Record of Events Leading to Dropping of Bombs on Hiroshima and Nagasaki', 'Events Leading up to the Use of the Atomic Bomb, 1945', Cherwell to Churchill, 29 January 1953.
5. Duff Hart-Davis (ed), *King's Counsellor. Abdication and War: The Diaries of Sir Alan Lascelles* (Weidenfeld and Nicolson, 2006), p.293.
6. TNA, PRO, PREM 11/565, 'Events Leading up to the Use of the Atomic Bomb, 1945', Cherwell to Churchill, 29 January 1953.
7. Ibid.
8. Peter Hennessy, *Never Again: Britain 1945–51* (Penguin, 2006), p. 86.
9. C.R. Attlee, *As It Happened*, (Heinemann, 1954), p. 135. See also Margaret Gowing, *Britain and Atomic Energy 1939–1945*, (Macmillan, 1964), p. 107.
10. Kenneth Harris, *Attlee*, (Weidenfeld and Nicolson, 1982), p. 277.
11. Francis Williams, *A Prime Minister Remembers*, (Heinemann, 1961), p. 73.
12. For the GEN 75 meeting of 25 October 1946 see TNA, PRO, CAB 130/2, GEN 75/15th meeting. For Bevin's 'Union Jack' remark see Peter Hennessy, *Cabinet* (Blackwell, 1986), pp. 126–7.
13. Iain Dale (ed), *Labour Party General Election Manifestos, 1900–1997* (Routledge/Politico's, 2000), pp. 123–4.
14. Hennessy, *Cabinet*, p. 126.
15. Peter Catterall (ed), *The Macmillan Diaries: The Cabinet Years 1950–1957* (Macmillan, 2003), pp. 327–8.
16. Peter Hennessy, 'A Bloody Union Jack on Top of It', in *Muddling Through: Power, Politics and the Quality of Government in Postwar Britain* (Gollancz, 1996), p. 100. For a full account see Margaret Gowing, *Britain and Atomic Energy, 1939–1945* (Macmillan, 1964), pp. 40–3, 46, 55–6, 60–1, 64, 86, 110, 367, 380, 383–4, 389–93.
17. Gowing, *Britain and Atomic Energy*, pp. 35, 43.
18. Ibid, p. 45.
19. Ibid, p. 48.
20. Margaret Gowing, *Independence and Deterrence: Britain and Atomic Energy 1945–1952, Volume 1 Policy Making* (Macmillan, 1974), pp. 1–2.
21. Ibid, p. 1.
22. Ibid, p. 5.
23. Ibid.
24. Gowing, *Independence and Deterrence, Volume 1*, p. 5
25. General de Gaulle, *War Memoirs: Unity 1942–44* (Weidenfeld, 1959), p. 245; Ronald. W. Clark, *The Greatest Power on Earth: The Story of Nuclear Fission* (Sidgwick and Jackson, 1980), p. 182.
26. The programme was broadcast on BBC2 on 29 September 1982.
27. Peter Hennessy, 'How Bevin saved Britain's bomb', *The Times*, 30 September 1982.
28. Gowing, *Independence and Deterrence, Volume 1*, p. 90.
29. Richard Aldrich and Michael Coleman, 'The Cold War, The JIC and British Signals Intelligence, 1948', *Intelligence and National Security*, Vol.4, No.3, July 1989, Appendix 2.
30. Gowing, *Independence and Deterrence, Volume 1*, p. 210.
31. TNA, PRO, CAB 128/12, CM (48) 31st conclusions.

32. TNA, PRO, CAB 195/6. Norman Brook's note simply reads:

CM 31 (48)

1. *Parliament*

Business for next week
Adjournment for Whitsun.

33. John P. Mackintosh, *The British Cabinet* (University Paperback, 1968), p. 469.
34. Gowing, *Independence and Deterrence, Volume 1*, p. 211.
35. House of Commons, *Official Report*, 12 May 1948, col.2117 (HMSO, 1948).
36. Gowing, *Independence and Deterrence, Volume 1*, p. 211.
37. Margaret Gowing, *Independence and Deterrence, Volume 2, Policy Execution* (Macmillan, 1974), p. 136.
38. Peter Hennessy, *What The Papers Never Said* (Politics Association, 1985), pp. 24–7.
39. Peter Hennessy, *Having It So Good: Britain in the Fifties* (Allen Lane, Penguin press, 2006), p. 328. Sir Michael said this during a conversation with Sir John Willis and the author at The National Archives, Kew on 6 May 2004 as part of a series connected to the TNA's 'Secret State' Exhibition.
40. Peter Hennessy, *The Secret State: Whitehall and the Cold War* (Penguin, 2003), pp. 3, 22–5, 46, 125.
41. Gerard De Groot, *The Bomb: A Life* (Cape, 2004), p. 146; Lorna Arnold, *Britain and the H-Bomb* (Palgrave, 2001), p. 9; David Holloway, *Stalin and the Bomb: The Soviet Union and Atomic energy, 1939–1956* (Yale, 1994), pp. 213–18.
42. TNA, PRO, CAB 134/3, AC (0) (50) 5, Official Committee on Communism (Overseas), 'The "Cold War", Note by the Joint Secretary, 21 February 1950 (Draft Lecture by Sir Gladwyn Jebb to the Imperial Defence College on 24 February 1950).
43. Tom Bower, *The Perfect English Spy: Sir Dick White and the Secret War 1935–90* (Heinemann, 1995), p. 96.
44. H. Montgomery Hyde, *The Atom Bomb Spies* (Hamish Hamilton, 1980), p. 222.
45. TNA, PRO, AB1/695, 'Perrin interviews with Dr Fuchs, January-March 1950'. 'Record of Interview with Dr K. Fuchs on 30th January 1950 by M. W. Perrin'.
46. Hennessy, *Having It So Good*, pp. 139–50.
47. TNA, PRO, PREM 11/292, 'Testing the First Bomb', Cherwell to Churchill, 14 December 1951.
48. Hennessy, *Having It So Good*, chapter seven.
49. Holloway, *Stalin and the Bomb*, pp. 305–9.
50. Hennessy, *Muddling Through*, pp. 105–6.
51. For Strath see TNA, PRO, CAB 134/940. HDC (55) 3, 'The Defence Implications of Fall-Out from a Hydrogen Bomb: Report by a Group of Officials', 8 March 1955. For the context in which Sir William Strath's group reported see Hennessy, *The Secret State*, chapter four, and Matthew Grant, 'Civil Defence Policy on Cold War Britain, 1945–68', unpublished PhD thesis, Queen Mary, University of London, 2006.
52. TNA, PRO, CAB 158/17, JIC (54) 42, 'Russian Capacity to Deliver Thermo-Nuclear Weapons: Report by the Directors of Intelligence', 22 April 1954.
53. *Defence: Outline of Future Policy, 1957*, Cmnd 124 (HMSO, 1957).
54. TNA, PRO, CAB 134/808, DP (54) 3rd Meeting, 16 June 1954, confidential annex.
55. Hennessy, *Having It So Good*, pp. 336–55.
56. Peter Catterall (ed), *The Macmillan Diaries: The Cabinet Years 1950–1957* (Macmillan, 2003), entry for 7 July 1954, pp. 327–8.
57. TNA, PRO, CAB 195/12. C 47 (54) 7 July 1954.
58. Churchill was an avid reader of the morning newspapers. For Soper's remarks see 'Methodists Seek A-Ban', *Daily Worker*, 8 July 1954.
59. TNA, PRO, CAB 195/12, C 47(54) 7th July 1954.
60. TNA, PRO, CAB 128/27, CC(54) 53rd Conclusions, 26 July 1954.
61. *Statement on Defence:1955*, Cmnd 9391 (HMSO, 1955).
62. Arnold, *Britain and the H-Bomb*, p. 84.
63. Ibid, p. 151.
64. See the photograph in Anthony Sampson, *Macmillan: A Study in Ambiguity* (Allen Lane, Penguin Press, 1967), between pp. 261 and 263.
65. Arnold, *Britain and the H-Bomb*, p. 145.

66. Alastair Horne, *Macmillan, 1957–1986* (Macmillan, 1989), p. 45; *Britain's Cold War Super Weapons*, Blakeway Productions/Channel 4 Television, 24 April 2005.

67. Arnold, *Britain and the H-Bomb*, p. 147.

68. Ibid, pp. 159–62.

69. Hennessy, *Having It So Good*, p. 581.

70. Arnold, *Britain and the H-Bomb*, p. 201.

71. Ibid, pp. 201–10.

72. As reported to the author by Victor Macklen, a member of the UK delegation to the Washington talks in August 1958. Hennessy, *Muddling Through*, p. 108.

73. TNA, PRO, CAB 164/988, Douglas-Home to Heath, 'Facilities for the U.S.A.', 18 September 1970. Annex, 'Facilities Made Available to the United States Forces and Information Exchange, Co-operative, Reciprocal, Shared and Joint Planning Arrangements'.

74. Hennessy, *Muddling Through*, p. 109.

75. Ian Clark, *Nuclear Diplomacy and the Special Relationship: Britain's Deterrent and America 1957–1962*, (OUP, 1994), pp. 176–89, 251–64, 353–73.

76. Michael Dockrill, *British Defence since 1945* (Blackwell, 1988), pp. 71–2.

77. Robert McNamara was speaking in the BBC Radio 4 *Analysis* series, *Moneybags and Brains*, broadcast in October-November 1990. Peter Hennessy and Caroline Anstey, *Moneybags and Brains: The Anglo-American 'Special Relationship' since 1945*, Strathclyde *Analysis* Paper, No.1 (Department of Government, University of Strathclyde, 1990), p. 11.

78. Ibid.

79. TNA, PRO, PREM 11/4412. 'Summary of tasks ahead: Prime Minister wrote to Private Secretary and Ministers'. 'Polaris'. Prime Minister's Personal Minute. M.343/62, 26 December 1962.

80. Horne, *Macmillan, 1957–1986*, p. 444.

81. Iain Dale (ed), *Labour Party General Election Manifestos, 1900–1997* (Routledge/Politico's, 2000), pp. 123–4.

82. Ibid, p. 124.

83. Hennessy, *Muddling Through*, p. 114.

84. TNA, PRO, PREM 11/4733, 'Talks on Defence Policy with Members of HM Opposition', Thorneycroft to Douglas-Home, 3 February 1964.

85. Hennessy, *Muddling Through*, p. 115.

86. Ibid, p. 116.

87. Denis Healey, *The Time of My Life* (Michael Joseph, 1989), p. 302.

88. Dale (ed), *Labour Party General Election Manifestos, 1900–1997*, p. 149.

89. Barbara Castle, *The Castle Diaries 1964–70* (Weidenfeld, 1984), p. 356.

90. Freedman, *Britain and Nuclear Weapons*, pp. 47–8.

91. TNA, PRO, DEFE 4/266, 'Strategic Nuclear Deterrent Force—"Poor Man's Deterrent"', Bondi to Carrington, 21 March 1972.

92. Ibid. 'Strategic Nuclear Matters'. Confidential Annex to COS 12th Meeting/72, 27 March 1972.

93. Helen Parr, 'Anglo-French Nuclear Collaboration and Britain's Policy Towards Europe, 1970–73', in Jan Van der Harst (ed), *Beyond The Customs Union: The European Community's Quest for Completion, Deepening and Enlargement, 1968–1975* (Bruylant, 2007).

94. John Campbell, *Edward Heath* (Cape, 1993), pp. 592–7.

95. Dale (ed), *Labour Party General Election Manifestos, 1900–1997*, 'Let us work together...', p. 191.

96. Ibid, 'Britain will win with Labour', p. 212.

97. Castle, *The Castle Diaries, 1964–1970*, pp. 227–8.

98. TNA, PRO, PREM 16/805, 'Sterling/dollar parity: IMF loan to support sterling; economic implications of IMF package...' Hunt to Stowe, 3 December 1976.

99. TNA, PRO, CAB 128/60, CM (76), 39th conclusions, 7 December 1976, 'Limited circulation Annex: IMF Negotiations', table of 'Public Expenditure Reductions'.

100. Hennessy, *Muddling Through*, p. 121.

101. Ibid.

102. Kenneth O. Morgan, *Callaghan, A Life* (OUP, 1997), pp. 605–6, 619–20; David Owen, *Time To Declare* (Michael Joseph, 1991), pp. 381–2; David Owen, *Personally Speaking to Kenneth Harris* (Weidenfeld, 1987), pp. 146–9.

103. Hennessy, *Muddling Through*, p. 123.

104. Ibid.

105. Hennessy, *Muddling Through*, p. 122.
106. Private information.
107. Hennessy, *Muddling Through*, p. 124.
108. Ibid, p. 125.
109. Ibid.
110. Morgan, *Callaghan*, p. 619.
111. Hennessy, *Muddling Through*, pp. 125–6.
112. Morgan, *Callaghan*, pp. 605–6.
113. Private information.
114. Hennessy, *Muddling Through*, p. 286.
115. Ibid, p. 126.
116. Ibid, p. 127.
117. Ibid, pp. 126–7.
118. Margaret Thatcher, *The Downing Street Years* (HarperCollins, 1993), p. 244.
119. Hennessy, *Cabinet*, p. 155.
120. Thatcher, *The Downing Street Years*, p. 245.
121. Hennessy, *Cabinet*, p. 155.
122. Thatcher, *The Downing Street Years*, pp. 246–7.
123. *"The Future of the United Kingdom Nuclear Deterrent Force"*, Defence Open Government Document 80/23 (Ministry of Defence, July 1980), p. 5.
124. Thatcher, *The Downing Street Years*, p. 247.
125. John Nott, *Here Today, Gone Tomorrow: Recollections of an Errant Politician* (Politico's, 2002), pp. 216–7.
126. Ibid, p. 217. See also Richard Hill, *Lewin of Greenwich: The authorised biography of Admiral of the Fleet Lord Lewin* (Cassell, 2000), pp. 327–9.
127. Dale (ed.), *Labour Party General Election Manifestos, 1900–1997*, 'new Labour because Britain deserves better', p. 380.
128. *Britain forward not back* (Labour Party, 2005), p. 88.
129. Private information
130. House of Commons, *Official Report*, 19 July 2005, col. 60.
131. Private information.
132. Private information.
133. Downing Street Press Briefing, Afternoon 4 December 2006, 'Press Briefing from the Prime Minister's Official Spokesman on: Trident'. http://www.number10.gov.uk/output/page10534.asp
134. *The Future of the United Kingdom's Nuclear Deterrent*, Cm 6994 (Stationery Office, December 2006), p. 7.
135. Ibid, p. 5.
136. Blair to Bush, 7 December 2006; Bush to Blair, 7 December 2006.
137. House of Commons, *Official Report*, 19 December 2006, col.141.
138. House of Commons, *Official Report*, 14 March 2007, cols 298–407; Christopher Adams, 'PM survives backbench rebellion,' *Financial Times*, 15 March 2007.
139. Ibid.
140. I am grateful to Mr Denham for sending me a copy. John Denham to Peter Hennessy, 18 April 2007.
141. Daniel Boorstin, *The Discoverers: A History of Man's Search to Know His World and Himself* (Random House, 1983), p. 675.
142. Sir Michael Quinlan in conversation with Sir John Willis and the author, the National Archives, Kew, 6 May 2004.
143. Alistair Cooke, *Letter from America 1946–2004* (Knopf, 2004), p. 93.
144. Clark, *The Greatest Power on Earth*, p. 298.
145. Michael Herman, 'The Role of Military Intelligence since 1945'. Paper delivered to the Twentieth-Century British Politics and Administration Seminar at the Institute of Historical Research, University of London, 24 May 1989.
146. Richard Aldrich and Michael Coleman, 'The Cold War, the JIC and British Signals Intelligence, 1948', *Intelligence and National Security*, Vol. 4, No. 3, July 1989. The document is reprinted in full in Appendix 2 of the article. The original can be found at the India Office Library in L/WS/1/1196.
147. Frank Panton, 'Government, Scientists and the UK's Nuclear Weapons Programme, 1957–1976'. Paper read at the British Rocket Oral History Project Meeting, 13 April 2007.

148. Quoted in Lorna Arnold, *A Very Special Relationship: British Atomic Weapons Trials in Australia* (HMSO, 1987), pp. 14–15.

149. For the text of the 'Modus Vivendi' see Gowing, *Independence and Deterrence*, Vol. I, pp. 266–72.

150. Lord Penney and Lord Sherfield (who, as Sir Roger Makins, had negotiated the 'Modus Vivendi' for the Foreign Office) were particularly helpful in explaining this to the author: see Peter Hennessy, *Whitehall* (Pimlico, 2001), p. 722.

151. TNA, PRO, AIR 8/2400, 'Russian Capacity to Absorb Damage'. Annex to DB (58) 10.

152. TNA, PRO, AIR 8/2201, 'Strategic Strike Planning by Bomber Command'.

153. TNA, PRO, CAB 158/45, Part 1, JIC (61) 77, 'The United Kingdom Nuclear Deterrent', 23 January 1962.

154. TNA, PRO, DEFE 10/402, SG (60) 13, 'Likely Effects of Nuclear Weapons on the People and Economy of a Country', 'Hypothesis 1', E. Anstey, 20 May 1963.

155. Catherine Haddon, 'British Intelligence Assessments of Soviet Nuclear Capabilities and Intentions', Queen Mary, University of London, PhD thesis (forthcoming).

156. TNA, PRO, CAB 158/61, JIC (66) 3, 'Soviet War Bloc Potential 1966–1970', 9 February 1966. See also TNA, PRO, CAB 182/23, JIC (M T) (WP) 5/66, Joint Intelligence Committee Missile Threat Co-ordination Sub-Committee Missile Threat Co-ordination Working Party, 'Assessment of New Soviet Air Defence System Deployment', 6 April 1966; TNA, PRO, CAB 158/66, JIC (67) 32 (Final), 'Soviet Intentions on Ballistic Missile Defence', 31 October 1967.

157. Private information.

158. Private information.

159. *The Future of the United Kingdom's Nuclear Deterrent*, p. 6.

LIST OF DOCUMENTS AND ILLUSTRATIONS

Documents

1. The Frisch–Peierls 'Memorandum on the properties of a radioactive "superbomb"' and 'On the construction of a "superbomb", based on a nuclear chain reaction in uranium'.
   TNA, PRO, AB 1/210

2. 'Report by M.A.U.D. Committee on the use of Uranium for a Bomb'.
   TNA, PRO, CAB 104/227

3. 'The Atomic Bomb: Memorandum by the Prime Minister', GEN 75/1, 28 August 1945.
   TNA, PRO, CAB 130/3

4. Minutes of a meeting of the Cabinet Committee on Atomic Energy, GEN 75, 18 December 1945.
   TNA, PRO, CAB 130/2

5. Minutes of a meeting of the Cabinet Committee on Atomic Energy, GEN 75, 25 October 1946.
   TNA, PRO, CAB 130/2

6. 'Note by the Controller of Production of Atomic Energy', Ministry of Supply, 31 December 1946.
   TNA, PRO, PREM 8/911

7. 'Research on Atomic Weapons': Bridges to Attlee, 7 January 1947.
   TNA, PRO, PREM 8/911

8. Minutes of the meeting of GEN 163, Atomic Energy, 8 January 1947; Confidential Annex.
   TNA, PRO, CAB 130/16

9. Joint Intelligence Committee report on 'Soviet Interests, Intentions and Capabilities', 6 August 1947.
   TNA, PRO, CAB 158/1

10. Undated brief for Attlee on 'Research on Atomic Weapons' for use at the meeting of GEN 75 on 12 March 1948.
    TNA, PRO, PREM 8/911

11. Joint Intelligence Committee report on 'Russian Interests, Intentions and Capabilities', JIC (48) 9 (0) Final, 23 July 1948.
    TNA, PRO, CAB 158/3

12. Churchill/Bridges exchanges on the financing of the atomic bomb project, plus correspondence with Cherwell, December 1951.
    TNA, PRO, PREM 11/297

13. Joint Intelligence Committee assessment of 'Soviet and Satellite War Potential, 1954–1958', JIC (54) 3 (Final), 15 February 1954.
    TNA, PRO, CAB 158/17 PART 1

14. Note of a meeting chaired by Sir Norman Brook in the Cabinet Office, GEN 465 (1st meeting), 12 March 1954.
    TNA, PRO, CAB 130/101

15. Note of a meeting of Ministers on Atomic Energy Development, GEN 464, 13 April 1954.
    TNA, PRO, CAB 130/101

16. Minutes of a meeting of the Cabinet's Defence Policy Committee, DP (54) 2nd meeting, 19 May 1954.
    TNA, PRO, CAB 134/808

17. 'United Kingdom Defence Policy' briefing by the Chiefs of Staff for the Defence Policy Committee (and later, minus detail on the number of bombs planned, for the full Cabinet), 31 May 1954. C (54) 249.
    TNA, PRO, CAB 129/69

18. Cabinet Minutes, CC (54) 47th Conclusions, 7 July 1954.
    TNA, PRO, CAB 128/27

19. Cabinet Minutes, CC (54) 48th Conclusions, 8 July 1954.
    TNA, PRO, CAB 128/27

20. Churchill to the Queen, 16 July 1954.
    TNA, PRO, PREM 11/747

21. Joint Intelligence Committee assessment of 'Sino-Soviet Bloc War Potential, 1960–64', JIC (60) 3 (Final), 1 March 1960.
    TNA, PRO, CAB 158/39

22. Cabinet Minutes, CC (60) 26th Conclusions, 13 April 1960.
    TNA, PRO, CAB 128/34

23. Cabinet Minutes, CC (60) 35th Conclusions, 20 June 1960.
    TNA, PRO, CAB 128/34

24. Joint Intelligence Committee assessment of 'Sino-Soviet Bloc War Potential, 1962–66', JIC (62) 3 (Final), 16 February 1962.
    TNA, PRO, CAB 158/45, Part 1

25. Cabinet Minutes, CC (62) 76th Conclusions, 21 December 1962.
    TNA, PRO, CAB 128/36 Part 2

26. Record of the Prime Minister's Admiralty House meeting on Polaris, 31 December 1962.
    TNA, PRO, PREM 11/4147

27. Telegram from Sir Pierson Dixon in Paris to the Foreign Office, 2 January 1963.
    TNA, PRO, PREM 11/4147

28. Cabinet Minutes, CC (63) 1st Conclusions, 3 January 1963.
    TNA, PRO, CAB 128/37

29. UK-made alternatives to Polaris: Amery to Thorneycroft, 15 January 1963; Thorneycroft to Amery, 28 January 1963.
    TNA, PRO, PREM 11/4148

30. Minutes of the meeting of MISC 16, 11 November 1964.
    TNA, PRO, CAB 130/212

31. Zuckerman's brief for Healey on the size of a UK Polaris force, 18 November 1964.
    TNA, PRO, PREM 13/26

32. Ministry of Defence memorandum for MISC 17 on 'The Size of the British Polaris Force', 20 November 1964.
    TNA, PRO, CAB 130/213

33. Minutes of the meetings of MISC 17, 21–22 November 1964.
    TNA, PRO, CAB 130/213

34. Cabinet Secretary's brief for the Prime Minister on 'Defence Policy', 25 November 1964.
    TNA, PRO, PREM 13/26

35. Cabinet Minutes, CC (64) 11th Conclusions, 26 November 1964.
    TNA, PRO, CAB 128/39

36. Minister of Defence's briefing on 'Polaris Submarine Building Programme', 12 January 1965.
    TNA, PRO, CAB 148/19

37. Minutes of the meeting of the Cabinet's Defence and Oversea Policy Committee, 29 January 1965.
    TNA, PRO, CAB 148/18

38. Minutes of the first meeting of the Ministerial Committee on Nuclear Policy, PN, 28 September 1966.
TNA, PRO, CAB 134/3120

39. Assignment of Polaris Submarines to NATO: Healey to Wilson, 3 August 1967.
TNA, PRO, CAB 164.713

40. 'British Nuclear Weapons Policy', report by the Defence Review Working Party, PN (67) 6, 1 December 1967.
TNA, PRO, CAB 134/3120

41. Minutes of a meeting of the PN Committee, PN (67) 4th meeting, 5 December 1967.
TNA, PRO, CAB 134/3120

42. Lord Rothschild's 'Minority Report' dissenting from the findings of the Kings Norton Working Party on Atomic Weapons Establishments, 18 July 1968.
TNA, PRO, CAB 134/3121, Part 2

43. Joint Intelligence Committee assessment of 'Soviet Bloc War Potential, 1969–73', JIC (A) (69) 3 (Final), 7 January 1969.
TNA, PRO, CAB 186/1

44. Carrington's brief on 'Improvement in Strategic Nuclear Deterrent', 10 September 1973.
TNA, PRO, PREM 15/2038

45. Trend's brief for Heath on 'The Nuclear Deterrent', 11 September 1973.
TNA, PRO, PREM 15/2038

46. Minutes of a meeting of 'The United Kingdom Nuclear Deterrent' Ministerial Group, 12 September 1973.
TNA, PRO, PREM 15/2038

47. Hunt's brief for Heath on 'Defence Expenditure', 29 October 1973.
TNA, PRO, PREM 15/2038

48. Minutes of a meeting of 'The United Kingdom Nuclear Deterrent' Ministerial Group, 30 October 1973.
TNA, PRO, PREM 15/2038

49. Hunt's brief for Heath on 'Super Antelope', 7 February 1974.
TNA, PRO, PREM 15/2038

50. Armstrong to Hunt on Super Antelope, 8 February 1974.
TNA, PRO, PREM 15/2038

51. Joint Intelligence Committee assessment of 'Soviet Bloc War Potential, 1974', JIC (A) (74) 3, 13 June 1974.
TNA, PRO, CAB 186/17

52. Report of Defence Studies Working Party for meeting of MISC 16 on 28 June 1974.
TNA, PRO, CAB 130/732

53. MISC 16 report for Cabinet's Defence and Oversea Policy Committee, OPD (74) 23, 15 July 1974.
TNA, PRO, CAB 148/145

54. 'Nuclear Testing': note by the Prime Minister, C (74) 85, 31 July 1974.
TNA, PRO, CAB 129/178

55. Confidential Annex to the Cabinet Minutes, C (74) 35th Conclusions, 12 September 1974.
TNA, PRO, CAB 128/55

56. Hunt and Roberts' brief for the OPD Committee, 'Defence Review—Critical Level', 13 September 1974.
TNA, PRO, CAB 148/145

57. Minutes of a meeting of the Defence and Oversea Policy Committee, OPD (74) 15th meeting, 18 September 1974.
TNA, PRO, CAB 148/145

58. 'Defence Review. Memorandum by the Prime Minister', C (74) 116, 28 October 1974.
TNA, PRO, CAB 129/179

59. Cabinet Minutes, CC (74) 47th Conclusions, 20 November 1974.
TNA, PRO, CAB 128/55

60. GEN 32 (76) 6, 'Nuclear Contacts with France' report, Annex D, 22 September 1976.
TNA, PRO, CAB 130/878

61. The Bush-Blair exchange of letters, 7 December 2006.

62. Beckett/Browne letter to dissenting Labour MPs, 14 March 2007.

Illustrations

330 A Trident D5 missile being test-fired by *HMS Vanguard*, October 2005. (Photo: © Crown Copyright/MOD. Reproduced with the permission of the Controller of Her Majesty's Stationery Office.)

332 Trident upgraders: Gordon Brown and Tony Blair. (Photo: News Group Newspapers Ltd.)